INDO-BANGLADESH BORDER TRADE

INDO-BANGLADESH BORDER TRADE

Benefiting from Neighbourhood

Edited by

Gurudas Das

C Joshua Thomas

AKANSHA PUBLISHING HOUSE

NEW DELHI - 110 002 (INDIA)

AKANSHA PUBLISHING HOUSE
4649/21-B, Ansari Road
Daryaganj, New Delhi - 110 002
Phones: 23263193, 9811582579, 09435116718
E-mail: ektabooks@yahoo.com

Indo-Bangladesh Border Trade

First Published, 2008
ISBN 978-81-8370-132-7

PRINTED IN INDIA

Published by Akansha Publishing House, New Delhi-110 002 and printed at Capital Offset Press, Delhi

CONTENTS

Indo-Bangladesh Border Trade: West Bengal-Bangladesh Sector

Indo-Bangladesh Border Trade: North Eastern Region-Bangladesh Sector

Minister of Panchayati Raj, Youth Affairs &
Sports and the Development of the
North Eastern Region
Government of India

FOREWORD

Indo-Bangladesh relations, unlike other bilateral relations, have a special significance. The people of India and Bangladesh due to a variety of reasons including linguistic and cultural affinities, shared history, shared borders, geographical interdependence, and so on, share a common emotional space and feeling of goodwill for each other. There is, undoubtedly, much higher expectation of the people of both the countries for stronger bilateral relations than what exists today. As a result, it is a stupendous challenge before the governments of these two nations to translate these desires into reality. Both India and Bangladesh can work together to improve the living conditions of the millions of people across the border. Both can evolve mutually beneficial programmes in areas like agriculture, industry, trade, technology, transit, tourism, common border management, security and share common resources. A strong bilateral cooperation in all these areas can make immense contributions in enhancing the welfare of the people of both the countries.

Besides bilateral cooperation, both nations can play important roles in regional fora like SAARC and BIMSTEC and facilitate cross-border development. To gain from the neighbourhood, both the nations need to shed traditional state centric security perceptions. For strong bilateral relations to take root, it is important to factor into each other's security concerns within the broader framework of cooperation. Besides traditional perceptions of security which are mostly related to militaristic threat perceptions, non-traditional security concerns like economic stability, energy security, food security, cultural security etc., need to be factored into. Usually bilateral framework of cooperation succeeds when programmes on economic cooperation are backed by both traditional and non-traditional security concerns of both the parties. I strongly feel that both India and Bangladesh, need to work out such a framework which adequately addresses both economic and security interests of the two countries.

Having the longest border between them, both, India and Bangladesh need to forge a strategy to develop the bordering regions that enhances the welfare of the people across the border. Border trade, thus, can be viewed as an instrument for achieving this goal. Together we need to arrive at equilibrium where trade, transit, tourism and security concerns are balanced for the greater good of the people in both the nations.

I extend my appreciation to ICSSR-NERC for bringing together the experts in this field, who have made valuable contributions in this volume. I wish, this volume gets a wider readership across business, industry, policy making agency and academia.

Mani Shankar Aiyar
Minister of Panchayati Raj, Youth Affairs &
Sports and the Development of the
North Eastern Region
Government of India

Date: 5 December 2007
Place: New Delhi

PREFACE

India and Bangladesh are not only bounded by geography (sharing about a little more than 4000 km long border) but also by history and culture. Being the lower riparian agricultural economy, the development of Bangladesh calls for bilateral cooperation as the Himalayan rivers flow through India before reaching Bangladesh. Similarly, as Bangladesh lies between the mainland India and her north eastern region, India requires the cooperation of Bangladesh for cost effective transportation of goods between the mainland and north east. Economic cooperation between them, thus, would prove to be beneficial for both.

As far as bilateral trade is concerned, an asymmetric trade relation has grown over time in favour of India. Although this asymmetry has developed mainly due to the limitations of the Bangladesh economy—narrow export basket as well as high import content of Bangladesh's export—India needs to find ways and means to bring a balance in the bilateral trade. Given the production structure and export basket of Bangladesh, it appears that there is not much room left for India to help Bangladesh in reducing her deficit trade balance through merchandise trade alone. The reduction of bilateral trade asymmetry, therefore, calls for comprehensive bilateral engagement covering transit, investment and trade in services. Expansion of merchandise trade, opening up of transit, Indian investment in Bangladesh and opening up of trade in services can only restore the balance in the long run.

State-centric traditional security perception often stands on the way of building bilateral economic partnership which often undermines the non-traditional security threats of a nation. While the countries around the world are moving away from state-centric security arrangement and building cooperative security network by forming regional groupings that can ensure both traditional and non-traditional security needs, countries in South Asia appears to have caught in the cogs of the wheel of history where military machine rules the roost. Both Bangladesh and India need to shake off state-centricism for the welfare of the people across the border.

This volume is the outcome of a two-day seminar on "Indo-Bangladesh Border Trade: Status, Problems and Potentials" held during July 12-13, 2005, organized by the Indian Council of Social Science Research, North Eastern Regional Centre, at North Eastern Hill University, Shillong. Although India and Bangladesh does not have any special 'Border Trade' agreement between them, but much of the bilateral trade flows across the land border. It is in this sense the term 'Border Trade' is used here which is synonymous to bilateral formal trade only.

Three sets of papers have been invited for presentations. First set of contributions deal with overall perspectives, status and issues relating to trade and transit. Second set of contributions deal with the status of trade and trade facilitation between West Bengal and Bangladesh sector while the third deal with the same between North Eastern Region of India and Bangladesh sector.

We are thankful to the Ministry of Commerce and Department of Development of North Eastern Region, Government of India, for providing generous financial support without which the seminar would not have been possible.

Gurudas Das
C Joshua Thomas

Shillong
June 10, 2007

INAUGURAL ADDRESS

P.R. Kyndiah

I deem it a great privilege to be invited to inaugurate the Seminar on Indo-Bangladesh Border Trade: Status, Problems and Potentials. It was indeed thoughtful of the Indian Council of Social Science Research, North Eastern Regional Centre, to organize a Seminar on this subject of great relevance to the economic development and prosperity of North Eastern Region.

India is today one of the dynamic and fast growing economies of the world. Even at the average growth rate of 6.5 per cent, our GDP is set to double every 11 years. It constitutes not only a vast and growing market, but also a competitive source of technologies and knowledge-based services.

Globalization has sharply reduced trade barriers and the process of integration of the world economy has encouraged an expansion in trade, foreign direct investment and flow of technology and talent. The explosion of information technology has created new business opportunities undreamt of ten years ago.

Potentials

The Seminar is timely and I would like to point out that economic, social and political implications of land border trade are very important as it facilitates economic activities and benefits the local people. Movement of goods along the land borders impacts livelihood of the people in the border areas in terms of (i) infrastructure development like roadways, railways and communications, and (ii) generation of demand in the service sector in areas like trade, hotels and restaurants, medical facilities, vehicle servicing, currency exchange, weigh bridges, information booths, etc. All these activities create new employment opportunities for the benefit of the people.

Borders are viewed as gateways to access market of the neighbouring countries and border trade is an important vehicle for the socio-economic development of the bordering territories.

Bangladesh is the largest trading partner of India in the region and 6th largest destination of our exports. The current bilateral trade is more than US$1.5 billion. Major items of exports from India to Bangladesh are fabrics, engineering goods, chemicals and pharmaceuticals, transport equipment, cement, limestone and coal. India's import from Bangladesh includes raw jute, leather, fabric yarn, jamdani sarees, etc.

Out of the country's total land border of 15,581 km with seven neighbouring countries viz. Afghanistan, China, Bangladesh, Bhutan, Myanmar, Nepal and Pakistan, the length of our border with Bangladesh is the longest. India shares 90 Land Customs Stations (LCS) with Bangladesh out of 138 authorized LCS along her land border with neighbouring countries. This indicates that India conducts significant volume of trade through land borders with Bangladesh.

A large part of formal bilateral trade flows across the land borders between India and Bangladesh through West Bengal and considerable trade also flows across the North Eastern Region. Unlike other regions in the country, four neighboring countries of Bhutan, China, Myanmar and Bangladesh bound the North Eastern Region (NER) and shares 98 per cent of the border with them and only 2 per cent with the mainland India. The region's border with Bangladesh spans about 1940 km. Besides being an important next-door neighbour, Bangladesh occupies a prominent place as one of India's trade partner with special reference to North East.

The region's export to Bangladesh mainly consists of mineral products like coal and limestone, boulders and stone chips and a few agro-horticultural produce.

During the period 1998-99 to 2002-03 about 98 per cent of the region's total official land route exports to neighbouring countries had gone to Bangladesh. This shows the importance of NER's trade with Bangladesh. The exports and imports to/from Bangladesh through the land route during the period 1998-99 to 2002-03 are as follows:

Export and Import to/from Bangladesh through LCS in NER

(Rs. in crore)

Year	*Export to Bangladesh*	*Import from Bangladesh*
A	*B*	*C*
1998-99	138.43	15.61
1999-00	169.71	9.51
2000-01	151.17	7.32
2001-02	222.01	5.47
2002-03	198.69	6.1

Problems

India shares a long and porous border with Bangladesh, Nepal and Pakistan. The artificial barriers have led to massive unrecorded trade through the porous borders. As Bangladesh is gradually becoming a trade partner of NE Region of India and West Bengal, informal trade between India and Bangladesh takes place along both the West Bengal and the

North Eastern borders. The current volume of the informal trade between the two countries suggests that there is abundant scope for beneficial mutual exchange through legitimate channels. This needs a careful study of items, volumes, direction, linkages, infrastructural gaps, a legal framework, inter-modal arrangements and customs and movements protocol.

The main items of exports in informal trade include handloom, bidis, sugar, betel nut and betel-vine, cattle, textiles and ganja etc. The items imported through informal trade mainly comprise of gold, pirated CDs, cassettes, processed food items, readymade garments etc.

Due to non-formalization of informal trade, the state exchequer receives nothing out of it and it leads to massive siphoning of resources and evil practices such as narcotic trade that have a negative effect on the society. Therefore formalizing the informal trade would be advantageous to both the countries and restrict the role of the mafia and bring forth the genuine traders for a sustainable and mutually beneficial exchange of goods and services.

A major concern to the growth of border trade is lack of required infrastructure in the NE States and accessibility to Bangladesh and other neighbouring countries. There are regular bus services between India and Bangladesh. Regular Kolkata-Dhaka and Agartala-Dhaka bus services operate between the two countries. However, this has been hampered by a high entry fel and the lack of double entry visa. There are two broad gauge rail links between the two countries but passengers' service is yet to commence.

Strategies

To improve and expand the economic relations with all our neighbouring countries including Bangladesh, the NER has a critical role to play in the 'Look East Policy' of the Government of India given its natural advantages. Only recently the Government of India has signed MOU with Singapore, Thailand and other South Asian countries having significance for future vibrant economic relationship. Earlier the Government of India has signed an agreement with Myanmar Government when the President of that country visited India. Bangladesh must, therefore, play a positive role in matters of trade and commerce and take economic advantage by improving its relationship with our country.

It must be remembered that we have in the North Eastern Region abundant plantation crops like rubber and tea, medicinal plants, bamboo, minerals like limestone and coal, forest products, fruits and handicrafts. These items can be exported to Bangladesh and to third countries through her. Similarly goods would be much cheaper for the region if it is imported from Bangladesh and what is required is to focus on each one's inherent strengths and to take advantage of it. The NE States and Bangladesh both have good reserves of hydrocarbons and there is a scope of cooperation in this field as well.

It must be ensured that NE Region does not remain as a mere transit route in matters of border trade and the goods and services exported to the neighbouring country are largely produced within this region.

A multi-pronged strategy is needed to tap the full potential of the border trade in this region:

(a) Mistrust and prejudices inherited from the past have to be shed and a mutually beneficial environment has to be created. This would require sensitivity towards the security concerns of both the countries.

(b) There has to be a realization that trade and commerce

are for mutual interest and restrictive regimes do not help growth.

(c) Business meets, trade shows and exhibitions should be organized to promote mutual awareness and understanding.

(d) Service sectors such as tourism, health and education should also be given adequate importance.

(e) Joint Ventures should be explored with equity participation from private entrepreneurs of both the countries.

Initiatives

Bangladesh is India's important trade partner and an export destination but the immense possibility to further trade between the two countries from the region has yet to be translated into reality. The Joint Economic Commission, representing the national interest of both the countries for promotion of bilateral trade and commerce has not made much headway in synergizing the transit and border trade issues. Bangladesh understandably is restive about its unfavorable balance of trade with India. It is demanding more access for her exports to Indian market and expecting India to allow duty-free imports of more commodities of Bangladesh's interest. India on the other hand is expecting Bangladesh to allow transit facilities for the two-way movements of goods between the north-eastern hinterlands and the mainland as well as to open up border trade across north-eastern region and Bangladesh sector. Once these issues are settled, the flow of bilateral trade will increase manifold.

The Government of India has accorded high priority for creation of infrastructure and a number of measures have been taken as a part of Prime Minister's New Initiative on North East. An empowered Inter-Ministerial Committee under the chairmanship of Commerce Secretary is coordinating the steps taken by various agencies for the development of trade in NE. A North East cell has been established in the Department of Commerce to promote exports from the North Eastern Region especially for boosting trade with the neighbouring countries like Bangladesh and Myanmar. An Export Development Fund has been set up with an initial contribution of Rs. 5 crore for assisting trade promotion activities in the North East. Eleven land customs stations have been prioritized for development of infrastructure in the NER. Ministry of DONER is also playing a crucial role in developing infrastructure under the Non-lapsable Central Pool of Resources, to boost trade and commerce in the Region.

During the last meeting of the North Eastern Council it was decided that measures be taken to launch and implement Border Trade Mission in consonance with Government of India's 'Look East Policy'.

The Ministry of Development of North Eastern Region also intends to convene the meeting of representatives of four states namely Assam, Meghalaya, Mizoram and Tripura bordering Bangladesh as a first step toward joint understanding to foster trade and commerce with Bangladesh. A joint meeting with Government of West Bengal would be explored as much of the Indo-Bangladesh trade flows through this state.

I would like to emphasize that a well-formulated plan of economic cooperation with neighbouring countries would greatly help the local economies of the region as a whole.

Once again I would like to thank the organizers for having given me this opportunity to inaugurate this seminar, which is a step in the right direction for the promotion of border trade with Bangladesh.

LIST OF TABLES

LIST OF FIGURES

LIST OF MAPS

CONTRIBUTORS

Chakraborti, Tusharbindu, Assistant Professor, Department of Defence Studies, BBM College, Agartala, Tripura

Chakraborty, Kiran Sankar, Regional Director, IGNOU, Agartala, Tripura

Das, Gurudas, Assistant Professor, Department of Humanities and Social Sciences, National Institute of Technology, Silchar, Assam

De, Prabir, Fellow, RIS, New Delhi

De, Utpal Kumar, Reader, Department of Economics, North Eastern Hill University, Shillong, Meghalaya

Deb Kar, Ajanta, Lecturer, Department of Economics, Don Bosco College, Tura, Meghalaya

Halder, Dilip, Professor, Institute of Business Management, Jadavpur University, Kolkata

Hossain, M Ismail, Professor, Department of Economics, Jehangir Nagar University, Dhaka, Bangladesh

Kakoty, Sanjeeb, Freelance Writer, Motinagar, Shillong, Meghalaya

Kar, Sadhan C, Lecturer, Department of Economics, Dinhata College, West Bengal

Kharlukhi, RDH, Inspector of Statistics, Directorate of Economics and Statistics, Government of Meghalaya, Shillong, Meghalaya

Khathing, JSR, Former Chief Commissioner, Customs and Central Excise, Shillong

Kundu, Pankaj, Lecturer, Department of Economics, Chachal College, Malda, West Bengal

Kyndiah, PR, Minister, Former Tribal Affairs and Development of North Eastern Region, Government of India

Pohit, Sanjib, Chief Economist, NCAER, New Delhi

Rahman, Md Habibur, Associate Professor, Department of Economics, MC College, Sylhet, Bangladesh

Ray, Santanu, Research Scholar, Department of Economics, North Eastern Hill University, Shillong, Meghalaya

Ray, Surya Narayan, Lecturer, Department of Commerce, Dinhata College, West Bengal

Raychaudhuri, Ajitava, Professor, Department of Economics, Jadavpur University, Kolkata

Rout, Lambodar, Lecturer, Department of Economics, Nongtalang College, Nongtalang, Meghalaya

Roy, Niranjan Reader, Department of Economics, Assam University, Silchar, Assam

Roy Chowdhury, Sunandan, Editor, Sampark Journal of Global Understanding, Kolkata

Sarma, DK, Secretary, NECCI, Guwahati

Suter, Sukharanjan, President, Techno International Ltd, Dhaka

PART I

INDO-BANGLADESH BORDER TRADE: STATUS, ISSUES AND PERSPECTIVES

1

INDO-BANGLADESH ECONOMIC RELATIONS: ISSUES IN TRADE, TRANSIT AND SECURITY

Gurudas Das

Economic relations between two countries are often structured based on the political/strategic relations between them. However, while this correspondence between political/strategic and economic relations seems to be strong under state-control-economies, it appears to be weak under market-led-economies. The strong Indo-Bangladesh economic relations exhibited in terms of trading engagement particularly during the post-liberalized era is a case in pointer. This paper argues in favour of stronger political/strategic relations between these two South Asian neighbours for fuller cross-border synergy and economic cooperation for the well being of the people across the border.

A plethora of research has already been done on Indo-Bangladesh trade particularly from Bangladesh point of view (Bakht: 1996; Rahman: 1997; Rahman: 1998; Eusufzai: 2000; Islam: 2004; Bhattacharya: 2004; Ahmed and Sattar: 2004; Rahman: 2005). As India being the largest source of Bangladesh's import, her trade relation with India has a significant bearing for the country's overall development.

However, such studies from Indian point of view are significantly conspicuous as India's Bangladesh trade is insignificant compared to her total trade.

This paper intends to analyze the nature of economic relations developed between India and Bangladesh since early 1970s. It attempts to study the trends and structures of Indo-Bangladesh trade in order to analyze the nature of persistent asymmetry in bilateral trade. It also focuses on the various options available with Bangladesh for the reduction of her trade deficit vis-à-vis India. It, then, analyzes the perceived security predicaments of Bangladesh in weighing some of the options which could, otherwise, have brought revolutionary change in her economy.

India-Bangladesh Peace and Friendship Treaty

The "Treaty of Peace and Friendship between the Government of India and the Government of the People's Republic of Bangladesh' signed on March 19, 1972 has laid the foundation of Indo-Bangladesh relations. The Treaty has been signed for 25 years and on expiry of the term, in spite of provision, has not been renewed due to the fact that Bangladesh found it to be some sort of transgression to her freedom. While the Treaty overwhelmingly dealt with political, social, cultural and security interests of both the countries, Articles 5 and 6 dealt with the pledge of economic cooperation. Mutual cooperation is sought to develop in 'economic, scientific and technical fields' as well as 'trade, transport and communication', 'flood control, river basin development and the development of hydro-electric power and irrigation' (Treaty:1972). Being the nascent state, Bangladesh needed the assistance from India in order to build infrastructure and war devastated economy. The Treaty, thus, made provisions for both trade and investment between the two countries.

India-Bangladesh 1972 Trade Agreement

The first Indo-Bangladesh trade agreement, viz., "Trade Agreement between the Government of India and the Government of the People's Republic of Bangladesh', was signed on March 28, 1972, just a week after the signing of the Treaty. This Agreement was signed for one year. It has two parts, viz, (a) formal trade, and (b) border trade.

(a) Formal Trade: A list of commodities (List-I) has been drawn which India will export to Bangladesh and another similar list (List-II) has been drawn which Bangladesh will export to India. For both the lists, money value ceiling of all exportables are agreed upon so that the total value of export and import exactly match with each other for both the countries. The total value that each country can export to other is kept at 25 crores. The major items that India would export include cement, coal, unmanufactured tobacco, asphalt, cotton yarn, stone boulders/lime stones/dolomite, etc. Major items that Bangladesh would export to India include fresh fish, cow hides, furnace oil, newsprint, raw jute and simul cotton. It may be noted that the bilateral trade between India and Bangladesh in 1970s was primarily rooted in reciprocal demand for raw materials rather than consumables and capital goods. Besides this regulated trade, trade in other goods not included in these two lists or excess imports/exports of listed goods will be permitted in accordance with the law of the land concerned.

(b) Border Trade: The Agreement provides for 'border trade' for the people living within the 16 kilometer belt of border between West Bengal, Assam, Meghalaya, Tripura and Mizoram on the one hand and Bangladesh on the other. Indo-Bangladesh border has been divided into 6 sectors, viz., Mizoram-Chittagong sector, Khasi Jaintia and Garo Hills-Sylhet Mymensing sector, Cachar-Sylhet sector, Tripura-Bangladesh sector, Rangpur (Bangladesh)-Assam (bordeing districts) Coochbehar/Jalpaiguri (West Bengal) sector, and Rest of Bangladesh—Rest of West Bengal sector. For each sector list of exportables and permissible quantities for both sides have been worked out. Modalities and modus operandi are laid down and the trade is made free from import, export, exchange control restrictions as well as customs duty and customs formalities.

Besides trade, Article V of the Agreement provides both the countries 'to make mutually beneficial arrangements for the use of their waterways, railways and roadways for commerce between the two countries and for passage of goods between two places in one country through the territory of the other'. Article VI provides MFN status to each other.

It may be recalled at this point that while India was engaging Bangladesh during the early 1970s, she was also simultaneously reorganizing the governance in her north eastern region by curving out new provinces from undivided Assam. While Meghalaya and Mizoram were curved out of Assam, Arunachal Pradesh was brought out of the influence of Assam, and Manipur and Tripura were conferred statehood as per the North Eastern Areas (Reorganisation) Act of 1971. As has been discussed in detail elsewhere (Das: 2002), both India's intervention in 1971 Bangladesh liberation movement and reorganization of her Noth Eastern Region were the resultants of her intense security threat perceptions arising out of her being cordoned off by the USA-China-Pakistan axis as part of the cold war stratagem. Irrespective of economic viability, small north eastern states were created only to accommodate smaller ethnic interests in order to defuse internal insecurity feelings. Being far away from national market centers, border trade for them can provide the necessary vent for their surplus produce (Das: 2000) and harmonization of transport and communication channels across India and Bangladesh can, to some extent, restore the traditional trade and commerce which suffered serious dislocation following the partition of the country.

From Indian perspective, had this Agreement been implemented in letter and spirit could have solved much of the isolation of her north eastern region. But unfortunately, before the provision of the Agreement could take off, the Government of Bangladesh complained in September, 1972, of large scale smuggling across the border, and in October,1972 asked for the 'border trade' to be scraped forthwith (Rajya Sabha Secretariat: 1998). Needless to say that scrapping of the 'border trade' provision could hardly contain smuggling across the border as can be seen from our subsequent discussion. It appears to be perplexing as to why Bangladesh scrapped the 'border trade' provision even without giving it a fair trial!

As this Agreement envisaged to promote bilateral trade on a 'statet-to-state' basis, not much headway could be done before it was replaced by another Agreement in 1973.

India-Bangladesh 1973 Trade Agreement

The 1973 Agreement made a departure from that of 1972 in that the former does not include the provision of 'border trade'. Moreover, unlike 1972 Agreement, the detail of 'balanced trade and payments arrangements' had not been included and left to be worked out later. Except 3 new Articles, it either repeated or rephrased the provisions of the 1972 Agreement. Among the three new Articles, Article 2 provides both the countries to conduct trade with each other 'in accordance with the evolving international commercial policy'. Article 3 provides space for negotiations between them for promoting exports of specific products to each other's market and Article 9 provides MFN treatment to merchant vessels of each other. However, unlike 1972 Agreement, this was signed for 3 years with effect from September 28, 1973. Like

1972 Agreement, it also envisaged to promote bilateral trade on a 'state-to-state' basis and hence could yield no better. It may not be out of place to ask, by way of digression, as to why both the Agreements envisaged promoting bilateral trade on a 'state-to-state' basis?

The answer lies with the model of economic development that Bangladesh followed at that time. On being independent in 1971, Bangladesh, like other developing countries in the world, adopted a model of 'import substitution industrialization' under heavy protection of domestic industries. The macroeconomic management primarily aimed at reviving the war-devastated economy under extensive state control. With the avowed ideology of state-socialism, the state not only became the *de facto* owner of a large number of enterprises that had been abandoned by their Pakistani owners (Mahmud: 2004), but also undertook efforts for massive nationalization of most of the production entities and introduced heavy trade controls. As Bangladesh was experimenting with a state guided socialistic type of economic development (Ahmed and Sattar: 2004), it was only natural that bilateral agreements sought to promote trade on a state-to-state basis. Meanwhile, by a protocol signed on December 17, 1974, rupee trade was replaced by freely convertible currency with effect from January 1, 1975.

However, with the end of Mujib era (1975), a gradual shift from 'state-guided-socialistic-economy' to 'aid-depended state-sponsored private capitalistic economy' had been initiated since 1976. The transition is marked with the beginning of the process of divestment of the abandoned state enterprises, promotion of private sector, economic deregulations encompassing goods and services sector, limited trade liberalization, etc. As a policy option, in harmony with the privatization strategy, inflow of foreign aid had been encouraged. Bangladesh Government adopted a soft credit policy primarily based on the foreign aid in order to encourage the private sector to come up speedily. Domestic industries were given adequate protection by way of high import tariff for the import competing sector. This change in internal development strategy necessitated a commensurate change in her trade agreement with India which has been formalized in 1980.

India-Bangladesh 1980 Trade Agreement

The 1980 Agreement has removed the clause 'on a state-to-state basis' for trade between the two countries. This is for the first time that the provisions of the Agreement were kept open for all the stake holders. Besides, it also removed the clause of 'balanced trade and payment arrangement'. By removing these two clauses, the Agreement had largely widened the scope of bilateral trade between the two countries. Article IV of the Agreement has formalized the use of 'convertible currencies' in trade between the two countries. Apart from these changes, the rest of the Articles of 1973 Agreement were incorporated. However, unlike 1973, this Agreement provides for bilateral consultation at least once in a year instead of once in six months. This Agreement has been signed for 3 years with effect from October 4, 1980 and renewed several times till the signing of another new Agreement in 2006.

Meanwhile, with the formation of South Asian Association for Regional Cooperation (SAARC) in 1985 and subsequently signing of SAARC Preferential Trading Arrangement (SAPTA) in 1995, formation of World Trade Organization in 1995 and consequent tariff reduction across the countries, liberalization of economies in both the countries since early 1990s, bilateral trade between India and Bangladesh took an upward turn. Bilateral trade Agreement of 1980 has lost much its relevance and trade between them has essentially been guided by the comparative and competitive advantages. It may be noted that trade agreements only provide the broad frameworks. No tariff negotiations have ever been initiated based on these Agreements. Indo-Bangladesh bilateral trade usually follows the exim policy of the respective countries based on multilateral WTO negotiations, Bangkok Agreement and SAPTA negotiations (SAFTA from July 1, 2006). Hence the bilateral Agreements could hardly influence the course of trade between these two countries.

Trends in Indo-Bangladesh Trade

Indo-Bangladesh trade, since inception, is characterized by almost unilateral export from India to Bangladesh. This is true for both formal and informal trade. The annual average export from India to Bangladesh for 1980-85, before the formation of SAARC, was US$75.14 million while the same for import from Bangladesh was US$17.65 million. India's average annual export has gone up to US$281.09 million in post-SAARC pre-SAPTA period (1986-94) while her average annual import from Bangladesh has gone down to US$14.02 million. For post-SAPTA as well as post-WTO but pre-SAFTA (South Asian Free Trade Agreement) period (1995-2005), India's average annual export to Bangladesh has further gone up to US$1122.41 million while the same for her import from Bangladesh has increased to US$72.48 million (Table 1.1). The general trend in Indo-Bangladesh trade is shown in Figure 1.1 and Table 1.2.

TABLE 1.1

India's Export to and Import from Bangladesh

(in US$ million)

Year	*Annual Average Export*	*Annual Average Import*
1980-85	75.14	17.65
1986-94	281.09	14.02
1995-05	*1122.41*	*72.48*

Source: Direction of Trade Statistics Yearbook, IMF.

TABLE 1.2

India's Export to and Import from Bangladesh

(in US $ Million)

Year	*Export to Bangla-desh*	*Total export*	*Export to Bangladesh as % of Total export*	*Import from Bangla-desh*	*Total import*	*Import from Bangladesh as % of total import*	*Trade balance (8)*
(1)	(2)	(3)	(4)	(5)	(6)	(7)	(8)
1980	105.52	8440.83	1.25	12.35	14822.20	0.08	(+)93.17
1981	49.01	6827.17	0.72	13.55	14549.80	0.09	(+)35.46
1982	60.18	8271.75	0.73	18.61	15634.80	0.12	(+)41.57
1983	41.97	7858.14	0.53	5.75	13892.70	0.04	(+)36.22
1984	89.97	8230.75	1.09	26.74	15115.30	0.18	(+)63.23
1985	104.19	8265.36	1.26	28.90	16329.00	0.18	(+)75.29
1986	112.59	9135.28	1.23	7.90	15051.40	0.05	(+)104.69
1987	145.49	10797.70	1.35	14.11	16838.00	0.08	(+)131.38
1988	169.99	13192.60	1.29	12.28	19034.70	0.06	(+)157.71
1989	176.23	15839.00	1.11	13.95	19297.50	0.07	(+)162.28
1990	297.11	17813.00	1.67	15.26	23991.40	0.06	(+)281.85
1991	324.56	17873.50	1.82	5.73	19509.40	0.03	(+)318.83
1992	353.18	19232.60	1.84	9.78	23196.60	0.04	(+)343.40
1993	429.62	20989.80	2.05	12.93	21268.80	0.06	(+)416.69
1994	521.00	24196.20	2.15	34.27	25485.80	0.13	(+)486.73
1995	959.62	30538.00	3.14	78.82	34486.50	0.23	(+)880.80
1996	832.45	32325.60	2.58	57.96	36054.80	0.16	(+)774.49
1997	807.13	34622.10	2.33	53.65	40896.40	0.13	(+)753.48
1998	943.33	33665.10	2.80	59.50	42162.10	0.14	(+)883.83
1999	726.13	35921.60	2.02	74.25	47900.50	0.16	(+)651.88
2000	860.33	42625.80	2.02	79.85	50336.10	0.16	(+)780.48
2001	1086.81	45225.70	2.40	66.88	59016.90	0.11	(+)1019.93
2002	1132.54	50496.30	2.24	61.32	58912.40	0.10	(+)1071.22
2003	1599.55	61118.50	2.62	73.73	74070.00	0.10	(+)1525.82
2004	1624.82	75385.20	2.16	60.57	99835.30	0.06	(+)1564.25
2005	*1773.85*	*99132.60*	*1.79*	*130.77*	*139458.00*	*0.09*	*(+)1643.08*

Source: Direction of Trade Statistics Yearbook, IMF.

Figure 1.1
India's Export to and Import from Bangladesh

(in US$ million)

Thus, as far as the official trade is concerned, there exists a huge trade surplus in favour of India. What is more important is that this Indian trade surplus is increasing over time. Figure 1.2 depicts this trend.

We do not have any precise data to study the trend in informal trade. However, available studies (Chaudhari:1995, Bakht: 1996, Rahaman and Razzaque: 1998, Taneja: 1999, Das: 2000, Pohit and Taneja: 2000, World Bank: 2006) indicate that, like formal trade, informal exports also flow almost unilaterally from India to Bangladesh and the volume of informal export from India to Bangladesh is guessed at almost equal to that of formal export. As a result, the real trade deficit that Bangladesh is having with India is almost double the formal trade deficit. It, thus, appears that the abrogation of "border trade" provision has in no way helped Bangladesh in stopping movement of goods across the border.

Figure 1.2

India's Trade Balance With Bangladesh

(in US $ Million)

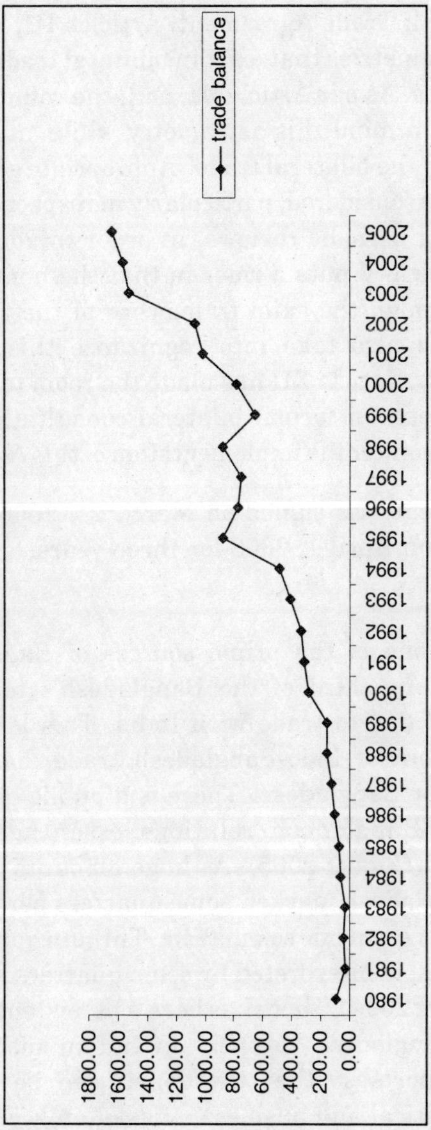

Source: Calculated from Direction of Trade Statistics Yearbook, IMF

India-Bangladesh 2006 Trade Agreement

This asymmetric trade relation has been focused in 2006 India-Bangladesh Trade Agreement. Articles III, V and XII refer to the asymmetries that exist in bilateral trade between the two countries. As par Article III, both the countries have agreed to keep in mind this asymmetry while 'augmenting and diversifying' the bilateral trade. 'Appropriate and special measures' will be considered, particularly in respect of specific products, during periodic reviews, in order to address this asymmetry. Article V puts a rider in that the normal trade that follows through the exim framework of the respective countries should also take into cognizance this bilateral trade asymmetry. Article XII has made the room to raise the issue of asymmetry in formal bilateral consultations to be held in order to monitor the implementation of this Agreement.

The Agreement was signed on March 21, 2006 and has come into force on April 1, 2006 for three years.

Issues in Trade

India being one of the prime sources of Bangladesh's import, almost one third of the Bangladesh's total trade deficit is caused due to trade with India. This large trade deficit, arising out of Indo-Bangladesh trade, has been a major concern for Bangladesh. There is a public perception that sees Indo-Bangladesh relations essentially as an exploitative one (Haque: 2005). As huge amounts of Indian goods flood Bangladesh market, some quarters perceive this as phenomenon of economic colonialism. This unequal trading relation, at times, is interpreted by some quarters as Indian hegemony (Islam: 2004). There has been a persistent demand on behalf of Bangladesh to open up Indian markets for Bangladeshi exports so that the deficit can be reduced. Bangladeshi political and business elites often accuse India not being sensitive enough in opening her markets for products having export interest of Bangladesh (Islam:2004).

TABLE-1.3

GDP Growth Rate of Bangladesh

Year	*Average Annual Growth Rate*	*Standard Deviation*
1974-1980	2.90	3.699008
1981-85	3.78	1.685497
1986-90	3.93	1.622335
1991-95	4.49	0.288062
1996-2000	5.20	0.494975
2001-2006	5.46	0.736885

Source: Alauddin: 2004, Bangladesh Bureau of Statistics, Bangladesh Bank and Asian Development Bank various issues.

Let us now consider the justification of these allegations leveled against India. Although overall trade deficit is more important than bilateral trade deficit, persistent bilateral trade deficit of significant magnitude has important political bearing for a nation only if it does not contribute to the productive capacity of the economy. Bangladesh's imports from India mainly consist of raw materials like cotton yarn, machine and equipments, base metals, chemicals and mineral products like coal, limestone, etc. These are all used in Bangladesh's ready made garments industry, fertilizer, pharmaceutical, chemical and cement industries. With the liberalization of imports and drastic reduction of import tariff on the industrial raw materials in Bangladesh, Indian products became highly competitive in Bangladesh markets leading to rise in imports from India. Overall export of Bangladesh has also started rising and percentage share of export to GDP has also started increasing overtime. With the growth of export, GDP started moving upwards and more and more imports could be financed due to higher exports. All these have transformed the Bangladesh economy from aid to trade dependence creating the necessary resilience for sustainable growth. Table 1.3 exhibits a secular rise in Bangladesh's average annual GDP growth rate along with declining variation indicating a march towards stable economic

Figure 1.3
GDP Growth Rate of Bangladesh

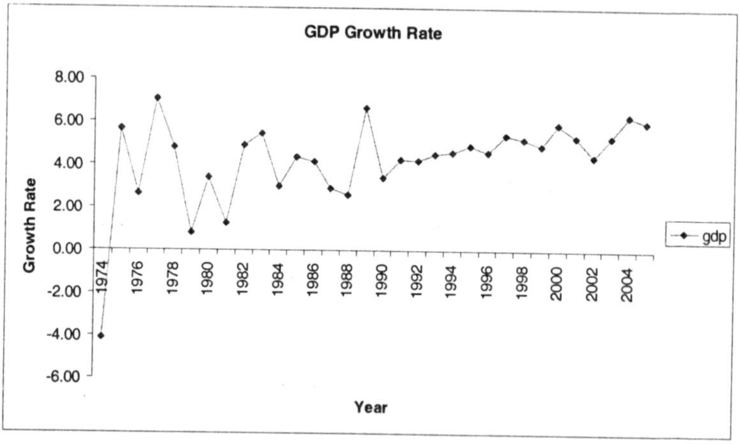

Source: Alauddin: 2004, Bangladesh Bureau of Statistics, Bangladesh Bank and Asian Development Bank various issues.

growth taking place particularly in post-liberalized era. The growth path is shown in Figure 1.3.

While export grew from US$ 790million in 1980 to US$ 1670 million in 1990, i.e., a rise by about 111 per cent, import grew from US$ 2610 million to US$ 3656 million, i.e., a rise of 40 per cent. Again export grew from US$1687 million in 1991 to US$ 5589 million in 2000, i.e., a rise by 231 per cent, while import grew from US$ 3421 million to US$ 9000 million, i.e., a rise by 163 per cent. Similarly, while export grew from US$ 5735 million in 2001 to US$ 8494 million in 2005, i.e., a rise by 48 per cent, import at the same time grew from US$ 9011 million in 2001 to US$ 13850 million in 2005, i.e., a rise by 54 per cent. The growth paths of export and import are shown in Figure 1.4. Thus, during the last quarter century, exports of Bangladesh have grown much faster than her imports except the early years of the present decade.

While in 1980, only 30 per cent of Bangladesh's imports

Figure 1.4
Growth of Export and Import of Bangladesh

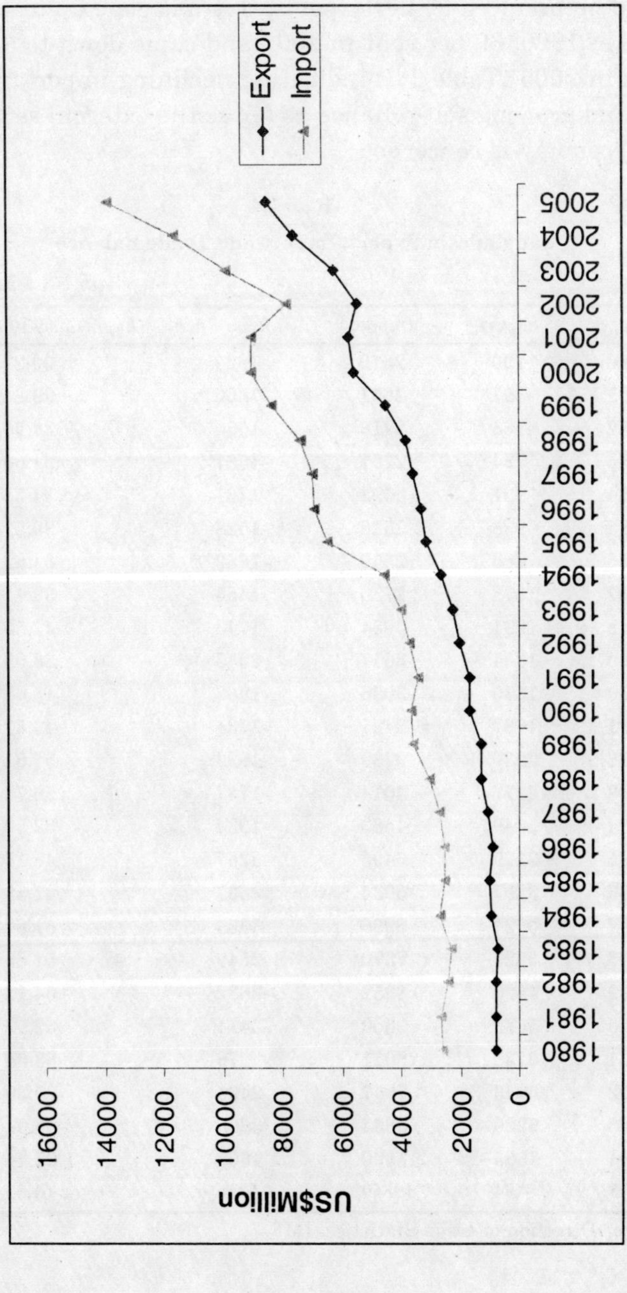

Source: Direction of trade Statistics, IMF.

could be financed by her exports, this has gone up to 46 per cent in 1990, 69 per cent in 2002 and came down to 61 per cent in 2005 (Table 1.4) indicating declining importance of aid and growing self-reliance as far as the external sector of the economy is concerned.

TABLE 1.4

Bangladesh: Export, Import and Trade Balance

(in US $ Million)

Year	*Export*	*Import*	*Trade balance*	*Export as %of Import*
1980	790	2610	-1820	30.27
1981	791	2651	-1860	29.84
1982	768	2418	-1650	31.76
1983	724	2291	-1567	31.60
1984	931	2692	-1761	34.58
1985	998	2526	-1528	39.51
1986	888	2550	-1662	34.82
1987	1076	2730	-1654	39.41
1988	1291	3034	-1743	42.55
1989	1304	3617	-2313	36.05
1990	1670	3656	-1986	45.68
1991	1687	3421	-1734	49.31
1992	2037	3730	-1693	54.61
1993	2277	4014	-1737	56.73
1994	2649	4583	-1934	57.80
1995	3129	6496	-3367	48.17
1996	3297	6934	-3637	47.55
1997	3627	6996	-3369	51.84
1998	3821	7370	-3549	51.85
1999	4520	8352	-3832	54.12
2000	5589	9000	-3411	62.10
2001	5735	9011	-3276	63.64
2002	5443	7847	-2404	69.36
2003	6229	9834	-3605	63.34
2004	7585	11590	-4005	65.44
2005	8494	13850	-5356	61.33

Source: Direction of trade Statistics, IMF.

TABLE 1.5

Composition of Imports of Bangladesh

(in percentage)

Year	*Food-grains*	*Consumer Goods*	*Intermediate Goods*	*Capital Goods*	*Others*	*Total*
1981	9.87	4.07	29.29	27.20	29.57	100
1982	11.08	2.95	30.64	34.06	21.27	100
1983	16.72	3.81	28.41	42.49	8.58	100
1984	16.91	3.78	27.20	26.18	25.92	100
1985	18.81	4.12	25.01	26.11	25.95	100
1986	9.31	5.75	25.80	42.43	16.71	100
1987	10.42	5.34	15.76	32.67	35.80	100
1988	16.38	7.20	17.55	36.50	22.37	100
1989	11.08	5.36	18.31	31.70	33.54	100
1990	9.12	5.69	15.83	34.48	34.88	100
1991	8.56	8.24	38.04	2.62	42.54	100
1992	7.65	7.68	42.65	2.08	39.94	100
1993	4.42	7.60	45.06	2.08	40.84	100
1994	3.71	6.31	48.65	3.19	38.13	100
1995	8.44	7.06	44.56	3.51	36.42	100
1996	8.79	5.61	43.91	4.48	37.21	100
1997	2.73	6.58	50.24	4.93	35.53	100
1998	5.25	6.22	47.82	4.06	36.66	100
1999	13.28	7.76	41.16	3.91	33.89	100
2000	4.94	7.36	46.82	4.07	36.81	100
2001	4.03	5.68	49.41	5.57	35.31	100
2002	2.35	6.39	48.03	7.00	36.22	100
2003	4.58	8.62	46.68	6.14	33.98	100
2004	4.30	8.64	49.67	7.28	30.11	100
2005	4.71	8.48	54.52	9.14	23.15	100
2006	3.05	6.99	57.61	11.25	21.10	100

Source: Bagladesh Bank, Annual Review of Imports Payments, 2004-05, (for 1991-2005),
CPD:1995(for 1981-1990), Bangladesh Bank Annual Report 2005-06 (for 2006)

Note: Figures since 1991 exclude imports of EPZs.

Commodity Structure of Imports of Bangladesh

An anatomy of Bangladesh's imports shows that import bill for the intermediate goods which are used as industrial inputs has been increasing over time. The annual average share of import of intermediate goods to total import has gone up from 24.22 per cent during 1980s to 41.79 per cent during 1990s and then to 50.39 per cent during the present decade. In 2006, the percentage share of imports of intermediate goods to total import bill of Bangladesh stands at 58 per cent. Import share of consumer goods has never been substantial. The annual average share of imports of consumer goods was 4.71 per cent during the 1980s which has slightly gone up to 6.87 per cent during the 1990s and then registered a marginal rise to 7.45 per cent during the present decade. Import share of food grains has substantially declined from an annual average import of 13.40 per cent during the 1980s to 7.20 per cent during 1990s and to 4 per cent during the present decade. Import share of capital goods has declined from an annual average of 33.26 per cent during the 1980s to 6.53 per cent during 1990s and then has slightly increased to 7.21 per cent during the present decade (Table 1.5 and Figure 1.5).

Thus, commodity structure of imports of Bangladesh exhibits the growing needs of industrial inputs particularly by the export sector. This is basically developmental import where export component of import is quite high. It is quite natural for the business to draw imports from the cheapest source and sale exports wherever the demands are. Bangladesh is importing more from India not because Indian firms have control over them but because buying from India is profitable for them.

This dimension of viewing Bangladesh's deficit trade balance with India in association with her growing economy and rising export is often missing in the literature of Indo-

Figure 1.5
Composition of Bangladesh's Imports

(in percentage)

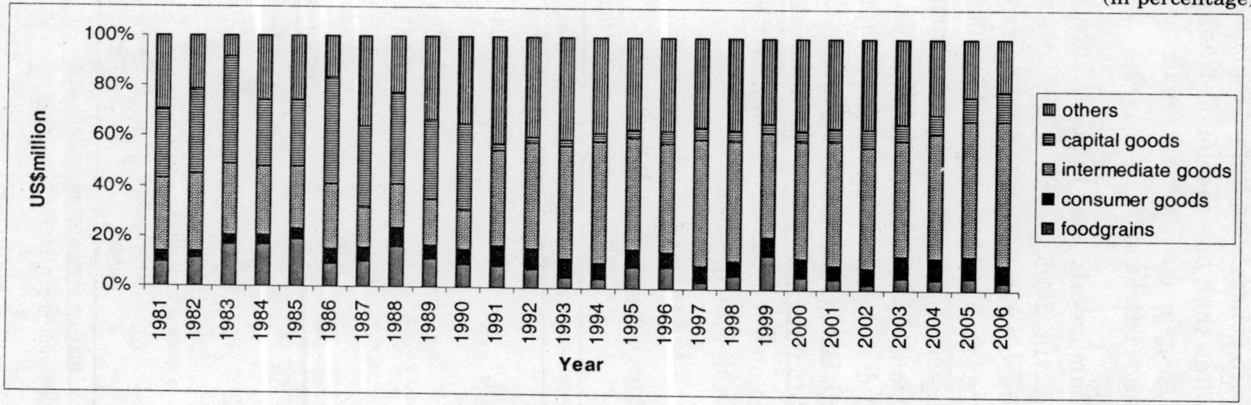

Source: Bagladesh Bank, Annual Review of Imports Payments, 2004-05, (for 1991-2005), CPD:1995 (for 1981-1990), Bangladesh Bank Annual Report 2005-06 (for 2006).

Note: Figures since 1991 exclude imports of EPZs.

Bangladesh relations in general and Indo-Bangladesh trade in particular. More often than not, the deficit-trade-balance issue is politicized to gain currency in domestic politics which suffer from Indo-centricism.

Besides India, Bangladesh also imports substantially from China. In fact, in 2005, while 17.77 per cent of Bangladesh's total import came from India, the same from China was 14.27 per cent. This has changed in 2006, while 15.78 per cent of Bangladesh's total import came from China, the same for India was 14.24 (Table 1.6). Thus, China has replaced India and has become the largest supplier to Bangladesh. Although Bangladesh is having almost the same trade deficit with China, then why is it that she makes it an issue in case of India and not in case of China? We shall get back to this question in a little while.

TABLE 1.6

Direction of Bangladesh's Imports

(in per cent of total import)

Country	*2005*	*2006*
China	14.27	15.78
India	17.77	14.24
Kuwait	4.59	7.73
Singapore	7.85	6.53
Hong Kong	4.66	4.81
Japan	4.85	4.69
Korea	3.66	3.63
Taiwan	3.88	3.61
USA	2.82	2.64
Malaysia	2.44	2.56
UK	2.53	2.51
Thailand	2.89	2.46
Others	27.81	28.82
Total	100.00	100.00

Source: Bangladesh Bank, http://www.bangladeshbank.org
Note: Only import under cash is considered

Figure 1.6
Trade Balance of Bangladesh with Major Trading Partners

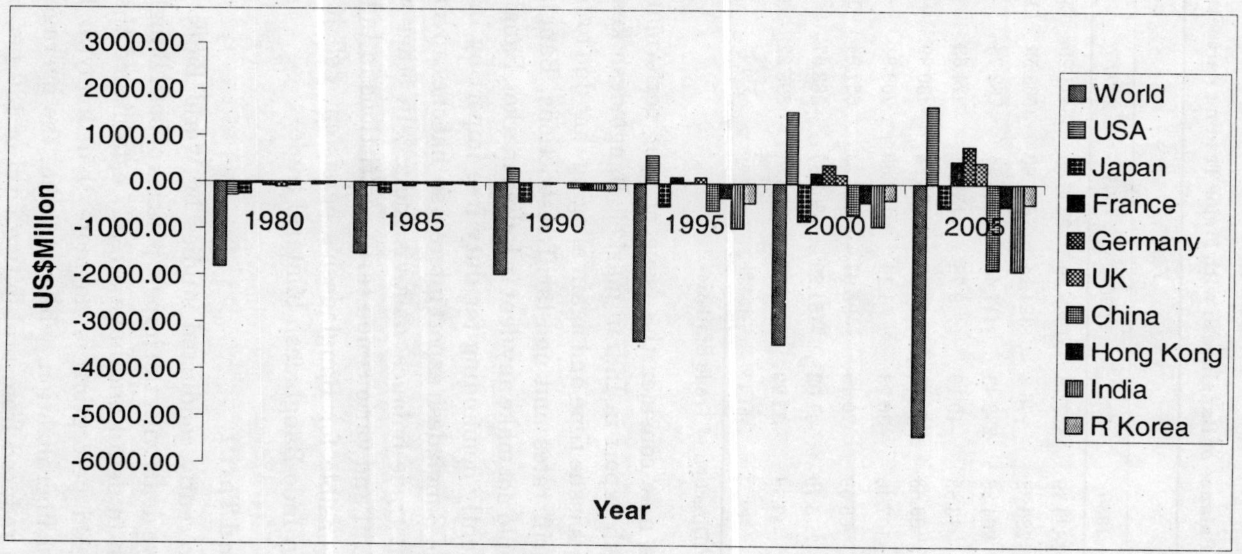

Source: IMF: Direction of Trade Statistics.

TABLE 1.7

Trade Balance of Bangladesh with Major Trading Partners

	Year					
Country	*1980*	*1985*	*1990*	*1995*	*2000*	*2005*
World	-1820.39	-1527.28	-1985.59	-3366.89	-3411.20	-5356.50
USA	-286.35	-76.3	324.14	604.60	1565.55	1676.94
Japan	-264.36	-238.43	-417.48	-494.54	-782.78	-506.63
France	-13.53	-19.19	9.78	131.01	224.63	488.74
Germany	-88.63	-69.67	-17.37	23.58	430.99	827.40
U K	-107.46	-36.73	1.14	143.60	200.81	472.05
China	-68.59	-70.15	-98.97	-582.29	-657.94	-1824.02
Hong Kong	6.79	-41.02	-151.29	-303.87	-383.07	-461.21
India	-47.58	-35.29	-148.59	-958.31	-895.32	-1832.36
Korea	-19.72	-61.13	-154.88	-409.16	-336.25	-423.30

Source: IMF:Direction of Trade Statistics.

Let us now consider the issue of poor performance of Bangladesh export in Indian market. Bangladesh keeps on raising this issue time and again alleging that due to India's higher tariff rates and non-tariff restrictions, Bangladesh exports could not make any dent in Indian market. Bangladesh is persistently demanding for duty free import by India of products of Bangladesh export interest so that she can improve her deficit trade balance vis-à-vis India. . In other words, higher tariff and various non tariff restrictions in India are held responsible for Bangladesh's persistent deficit trade balance in Indo-Bangladesh bilateral trade.

Trade and Tariff

Two recently conducted studies by World Bank (2004, 2006) have dealt with the import policies of both Bangladesh and India in detail and have already established that this Bangladeshi perception is no more than a myth. In the process of liberalization, while in India, the average tariff has been reduced from prohibitive level of 130 per cent in

1990-91 to 35 pre cent in 1997-98 and then to 15 per cent in 2005-06 and finally to 12.5 per cent in 2006-07: in Bangladesh the same has been reduced from 73.6 per cent in 1991-92 to 32 per cent in 1995-96 and then to 24.3 per cent in 2006-07 (World Bank: 2006). Although base level tariff was higher in India, but the depth of tariff reduction is also higher in India. Under SAPTA, India has provided tariff preferences to SAARC LDC members on approximately 2925 tariff lines, about 58 per cent of the total number of its approximately 5000 6-digit H S which came into force since 2000-01. In most cases tariff preferences were 50 per cent. This means while average MFN tariff rate was 35 per cent in 2000-01, for Bangladesh it was 17.5 per cent. Subsequently, following another two rounds of tariff reduction in 2005-06 and 2006-07, tariff on Bangladesh import has become negligible. Thus, while the hypothesis of higher Indian tariff as the cause of poor export of Bangladesh products in Indian markets partially explains the asymmetric bilateral Indo-Bangladesh trade in the 1980s and 1990s, it can hardly explain as to why this asymmetry has further increased during the current decade (Table 1.2 and figure 1.2) in spite of the fact that effective average tariff is much lower in India than in Bangladesh. The World Bank study (2006), thus, concludes that "the explanations for the stagnation of Bangladesh exports to India have to do with comparative advantage and supply side factors in Bangladesh, not lack of demand or protection in India".

Commodity Structure of Exports of Bangladesh

In order to better understand the nature of these 'supply side factors', let us have a look at the commodity structure of exports of Bangladesh. It can be seen from Table 1.8 and Figure 1.7 that Bangladesh's export basket is too narrow. Four commodity groups namely raw jute and jute goods, leather, frozen shrimps and fish and ready made garments constitute bulk of Bangladesh's export. During the 1980s,

TABLE 1.8

Composition of Bangladesh's Export

(in percentage)

Year	*Raw Jute and Jute Goods*	*Leather*	*Frozen Shrimps and Fish*	*Ready Made Garments*	*Others*	*Total*
1981	68.21	8.02	5.63	0.42	17.72	100
1982	63.80	10.05	8.45	1.12	16.59	100
1983	62.39	8.45	10.50	1.60	17.06	100
1984	58.45	10.48	9.49	3.95	17.63	100
1985	57.92	7.49	9.31	12.42	12.85	100
1986	50.92	7.45	13.80	16.00	11.84	100
1987	37.80	12.57	12.66	27.84	9.12	100
1988	31.03	11.94	11.37	35.26	10.40	100
1989	26.98	10.65	10.96	36.63	14.77	100
1990	29.72	11.75	9.06	39.96	9.51	100
1991	26.91	7.80	8.21	42.87	14.21	100
1992	19.37	7.23	6.52	53.39	13.50	100
1993	15.37	6.21	6.93	52.06	19.44	100
1994	13.46	6.63	8.72	61.43	9.75	100
1995	11.20	5.82	8.81	64.29	9.88	100
1996	10.66	5.44	8.06	65.58	10.25	100
1997	9.71	4.41	7.24	67.93	10.71	100
1998	7.46	3.68	5.68	55.09	28.10	100
1999	7.00	3.16	5.16	56.17	28.50	100
2000	5.79	3.39	5.96	53.58	31.28	100
2001	4.58	3.91	5.61	80.45	5.44	100
2002	5.05	3.46	4.61	82.44	4.44	100
2003	5.16	2.92	4.90	75.86	11.16	100
2004	4.26	2.78	5.13	75.68	12.15	100
2005	4.66	2.54	4.85	74.89	13.06	100
2006	4.84	2.44	4.36	75.81	12.55	100

Source: CPD: 1995, IMF: 2003 and Bangladesh Bank Annual Report 2005-06.

jute and jute goods had been the principal export items contributing on an average about 51 per cent of annual export earnings of Bangladesh. This had declined to 15 per cent during the 1990s and then to merely 5 per cent during the present decade. Export of ready-made garments that include woven garments and knitwear has substituted the export of raw jute and jute products over the years. During the 1980s, on an average ready-made garments contributed around 15 per cent of annual export earnings of Bangladesh. This had gone up to 56 per cent during the 1990s and then to 74 per cent during the present decade. In 2006, about 76 per cent of total export earnings has come from the ready-made garment sector, while raw jute and jute products contributed only 5 per cent, leather contributed 2 per cent, frozen shrimps and fish contributed 4 per cent and export of other commodities together contributed 13 per cent of the total export earnings.

Thus export basket of Bangladesh was all along dominated by single product— raw jute and jute goods during the 1980s and ready-made garments since 1990s whereas the export basket of India is much diversified. It is precisely because of this, Bangladesh, in spite of enjoying preferential tariff on 2925 tariff lines which are, in most cases, 50 per cent lower than MFN tariff rates, could not make any dent into Indian market.

Competitive Nature of Export baskets

Moreover, commodity structure of exports of Bangladesh is competitive rather than complementary to that of India. Like Bangladesh ready made garments, leather manufactures and jute manufactures are also important items of export of India. While in 2000-01, the share of ready-made garments, leather goods and jute manufactures was 12.58, 4.40 and 0.46 per cent of India's total export respectively, the same for 2005-06 amounts to 8.18, 2.6 and 0.29 respectively. Although Bangladesh has comparative advantage in ready made garment

Figure 1.7
Composition of Bangladesh's Export (in percentage)

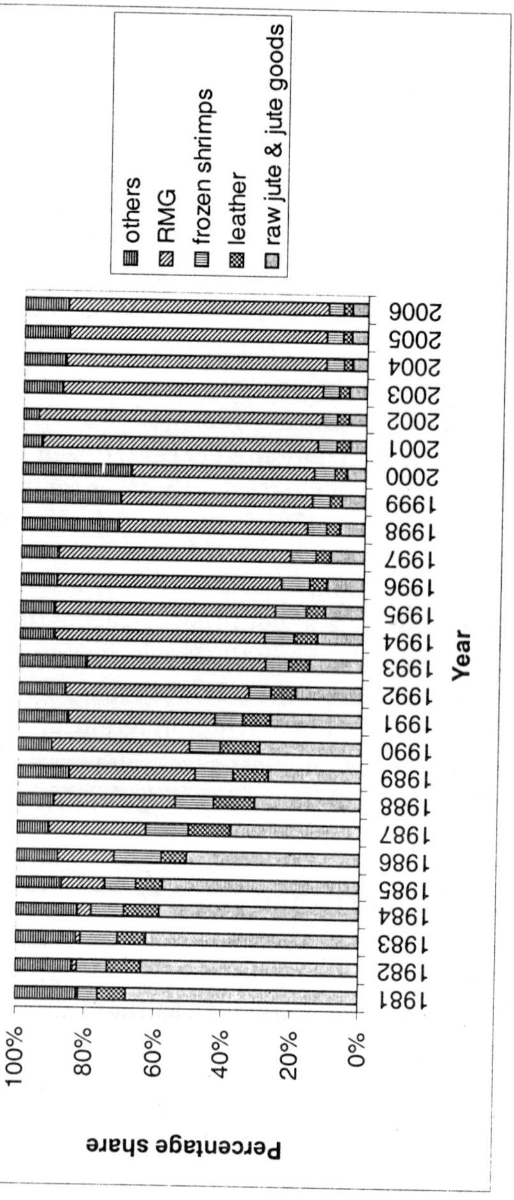

Source: CPD: 1995, IMF: 2003 and Bangladesh Bank Annual Report 2005-06.

sector, it is difficult for India to allow free access in this market segment as it may out compete Indian industries. As a result, just before the withdrawal of import licensing from textiles and garments in 2001, India imposed specific duties on a large number of textile fabrics and garments in order to protect domestic producers against low price import competition (World Bank: 2006). Use of para-tariff, however, does not violate the principles of RTA or WTO. Countries adopt them to secure national interest as short and medium term measures. Bangladesh has also imposed a number of para tariffs like regulatory duties (discontinued since 2004-05), license fee (withdrawn in 2002-03), infrastructure development surcharge (in practice), supplementary duties (in practice), etc. However, SAPTA preferences given by India to Bangladesh are also applicable to these specific duties while the same given to India by Bangladesh are not applicable in case of para tariff.

Besides para tariff, the rules of origin clause under SAPTA also stands on the way of Bangladesh RMG export to India. In order to qualify for India's SAPTA preferences, the cif value of non-SAPTA imported inputs included in the exported product should not exceed 70 per cent of the fob price, i.e., national value added should be no less than 30 per cent of the fob price (World Bank:2006). As the value added margins in cutting, sewing assembling garments from imported fabrics are typically around 30 per cent (or even less) of fob prices, if Bangladesh firms import fabrics from non-SAPTA countries like China, this limits their ability to compete in exporting to India (World Bank:2006).

What are the options, then, available with Bangladesh to narrow down the deficit balance of trade with India?

Options for Bangladesh

Firstly, as short term measure, Bangladesh can buy

fabrics from any of the SAPTA member countries so that it can export RMG to Indian market at preferential rate. This will enable Bangladesh to export more in Indian market and thereby reduce the deficit trade balance with India. Imports of fabrics and textile articles constitute about a quarter of Bangladesh's total annual imports. In fact in 2004-05, the share of fabric and textile articles to total imports was 24 per cent and the same for 2005-06 was 23.5 per cent (Bangladesh Bank: http://www.bangladesh-bank.org/econdata/import/imp_pay_comodity.php/txtperiod=2). Bangladesh imports fabric and yarn from a number of countries like China, India, Hong Kong, Singapore, Japan, Republic of Korea, Taiwan, USA, Malaysia, UK and Thailand. However, China, India and Hong Kong are the three most important sources of supply. As both China and Hong Kong are non-SAPTA countries, Bangladesh is left with the only choice to increase its import from India. But as the export strategy of Bangladesh RMG sector is based on the US and EU markets, more than 50 per cent of total woven garments are exported to USA and about 70 per cent of the knit wear are exported to EU (Razi: 2006), availing of SAPTA preferences appears not to be very high in Bangladesh's import agenda as China has already replaced India as the preferred source of supply of fabrics and yarn in recent years.

Secondly, as a long term measure, Bangladesh needs to expand her export basket with products having ability to compete with Indian industries at home. For this to happen there has to be all-round improvement in productivity, efficiency and technology.

Transit

Thirdly, as a medium term measure, Bangladesh can earn a hefty amount if she chooses to provide transit facilities to India for sending goods from mainland India to her north eastern region. A rough estimate suggests that Bangladesh can earn an annual transit fee of Rs 1000 croes (Thapar: 2005), i.e., roughly US$247 million, as well as can attract substantial investment in infrastructure sector. As Bangladesh is located not only between the mainland India and her north eastern region but also between India and the South East Asia, with India's look east policy gaining ground, transit routes and transit trade through Bangladesh will play a more important role in future. Transit through Bangladesh will benefit both India and Bangladesh. India will be gaining in terms of reduced transport cost and Bangladesh in terms of huge transit fees. Presently, Assam's tea travels 1400 km to Kolkata port while it could have curtailed about 60 per cent of the distance if access to Chittagong port was available. Goods from Agartala travel 1645 km to Kolkata while direct distance would be about 350 km through Bangladesh. A rough estimate suggests that in the next 20 years movement of goods to north east region could be around 30 million tones and if even 20 million tones could move through Bangladesh this would be several times the annual freight handling of Bangladesh railways(Thapar: 2005). Besides transit income accruing from India, the same can also be accrued from Nepal and Bhutan if Bangladesh opens up its ports for these two land-locked Himalayan countries. Apart from transit fees that can accrue from opening up of Bangladesh's roadways, railways and ports, she can also earn US$125 million (Srivastava: 2005) as transit fee from the proposed tri-nation gas pipe line running from Myanmar to India through Bangladesh. It is not that Bangladesh is not aware of the commercial value of her geo-strategic location. It is well known what role transit/ transshipment can play in revolutionizing the Bangladesh economy once her multi-modal transportation network is linked and made accessible for regional and inter-regional trade and economic cooperation (Choudhury: 2005; Mohammed: 2006). Besides transit fee, Indian investment in infrastructure sector, growth of ancillary transport industry and services, indirect employment and income generation from hospitality services can largely reduce Bangladesh's deficit trade balance vis-à-vis India.

In spite of sound economic logic for transit traffic and bilateral framework agreement on this issue already in place (India-Bangladesh Trade Agreement: 1972, 1973, 1980, 2006), why is it that Bangladesh hesitates to finalize a concrete deal with India?

Security

It is well known that this issue is rather political than economic and has direct bearing on the security perception of Bangladesh. National consensus within Bangladesh could not be arrived at on this issue due to the divergence of security perception of the different stakeholders like political parties, military, intelligence agencies and civil society organizations. State-centric security perception, foremost in the minds of certain sections, considers the grant of transit facilities would be tantamount to cut Bangladesh in two to make for an Indian corridor (Mohammed: 2006). The security doctrine of certain quarters in Bangladesh interprets that for India Bangladesh remains as a strategic hinterland which is a major hurdle in its national integration particularly in relation to her north eastern states. India perceives Bangladesh to be a hurdle in attaining social, political and economic stability in her north eastern states. Issues relating to cross border illegal immigration, cross-border movement of insurgent activists, arms trade—all pose a great threat to Indian security (Hussain: 2005). Besides the security concern arising out of her geo-strategic location, in some section, Indian hegemony in bilateral relation is also viewed as a threat to the existence of independent Bangladesh (Choudhury: 2005).

The China Factor

To counter Indian hegemony and to strengthen her strategic value, Bangladesh has developed a deep politico-military relationship with China over the last 3 decades. In fact China currently plays a role in the maintenance of Bangladesh's security that no other country does. China is the largest and most important provider of military hardware and also trains Bangladesh armed forces (Kibria: 2006). Bangladesh army's artillery is equipped with the Chinese semi-automatic assault rifle (Type 567.62 mm) which is a variant of the AK-47. This is due to be replaced by the automatic Chinese assault rifles (Type 817.62) to be manufactured at the Bangladesh Ordnance Factory in Ghazipur, near Dhaka. The deal with China to this end has already been finalized in 2003. A licensed production agreement with China North Industries Corporation (NORINCO) is on the card for production of this new assault rifles (BDN:March, 2006). Bangladesh army is also contemplating to buy 100 main battle tanks from China and the government has already entered into agreement to upgrade 58 existing tanks out of 232 under Chinese loan for Chinese expertise (BDN: May, 2006). Bangladesh is also contemplating to buy Chinese made PLZ-45 self-propelled howitzers (BDN: August, 2005)

Bangladesh army's air-defence brigade is equipped with Chinese HN-5/HN-5A man portable surface-to-air (SAM) supplemented by several types of anti-aircraft artillery systems of Chinese origin. The HN-5/HN-5A is due to be replaced by QW-2, low-altitude SAM system produced by China National Precision Machinery Import and Export Corporation. A contract to this end was concluded in last September 2004 (BDN: March, 2006). Recently Bangladesh has procured 16 F-7 fighter aircraft from China (BDN: March, 2006). Bangladesh is also exploring the possibilities to produce naval patrol boats with Chinese assistance (BDN: March, 2006)

All these show the depth of Sino-Bangladesh defence cooperation. In fact, all the three wings of Bangladesh army are equipped with Chinese armour and depend on China for manpower training as well as upgradation and service of the inventory.

Besides military cooperation, China has agreed to provide assistance to Bangladesh for peaceful uses of nuclear energy for electricity and medicine. It has assured its help for the installation of Rooppur nuclear power project in Pabna which was conceived even before the birth of Bangladesh in 1961 but could not be materialized due to the shortage of fund (BDN: August, 2005). China has also extended assistance for the development of infrastructure in Bangladesh. It has already funded the construction of 6 "Friendship Bridges' and has agreed to develop Chittagong town and its link with Kunming. It has already signed Memoradum of Understanding to develop natural gas and petroleum as well as water resources in Bangladesh. Sino-Bangladesh engagement has already paid dividend to China as it has recently replaced India as the prime source of import.

China has fourfold interest in cultivating Bangladesh. First, like Pakistan and Myanmar, China wants to have access to the Indian Ocean through Bangladesh. Development of the friendship city of Chittagong and its link with Kunming will provide that much haunted southern sea route to China and bring the Chinese sea lane of communication under better surveillance. It may be noted that 80 per cent of China's oil import is from the Gulf region and the rest is from Africa and is transported through the sea lane of the Indian Ocean (Hussain:2006). As a result, surveillance of the Indian Ocean sea lanes in general and the Strait of Malacca in particular is very important from Chinese energy security point of view. Moreover, if China could develop the Chittagong port *a la* Gwadar port in Pakistan which is connected with China through the Karakoram Highway and acting as the alternative route for import of oil from the Gulf and Africa, then it can open up another cost-effective Chittagong-Kunming route to enhance its energy security in the long run as well as the same can be used as an outlet for South-West Chinese products for the global market. Construction of road links between Bangladesh and China through Myanmar could also serve military purpose in future as the China-Myanmar-Bangladesh triangle will have potential to draw India's north east into its *de facto* sphere of influence (Kibria: 2006).

Second, befriending Bangladesh is a part of grand Chinese strategy to contain India within its border (Pant: 2006). With Chinese penetration in Bangladesh the strategy of containment-of-India comes to full circle as China has already made Pakistan and Myanmar her strategic partners. Moreover, by developing close relationship with India's neighbours in South Asia, China amply demonstrates her interest to play the balancing role in the region vis-à-vis India. In fact, the role India is playing in ASEAN, China intends to play the same in SAARC. It has already acquired the 'observer' status in SAARC and is destined to play crucial role in the days to come. In fact, the principal Chinese goal is to prevent the rise of any peer competitor in Asia that can challenge China's role in the Asia-Pacific region (Kibria: 2006).

Third, opening to Bangladesh via Kunming-Chittagong route will enable China to flood Bangladesh and Eastern India markets with cheap Chinese merchandise. Already Chinese exports to Bangladesh has surpassed that of India and Chinese consumables are making their way to north eastern states of India via Myanmar.

Fourth, China has deep interest in Bangladesh's natural gas reserves. Bangladesh has a proven reserve of 15 trillion cubic feet (Tcf) of natural gas in the 13 explored fields. About 9 other gas blocks are yet to be explored. The US Geological Survey has estimated that Bangladesh contains 32 Tcf of additional "undiscovered reserves". Thus, Bangladesh has the potential to become a major producer of natural gas. A conservative estimate based on 11.47 Tcf of proven reserve and current rate of consumption forecasts that the reserve will last for 27 years (Rahman: 2004). If the reserve is approximated at 47 Tcf (proven plus potential), then at the current rate of consumption it will last for more than 100 years. Even when annual growth rate of national demand for gas is factored into, gas export by Bangladesh appears viable. China requires to import huge oil and gas to support the growing need of her economy. Already China has surpassed Japan to become the world's second largest consumer of oil (Bhattacharya: 2006). The competition between India and China for oil and gas has already intensified. Bangladesh's role in tri-nation gas pipeline may well be understood in terms of China factor.

Bangladesh also has its own strategic interest for engaging China. The militaristic perception of national security suffers from a perceived threat from India. As China is not only an Asian power but also one of the leading global players, engaging China will not only enhance the strategic value of Bangladesh but also neutralize 'Indian domination' in her internal affairs. In fact, immediately after the assassination of Mujibur Rahman on August 15, 1975, military rulers of Bangladesh established diplomatic relations with China on October 4, 1975. They anticipated Indian intervention following the assassination of Mujibur Rahaman who was considered to be pro-Indian and played the China card to avert any such eventuality. This policy of balancing China against India has been further strengthened by the military rulers like Zia ur Rahaman, Hussain Mohammad Ershad and later Khaleda Zia, the widow of Zia-ur Rahman and has become the mainstream strategic thinking in the security discourse of Bangladesh.

Thus the Chinese strategic interest of "bottling up" India converges with Bangladesh's interest of "balancing India". Bangladesh's India policy could not be well understood without this China factor. As a long term strategy, this Bangladeshi militaristic security doctrine views that Bangladesh will be only gainer if China continues to grow at the present rate and eventually becomes the major Asian power. With the present US role of global policing and fighting terrorism across the world which will continue to bleed US, the influence of US is destined to decline. In that case, it will be difficult for US to contain China and India will then have to accommodate the Chinese interest in the Asia-Pacific region. If this futuristic strategic calculation goes well, then Bangladesh, already in good book of China, will only benefit by endorsing Chinese strategic interest which she can not do now fully due to her present geo-political limitations (Kibria: 2006).

This militaristic doctrine of national security has a bearing on Bangladesh's denial of transit facilities to India. In fact, India had transit facility through former East Pakistan till 1965 Indo-Pak war. One former Bangladeshi diplomat to China, Enayetullah Khan, has confessed that Pakistan had denied this transit right to India following the 1965 Indo-Pak war at the insistence of China (Pattanaik: 2005). Khan is of the view that the issue of transit is a strategic one and not economic. In the event of any future Sino-Indian conflict, then Bangladesh will become vulnerable. Moreover, Bangladesh can give transit to India only at the cost of her friendship with China (Pattanaik: 2005). It is, thus, obvious that the China factor lies at the back for citing apparently unfounded security threats to Bangladesh in the event of allowing transit to India.

One is not sure whether this Chinese factor is working at the back of Bangladesh's mind in delaying the contract of tri-nation gas pipe line project for bringing gas from Myanmar to India through Bangladesh. The project would have been proved beneficial for all the three stakeholder countries. Myanmar could have sold its gas and earned revenue while Bangladesh would have earned transit fee as well as realized value for the stranded gas in north eastern Bangladesh and India could have gained energy to feed her growing economy as well as could have tapped the stranded gas in the north eastern region (Kumar: 2006). In spite of the fact that all the three nations have agreed in principle on this $1billion project in January 2005, subsequently Bangladesh took a position that her participation in this project is contingent upon (i) India's providing unhindered corridor to Bangladesh for trade with Nepal and Bhutan, (ii) allowing transit passage to Bangladesh for transmission of hydro-electricity from Nepal and Bhutan, and (iii) reduction of trade deficit of Bangladesh arising out of bilateral trade with India (Srivastava: 2005) Meanwhile, due to the delay, Myanmar signed an agreement with Hong Kong-listed Petrochina to sell 6.5 Tcf gas from A-1 block reserve (for which India was negotiating) which is near to Teknaf of Bangladesh through an overland pipeline to Kunming (China) for 30 years (Kumar: 2006). Although Myanmar is still willing to supply gas to the proposed tri-nation gas pipeline from other gas blocks, the project cost will go up manifold as to reach up to the nearest gas block bordering Bangladesh (A-2) will require at least an additional 150 km pipeline (Kumar: 2006).

Security and Development

Thus, the geo-economic advantage that Bangladesh could have used for her economic development has become hostage to geo-strategic concern of the militaristic security perception. This overriding traditional security concern undermines non-traditional security threats arising out of the economic, social and political factors. The external sector of Bangladesh suffers from severe limitations like extremely narrow export basket (mainly ready-made garments), extreme concentration of export markets (mainly US and EU), and also extremely limited sources of import (mainly China and India). This, in turn, has severe implications for foreign policy making in Bangladesh.

There is also an alternative liberal perspective of national security of Bangladesh that sees no justification for Bangladesh either to align with China or India. Bangladesh should be friendly to both and enemy to none (Bakht: 2005). It should take maximum advantage of her geo-strategic locations for geo-economic gains. It should open up to neighbouring countries in order to transform herself into a hub of regional transit traffic, investment and trade. Since military movement through the corridor is out of question, providing the same in no way impact upon the country's security concern. An economically well off Bangladesh, then, can play effective strategic role in the region (Choudhury: 2005). Besides economic gains, transit traffic has significant political, diplomatic and strategic significance. As Bangladesh becomes a centre of regional communications network and a cross road of inter-state traffic, her importance in the geo-politics will naturally increase. Her international image will undergo a metamorphosis. Instead of a country perennially at the receiving end, Bangladesh will have something to offer to others. Peace, prosperity and stability of Bangladeh will be a matter of concern not only of Bangladeshis, but of all with a stake in trade and transit. Bangladesh's security will be strengthened by getting others beyond the region interested in her security and and well being (Choudhury: 2005). Since Bangladesh is not competing with India for regional power, there is no reason for her to play off China against India and to become a chess board for powers aspiring for regional/ Asian hegemony. It is imperative for Bangladesh to pursue a foreign policy conducive to her economic growth and this can best be achieved through multilateral and bilateral engagements with as many countries as possible. Cementing of Sino-Indian relations will better serve the interest of Bangladesh than their rivalries (Bakht: 2005). Since in spite of much differences and having competitive relationship between them, China and India are engaging with each other, what purpose does it serve for Bangladesh in being India-phobic?

Conclusion

The asymmetry in Indo-Bangladesh bilateral trade in favour of India is mainly due to the very narrow export basket of Bangladesh. Competitive nature of the export baskets of India and Bangladesh has made it further difficult to resolve this asymmetry through merchandise trade between the two countries. Since India enjoys competitive advantage in most lines of production, even in case of free trade between them, it will be difficult for Bangladesh to significantly increase her export to Indian market (World Bank: 2006; Bhattacharya: 2004). The resolution of this asymmetry calls for comprehensive bilateral agreement including transit, investment, joint ventures and other forms of economic cooperation. This all out bilateral engagement needs to factor into security concerns of each other. State-centric security perception should give way to cooperative security management and non-traditional security concerns should be factored into the foreign policy making of both the countries.

[*Acknowledgement:* Author is thankful to Mr K Gyanendra Singh, Research Scholar, Department of Humanities and Social Sciences, National Institute of Technology, Silchar, for providing secretarial assistance for the preparation of this paper].

REFERENCES

Ahmed, Sadiq and Zaidi Sattar, 2004, "Impact of Trade Liberalization: Looking at the Evidence", *Economic and Political Weekly,* September 4, 2004.

Alauddin, Mohammad, 2004, "Recent Developments in the Bangladesh Economy", *ASARC Working Paper,* 2004/13.

Bakht, Farid, 2005, "And Don't Forget Bangladesh", *Asia Times* (Online), April.

Bakht, Z, 1996, *Cross Border Illegal Trade in Bangladesh : Composition, Trends and Policy Issues*, Bangladesh Institute of Development Studies, Dhaka.

Bangladesh Bank, Annual Report 2005-06, http://www.bangladesh-bank.org

Bangladesh Defence News (BDN): August, 2005; March 2006, May 2006.

Bhattacharya, Abanti, 2006, "China's Foreign Policy Challenges and Evolving Strategy", *Strategic Analysis*, Vol 30, No 1, January-March.

Bhattarcharya, Swapan K, 2004, "Does Bangladesh Benefit from Preferential Trade with India: A Gravity Analysis", *Economic and Political Weekly*, November 27.

Choudhury, Ishfaq Ilahi, 2005, "Transit and Beyond: Economic and Strategic Significance", in http://www.thedailystar.net

Chaudhari, Sudhakar K, 1995, *Cross Border Trade Between India and Bangladesh*, Working Paper No 58, NCAER, New Delhi.

Centre for Policy Dialogue, 1995, *Experiences with Economic Reforms: A Review of Bangladesh's Development,* University Press Ltd, Dhaka.

Das, Gurudas, 2000, "Trade Between the North Eastern Region and Neighbouring Countries: Structurs and Implications for Development", in Das, Gurudas and R K Purkayastha (eds), *Border Trade: North East India and Neighbouring Countries*, Akansha Publishing House, New Delhi.

Das, Gurudas, 2002, "India's North-East Soft Underbelly: Strategic Vulnerability and Security", *Strategic Analysis*, 2002, Vol. 26, No 4.

Eusufzai, Zaki, 2000, *Liberation in the Shadow of a Large Neighbour: The Case of Bangladesh-India Economic Relations,* Loyola Marymont University, USA.

Haque, Anwarul, 2005, "Indo-Bangladesh Relations: Time for Re-thinking and Reconciliation", in *The Daily Star*, Strategic Issues, November 25, 2005, http://www.thedailystar.net/strategic/2005/11/01/strategic.htm

Hussain, M Sakhawat, 2005, "Strategic Factors in Indo-Bangla Relations", in *The Daily Star*, Friday, January 21,http://www.thedailystar.net/strategic/2005/01/02/strategic.htm

Hussain, M Sakhawat, 2006, "China-India-US Strategic Tangle: Challenges for Bangladesh", in *The Independent* (Internet ed), Issue No 1521, April 28, Dhaka, Bangladesh.

International Monetary Fund (IMF), 2003, IMF Country Report No. 03/194, Bangladesh Statistical Appendix, Washington DC.

Islam, Asadul, 2004, "South Asian Free Trade Agreement: Perspectives of the Private Sector and Government of Bangladesh", Paper presented in the Commonwealth Business Council SAFTA Roundtable on 'Achieving the South Asia Free Trade Agreement: A Public-Private Partnership', held during December 15-16, 2004, organized by Commonwealth Business Council, at New Delhi.

Islam, Nurul, 2004, "Indo-Bangladesh Economic Relations: Some Thoughts", *Economic and Political Weekly*, September 4.

Kibria, Ruksana, 2006, "Strategic Implications of Bangladesh-China Relations", in Bangladesh and the World, 15th Anniversary Special, *The Daily Star*, Dhaka.

Kumar, Anand, 2006, "Myanmar-Petrochina Agreement: A Setback to India's Quest for Energy Security", Paper No 1681, South Asia Analysis Group, http://www.saag.org

Mohammed, Mostafa Farque, 2006, "The Ups and Downs of Bangladesh-India Relations", in Bangladesh and the World, 15th Anniversary Spesial, *The Daily Star*, Dhaka.

Mahmud, Wahiduddin, 2004, "Macroeconomic Management:From Stabilization to Growth", *Economic and Political Weekly*, September 4, 2004.

Pant, Harsh V, 2006, "Indian Foreign Policy and China", *Strategic Analysis,* Vol 30, No 4, October-December.

Pattanaik, Smruti S, 2005, "Internal Political Dynamics and Bangladesh's Foreign Policy towards India", *Strategic Analysis*, Vol 29, No 3, July-eptember.

Pohit, Sanjib and Nisha Taneja, 2000, *India's Informal Trade with Bangladesh and Nepal: A Qualitative Assessment,* Working Paper No 58, Indian Council of Research on International Economic Relations, New Delhi.

Rahman, M: 1998: "Bangladesh-India Bilateral Trade: Current Trends, New Perspectives, New Challenges", *BIISS Journal*, Vol 9, No 1.

Rahman, Mohammad Mafizur, 2005, "Bangladesh-India Bilateral Trade: Causes of Imbalance and Measures for Improvement", www.etsg.org/ETSG2003/papers/rahman.pdf

Rahman, Nabeela Afrooz, 2004, "Sustainable Energy Development: Bangladesh Perspective", paper presented in the 19th World Energy Council Congress, 5-9 september, Sydney, Australia.

Rahman, S, 1997, "Non-Reciprocity in Bangladesh-India Bilateral Trade: A Case for Market Access and Domestic Competitiveness", *BIISS Journal,* Vol. 18, No. 3.

Rahman, A. and M.A, Razzaque, 1998, *Informal Trade Between Bangladesh and India: An Empirical Study in Selected Areas,* The Asian Foundation, Dhaka.

Rajya Sabha Secretariat, 1998, *Thirty Sixth Report on Development Potential of Commerce in the North-Eastern Region,* Commerce No 65/98, Department-Related Parliamentary Standing Committee on Commerce, Parliament of India, Rajya Sabha, New Delhi.

Razi, Zillul, Hye, 2006, "Future of Clothing Exports from Bangladesh: Disaggregated Scenario", *The Daily Star*, Vol 5, No 745, http://www.thedailystar.net/2006/07/02/d60702050376.htm

Srivastava, Siddharth, 2005, "India Looks East for Gas", in *Online Asia Times*, September 28, http://www. atimes.com/atimes/South_Asia/G128Df02.html

Taneja, Nisha, 1999, Informal Trade in the SAARC Region, Working Paper No 47, Indian Council of Research on International Economic Relations, New Delhi.

Thapar, K L, 2005, Speech at "India-Bangladesh Dialogue on Trade,

Investment and Connectivity", January 18-19, First Meeting, Delhi.

Treaty of Peace and Friendship between the Government of India and the Government of the People's Republic of Bangladesh, 1972, March 19, Dacca.

World Bank/IMF, 2004, *Promoting Regional Integration in South Asia: a Private Sector Perspective,* South Asia Regional Integration, Bangladesh Country Note, Washington DC.

World Bank, 2004, *Trade Policies in South Asia: An Overview,* (3 Vol), Report No 29949, www.worldbank.org

World Bank, 2006, India-Bangladesh Bilateral Trade and Potential Free Trade Agreement, Bangladesh Development Series, Paper No 13, The World Bank Office, Dhaka, www.worldbank.org.bd/bds

2

BANGLADESH - NEI TRADE: CAN THERE BE A BETTER FUTURE?

M Ismail Hossain
Md Habibur Rahman

Introduction

India is Bangladesh's nearest and by far the largest neighbour with borders on three sides of the country. Quite naturally, substantial share of total external trade of these countries should occur between themselves. In 2002-03, Bangladesh imported US $1357.79 ml worth of goods from India, which is about 16 percent of her total imports. During the same period Bangladesh's export to India comprised 0.7 percent of her total exports. This shows the low level of trade between these two countries especially Bangladesh's export to India. If the current trade is a reflection of mutual comparative advantage with unhindered flow of goods, perhaps little can be done to enhance trade beyond its current trend. The available studies (e.g., Bayes (2002); Chittagong Chamber of Commerce and Industry and Tripura Chamber of Commerce and Industry, 2002) indicate potential for more trade between these two countries. In this context, potentials for increased trade and measures for enhancing trade needs to be examined.

Bangladesh has traditionally focused its attention on

trade with vast India that lies on the western side of its border. There is a growing realization that Bangladesh's export potential in North East India has remained relatively unexplored. A similar realization regarding export potentials of these states to Bangladesh also prevails in North East India.

There are some factors which create conditions for trade between Bangladesh and NEI. First, Bangladesh has close historical, social and economic links with these states. Many people feel a psychological bond that binds the peoples of two sides of the border. The prevalence of Bangla in Tripura and some parts of Assam make it especially easy to establish contacts with traders. Secondly, these states have low production base not only for manufactured goods but also for agricultural goods like poultry, livestock and fish. Being deficient in supply to meet internal requirements, they depend on supplies from other states of India for a whole range of both agricultural and manufactured goods. Bangladesh can supply some of these goods. Similarly, Bangladesh is deficient in mineral resources like coal, sandstone, limestone, boulders, and fruits in which these states are richly endowed with. Thirdly, the major source of supply of goods for these states is Kolkata, which lies at a distance of 1,151 km from Guwahati. This involves high transport charges and long transportation time. For example, trucking charge from Kolkata to Guwahati is Rs. 3.00 per kg and it takes 7-8 days time for transportation. Other states are even further away from Kolkata which involves higher transportation charge and time. On the other hand, transport charge is lower for importing goods from Bangladesh. For example, per kg transport charges from different land customs stations along Bangladesh border to Guwahati are estimated to be (in May 2004): Sherpur: Re 0.60; Tamabil: Re 0.70; Agartala: Rs 1.25; Burimari: Rs. 1.0. There will also be enormous saving of time if goods are brought from Bangladesh. This will reduce spoilage of goods in transit and time for which funds are held up.

Basically, distance and transport cost will be a determinant of Bangladesh's export to seven sisters. There are examples of trade of this kind in the world. Trade between Canada and the United States on the eastern and the western region are based on this principle. Goods are imported to Canada from the States in the eastern region and similar goods are exported to the United States from Canada in the western region. It is more rational for the two friendly states to do this than to transport goods from the east coast to the west coast and vice versa.

Fourthly, India's opening up of the economy in the recent years, liberalization of trade in Bangladesh, and progressive economic development of the North Eastern states as well as that of Bangladesh has created possibilities of expanded trade between the two regions. The objective of this paper is to examine the current pattern of trade and identify the potentials of enhanced trade between Bangladesh and North East India.

The paper is structured in the following way: Section 1 is the introduction. Section 2 provides information on India-Bangladesh border area. The socio-economic profile of seven North Eastern Indian states and Bangladesh are presented in section 3. Section 4 discusses the structure of trade, both formal and informal, between Bangladesh and India focusing particularly on Bangladesh's exports to and imports from North East India. In section 5 rules and agreements governing Bangladesh's trade with India have been discussed. Section 6 deals with the probable strategies for enhancing trade in the region. In this regard a set of core and supportive strategies have been discussed here. Section 7 is the concluding part of the paper.

2. Bangladesh-India Border

That it is so natural for Bangladesh to trade with India can be appreciated from the fact that Bangladesh has 4096.7 km long border with India. Of this 1880 km is shared by four of the North Eastern states, viz., Assam, Meghalaya, Mizoram and Tripura, and the rest is with West Bengal. Bangladesh's border with North-Eastern states is as follows:

TABLE 2.1

Bangladesh's Border with North East India

States	*Border Type*	*Length (km)*
Assam	Land	160
	Riverine	103
	Sub-total	263
Meghalaya	Land	443
Tripura	Land	773
	Riverine	83
	Sub-total	856
Mizoram	Land	58
	Riverine	260
	Sub-total	313
Total		1880

Source: Gurudas Das and RK Purkayastha (eds) *Border Trade: North-East India and Neighbouring Countries*, 2000.

Long land and riverine borders mean that both land and riverine routes can be used for trade. In fact land routes and river ways are being used in several places for trade between Bangladesh and North Eastern states. The borders with Meghalaya and Mizoram are hilly, the latter state being relatively less accessible for trade.

3. Socio-economic Profiles of Seven Sisters and Bangladesh

The socio-economic profiles of North Eastern states and that of Bangladesh will indicate the type and level of trade that can be expected in this region. It is generally observed that trade between two developing countries is complementary in nature while trade between two developed countries is mostly in differentiated products. Similarly, large and diversified economies often trade less with outside world than small countries.

3.1 Area, Population and Income

There are differences among the seven states in terms of geographical area, population, income, and language. While Arunachal has a land area of 84 thousand sq. kms.

TABLE 2.2

Socio-economic Profile of NEI and Bangladesh, 2000/01 or Latest Available Year

	Arunachal	*Assam*	*Manipur*	*Meghalaya*	*Mizoram*	*Nagaland*	*Tri pura*	*Bangladesh*
Area (000'sq km)	84	78	22	22	21	17	11	148
Population (million)	1.1	26.6	2.4	2.3	0.9	2.0	3.2	137.1
Population density(per sq km)	13.0	341.5	108.6	104.8	42.4	117.0	290.1	929.7
Per capita income (US $)	336	233	284	323	333	270	331	444
Literacy rate (percent)	54.7	64.3	68.9	63.3	88.5	67.1	73.7	62.7
Bangla speaking population(lakh)	0.07	48.86	0.02	0.15	0.06	0.04	1.9	1370
Languages	Tribal	Assamese	Manipuri	Khasi Garo Jaintia	Mizo English	Nagamese English	Tripuri Manipuri Bangla	Bangla

Source: NEDFi, Databank Quarterly, 2003; A. Bayes, Trade between Bangladesh and North East India: Prospects, Problems, and Policy Prescriptions, Ministry of Finance, Bangladesh Economic Review, 2004.

Tripura has a land area of only 11 thousand sq. kms. The total land area of the region amounts to 255 thousand sq.

km. One fourth of the area is hills and mountains and the rest is plains and alluvium deposits.

Of the total population of 38.5 ml in the region, about 26 percent live in the urban areas while the rest live in villages scattered in plains and hills.

Per capita income varies among the states between US $336 and US$ 233 averaging US $ 257 for the region as a whole.

Bangladesh has a total population of 137 million living in mostly plain land area of 147 sq kilometers with a per capita income of US $ 444.

3.2 Structure of the Economies

The economies of NEI are basically agrarian in nature. Agriculture's contribution to NSDP varies from 25.96 percent in Meghalaya to 36.84 percent in Assam. The contribution of agriculture to NSDP is falling with the level of development of the economies. Some of the states like Arunachal, Mizoram, and Tripura have small mining and quarrying sector.

TABLE 2.3

Sectoral Distribution of NSDP 2000-01

States	*Agri-culture*	*Mining and quarrying*	*Manu-facturing*	*Construction*	*Services*
Arunachal	34.55	0.7	3.11	16.73	44.91
Assam	36.84	6.31	8.84	4.16	43.85
Manipur	30.32	00	10.41	10.52	48.75
Meghalaya	25.96	6.63	2.07	9.73	55.61
Mizoram	27.62	0.12	00	10.93	61.33
Nagaland	29.09	00	2.15	10.99	57.77
Tripura	28.92	1.83	0.84	13.80	54.61
Bangladesh	22.83	1.10	16.25	8.86	50.96

Source: NEDFi, NEDFi Databank Quarterly, Vol. 2, Issue III, June 2003, Ministry of Finance, Bangladesh Economic Review, 2004.

Each of these states has small manufacturing sector and relatively large services sector. Manufacturing contributes less than 3 percent of NSDP in Meghalaya, Mizoram, Nagaland, and Tripura, and about 3 percent in Arunachal.

Only limited number of heavy and medium scale industries has developed in the region. The industries are mostly in Assam (80%), Nagaland (10.4%) and Arunachal. The type of industries are tea, plywood, oil refinery, jute, petrochemical, paper industry, and fertilizer. Some agro-based and forest based small scale industries have developed and are scattered in different states, about half in Assam followed by Manipur and Tripura (Bhuyan 2003). Construction sector has sizeable contribution to NSDP in all the states – 10 percent or more except in Assam where the contribution is about 4 percent. Because of small goods production base, the region has to depend on sources outside the region not only for the manufactured goods but also for agricultural goods to meet its requirements.

The economy of Bangladesh is also agrarian in nature. Manufacturing contributes 16.25 percent to its GDP while the share of services sector in GDP is 50.96 percent.

4. Trade between Bangladesh and India

4.1 Trends in Bangladesh-India Trade

Bangladesh's trade with India is highly imbalanced. Exports doubled from an average of US$25 million in the period from 1993/94 to 1996/97 to about US$50 million in 1997/98. However, it has remained stuck at this level till 2002-03. On the other hand imports crossed the US$1 billion mark in 1995/96. The highest level of imports of US$1357.79 million was attained in 2002/03. Deficit in trade balance has increased considerably during the period since 1994/95 because of the higher import growth as opposed to exports. However, during the period since 1990/91 trade deficit got to the peak in 2002/03 which is estimated at US$ 1310.42 million.

TABLE 2.4

Bangladesh – India Trade, 1990/91 – 2002/03

Year	*Export (ML US$)*	*Import (ML US$)*	*Trade balance (ML US$)*
1990/91	24.21	180.63	- 156.42
1991/92	7.66	231.32	- 223.66
1992/93	7.58	341.97	- 334.39
1993/94	21.37	414.39	- 393.02
1994/95	28.62	688.54	- 659.92
1995/96	24.44	1100.14	- 1075.70
1996/97	28.01	922.16	- 894.15
1997/98	49.92	934.14	- 884.22
1998/99	48.24	1234.82	- 1186.58
1999/00	58.67	832.60	- 773.93
2000/01	56.92	1183.99	- 1127.07
2001/02	43.60	1021.60	- 978.00
2002/03	47.37	1357.79	- 1310.42

Source: Annual Export Receipts and Annual Import Payments 2002-03, Statistics Department, Bangladesh Bank.

4.2 Bangladesh's Trade with Seven Sisters

Currently active land customs stations in Bangladesh through which both import and export trade are taking place are Juri (Moulavibazar), Bibirbazar (Comilla), Seola (Sylhet) and Akhaura (Brahmanbaria). The other LC stations located in the border areas with NEIs namely, Borosora, Chatak (Sylhet), Tamabil (Sylhet), and Zakignaj (Sylhet) are considered as the import points as little or no export is done through them.

Exports of Bangladesh to NEI comprise hilsha fish, dry fish, small fish, fresh fish, fruit juice, soft drink, condensed milk, tomato ketchup, biscuits, potato, potato crackers,

TABLE 2.5

Trade with North - East India

(Thousand US$)

	2001-02		*2002-03*		*2003-04*	
	Export	*Import*	*Export*	*Import*	*Export*	*Import*
Juri (Batuli), Maulavibazar	9.30	1.89	11.17	70.60	30.21	33.12
Bibirbazar, Comilla	nil	16.14	2.16	56.94	190.86	25.00
Sheola, Sylhet	139.40	6.99	55.2	7212.39	760.90	9688.26
Akhaura, Brahmanbaria	904.07	257.13	209.63	51.37	1486.25	54.48
Borosora	nil	3,928.62	nil	11279.02	nil	9527.36
Chatak, Sylhet	nil	480.38	nil	1418.71	nil	2063.17
Tamabil, Sylhet	nil	2,815.76	nil	22420.67	2.75	17637.76
Zakiganj, Sylhet	nil	459.95	25.96	1506.28	6.31	555.10
Others	—	—	nil	4831.03	nil	5144.07
Total	—	—	304.12	48847.01	2477.28	44728.32

Source: Different LCSs, 2004, and BEI-SEDF, Bangladesh North East India Trade Quarterly, Issue 2, March 2005.

pickle, milk powder, ice cream, tin foil, ready made garments, fabrics (other), waffles and wafers, synthetic fibres, fittings for furniture, electric goods, woven fibres of paper yarn, separator (electric), plastic doors, Jamdani saree, cold drinks, vegetables, molasses, battery plate, corrugated tin, motor parts, bricks, tobacco leaf, toilet soap, soybean, mosquito-net, cosmetics, polythene, cement, raw jute, PVC pipe, cast iron scrap, MS rod, and PP filter.

Bangladesh's import from NEI consists of rice, ginger, garlic, onions, turmeric, dry chilli, methi, soybeans, lentils, potato, betel leaf, tomato, apple, grapes, oranges, pears, citrus fruits, banana, pineapple, rohu fish, chocolates, paper, tube light, umbrella, synthetic saree, electric goods, clothes, ply wood, ceramics, glass, wooden materials, wall clock and table clock, tape recorder, bicycle, audio cassette recorder, sanitary items, mooli bamboo, potato seeds, coal, ferrous waste, stone chips, crushed stone, sand stone, limestone, cement, boulder, crude marble, automotive parts, bangles machine, and motor parts.

The list of commodities reveals that Bangladesh imports a range of consumer goods – both agricultural and manufactured which supplements domestic production. It also imports from NEI few manufactured goods. The most important imports are natural resource products which act as intermediate products for industry. Similarly, Bangladesh's export to NEI comprises consumer goods most of which are manufactured goods. These goods supplement domestic production. But most importantly, they provide variety to the consumers. Bangladesh exports a few intermediate goods or raw materials. This reveals some degree of complementarity in the region.

It should be noted that the list is not an exhaustive one and the share of commodities in both export and import vary over time. Rohu fish was once an important import; it is no longer so.

4.3 Informal Trade

An important aspect of trade links between Bangladesh and India is the existence of large scale informal trade between these two neighbours. The persistence of informal trade indicates the operation of strong factors which create incentive for evasion of trade through formal channel. Several studies on informal trade between India and its neighbours including Bangladesh have been undertaken (e.g., Barua 1998; Pohit and Taneja: 2002; Government of India 2002). There have also been some studies in Bangladesh on informal trade between Banladesh and India (e.g. Bakht 1996, Ministry of Commerce 1999, Rahman and Razzaque 1998). These studies suggest a few items are exported from Bangladesh through the informal channel and they are in small amounts. On the other hand, a wide variety of products are imported from India and in large quantities. The following items are at present informally traded between Bangladesh and NEI.

TABLE 2.6

Informally Traded Goods

Exports from Bangladesh	*Imports from India*
Vegetable oil, hilsha fish, dry fish, small fish, garlic, winter clothes, juice, biscuits, medicine, soap, pulses, fuel, readymade garments, tea, mosquito net, bicycle, electronic goods, soybean oil, under clothes, toiletries, cement, poultry feed, battery, show pieces, potato chips, brass pitcher, eggs, turtle, rice, corrugated tin, cement, shallow tube-well engine.	Computer, medicine, spices, cotton saree/lungi, milk powder, cattle, coal, bidis, rohu fish, engineering goods, sugar, steel utensils, rice, bicycle, auto parts, bamboo, dry fish, ginger, orange, potato, pineapple, petrol / diesel, liquor.

Several observations can be made on the Table 2.6: (i) some of the commodities traded through the formal channel are also traded through the informal channel; (ii) some of the commodities which are exported are also imported. This may happen depending on local demand-supply situation. (iii) Some of the goods are exported from Bangladesh which are not produced in the country. For example, fuel, soybean oil, shallow tube-well engine. It may be mentioned that informal exports from Bangladesh is estimated at US $ 10 million while informal imports from NEI is estimated at US $ 26 million.

Researchers have interpreted existence of informal trade as an indicator of potential trade between the two countries. If the existing factors which underlie the informal trade are dealt with, formal trade will expand benefiting both countries. Generally speaking, the barriers to trade can be of two types. First, barriers imposed at the border – tariff and non-tariff barriers, regulations relating to foreign commercial presence and foreign investment, exchange controls and other restrictions on the transfer of funds, restrictions on the movement of people and their ability to visit or work in foreign countries. Second, barriers imposed internally - in the form of differential regulations or taxes on foreign producers or products. Both these barriers discriminate against foreigners (Snape 2003).

5. Rules and Agreements Governing Bangladesh-India trade

Trade between Bangladesh and NEI is governed by the trade policies in the two countries, the trade agreements between them and existence of facilities required for low cost trade. Fortunately, both countries embarked on trade liberalization since 1991 making their trade regime more open than before the liberalization began. The highest tariff rate and number of tariff slabs have declined. Quantitative restrictions have been gradually reduced in both countries and they have been completely eliminated in India in April 2001. However, India has been increasingly making use of GATT- compatible controls, e.g., (i) technical standards and regulations, (ii) sanitary and phytosanitary rules, and (iii) other health and safety regulations.

5.1 Regional Trade Agreements

Bangladesh – India trade can be rationally expected to be influenced by the various trade agreements – bilateral as well as regional. Three regional trading arrangements (RTA) in which both Bangladesh and India are members are - the Bangkok Agreement, the South Asian Preferential Trading Agreement (SAPTA), and the Global System of Preferences (GSP). SAPTA which was operationalized from December 1995 has been succeeded by South Asian Free Trade Agreement (SAFTA) which was signed in 2004. Bangladeshi products enjoy tariff concessions offered by India and similarly Indian products enjoy tariff concessions in Bangladesh market. Bangladesh's list of products is much smaller than the Indian list. Researchers have assessed the impact of these various agreements on the actual flow of commodities and observed very little impact (e.g. Mukherjee 2002, Bhuyan, 2003).

5.2 Some more Constraints

Bangladesh's trade with NEI also faces some special constraints. These have been well documented in some recent studies. The most important of these bottlenecks is lack of infrastructural facilities at the customs stations including facilities such as warehouses, parking, dumping space, guest houses, sheds, and utilities like electricity, gas, water, and telecommunication. Besides, the conditions of roads leading to the customs stations connecting the land customs stations are generally unsatisfactory on Bangladesh side. There are other issues which have been raised include distance of the nearest banks for opening letter of credit, payment of VAT and other taxes and insurance costs, release time of goods, lack of human resource at LCSs, mismatch of timing between Bangladesh and Indian customs and weekly holidays, delay in payments for exports by banks.

Because of lack of communication between Bangladesh and India less is known in NEI about Bangladeshi products. The further one lives from the border the greater is the level of ignorance. As a result, people do not fully know about the goods in Bangladesh – the type of goods, the price of goods and quality of goods. Businessmen, exporters and general people visiting Bangladesh are gradually becoming acquainted with Bangladesh.

6. Strategies for a Better Future for Trade

The foregoing discussion shows that there exists potential for trade in the region which has not been fully exploited. It is imperative that both sides of the border undertake suitable policies and strategies for exploitation of the trade opportunities which would contribute to economic development and poverty reduction in both Bangladesh and NEI.

6.1 Core Strategies

i) Reduction of Tariff and Para Tariff Barriers

Bangladesh's current exports face tariff rates between 15% and 35% with the exception of mustard oil and soybean oil which face 85% and 45% tariff rates respectively. Tariff rates on the agro-based products are on the higher side. Besides, many products are subjected to countervailing duties (CVD) and special additional duties (SAD). High tariff and para-tariff barriers reduce market access for Bangladeshi products. In order to overcome this problem, Bangladesh should negotiate with India for reducing/removing CVD and SAD under bilateral or regional trading arrangements; increasing concession rates on exports under bilateral or regional trading arrangements; reducing tariff on potential export products on bilateral basis. Similarly, Bangladesh should examine the customs duty structure facing products from NEI and reduce barriers for increased trade through legal channel.

ii) Reduction of Non-Tariff Barriers

Bangladesh should try to persuade India not to use the new protectionist measures like countervailing duties and anti-dumping measures against Bangladesh. Though these measures are WTO compatible, indiscriminate use of these measures undermines the spirit of trade liberalization. Being small producers, many exporters lack resources to challenge the measures for settlement. Besides, it creates an image of India which is protectionist within a liberalized environment.

6.2 Supportive Strategies

i) Development of Infrastructure for Trade

Development of infrastructure at the land customs stations is needed to facilitate trade. Infrastructure on the Indian side is in relatively better shape and is being developed further. Bangladesh needs to develop infrastructure on its side. Bangladesh seems to have neglected infrastructure development in the border areas on two major grounds. First, the volume of traffic does not justify improved infrastructure. Second, bad road is a natural security check. But experience shows that good transport and communication system leads to greater traffic.

Because of limitation of resources Bangladesh has to develop infrastructure in phases. In the first phase the LCS which have emerged as important export routes will have to be developed. These are: Akhaura, Bibirbazar, Juri and Sheola. A fully functioning and well developed LCS needs office building, electricity and water supply, telephone and fax, warehouse, transshipment platform, weigh bridge, truck-parking area, truck-servicing center, rest house, cold storage, banking and insurance facilities. These facilities will have to be created where they do not exist now. Further, the following approach roads need improvement (Pacca construction/ widening/straightening):

Bharkhar to Akhaura (30 kms). The alternative route connecting Sultanpur (Brahmanbaria) and Akhaura needs to be constructed as fast as possible.

Phultali – Batuli (Juri) road. The construction of the alternative route connecting Kulaura and Phultali via Gazipur which is under construction, should be completed soon.

Sheola bridge to Sheola LCS including the culvert on the road. The culvert needs immediate re-construction.

In the second phase LCS should be developed which has potential as an export route. An example of such potential LCS is Tegamukh in Rangamati district which can open formal trade with Mizoram.

ii) Visa Office and Multiple Entry Visa

Bangladesh should open a visa office in Guwahati in addition to the one in Agartala. Pending this arrangement the current visa office can work 2-3 days in Guwahati. Besides, both Bangladesh and India should issue multiple entry visa for one year to business persons. This will facilitate easy flow of business persons between the two countries leading to enhancement of trade.

iii) Harmonization of Product Standards and Tests

Both Bangladesh and India should adopt Mutual Recognition Agreements (MRAs) between Conformity Assessment Bodies (CABs) of Bangladesh and India. This would help in mutual acceptability of goods in either country.

iv) Training of Exporters and Importers

The current business world is information-intensive. Information can be used to the advantage of those who possess it. Both exporters and importers should be aware of the Acts, Agreements, Rules governing trade between Bangladesh and India. The Bangladesh Foreign Trade Institute in collaboration with Foreign Trade Institute of India can arrange training programmes for businessmen from both sides of the border.

v) More Interaction between Stakeholders of Two Countries

The stakeholders from the two countries should meet at regular intervals to discuss issues relating to exports / imports and try to resolve the issues in an atmosphere of mutual cooperation and understanding.

vi) Joint Ventures

Bangladesh will face difficulties in raising exports to NEI because of its narrow export base. An important step should therefore be to encourage joint venture projects with a view to exporting to NEI under buy-back arrangements. Enormous opportunities and potential are believed to exist of joint venture operations based on the vast untapped resources of the eastern region of Bangladesh and the adjoining Eastern and North Eastern States of India. These joint ventures could be in the form of mutual collaboration of equity participation, transfer of technology, provision of machinery and capital equipment, and exchange of managerial and professional expertise. Studies may be undertaken to identify actual opportunities based on the natural resource endowments in this region.

vii) Direct Investment and Technology Flows

Apart from joint venture operation, direct investment by India in Bangladesh can contribute to expansion of Bangladesh's exports both to India and to the outside world. Indian investment in the country at present is very low. A reason perhaps is that Indian investors are more interested in investing inside India, given the large size of its domestic market.

Other factors that might have held Indian investment in Bangladesh at low levels are probably restrictive rules regarding capital flow, unstable economic policies, and lack of information about sectors where returns to investment will be high. This calls for streamlining the investment regime by laying down explicit rules on issues like national treatment, application of MFN clauses in both pre- and post-entry stages, repatriation of profits, currency convertibility, ownership and licensing restrictions, double taxation and dispute settlement mechanisms.

Apart from setting in place investment related policies, there is the need to adopt appropriate measures to remove the constraints in power, energy, transport, communications, port facilities, human resource development, technology etc. and also address direct investment facilitation measures such as reduction of paperwork, procedural simplification, reduction in bureaucratic hurdles, and so on (RIS, 2001). One concrete measure that may facilitate Indian investment in Bangladesh is to coordinate the exchange rate policies of the two countries. This may complement efforts at expanding their bilateral trade as well.

It may be noted that TATA group of India has shown keen interest in making huge investment in power and steel in Bangladesh.

viii) Holding Trade Fairs

In order to enhance trade prospects, the Government of India may allow the Government of Bangladesh to open trade centres and allow private banks of Bangladesh to open branches in specific locations of India. Trade fairs will enhance the interaction among investors of the two countries and help familiarize them with each other's products. Ignorance about Bangladeshi products is one of the main reasons for low Indian imports from Bangladesh. Bangladesh industrialists should be allowed to effectively participate in trade fairs organized in India to provide Indian consumers an idea about the variety of Bangladeshi products and their quality.

ix) Tourism Development

Tourism has good potential on both sides of the border. Bangladesh has important tourist spots that should be able to attract Indian tourists. Some of these are: Mainamati Ruins, an important centre of Buddhist culture; Somapati Bihara, formerly the largest Buddhist Monastery in the south of Himalaya; Sundarban National Park; Puthia, home to the largest number of historically important Hindu structures; St. Martin's Island, the small and beautiful coral island; the capital city Dhaka on the banks of exquisite Buriganga; the second largest city Chittagong; and the world's longest sea-beach at Cox's Bazar.

The tourism industry can be developed to its full potential through suitable public and private sector efforts. Promotional measures should be adopted for making tourism attractive, not only to Indian but also to international visitors.

x) Other Areas of Cooperation

A road transhipment arrangement and alternatively entrepot trade, export of natural gas to India and gas pipeline from Myanmer to India through Bangladesh are some of the possibilities for trade and economic cooperation between these two countries. The economic viability of these options should be closely examined and appropriate decisions taken keeping in view the best interest of Bangladesh consistent with that of her trading partner.

Conclusion

The current level of trade between Bangladesh and NEI is relatively low. There is no reason why such low level of trade should persist especially in view of the potential of mutually beneficial trade to promote economic development and reduce poverty in this region. A number of strategies which include reduction of tariff and non-tariff barriers, joint venture, FDI, and tourism development can be adopted to enhance trade.

REFERENCES

Barua, Srinath (1998). *India's Border Trade with Selected Neighbouring Countries*, RIS, New Delhi.

Bayes, A (2002). Trade Between Bangladesh and India: Prospects, Problems and Policy Prescriptions, Chittagong Chamber of

Commerce and Industry (CCCI) and Tripura Chamber of Commerce and Industry (TCCI), In Association with South Asia Enterprise Development Facility (SEDF), Draft Report.

Bakht, Zaid, 1996, *Cross-Border Illegal Trade in Bangladsh:* Composition, Trends and Policy Issues, Bangladesh Institute of Development Studies, Dhaka, (mimeo).

Bhuyan, Md. Ayubur Rahman, 2003. Bangladesh's Bilateral Trade with India: Issues and Concers. BIISS Study on Free Trade: Options for Bangladesh, Bangladesh Institute of International and Strategic Studies, Dhaka, Mimeo.

Das, Gurudas (2000). "Trade Between the North-Eastern Region and Neighbouring Countries: Structures and Implications for Development", in Gurudas Das ad R K Purkayashta (eds), *Border Trade: North-East India and Neighbouring Countries,* Akansha Pub. House, New Delhi.

Dutta, G. (2002). Enhancing the Prospects of Border Trade with North East India and Bangladesh, Chittagong Chamber of Commerce and Industry (CCCI) and Tripura Chamber of Commerce and Industry (TCCI), In Association with South Asia Enterprise Development Facility (SEDF), Draft Report.

EPB. Export Statistics of Bangladesh, 1999-2000.

Government of India (2002). Report of the Committee on Informal Cross Border Trade, Ministry of Commerce and Industry, Delhi.

Ministry of Commerce, Government of the Peoples' Republic of Bangladesh, 1999, Promotion of Regional Trade in South Asia, (mimeo).

Mukherjee, I.N. 2002. Charting a Free Trade Area in South Asia: Instruments and Modalities, in T.N. Srinivasan, ed., *Trade, Finance and Investment in South Asia,* Social Science Press, New Delhi.

Pohit, Sanjib and N Tanejia (1999). *India's Informal Trade with Bangladesh and Nepal: A Comparative Study,* Working Paper No.47, ICRIER, New Delhi.

Rahman, Atiur and M A Razzaque (1998). *Informal Trade Between Bangladesh and India: An Empirical Study in Selected Areas,* The Asian Foundation, Dhaka.

Research and Information System (RIS) for the Nonaligned and other Developing Countries, (2001). Economic Impact of Trade and Investment Facilitation and Liberalization in South Asia (BBIN) Growth Quadrangle: A Development Perspective, New Delhi, December 2001 (Mimeo).

Snape, Richard H (2003). Reaching Effective Agreements Covering Services in Anne O. Krueger (ed.). *The WTO as an International Organization*, Oxford, Delhi.

World Bank (2003). *Trade Policies in South Asia: An Overview*, June 2003.

3

WIDENING INDIA-BANGLADESH COOPERATION AGENDA IN CONTEXT OF SOUTH ASIAN REGIONAL COOPERATION: ISSUES AND TASKS AHEAD

Prabir De

1. Introduction

Despite the trusted and tested relationships between India and Bangladesh over a long period of time, why still we need to discuss and debate on economic cooperation and integration agenda between India and Bangladesh. Perhaps, the reason is very well captured in Basu's following remarks on Indian economy (Basu, 2001: 3838).

> If in an economy some people control all the water, some all the food and some all the energy, even if the total amount of water, food and energy is very large, if this society does not learn how to exchange and trade, it will be a very poor society; indeed so poor that all may die. In a modern nation, it is not enough for there to be a lot of medical knowledge and engineering knowledge and knowledge of information technology. If the nation does not have the organization to share and exchange this knowledge and to harness it where it is needed, it will be a miserable and poor nation.

India and Bangladesh are the most trusted neighbours in the world. They were once sharing the same land. It got separated from Indian landmass and later emerged as an independent nation in 1971.

Today, India and Bangladesh boast a total population of more than 1 billion, and their rapid domestic economic development have demonstrated broad prospects for cooperation. India has become Bangladesh's largest trading partner in South Asia. A remarkable growth in two-way trade between India and Bangladesh has resulted in robust growth of the economies in South Asia. Even though, India and Bangladesh are still characterized by its low level of economic integration, despite the fact that the economies are complementary to a large extent and could potentially benefit substantially from economic integration. However, compared with their strength, there still exists much space and huge potential for the development of trade and economic relations between the two countries.

Notwithstanding the development witnessed by India and Bangladesh in recent years, the two countries together still contain, 1/3rd of world's poor; approximately 35 percent of their total population (409 million in 2001[1]) still living with one dollar a day. This is the real challenge posed before the two nations. It is not easy to think of another region of the world which can surpass India and Bangladesh in terms of resource endowments. Despite its vast resources, perhaps due to absence of organisational capital, this region has miserably failed to convert its resources into productive and collective wealth.

Lack of organisational capital is more vivid when we look into India-Bangladesh trade. Today's India-Bangladesh trade issues go beyond the traditional mechanisms of tariffs and quotas and include "behind-the-border" issues, such as the role of infrastructure and governance in supporting a well-functioning trading economy. For instance, studies[2] show that international transport services liberalisation foster international trade very much the same way tariff liberalisation does. India and Bangladesh (and also other countries in South Asia) will have to acquire quickly the needed expertise on the whole lot of complex issues of trade facilitation, so that they can negotiate more effectively and ensure that agreements serve their objective of poverty reduction. For example, one of the major obstacles to economic integration between India and Bangladesh is the lack of integrated and poor quality transport infrastructure.[3] For instance, ships moving from Bangladesh to the ports of India's east coast levy higher freight charges than for the movement to Singapore or Hong Kong. Although this may partly due to inadequate harbour facilities, a larger part is due to lack of mutual cooperation. Much more intense is the case of trade between India's North Eastern Region (NER) and Bangladesh, where there is at present no multimodal linkage, though existed half a century back. For example, NER's imports are carried through Haldia port, instead through Bangladesh. Had NER imported through Chittagong (in Bangladesh), both landed cost and delivery time would have been lower. On the other hand, Bangladesh imports pulp and paper board from China, Indonesia, and Malaysia instead of from NER, which, again imports fertilizer and cement respectively from Gulf and Southeast Asia rather than from Bangladesh. On the whole, the real problem that India and Bangladesh are faced with is not demographic but economic in nature: how to ensure good quality of trading infrastructure (both visible and invisible) for people in the region which are willing and able to share for the benefit of others. Working together for trade facilitation, an essential element to promote international trade, will pave the way for "win-win" situation.

It is fairly established that adequacy of trade facilitation measures determines one region's success and other's failure. For instance, it is the transport infrastructure and user-friendly trading instruments that helped European countries to unite, whereas the lack of integrated transport network prevents South Asia to integrate. South Asian countries in general and India and Bangladesh in particular have taken some trade facilitation measures aiming to reduce current physical and non-physical barriers to trade – by means of both visible infrastructure (such as multi-modal corridors and terminals) and invisible infrastructure (such as reformed policies and procedures, regulations), but overall progress is unsatisfactory (De and Ghosh, 2001).

Transit and transhipment between India and Bangladesh are the two long standing unresolved bilateral issues. This has rationally provoked neighbouring country(s) to enjoy a 'free ride' on local market–the costs of our non-cooperation. It may be noted that today, trade between Bangladesh and China has been growing faster than that of India and commodities which were predominantly supplied by India to Bangladesh are fast being replaced by China. As a matter of fact, third country products are entering India with the help of porous border and inefficient bureaucracy. Therefore, transportation obstacles are posing great threat to the bilateral cooperation between India and Bangladesh.[4] Hence, reshaping the economic cooperation agenda between India and Bangladesh is of immediate requirement.

However, there are some positive changes taking place towards reshaping the regional integration process in South Asia in recent period.[5] When South Asian countries are all set to open South Asian Free Trade Area (SAFTA) with effect from 1st January 2006,[6] improved and integrated infrastructure facilities will help these countries not only to reduce transaction costs but also to generate higher intra-regional trade. Reducing the cost of intra-regional transportation of goods and services and improving the quality of transportation services will enhance South Asia's intra-regional trade and also international market access.[7]

It is against this backdrop that this chapter reviews the prevailing profile of transport infrastructure sector of India and Bangladesh. This chapter attempts to identify the potentials for economic cooperation in different segments of trading infrastructure. Finally, underlining the importance of the trade facilitation in the growth of bilateral and regional cooperation, this chapter concludes with few remarks on policy perspectives in order to deepen economic integration.

2. Infrastructure, Trade, Growth and Poverty Reduction

It stems from the experience of nations everywhere since the end of World War II: openness to external trade and foreign investment permits more rapid economic growth than protectionist regimes achieve. Countries, which have chosen to integrate with the global economy, have done better in reducing poverty in long run.

In South Asia, during 1990s, as India and Bangladesh followed Sri Lanka into the ranks of countries known as rapid globalizers, strong growth tallied with sharp drops in poverty incidence – from 51 percent in 1977-78 to 27 percent in 1999-2000 in India, and from 45 percent in 1991 to 34 percent in 2000 in Bangladesh (World Bank, 2004). Table 3.1 shows that Bangladesh done well in 1990s in raising her per capita income compared to her performance in previous three decades. In fact, in 1990s, her per capita income growth crossed not only that of Pakistan's but also South Asia's average, and the momentum has also been continued in next four years. At the same time, the country has made considerable gains in poverty reduction and primary education. With respect to universal primary education, there are equal number of girls and boys in primary and secondary school. Its infant mortality rate is lower than India and it could achieve the Millennium Development Goal of two-third reduction by 2015 (World Bank, 2005). However, over 63 million people are still living in poverty, making the country one of the poorest in the world. And access to education, health care and jobs are still unequal. In general, for the South Asia region as a whole, the period 1980–2000 saw significantly high per capita GDP growth performance, although Pakistan (political instability) and Sri Lanka (ethnic conflict) suffered setbacks in 1990s. Therefore, the effect on reduction in poverty in India and Bangladesh was dramatic and growth became the principal driver of poverty reduction. When India and Bangladesh (also rest of South Asian economies) are well endowed with labour, trade openness is expected to stimulate production and expansion of labour-intensive exports, thus generating employment, raising wages, and thereby reducing poverty.

TABLE 3.1

Average Annual Growth Rates of Real GDP Per Capita[1]

Countries	*1960-2003 (%)*	*1960-70 (%)*	*1970-80 (%)*	*1980-90 (%)*	*1990-2000 (%)*	*2000-03 (%)*
Bangladesh	1.39	1.48	-1.57	1.19	3.42	3.27
India	4.45	1.83	0.70	4.21	4.27	4.49
Nepal	1.75	0.58	0.02	2.70	2.87	0.34
Pakistan	4.50	5.19	1.58	4.09	1.51	0.95
Sri Lanka	5.34	2.33	2.96	3.53	4.65	1.36
South Asia	3.48	2.28	0.74	3.15	3.34	2.08

Note: 1. Taken at constant US$ (at 2000 international prices).

Source: Compiled from *World Development Indicators CD ROM 2005*, World Bank.

The benefit of globalization in terms of trade liberalization is expected to flow to abundant factors, and, therefore, to unskilled labour in developing countries, such as India and Bangladesh. However, a recent study (Banerjee and Newman, 2004) suggests that removing trade barriers may adversely affect the wages of unskilled labours in labour abundant developing countries. In the long-run, economic integration could foster rapid economic growth and significant rise in standard of living and hence decrease in poverty. But in the transition period, the burden of adjustment might fall disproportionably to poor people. Another recent study (Topalova, 2005) on impact of trade liberalization on poverty reduction in Indian districts concludes that the effects of trade liberalization were not uniform over districts. There were insignificant benefits of liberalization (or a disproportionate share of burden) with respect to poverty reduction for those districts with more exposure to potential foreign competition. Therefore, appropriate policies may be required to address the social cost of inequality through redistribution of gains of trade liberalization. Strengthening labour mobility in short-to medium-term is crucial to reduce the adjustment burden of liberalization.

The linkage between greater trade openness and poverty reduction need not be direct, but rather through the positive impact of trade expansion on growth performance – a correlation that has been established in extensive empirical research. Cross-country studies on the relationship between growth performance and poverty reduction lead to the conclusion that there exists a close correspondence between growth of per capita income and growth of per capita infrastructure stocks, though not all growth is necessarily pro-poor. More importantly, trade openness is a necessary but not a sufficient condition for rapid growth. Trade policy reforms generally need to be accompanied by complementary measures for ensuring macroeconomic stability and efficient financial intermediation, improving infrastructure services, improving investment climate for private enterprises and removing barriers to trade or what we call trade facilitation.

In spite of strong growth in per capita GDP in 1990s, India's and Bangladesh's progress on infrastructure sector has failed to keep pace with its growth in trade (Ghosh and De, 2000; De and Ghosh, 2003, 2005; De, 2005). There is now broad consensus that openness to trade coupled with improved infrastructure must be a key component of policies to accelerate economic growth in South Asia. Therefore, faster progress in infrastructure development will be crucial to sustaining South Asia's competitive advantages.

TABLE 3.2

Selected Economic and Social Indicators in 2002

Particulars	*Unit*	*Bangladesh*	*India*	*South Asia*
Population	Million	135.68	1048.64	1373.46
Population Growth[1]	%	1.91	1.92	2.01
Population Density	Per sq. km.	1042	353	431
Poverty Headcount[2]	%	33.70	28.62	31.63
GDP per Capita[3]	US$	396.2	493.27	770.08
GDP per Capita PPP[4]	US$	1501.34	2364.61	1992.37
Trade in Goods[5]	%	29.45	20.78	44.87
Gross FDI[6]	US$ Bln.	0.95	22.59	31.96
Gross CAB[7]	US$ Bln.	0.74	4.66	8.75
Gross FCF[8]	%	23.09	22.14	25.15

Notes: 1. Decadal population growth rate for the period 1991-2001. 2. Taken in percentage of population. 3. Taken in constant 1995 US$. 4. Taken in constant 1995 US$. 5. Taken as percentage of GDP. 6. Gross cumulative foreign direct investment, taken at current US$ billion for the period 1991 to 2002. 7. Gross current account balance, taken at current US$ billion. 8. Gross fixed capital formation, taken in average as percentage of GDP for the period 2000 to 2002. 9. Data relates for the year 2001.

Source: World Development Indicators CD ROM 2005, World Bank.

Low quality of infrastructure coupled with high logistics costs for India and Bangladesh are derived from poor transport infrastructure, underdeveloped transport and logistics services, and slow and costly bureaucratic procedures dealing with bilateral trade. The opportunities for improvement of infrastructure facilities are immense when India and Bangladesh offer some similar characteristics: high population growth and high incidence of poverty (see Table 3.2). India and Bangladesh can reinforce the economic strength of each other by synergising their complementarities in the areas of industry, services, trade and technology provided these economies put in place adequate and improved infrastructure facilities. Interestingly, setting in place adequate infrastructure is getting momentum due to (a) rising stock of intra-regional capital, represented by current account balance (US$ 8.75 billion in 2002), and (b) growing fixed capital formation (25.25 percent of GDP in 2002). Bangladesh and India have realised that without having proper infrastructure in place, foreign direct investments (only US$ 23.55 billion for the period 1991 to 2002) may not flow in large amount despite the region's labour cost advantage (Kumar, 2002). Table 3.2 briefly captures these findings.

The relative paucity of integrated and improved infrastructure networks within South Asia is not difficult to remove, given the outward-looking policies and increasing openness. Over and above, liberalisation process in India has infused dynamism in the region's economies in several ways. South Asia is becoming more open, outward-oriented, and more receptive to foreign investment and trade. At this juncture, working together for the improvement of infrastructural facilities, an essential element to enhance intra-regional trade, will pave the way for the region's international market access and through this to higher income.

The key objective of the cooperation in trade and investment is to achieve more rapid growth in exports through improvements in product design, marketing, financing, and logistics. Appropriate industries with potential comparative advantage need to be identified. Associated soft infrastructure to support the trade and investment should be in place. These include: (i) approval and implementation of required legal and policy reforms; (ii) implementation of effective border crossing and transport services; (iii) effective agreement on trade and transit treaties between participating countries in SAARC and BIMSTEC context; (iv) establishing a facility to encourage investments in SME exporters and to improve their market access; and (vi) promote human resource development, better education and appropriate technology transfer.

Therefore, the aim of cooperation in the infrastructure sector among South Asian countries in general and between India and Bangladesh in particular should be to utilise the available resources optimally for the maximisation of welfare of the region as a whole. Naturally, the rationale for this type of cooperation lies in developing regional public goods in an integrated manner, removing visible and invisible trade barriers and exploiting the complementarities for mutual benefit of all.

3. Infrastructure and Regional Development

In general, infrastructure facilities can be understood largely as public infrastructural inputs from the supply side. However, depending on the nature of services delivered, infrastructure can be broadly divided into physical, social and financial categories - all economically desirable. The first of these consists of transport (railways, roadways, airways, and waterways), electricity, irrigation, telecommunication, water supply and the like. Notwithstanding their very direct impact on production through external economies, they are beneficial for "crowding in" of private investment (both domestic and foreign) in the concerned geographical region. In a "cumulative causation" fashion, physical infrastructure contributes to economic growth through lower transaction cost, and generates "multipliers" of investment, employment, output, income and ancillary development. On the other hand, social infrastructure through enrichment of human resources in terms of education, health, housing, recreation facilities and the like improves the quality of life. This is primarily responsible for higher concentration of better human resources in a region, and helps improve productivity of labour. Financial infrastructure incorporating banking, postal and tax capacity of the concerned population represents the financial performance of a country. These three taken together represent the relative income generating capability of a country or a region. The adequacy of infrastructure helps determine one country's success and another's failure – in diversifying production, expanding trade, coping with population growth, reducing poverty, improving quality of life, or improving environmental conditions (Munnell, 1990). Although infrastructure capacity grows step by step with economic output, the precise linkage between infrastructure and development are still open to debate (World Bank, 1994). And as countries develop, infrastructure must adapt to support changing patterns of demand, as the shares of power, roads, railways, airways, and telecommunications in the total stock of infrastructure increase relative to those of such basic traditional services.

As is well known, building up of additional infrastructural facilities at the initial stage may not have immediate, high and positive impact on income. After the critical minimum level of overhead infrastructure level is crossed, the impact of infrastructure stock on per capita income exponentially helps increase income. The economic rationale behind this may be that at the initial scale building up of infrastructure facility may act as a downward pressure (or burden) on income thereby implying a sort of sacrifice, and beyond that level various external economies may multiply the contribution of infrastructure to income exponentially (Krugman, 1995).

The literature offers substantial evidence linking improvements in infrastructure directly to improvements in export performance of a country or a region. The effects are especially strong when importers have access to multiple suppliers of highly substitutable commodities.[8]

Figure 3.1
Potential Contribution of Infrastructure to Openness in South Asia

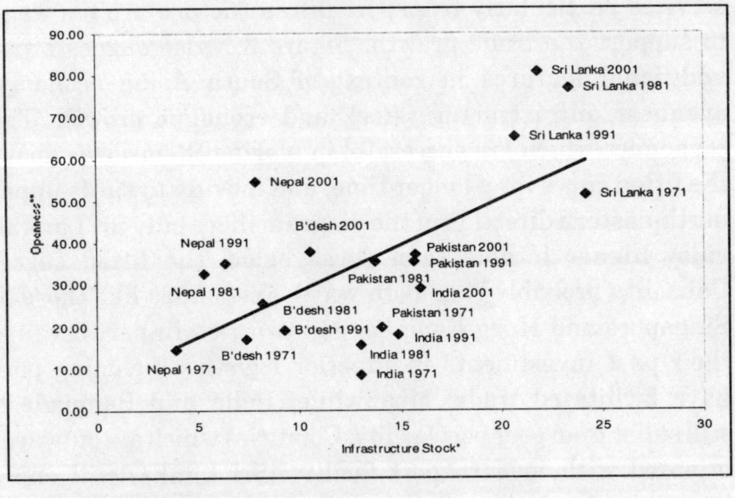

Notes: *The measures of infrastructure stock are based on those indicated in the De and Ghosh (2003) ** Openness considers trade as percentage of GDP.

Sources: De and Ghosh (2003) for infrastructure stock, and *World Development Indicators CD-ROM 2004*, World Bank for openness.

Now that we have seen that several studies show quality of transport infrastructure improves international market access of a region and leads directly to increased trade and through this to higher incomes, the question is whether or not improved infrastructure matters. The answer is: it does.

Figure 3.1 explains the proposition in the context of South Asia. Those countries lying above the fitted line score high on measures of openness, and are accessible to world markets in the sense of having superior infrastructure facilities. Some of these countries in South Asia in recent period are Sri Lanka, Bangladesh and Nepal. India and Pakistan lie below the fitted curve. That is, economies with higher openness thereby meaning economies with fewer political barriers to trade can enjoy greater returns to infrastructure investments than those whose political system and poor infrastructural facilities would prevent trade growth. Similarly, benefits from free trade may be of limited value if infrastructure services particularly transport infrastructure are too weak to support the trade growth. Figure 3.1 also suggests two additional features in context of South Asian economy: openness, infrastructure stock and economic growth. The economies which are successful in placing themselves above the fitted curve for a longer time, and moving towards upper north-eastern direction of the diagram (here only Sri Lanka), enjoy higher income than those below the fitted curve. Causality probably runs both ways. Economies like those of Singapore and Hong Kong have grown rich in part because their past investments in superior logistics including port have facilitated trade. Meanwhile, India and Bangladesh still suffer from poor port facility. Countries which are outward-oriented with modern port facility (Sri Lanka) will enjoy benefits of borderless global trade than countries which are open but equipped with relatively poor facility (Bangladesh). Ghosh and De (2000) and De and Ghosh (2003, 2005) using several infrastructure facilities across the South Asian countries over last two decades have shown that differential endowments of infrastructural facilities were responsible for rising regional disparity in South Asia. Naturally, here comes the need for mutual cooperation in the region for catching up those who are ahead of South Asian countries. Therefore, establishment and existence of well functioning, efficient and integrated transport infrastructure facility is essential for economic development and trade growth of a country and also a region.

4. Trade and Trade Costs

The performance of South Asia is poor in terms of intra-regional trade. Countries within the SAARC do not have significant trade with one another in spite of their proximity and income levels. For instance, intraregional trade in ASEAN at present is approximately 20 percent per annum, which was increased from mere 5 percent in beginning of 1990s, whereas the same in South Asia is just 4 percent and that too is hovering for last one decade. At present, the intraregional official trade in South Asia is around US$ 6.25 billion[9] where India alone contributes more than 45 percent of total intraregional trade, and the rest is distributed among Bangladesh, Nepal, Pakistan and Sri Lanka. Table 3.3(a) shows the trends of intra-regional trade in South Asia for three cross-section points (1991, 1995 and 2002). It is very

TABLE 3.3(A)

Intra-South Asia Trade

Countries	*Trade with World US$ Million*			*Trade with SAARC US$ Million*			*Intra-SAARC Trade %*		
	1991	*1995*	*2002*	*1991*	*1995*	*2002*	*1991*	*1995*	*2002*
Bangladesh	5108	9625	13290	335	1234	1295	6.56	12.82	9.74
India	37381	65021	115407	718	1742	2739	1.92	2.68	2.37
Maldives	216	407	599	33	58	109	15.28	14.25	18.13
Nepal	757	1091	1419	120	164	462	15.85	15.03	32.55
Pakistan	14925	19452	21124	339	419	457	2.27	2.15	2.16
Sri Lanka	5048	8282	10703	369	646	1189	7.31	7.80	11.11
South Asia	63435	103878	162541	1914	4263	6251	3.02	4.10	3.85

Source: Direction of Trade Statistics Yearbook, Various Issues, IMF.

clear that despite overall economic progress in South Asia since 1991, economies in South Asia have not yet engaged in higher trading among themselves; 3.85 percent of intra-regional official trade in 2002 is nonetheless disappointing, which was even mere 3.02 percent in 1999, increased to over 4 percent in 1995 and thereafter seen sharp decline. Except Pakistan, rest of South Asian countries have engaged into comparatively higher trading among themselves during 1991 to 2002. Nonetheless, the overall growth of intra-regional trade in South Asia is rather slow.

TABLE 3.3(B)

India – Bangladesh Trade Matrix

Export	*Bangladesh*			*India*		
	1991	*1995*	*2002*	*1991*	*1995*	*2002*
Bangladesh				23.00	36.00	39.33
India	325.00	960.00	1042.00			
Import	*Bangladesh*			*India*		
	1991	*1995*	*2002*	*1991*	*1995*	*2002*
Bangladesh				189.00	994.00	1145.83
India	6.00	79.00	43.00			
Total	*Bangladesh*			*India*		
	1991	*1995*	*2002*	*1991*	*1995*	*2002*
Bangladesh				212.00	1030.00	1185.16
India	331.00	1039.00	1085.00			

Note: Trade is taken in terms of US$ million.

Source: Direction of Trade Statistics Yearbook, Various Issues, IMF

Bilaterally, from India's point of view, India-Bangladesh two-way trade has grown over 6 percent annually during 1991 to 2002 whereas the same for Bangladesh's trade with India has increased by more than 42 percent since 1991 thereby showing huge trade imbalance between the two countries (see, Table 3.3(B)). In general, India-Bangladesh bilateral trade has expanded, presumably due to trade liberalisation, initiated unilaterally, bilaterally and regionally (SAPTA). However, the growing trade imbalance is cause of great concern to Bangladesh (and also to India) primarily on two aspects – (a) whether huge imports from India is helping Bangladesh in increasing her trade intensity with rest of the world, and (b) whether the rising import from India is strengthening Bangladesh's international competitiveness in the era of globalisation.[10] In order to deepen bilateral economic relations between the two countries, policy makers should explore these two issues extensively.

Another important reason for persistently low intra-regional trade in South Asia is inadequacy in appropriate trading instruments (both visible and invisible) (De and Ghosh, 2005). Today, South Asian economies together pay about 8.46 percent as trade costs (interchangeably, transaction costs) for its US$ 6.25 billion of intra-regional annual trade, which is usually moving around 8–10 percent since 1995 (Table 3.4).

Incidence of transaction costs between India and Bangladesh for approximately US$ 1 billion two-way official trade is too high; in 2002, people in India and Bangladesh incurred approximately US$ 108-118 million as bilateral transaction costs. Costs for not having improved transit and transport infrastructure facilities may be more if we add several invisible and unaccountable incidences to it. To a great extent, as an effect of high trading costs, bilateral and intra-regional trade between India and Bangladesh and among South Asian countries respectively are not taking a good shape as yet, compared with predominant regional trading blocs such as ASEAN, EU and NAFTA. Those countries which have removed the common barriers to trade have done well in raising per capita income from rising trade. It

TABLE 3.4

Intra-SAARC Transaction Costs

Particulars	*Transaction Costs*[1]	
	1995 %	*2002* %
Trade between India and Bangladesh	7.73	9.94
Trade between India and Sri Lanka	22.41	10.09
Trade between India and Nepal	9.85	9.63
Trade between India and Maldives[2]	158.33	10.92
Trade between India and Pakistan	15.71	10.15[1]
Trade between Bangladesh and Pakistan[2]	34.62	14.05
Trade between Bangladesh and Sri Lanka[2]	*	100.52
Trade between Sri Lanka and Pakistan[2]	16.28	10.96
Trade between Sri Lanka and Maldives	28.00	10.00
Trade between Bangladesh and Nepal	7.14	10.11
Trade between Pakistan and Nepal	*	18.77
SAARC Total	10.94	8.46

Notes: 1. We have also considered inter-country transaction costs (TC), represented by the difference of CIF (cost, insurance and freight) and FOB (free on board) values which are reported in Direction of Trade Statistics Yearbook of IMF, using $TC_{ijt} = (IM_{ijt} / EX_{jit}) - 1$, where TC_{ijt} represents transaction costs between country i and j for the period t, IM_{ijt} stands for import (cif price) of country i from country j for the period t, EX_{jit} denotes export (fob price) of country j to country i for the period t. Many measures have been constructed to measure transaction (transport) cost. The most straightforward measure in international trade is the difference between the so-called cif and fob quotations of trade. The difference between these two values is a measure of the cost of getting an item from the exporting country to the importing country. Transaction costs have been estimated here for two-way trades between a pair of countries. 2. Estimated for one-way trade only. * Data not available

Source: Author's own calculation based on various issues of *Direction of Trade Statistics Yearbook*, IMF

should be noted that by removal of common borders between Germany and the Czech Republic, and also between the United States and Mexico, have had substantial effects on predicted income per capita in the smaller countries; income per capita in Czech Republic and Mexico have gone up by 26 percent and 27 percent, respectively, presumably as a result of integration (Redding and Venables, 2004).

Therefore, to attain higher trade between India-Bangladesh and within South Asian countries, economies in the region need to minimize trade costs by removing visible and invisible barriers to trade. Countries can reduce rising trade costs through improved and integrated trading infrastructure which is responsible for faster movement of goods and services not only within countries but also across the region.

5. Issues and Ways Forward

India and Bangladesh with their geographical contiguity have great potential for strengthening trading instruments. Over the years a number of initiatives have taken by India and Bangladesh (and also other South Asian countries) to remove 'invisible' trade barriers such as elimination of tariffs and non-tariff restrictions at unilateral, bilateral and regional levels (Pandian, 2002). Despite these initiatives the intra-South Asia trade is not growing at the expected pace. Therefore, there is need to remove the region's 'visible' trade barriers by strengthening and interlinking the region's trading instruments. Even South Asian countries depend on transport infrastructure in a major way but there is clear absence of interlinked networks in the region. While India and Bangladesh have cooperate in IWT, the same between India and Pakistan is not yet formulated. Similarly, in the road sector, even if there is a treaty among Bangladesh, India and Nepal for allowing free flow of trade through a tiny transit corridor at Phulbari (in West Bengal) between Bangladesh and Nepal, it is not even functioning properly due to some unknown reasons. In today's world where competitiveness is the key factor for a country's or a region's success or failure, strengthening of bilateral or regional trading infrastructure networks will pave the way for faster enhancement of bilateral and regional integration thereby international competitiveness. To improve the competitiveness, India and Bangladesh have to cooperate with each other and share their experiences in building and operating cross-country infrastructure facilities such as rail, road, airport, port, waterways, etc. For example, cooperation in the field of road network will help Nepal and Bhutan, using Indian soil, can access Bangladeshi road thereby ports and, similarly, India, using Bangladeshi soil, to access its NER. Again, incurring huge road transportation costs, some of the break-bulk items generated in the Northern India, such as cycle parts, newsprints, and spare parts are presently exported to Bangladesh by roads through border trade points. Denim and related items, originating at Western India, are also transported by roads in every month to Bangladesh. Ideally, this entire cargo can easily be transported by rail at lower costs to Bangladesh had there been integrated and harmonised railway network in place between the two countries. Cooperation in the emerging issues in the infrastructure sector is thus very much important for the integration of South Asian economy.

These new issues also have potentials to strengthen the bilateral relations because substantial complementarities characterize the economic structures of India and Bangladesh. Bangladesh could become economic hub in Eastern South Asia[11] on the backdrop of India's growing integration with East provided the country attempts to widen its cooperation with India. In a sense, these synergies now being rejuvenated centering around shared vision towards economic development. In view of the above discussion, following important areas of bilateral and regional cooperation need special attention from the governments and policy makers of this region.

(i) Improving Road Networks

In last decade, roads in South Asia have grown in

prominence as a means for moving goods and people. With 3.82 million km. road network in 2002, South Asian countries share 10 per cent of the world road network. Even though each sq. km. of surface area in South Asia is now served by one km. of road in some of the countries of this region such as Bangladesh, India and Sri Lanka, there are still doubts about the general quality of roads particularly those stretches of roads leading to borders in South Asia. Is there any expressway that immediately starts (ends) from (at) the border custom stations between India and Bangladesh or between Indian and Pakistan? Not, as yet.[12] Therefore, goods have to travel extra miles and people have to incur huge time, costs and harassments to get access to border.[13] Both the countries need to extend their expressways up to their own border custom stations. Also we need to look into road standard and carriageway capacity in South Asia.[14] It would be quite appropriate if we think for setting up an inter-Ministerial regional advisory committee, taking representatives from Road and Highway Ministries of the South Asian countries, to look after the region's road standard convergence and also execution of new regional highways. Best example to follow the mechanism of ASEAN, where similar arrangement has helped LDCs in ASEAN to improve their road networks thereby raising intra-regional trade.[15]

(ii) Strengthening Railway Networks

Railway network in South Asia is one of the largest railway systems in the world. It has an extensive network which is spread over 75,002 km., comprising 70 percent of broad gauge network. Before 1947, railways historically played an important integrating role in the social and economic development in South Asia. At present, approximately 30 percent of freight and 20 percent of passenger traffic are carried by railways in South Asia whereas the same for road sector are 70 percent and 80 percent respectively. There is growing modal imbalance between railways and roadways in South Asia (World Bank, 2002). The penetration of railway network in South Asia is much lower than that of road sector. India and Pakistan have quite stable broad gauge railway network whereas the same in Bangladesh is miserably poor, fragmented, and unstable[16]. Bangladesh with a total 2,734 km of railway network has only 901 km of broad gauge track (only 33 percent of total network) thereby making it as least developed railway system in South Asia (CPD, 2003). Nepal, Bhutan and Maldives are still not endowed with railway system.

Except some periodic trial runs, exporters and importers were never encouraged to use railway system for their trade in South Asia. For instance, there is no container train running between India and Pakistan, and between India and Bangladesh. As a matter of fact, trading of bulk items between India and Pakistan and India and Bangladesh is not getting the due momentum. Had there been an adequate system placed in the region, cost of intra-regional movement of goods such as cement, logs, food grains, salt, etc. would have been cheaper. While there is similarity in railway gauge to some great extent between India and Pakistan, the same is highly missing between India and Bangladesh. Mutual cooperation among these countries will pave the way for having 'one track system' in South Asia.

Unlike EU, where uninterrupted and uniform railway network alone carries the major portion of intra-regional merchandise and people, South Asia suffers from harmonisation of railway standard. In general, India – Bangladesh border trade occur through roadways and very negligible freight is carried by railways. Cross-country railway network is completely missing between India and Bangladesh, though it was fairly established pre-1947 period.

South Asian countries need to follow the EU model in setting up uniform railway network. India, with her vast experiences, can play a major role in total overhauling of the railway systems in South Asia in general and Bangladesh in particular, and extending railway networks up to all border customs points.[17] An inter-Ministerial Committee of Railway Ministries of South Asian countries can be formed to look after the development of railway network in the region.

(iii) Liberalising Aviation Services

Liberalisation of international transport services (such as air transport services) fosters international trade very much the same way tariff liberalisation does. The civil aviation sector in South Asia has made significant strides in coping with the growth of international and domestic traffic. It is increasingly acknowledged that aviation sector makes an important contribution to the economic development of this region and is crucial for sustainable development of trade and tourism.

Open skies policy has allowed private players to run domestic airlines in this region, which has attracted more passengers to fly within the national territory. Even private airlines from India are now allowed to operate within South Asia as well as abroad. In fact, airlines in South Asia have carried more passengers than freights in 2001, compared to that of 1991 (De, 2005; RIS, 2004). Rise in passenger traffic is phenomenal in small countries like Bhutan and Maldives. Today, more foreign airlines are now operating in South Asia, resulting in higher number of foreign tourists in the region. However, there are still bottlenecks in airport infrastructure and related back up facilities, particularly in congested airports in the region, which have to be fully revamped. Moreover, there should be direct flight connecting India's NER with its neighbouring countries such as Bangladesh, Bhutan, Myanmar and Nepal. Besides, national air carriers should also be given additional access right to fly to major cities in South Asia and abroad.

Therefore, governments in South Asia should aim at providing adequate capacity in accordance with demand by first restructuring of their national carriers and maximizing their equal participation in the South Asia air transport segment. Adequate capacity will certainly lead to development of trade and tourism among South Asian countries. Liberal regional rights should also be given for promoting international operations at NER to promote trade and tourism.

To encourage South Asian tourists to travel within South Asia freely, private airlines in the South Asia may be encouraged to fly in major tourist destinations in the region. Flying of private airlines within South Asia, such as India's in Sri Lanka and Nepal, and Bangladesh's in India, could be an example of such successful initiative, but their frequencies have to be increased. Similarly, private airlines of Nepal and Bangladesh should also be allowed to fly into NER's popular tourist places, which will promote tourism thereby generate employment. When people in NER want to enjoy sea beaches of Cox Bazar in Bangladesh or people in Bangladesh are interested to visit Darjeeling in India, such a network will enhance tourism activities in the region. Therefore, a much more vigorous open sky policy will certainly foster 'people to people' contact and also enhance service trade in the region. Mutual cooperation should also be initiated for upgradation of airports without which open sky policy will not generate desired results.

We also have to acknowledge that tourism and trade sectors are closely linked to civil aviation sector. Therefore, it is important that airport infrastructure and air services are planned keeping in view the requirement and promotion of these sectors. Multi-modal approach should be used for planning to ensure better connectivity. Efforts should also be made to issue visa on arrival at the airport in case passenger coming from South Asia. Airlines in South Asia should introduce EDI (Electronic Data Interchange) interlinking trade agencies, customs, and immigration for faster efficient trade transactions. Private sector participation in cargo handling for increasing competition and improved services should be welcomed.

(iv) Linking Inland Waterways

Waterways have been found as the cheapest source of movement of goods and passengers in remotest parts of South Asia. Today, though Bangladesh, India, Nepal, Pakistan and Sri Lanka together have approximately 25,000 km. of navigable waterways consisting of a variety of rivers, canals, backwaters, etc., only 10,740 km in the major rivers and 700 km of canals are suitable for operation of mechanised crafts. Due to lack of proper water transport infrastructure, organised inland water transport (IWT) services in South Asia constitutes a very small part of the total transport network of the region. IWT is still not the preferred mode of transport in South Asia. Out of total freight traffic of about 900 million tonnes by all modes of surface transport in 2001-02, IWT accounts only 25 million tonnes and thereby shares only 3 percent of total South Asian freight traffic. If absence of all weather navigability is a cause of low freight traffic in IWT then lack of awareness towards its energy conservation potential is too a reason to blame.[18] In South Asia, movement of goods by IWT system is yet to gain momentum. Against share of IWT in the level of 8 percent to 20 percent of total inland cargo in countries like USA, Netherlands, China, etc., share of IWT in South Asia is around 0.1 percent only. Although there is a rise in movement of IWT traffic in bulk and break bulk categories, movement of containers, apart from some periodic trial runs, has not made any foray in the IWT sector in South Asia (De, 2003).

India's National Waterways 2 (NW 2)[19] cutting across Bangladesh links NER with West Bengal. Absence of all weather navigation facility coupled with inadequate depth of river prohibit high speed vessels to ply in NWs thereby making little contribution in merchandise trade between the two countries. When India's West Bengal, NER and Bangladesh are well covered by inland waterways, requirement is interlinking major waterways for navigation, and also bringing new waterways within the India-Bangladesh Waterways Treaty to enhance bulk movement of goods in remotest corners where road and railways can not even penetrate.

(v) Liberalising Maritime Facilities

South Asia is endowed with approximately 9,000 km of coastline which is dotted with more than 250 ports. Although there exists large number of sea and river ports across South Asian coast, only 25 are in operation and can be treated as prominent ports of the region. All these ports together presently handle more than 400 million tonnes of cargo including 6 million TEUs of container.

Ports are a key component of infrastructure in South Asia, where recent policy initiatives have ushered in new institutional arrangements, and have yielded results in terms of measurable outcomes such as the delays at ports. Most of the busy ports in South Asia have partly privatised such as the case may be Jawarlal Nehru (in India), Karachi (in Pakistan), Colombo (in Sri Lanka) resulting in higher efficiency in operation. Some of world leading port companies are also running container terminals in Pakistan, Sri Lanka and India except Bangladesh.[20]

Since most of the intra-regional trade among South Asian countries is routed through seaports, due to rising handling costs at ports coupled with operational inefficiency, intra-regional trade in South Asia is not picking up at the desired level. The year-wise movement of containers between Calcutta, Haldia and Chittagong ports is low. Due to absence of direct calls between the ports of India and Bangladesh, containers shipped to Bangladesh from the West Indian ports are normally transhipped at Colombo and/or Singapore thereby imposing additional costs to the users and hampering intra-regional trade growth. Sharing performance of port of Jawaharlal Nehru (in India) could be a way to encourage private-public partnership for development of efficient port network in Bangladesh.

NER is very much near to Bangladesh's Chittagong port. No progress has been made to give access to NER to use Chittagong port for international and coastal trade, despite clear indications of transhipment benefits in favour of Bangladesh. Cost of non-cooperation in maritime sector is likely to be havoc, when seeing Bangladesh's noncommittal attitude towards NER's transhipment facility. India has taken new initiatives to link NER with ports in Myanmar. Therefore, by allowing Chittagong port for NER's trade will pave the way in strengthening bilateral relations between the two countries, failing which cooperation momentum will certainly be slowed down.

(vi) Liberalising Trade Services

Today, trade services (or trade facilitation) are at the forefront of the development agenda, and it is a critical element of any strategy to fight poverty.[21] Today's trade issues go beyond the traditional mechanisms of tariffs and quotas and include "behind-the-border" issues, such as the role of infrastructure and governance in supporting a well-functioning trading economy. Some studies have indicated that the cost of trade facilitation, specifically trade documentation and procedures, is high, between 4 and 7 per cent of the value of goods shipped. In 1996, APEC conducted a study that highlighted the gain from effective trade facilitation. For example, the gains from streamlining customs procedures exceeded those resulting from trade liberation such as tariff reduction. Gains from effective trade facilitation accounted for about 0.26 per cent of real GDP of APEC members (about US$ 45 billion), while the gains from trade liberalization would be 0.14 per cent of real GDP (about US$ 23 billion) (UNESCAP, 2005).

Inadequate trade facilitation measures are very much prominent between India and Bangladesh border trade. In the road sector, a trade consignment takes minimum 4 to 6 days for clearance from Indian border to Bangladesh side and vice versa. The present legal arrangement between India and Bangladesh prohibits Indian vehicle (or Bangladeshi vehicle) to cross each other's border for delivering the consignment to the ultimate user(s). Generally a consignment needs minimum 22 documentations, more than 55 signatures, and minimum 116 copies for the final approval taking into account both sides. Due to this complex, lethargic and primitive procedure, pilferage is rising high day-by-day, which often changes the composition and direction of trade (Subramanian, 1999). Procedural complexities very often work as deterrent to India–Bangladesh trade.

(vii) Renovating Land Customs Stations (LCSs)

LCSs are the gateways for the transit of goods, services and human beings between India and Bangladesh. Most of the India-Bangladesh traders and service providers use LCSs. Unfortunately, not a single LCS between India and Bangladesh offers services of international standard.[22] The physical environment at LCSs is anything but not conducive for trade and services. Several measures have already taken for upgradation of LCSs in NER, but effects are still limited.[23] As on date, the 11 LCSs, as shown in the Table 3.5, have been prioritized for development of infrastructure,[24] out of which development of 4 LCSs, namely Moreh, Sutarkandi, Dawki and Zokhawthar were given highest priority.[25]

The Central Warehousing Corporation (CWC) has conducted studies on requirement of infrastructure facilities at Moreh (Manipur), Dawki (Meghalaya) and Sutarkandi (Assam) for improvement of LCS. CWC is the appointed agency for the development of Moreh, Dawki and Sutarkandi LCS, whereas the Zokhawthar (Mizoram) will be developed by the Borders Road Organisation (BRO) in cooperation with the Mizoram Government (Government of India, 2005). In order to enhance the overland trade between India and Bangladesh, utmost priority should be given to improvement of LCSs because a major proportion of the bilateral trade in goods and services passes through these stations.

TABLE 3.5

LCS Under Renovation/Development in NER

Sr. No.	*Land Custom Station*	*State*	*Neighbouring Country*
1.	Agartala	Tripura	Bangladesh
2.	Borsorah	Meghalaya	
3.	Dawki	Meghalaya	
4.	Demagiri	Mizoram	
5.	Ghasuapara	Meghalaya	
6.	Karimganj Steamer Ghat	Assam	
7.	Moreh	Manipur	Myanmar
8.	Old Raghana Bazar	Tripura	Bangladesh
9.	Srimantapur	Tripura	
10.	Sutarkhandi	Tripura	
11.	Zokhawthar (Champai)	Mizoram	Myanmar

Source: Government of India (2005).

Finally, India and Bangladesh, bilaterally and regionally, will have to quickly acquire the needed expertise on the whole lot of complex issues of trade facilitation, so they can negotiate more effectively and ensure that agreements serve their objective of poverty reduction.

6. Conclusions and Policy Recommendations

Today's trade issues go beyond the traditional mechanisms of tariffs and quotas and include "behind-the-border" issues, such as the role of infrastructure and governance in supporting a well-functioning trading economy. International transport services liberalisation foster international trade very much the same way tariff liberalisation does. Developing countries will have to acquire quickly the needed expertise on the whole lot of complex issues of trade facilitation, so that they can negotiate more effectively and ensure that agreements serve their objective of poverty reduction. The adequacy in trade facilitation measures (both visible and invisible) helps determine one region's success and another's failure. For instance, it is the transport infrastructure and user-friendly transaction instruments helped European countries to unite, whereas the lack of integrated transport network preventing South Asia to integrate. Therefore, working together for trade facilitation, an essential element to promote international trade, will pave the way for "win-win" situation.

South Asian economies are aiming to undertake trade facilitation measures which will greatly reduce current physical and non-physical barriers to transportation and transit – by means of both visible infrastructure (such as multi-modal corridors and terminals) and invisible infrastructure (such as reform policies and procedures, regulations). We also have to acknowledge that due to lack of adequate research on trade facilitation on South Asia, there is not much information available at present on existing profile of trade facilitation measures (both at border and capital) in South Asia. This is a research area which needs special attention from policy makers and researchers in South Asia.

Considering this region's emergence as a free trade area from 2006 onward, reform in the transport sector will help South Asian countries to assess potential benefits of moving to a deregularised transport sector under a liberal trading regime when transport sector is the one of the prime instruments for promotion of intra-regional trade. Hence, countries in this region should take immediate steps in not only integrating their transport system but also reforming the entire systems so that it works as 'engine of growth' rather than posing as 'trade deterrent'. The Government of Bangladesh should try to remove the structural asymmetries in the rail and maritime transportation sector, which are found to be quite significant.

There exists severe transport and transaction cost barriers for effective cross-border trade between India and Bangladesh. Therefore, they need to develop regional transportation and transit system that offers efficient transportation options and low 'transaction costs' that are competitive with those found elsewhere. As the 'full life' of many new products become shorter and shorter and the spatial distribution of supply and demand points changes rapidly in such a system, what is transported, how it is transported, and to where and from where transported, are all rapidly changing. The price of admission for a region to this dynamic global system is a transportation and transit system that offers an exporter short time spans between order and delivery, and predictable and reliable deliveries. In order to plug into this wealth-creating machine, India and Bangladesh must develop a transportation and transit facilitation system that will greatly reduce current physical and non-physical barriers to transportation and transit – by means of both physical infrastructure (such as multi-modal corridors and terminals) and non-physical infrastructure (reform policies and procedures, regulations, and incentives for efficient transportation and transit).

India being large in size has special role to play in deepening bilateral cooperation with Bangladesh through transport infrastructure sector. First, India may invest in infrastructure as a response to serious bottlenecks taking place due to an expansion of private sector. This leads to a passive strategy: transport infrastructure is following private investment. Another option is that Governments of India and Bangladesh use transport infrastructure as an engine for regional development. This implies an active strategy where transport infrastructure is leading and inducing private investment. Although both the approaches have some pros and cons, many countries have used the latter approach to attract private investments vis-à-vis regional development.

Trade liberalisation is a necessary but not a sufficient condition. To achieve any substantial progress in bilateral as well as regional trade among the countries in South Asia, we must give utmost priority for the development of infrastructural facilities. Added to this, complimentary policy reform, accompanied by improved procedural and operational efficiency, in the transport sector is essential to support trade liberalisation of South Asia.

In context of India and Bangladesh bilateral economic cooperation, some of the immediate issues which need urgent focus are (a) harmonisation of technical standards such as truck size and weight regulations, railway gauge and rolling stocks, (b) harmonisation of road transportation and motor vehicles rules and regulations, (c) free movement of vehicles, registered in India and Bangladesh, within the region subject to fulfilment of road transportation rules and regulations, (c) abolition of residual economic regulations, especially in the form of sabotage rules and restrictions on the movement of certain goods, (d) faster border inspection except strategic areas, (e) simplification of documentation and custom procedures; (f) application of information technology in monitoring cross-border movement of goods and services, (g) open sky policy for airlines, (f) movement of container train from one port of one country to another port of another country, (h) intra-regional transit and transportation facilities, (i) cover border customs points under national road and highway development programme, (j) rebuilding LCSs to international standards, and finally, (j) a well balanced inter-governmental regulatory body in line with European Union to monitor the integrated development of transport sector in the region.

NOTES

1. Specifically, 48 million in Bangladesh and 361 million in India. Calculated based on the population living below US$ 1 a day in terms of percentage of the population living on less than US$ 1.08 a day at 1993 international prices (World Bank, 2005).
2. See, for example, Andriamananjara (2004).
3. See, for example, De and Ghosh (2001, 2003).
4. This does not mean narrowing down other important issues between the two countries.
5. There are several studies which support this argument. To name a few, Das (1996), Paranjpe (2002), Srinivasan (2002), Shrestha and Upadhyay (2004), World Bank (2004), De and Ghosh (2005), and De (2005).
6. There are secondary reports which indicate uncertainty to opening SAFTA from 1st January 2006.
7. In a recent paper, De (2004) shows that for most Asian countries, transaction cost works as a strong barrier to trade integration than import tariff. By estimating a structural model of economic geography using cross-country data on income, infrastructure, transaction costs and trade of selected Asian economies, this paper provides evidence that transaction cost is statistically significant and important in explaining variation in trade in Asia. In addition, this study also finds that port efficiency and infrastructure quality are two important determinants of transaction costs.

8. Comparing sales by manufacturers of similar products, Hummels (1999) estimated that exporters with 1 percent lower shipping costs will enjoy a 5-8 percent higher market share. Limao and Venables (2001) found differences in infrastructure quality account for 40 percent of the variation in transport costs for coastal countries and up to 60 percent for landlocked countries. Fink et. al. (2002) estimated that liberalising the provision of port services and regulating the exercise of market power in shipping could reduce shipping costs by nearly a third.
9. There are several studies which show that there is considerable informal trading in South Asia, which has evolved due to several geo-political and commercial reasons. See, for example, (Chaudhury, 1995; Taneja, 1999; Pohit and Taneja, 2000).
10. Studies indicate that India Bangladesh trade pattern does not follow strictly the principle of comparative advantage. According to Raychaudhuri (2005), India Bangladesh trade promotes some activities which may be consistent with relative comparative advantage but not global.
11. What we know as South Asian Growth Quadrangle (SAGQ). See, for instance, Dubey et al., (1999) for the framework of SAGQ.
12. The National Highway Authority of India (NHAI), under the Ministry of Road Transport and Highways, Government of India, is implementing the NHDP, comprising of the Golden Quadrilateral (5846 km) and North-South & East-West Corridors (7300 km), which entails expansion of the existing two-lane highways to four/six-lanes. In addition to the projects under NHDP, the NHAI is also currently responsible for about 1,000 km of highways connecting major ports and also on National Highways 8A, 24, 6, 45 and 27. Approximately 2093 km, consisting of the 1408 km of GQ, 557 km of NS-EW and 56 km of PC and 153 km of other highway projects, have already been four laned, and 5133 km are under implementation. Unfortunately, not a single NHDP component covers India-Bangladesh border custom points. Similarly, under Khushal Pakistan Programme (KPP), all lower grade roads are also being upgraded to higher grades by National Highway Authority (NHA) of Pakistan for last two years

without India-Pakistan border customs points. Similar attitude has also prevailed in Bangladesh.

13. For instance, exporters (through vehicle attendants) are forcefully made to pay US$ 12 per vehicle carrying goods to Bangladesh using Petrapole LCS (India) to unauthorised local youths at a place called Bangon, West Bengal. This is according to author's eyewitness when the author visited the border LCS on 14 September 2005, and later also reconfirmed from representatives by the Western Group, Kolkata, which is a leading freight forwarding company in India.

14. To some extent, this is covered under UNESCAP's Asian Highway project where most of the South Asian countries are the signatories.

15. For instance, we need to learn from the regional highway that originates at Thailand (Bangkok) and ends at Vietnam (Hanoi), cutting across Lao PDR.

16. Sri Lankan broad gauge railway system, though was quite stable, needs complete overhaul which was badly damaged by Tsunami in 2004.

17. Countries in South Asia are signatories of UNESCAP's Trans-Asian Railway (TAR) system, which does not cover all the border customs points among South Asian countries.

18. Among South Asian countries, India's progress in IWT is notable, though Bangladesh has also made considerable progress in this sector. India has established the Inland Waterways Authority of India (IWAI) in 1986 by promulgating the Inland Waterways Authority of India Act in 1985 for regulation and development of inland waterways for the purpose of shipping and navigation. At present, IWAI is responsible for development and maintenance of India's three National Waterways, and Bangladesh Inland Waterways Authority (BIWA) for its waterways.

19. Specifically, NW 2 links Ganga with Bramaputra through Bangladesh.

20. For instance, P&O Ports, from its regional head quarter located in Mumbai, are running couple of container terminals in South Asia such as at Jawaharlal Nehru, Chennai, Mundra ports (all in India), Colombo port (in Sri Lanka), Qasim port

(in Pakistan). There are few more terminals running by noted private port companies like Port of Singapore Authority, A P Moller, Dubai Port, etc. in India.

21. In general, there is no official definition of trade facilitation. According to WTO, trade facilitation is the specification and harmonization of international trade procedures, where trade procedures are the activities, practices and formalities involved in collecting, presenting, communicating and processing data required for the movement of goods in international trade. These procedures are required government agencies, importers and exporters to monitor and control the movement of goods, performance of services and the payment for such goods and services. They also allow for the collection of statistics for policy formulation, market research and operational purposes (UNESCAP, 2005).

22. By international standard, we mean the guidelines issued by the World Customs Organisation.

23. The Government of India continues to accord high priority to the development of trade and exports in the NER. Following the announcement made by the Prime Minister in respect of measures for the development of exports from the NER in Shillong during 21-22 January, 2000, an Export Development Fund (EDF) has also been set up with the objective of using the resources for the development of exports from NER. An Empowered Committee has been set up under the Chairmanship of the Additional Secretary, Infrastructure, Department of Commerce, Government of India for approving projects to be funded from the Export Development Fund. The funds are released to the Agricultural & Processed Food Products Export Development Authority (APEDA), which has been nominated as the nodal agency for the Scheme. Adequate infrastructure being an essential requirement for sustained growth of trade, the Government of India has been assisting the NER states for creation of infrastructure under the Assistance to states for Development of Export Infrastructure and other activities (ASIDE) scheme. During 2004-05 an amount of Rs. 360 million, constituting 10 percent of the outlay under the scheme, has been allocated for the NER (Government of India, 2005). On the other hand, it is also

true that paucity of funds restricts the State Governments in NER to invest in LCSs, but, very often they expose their inability to develop LCSs indicating the bilateral trade is a Central subject.

24. It has been decided that requirement of funds for the development of infrastructure at 11 LCS would be met from the central component of ASIDE. RITES Ltd. has been asked to conduct a study on the development of infrastructure at Borsorah and Agartala LCS in NER. An Inter- Ministerial Committee for the development of LCSs has been constituted under the Chairmanship of the Additional Secretary (Infrastructure), Department of Commerce with representatives from the Ministry of External Affairs, Ministries of Home Affairs, Railways, Road Transport and Highways, Telecommunications, Department of Revenue, Reserve Bank of India, Central Warehousing Corporation, National Highways Authority of India, Border Roads Organization and the concerned State Governments. Coordination Committee at each of the LCSs have also been constituted under the Deputy Commissioner of Customs / Assistant Commissioner of Customs for deliberating on local issues connected with day to day functioning of the Station (Government of India, 2005).

25. The Central Warehousing Corporation (CWC) has conducted studies on requirement of infrastructure facilities at Moreh (Manipur), Dawki (Meghalaya) and Sutarkandi (Assam) for improvement of LCS. CWC is the appointed agency for the development of Moreh, Dawki and Sutarkandi LCS, whereas the Zokhawthar (Mizoram) will be developed by the Borders Road Organisation (BRO) in cooperation with the Mizoram Government (Government of India, 2005).

REFERENCES

Andriamananjara, S. 2004. "Trade and International Transport Services: An Analytical Framework", *Journal of Economic Integration,* Vol. 19, No. 3, pp. 604-625.

Banerjee, A. and A. Newman. 2004. *Inequality, Growth and Trade Policy*. Mimeo, Massachusetts Institute of Technology.

Basu, K. 2001. "India and the Global Economy: Role of Culture,

Norms and Beliefs", *Economic and Political Weekly*, Vol. 36, No. 40, 2001, pp. 3837-3838.

Centre for Policy Dialogue. 2003. *Developing a Policy Agenda for Bangladesh: Civil Society's Task Force Reports 2001*, The University Press Limited, Dhaka, p. 132.

Chaudhari, S.K. 1995. *Cross Border Trade between India and Bangladesh*, Working Paper 58, National Council of Applied Economic Research, New Delhi.

Das, K.C. 1996. "The Political Economy of Regional Cooperation in South Asia", Pacific Affairs, Vol. 69, No. 2, p. 4.

De, P. 2003. "Movement of Containers through National Waterways", *Indian Ports*, Vol. 35, No. 1, pp. 5 – 16.

De, P. 2004. *Transaction Costs as Barriers to Economic Integration in Asia: An Empirical Exploration*, Discussion Paper 77, Research and Information System for Developing Countries, New Delhi.

De, P. 2005. "Cooperation in Infrastructure Sector: A South Asian Perspective", *Contemporary South Asia*, Forthcoming.

De, P. and B. Ghosh. 2001. "Transport Infrastructure and Economic Performance of Bangladesh and Indian Bordering States", *BIISS Journal*, Vol. 22, No. 4, pp. 414-462.

De, P. and B. Ghosh. 2003. *How Do Infrastructure Facilities Affect Regional Income? An Investigation with South Asian Countries*, Discussion Paper 66, Research and Information System for Developing Countries (RIS), New Delhi, Available at www.ris.org.in

De, P. and B. Ghosh. 2005. "Effects of Infrastructure on Regional Income in the Era of Globalization: New Evidence from South Asia", *Asia Pacific Development Journal*, Vol. 12, No. 1, pp. 81-107.

Dubey, M., L R Baral, and R. Sobhan. 1999. *South Asian Growth Quadrangle: Framework for Multifaceted Cooperation*, Macmillan, New Delhi.

Fink, C., A. Mattoo and I.C. Neagu. 2002. "Trade in International Maritime Services: How Much Does Policy Matter?" *The World Bank Economic Review*, Vol. 16, No. 1, pp. 451-479.

Ghosh, B. and P. De. 2000. "Infrastructure, Economic Growth and Trade in SAARC", *BIISS Journal*, Vol. 21, No. 2.

Government of India. 2005. *Annual Report 2004-05,* Ministry of Commerce and Industry, New Delhi.

Hummels, D. 1999. *Have International Trade Costs Declined?,* Working Paper, University of Chicago Business School, Chicago.

Krugman Paul. 1995. *Development, Geography, and Economic Theory,* MIT Press, Cambridge, p. 47.

Kumar, N. 2002 *Globalisation and Quality of FDI: A Quantitative Analysis of the Role of Host Country Characteristics and WTO Regime,* Oxford University Press, New Delhi.

Limao, N. and A.J. Venables. 2001. "Infrastructure, Geographical Disadvantage, Transport Costs, and Trade", *The World Bank Economic Review,* Vol. 15, No. 3, pp. 451-479

Munnell, A.H. 1990. "How does Public Infrastructure Affect Regional Economic Performance?", *New England Economic Review,* September/October, pp. 11-32

Pandian, S.G. 2002. "Moving South Asia's Economies beyond the Indo-Pakistan Paradigm in the South Asian Regional Association for Cooperation", *Contemporary South Asia,* Vol. 11, No. 3, pp. 329 – 344.

Paranjpe, S. 2002. "Development of Order in South Asia: Towards a South Asian Association for Regional Cooperation Parliament", *Contemporary South Asia,* Vol. 11, No. 3, pp. 345-346;

Pohit, S. and N. Taneja. 2000. *India's Informal Trade with Bangladesh and Nepal: A Qualitative Assessment,* Working Paper 58, Indian Council for Research on International Economic Relations, New Delhi.

Raychaudhuri, A. 2005. *India Bangladesh Border Trade: Some Analytical Issues,* Conference Proceedings of the International Conference '*Indo-Bangladesh Border Trade: Status and Pros*pects', Organised by the ICSSR-NERC, held at Shillong on 12-13 July 2005.

Redding, S. and A.J. Venables. 2004. "Economic Geography and International Inequality', *Journal of International Economics,* Vol. 62, No. 1, pp. 53-82.

Research and Information System for Developing Countries (RIS). 2004. *South Asia Development and Cooperation Report 2004,* New Delhi.

Shrestha, H.K. and M.P. Upadhyay. 2004. "Political Economy of Regional Trading Arrangements in South Asia", *Journal of Economic Integration,* Vol. 19, No. 3, pp. 427-446.

Srinivasan, T.N. 2002. *Trade, Finance and Investment in South Asia,* Social Science Press, New Delhi.

Subramanian, U. 1999. *South Asia Transport: Issues and Options,* Paper presented at the international workshop on 'Regional Initiative on Transport Integration of South Asia Region', organised by UNESCAP, held at Bangkok, 19- 21 April.

Topalova, Petia, 2005. *Trade Liberalization, Poverty and Inequality: Evidence from India Districts,* Working Paper No. 11614, National Bureau of Economic Research, Cambridge, Available at http://www.nber.org/papers/w11614.

UNESCAP. 2005. *ESCAP Trade Facilitation Framework:* A Guiding Tool, UNESCAP, Bangkok.

World Bank. 1994. *World Development Report 1994: Infrastructure for Development,* Oxford University Press, New York, pp. 1-12.

World Bank. 2002. *India's Transport Sector: The Challenges Ahead,* New Delhi, pp. 45-49.

World Bank. 2004. *Trade Policies in South Asia: An Overview,* Report No. 29949, Washington D.C.

World Bank. 2005. *World Development Report,* Washington D.C.

4

COOPERATION THROUGH COMMUNICATION: AN APPROACH TO NER OF INDIA-BANGLADESH TRANSPORT LINK

Sukharanjan Suter

Introduction

Communication is the key to development. Communication is an all-embracing term to include infrastructure, services and regulatory framework for all modes—road, rail, air, maritime and waterway transport. Improvement of transport communication is a must to develop the physical links as well as to improve the cooperation between and within the countries and regions. Communication guides the communities, regions, and countries in achieving the main development goals i.e. economic and social development. An improved communication system is required for physical access to jobs, health, education and other social amenities and essential for economic growth, trade and fosters integration.

The broad development objectives for improvement of the transportation linkages are: to provide access for trade, commerce and mobility for all people in society; to foster sustainable economic and social development between the countries and regions; to facilitate integration between and within countries, and linking landlocked countries to regional and international trading routes; to integrate countries into the world economy.

Bangladesh is located between two parts of India and the Bay of Bengal. Because the two parts of India are divided by Bangladesh, physical communication between West Bengal and the seven Eastern and North-Eastern Indian States takes place through a rather long corridor of Siliguri, bypassing Bangladesh. Therefore, it may be beneficial for both Bangladesh and India to develop transshipment services through Bangladesh territory. The eastern and north-eastern states are now connected with the western parts of the country by railways and long-winding, hazardous, mountainous roads along the Siliguri corridor, transportation along which involves huge costs to the Indian economy in terms of time and resources. Any transshipment/communication agreement between the two countries is likely to reduce these costs significantly.

At the same time, Bangladesh, which has large and growing balance of payments deficits with India, might be in a position to meet part of these deficits through raising its services exports to India in the form of transshipment freight and transport-related services, transit fees, and other charges. Indirect benefits may accrue in the form of employment generation, modernization and development of the country's transport infrastructure, increased opportunities for Indian investment in Bangladesh, and growth of ancillary services in the country. On the other hand, there are costs for administering the facility, costs of wear and tear of roads and their maintenance, environmental costs, and costs of maintaining security along the transshipment routes.

Bangladesh and India are two independent countries of the Indian sub-continent consisting of major population in this region. Bangladesh shares her border mainly with India and partly with Myanmar. At present, the sub-continent is divided by invisible lines of political divisions. Transportation network within the countries have been developed in a large scale but the state of transport between NER-India and Bangladesh still constrains overall development. Moreover, communication system among developed countries reflects the higher demand of transport linkage between NER-India and Bangladesh. For the need of globalization and socialization, it is time to establish common interest on regional cooperation among the neighbors. Transport linkages may contribute to the campaign against poverty and strengthen the cooperation between NER-India and Bangladesh. This approach needs to be built on a framework of principles to achieve the wider development goals, which will deliver a safe, economically viable, institutionally sustainable, environmentally sound and socially aware transport system.

In order to understand the importance of transportation system between Bangladesh and NER-India we need to review few concepts and comprehend the importance of this concept in terms of transportation linkage between NER-India and Bangladesh.

2. Geography of Bangladesh and North Eastern Region of India

Bangladesh, with around 140 million population, is surrounded in the west, north-west and east by India and shares a south-eastern border with Myanmar. To the south is the Bay of Bengal. Bangladesh has a total area of 143,998 square kilometers. The topography is characterized by alluvial plains, bound in the north by the submontane regions of the Himalayas, and the predominate areas in the north-east and the eastern fringes adjacent to Assam.

The alluvial river plains, which dominate 90 percent of

the country, are very flat and never rise more than 10 m above sea level. The two hilly areas are the hills of sedimentary rock around Sylhet, which mark the beginnings of the hills of Assam, and the short, steep ridges of the Chittagong Hill Tracts, which run along the Myanmar border.

The North Eastern Region, comprising the states of Arunachal Pradesh, Assam, Manipur, Meghalaya, Mizoram, Nagaland, Sikkim and Tripura, spreads over a vast expanse of over 260,000 square kilometers with about 40 million people. The region is characterized by heavy precipitation; extremely rich biodiversity; fragile hills; high seismicity; and a drainage pattern marked by lateral valleys in the north and transverse valley in the south, dissected by huge rivers and raging torrents. The northeastern states have suffered from lack of adequate roads, rail, inland waterways, and civil aviation to other parts of India, as well as poor municipal infrastructure. These have contributed to poverty and impaired economic development. In terms of per capita state domestic product and other development indices, such as power and road length, the region ranks well below the national average. Nearly 32% of the region's population was below the poverty line, which was higher than the national average (26%), in 1999–2000. The region has been affected by insurgency.

3. Bangladesh-India Border

Trade of Bangladesh with India can be appreciated from the fact that Bangladesh has 4,096.7 km long border with India. Of this 1,880 km is shared by four of the North Eastern states, viz., Assam, Meghalaya, Mizoram and Tripura, and the rest is with West Bengal. Bangladesh's border with North-Eastern states is as follows:

TABLE 4.1

Bangladesh's Border with North Eastern States of India

States	*Border Type*	*Length (km)*
Assam	Land	160
	Riverine	103
	Sub-total	263
Meghalaya	Land	443
Tripura	Land	773
	Riverine	83
	Sub-total	856
Mizoram	Land	58
	Riverine	260
	Sub-total	313
Total		1880

Source: Gurudas Das and R.K. Purkayastha (eds) *Border Trade: North-East India and Neighbouring Countries*, 2000.

Long land and riverine borders mean that both land and riverine routes can be used for trade. Land routes and river ways are being used in several places for trade between Bangladesh and North Eastern states. The borders with Meghalaya and Mizoram are hilly, the latter state being relatively less accessible for trade.

4. Historical Experience of Bangladesh in Transit

The transit passage connecting the North-Eastern part of India with its Southern and Western parts had started during the British rule in the subcontinent. The industrial transportation network in the Indian subcontinent was developed by the British colonial power for its economic and strategic needs. Calcutta was the main port on the Indian subcontinent after Bombay, serving all the eastern parts of British India, including the present day Bangladesh. Chittagong, on the other hand, developed much slower and became the port for export of tea from Assam and other parts of Eastern India.

The independence from colonial rule and the partition of India into India and Pakistan had significant impact on the transportation network. Especially after the India-Pakistan war most transport links between East Pakistan and India were cut. This left East Pakistan without access to its former main port Calcutta. The need to build and develop its own national transport network became obvious.

The war of independence in 1971 caused mass destruction in Bangladesh. Apart from tremendous losses in lives, most of the country's transport infrastructure was systematically destroyed by the Pakistan army. After the war the whole transportation network had to be rebuilt. The port of Chittagong emerged as the leading international seaport of Bangladesh. It became one of the cornerstones of an independent national transportation system.

5. The Present Situation of the Bangladesh Transport Sector

The transport system of Bangladesh consists of roads, railways, inland waterways, two sea ports, maritime shipping and civil aviation catering for both domestic and international traffic. Presently there are about 21,000 km of paved roads; 2,858 km of railways; 3,865 km of perennial waterways, which increases to 5,968 km during the monsoon, 2 sea ports, and 2 international (Dhaka and Chittagong) and 8 domestic airports.

6. Infrastructure Facilities in North Eastern Region

6.1 Transport Infrastructure

The North Eastern region of India has a mixed level of infrastructural facilities. The major cities in the region, the center of trade and commerce, are connected by airways as well as by national highways and roads. The conditions of these roads are not uniformly good because of lack of proper maintenance. Further, because of hilly areas with coiling roads, transportation is more time consuming than in the plain lands. Except in Assam and Nagaland there is hardly any railway in other states.

TABLE 4.2

Road and Railway in North-Eastern Region

State	*Road length(km)*	*Railway length(km)*
Arunachal Pradesh	13,868	1.26
Assam	33,343	2,392
Manipur	7,172	1.35
Meghalaya	1,944	Nil
Mizoram	1,871	1.5
Nagaland	9,499	768
Tripura	6,496	45
Sikkim	2,338	Nil

Source: NEDFI Databank website.

6.2 Land Customs Station (LCS)

Bangladesh has more than 30 notified land customs stations (LCS) along its border with North Eastern India. Similarly, India has 32 LCS along its border with Bangladesh. However, on Bangladesh side only the following are functional:

TABLE 4.3

Land Custom Stations in Bangladesh along Indo-Bangladesh Border

Official entry \point in Bangladesh side	Akhaura of Brahman-baria	Bibir-bazar of Comilla	Seola of Sylhet	Juri (Batuli) of Mawlavi bazaar	Tamabil of Sylhet	Karaitala and Gobrakura at Haluaghat of Mymensingh
Official exit point in India side	Agartala of Tripura	Srimanta-pur of Tripura	Sutark-andi of Assam	Old Ragh-nabazaar of Tripura	Dawki of Meghalaya	Ghasuapara of Meghalaya

Source: Study on the Possibility of Market Access to Seven Sisters in India, IBTCI/ UCIL, 2004.

6.3 Infrastructure Facilities at the Land Customs Stations

The LCSs should have adequate facilities for handling both exports and imports. The LCSs on the India side of the borders have better infrastructural facilities though not yet fully equipped. The condition of LCS on Bangladesh side is anything but satisfactory. The approach road is satisfactory only in Tamabil. The LCS's lack most of the needed facilities. Though the traders carry on their business even in this unsatisfactory environment, they would prefer a better environment to facilitate exports/imports.

Bangladesh has functional LCS with all bordering states in NEI except Mizoram. Current level of formal trade with Mizoram is small. Some of the goods entering into India through Sheola and Akhaura LCS find their ways to Aizawl in small quantities. An LCS along Mizoram border would help exploit the potential of trade with this state. Situated at the farthest point of India on hilly terrain, it is also rational for Mizoram to trade with Bangladesh. There is a notified LCS at Tegamukh but it is not functional. Due to the lack of formal trading post, informal trade takes place in this region.

7. Transshipment

The concept of transshipment refers to the transfer of cargo from one ship or carrier to another. Transshipment is distinctly different from 'transit' and 'corridor use'. In the case of 'transit' and 'corridor use', one country's cargo may be moved from one point of that country to another country through a third country by the first country's own transport vehicle or carrier using a specific corridor or different corridors/ routes. But transshipment relates to transfer of cargo from one carrier to another. Theoretically, these carriers may belong to the country which transships cargo from one part of the country to another part of the same country through a third country's territory, or these carriers may belong to the country through which goods are to be moved. The carriers may relate to land routes, waterways or railways.

It may be noted that in the case of 'transit' and 'corridor use', the question of entry and exit of the sending country's transport vehicle is directly involved, whereas in the case of transshipment the involvement of that country's vehicle may be avoided altogether. If the goods are directly moved along the routes/corridor of a country, the personnel and the transport vehicles of the sending country may have the access into the country through which goods are to be moved. But in the case of transshipment, access of personnel and transport vehicles of the sending country may not be needed. The country through which goods are to be moved may provide the transport vehicles and the personnel associated with transshipment.

It is important to note that the transshipment arrangement between Bangladesh and India is restricted to the transfer of cargo from Indian road/rail transport to the road transport of Bangladesh. An efficient and cost effective reloading is necessary to make transshipment competitive.

7.1 Possible Land Routes and Entry/Exit Points for Transshipment

It is well known that there are several entry and exit points both on the western and the eastern boundaries of Bangladesh with India. If the transshipment arrangement takes place between Bangladesh and India, several routes may possibly be used. These routes will connect one border to another. The possible routes that can be used for transshipment are indicated below:

(a) Goods from India may enter through Benapole–Petropole border and may reach Tamabil–Meghalaya border via Dhaka. Total length of this route is about 686 km. This route may serve specially Meghalaya, Assam, Arunachal Pradesh, Nagaland and Manipur. The distance between these North-Eastern States and other parts of India will significantly be reduced if transshipment is arranged.

(b) Goods from Benapole–Petropole border may also be moved to Akhaura–Agartala border via Dhaka and Brahmanbaria. Distance between Benapole and Akhaura–Agartala border is about 437 km. The Benapole – Akhaura route will be extremely useful for Tripura, Mizoram, Manipur and Nagaland and will shorten the route distance between West Bengal, Orissa, Bihar and other States of India.

(c) Indian goods through Hilli–Balurghat may be transshipped to Tamabil–Meghalaya border as well as to Akhaura–Agartala border in the East. Distances between Hilli–Tamabil and Hilli-Agartala are 650 km and 404 km respectively. This route may equally serve all the North-Eastern States of India by crossing the Jamuna Multipurpose Bridge.

(d) Indian goods may also be transshipped through Rohanpur-Sindbad border to Tamabil and Akhaura borders. The distance between Rohanpur and Tamabil is about 763 km while the distance between Rohanpur and Akhaura border is roughly 416 km. These two routes may well serve the North-Eastern States of India.

Apart from these two routes originating from Benapole and Hilli and terminating at Tamabil and Akhaura, the routes from Banglabandh may also be used for reaching Tamabil and Akhaura. Distances between Banglabandh and Tamabil, and between Banglabandh and Akhaura are 876 km and 627 km, respectively. These routes are the longest between the western border of Bangladesh and its eastern border.

7.2 Benefit of Transport Linkages and Transshipment for Bangladesh

The benefits from transport linkage and transshipment for Bangladesh could be in many different forms. However the benefit of transshipment linkage could be more to Bangladesh compared to benefit from Transit Linkage (Study on Transshipment Agreement with India, IBTCI/UCIL, 2000)

7.2.1 Direct Benefit

The direct benefits that might straightaway accrue to the government exchequer may include:

(i) *Annual Royalty*— The Government of Bangladesh may charge royalty for allowing movements of Indian goods through Bangladesh. The actual amount of royalty may be determined through negotiation between the two governments. The starting point for such negotiation may be the costs currently incurred by India for transporting goods through Shiliguri corridor and the savings in these costs that may be achieved by transshipping goods through Bangladesh.

(ii) *Sharing of Maintenance Cost*—The Bangladesh Government might convince/influence the Indian Government to share the maintenance and rehabilitation cost since the road would also be used for carrying Indian goods.

(iii) *Tolls and Ferry Charges*—Every year RHD in Bangladesh collects substantial amount of tolls and ferry charges from the transport vehicles passing through different routes of the country. In 1998 RHD collected revenue amounting to BDT 532 million as tolls and ferry charges. In addition, tolls from Jamuna

Multipurpose Bridge (JMB) constitute a significant portion of the total revenue collected from bridge tolls in Bangladesh. Considering the daily additional truck movement along the JMB and other segments of selected routes, the total revenue from tolls and ferries from additional trucks carrying Indian good might be of very significant amount.

(iv) *Duties and Taxes on Goods Passing through Bangladesh*—Government may impose duties and taxes on the goods passing through Bangladesh. It is assumed that the additional volume of traffic which will be generated due to diversion of traffic from Siliguri corridor to routes in Bangladesh may be charged duties for entering into Bangladesh. Fixation of duties is a complicated issue and it may be detailed out by negotiation between the two governments.

(v) *Charges for Warehousing / Storage Facilities*—Goods coming from India may have to be stored in warehouses for some time, because immediately after arrival at entry and exit points, trucks may not be available for carrying goods. In that event, storage space and warehousing facilities will have to be provided. The government may realize some charges for rendering these facilities. This charge should entail charge for providing warehousing/storage facilities and protection of goods stored in the warehouse. If BDT 100 is charged per truck per day for warehousing and storage facilities, then the total revenue from these facilities may yield BDT 36.5 million per year.

7.2.2 *Indirect Benefits*

Indirect benefits from transshipment may include:

(i) Earnings from trucking services and new employment in the trucking services.

(ii) New employment opportunities in the truck manufacturing and repairing industries.

(iii) Increase in the number of fuel stations and creation of employment opportunities therein.

(iv) Establishment of Rest House, Hotel and Restaurant and creation of employment in those establishments.

(v) New employment in the road maintenance and rehabilitation works which will take place due to more frequent and intensive use of roads by significantly larger number of trucks.

7.2.3 Benefit from Trade

Better access to the global market is an important issue for Bangladesh. The country's export basket is highly concentrated in terms of both commodity composition and market destination. Ready Made Garments (RMG) accounts for 75 percent of the country's total exports and North America and EU together account for 86 percent of the export market.

Being the closest neighbor with borders on three sides of the country, India is Bangladesh's natural trading partner. Though Bangladesh's imports from India is quite large, its exports to India is very small; the export-import ratio being 1:28 in 2002-03. However, there is a growing realization that Bangladesh can improve its export performance in India if it focuses more on North Eastern Region of India. Bangladesh has a 1,880 km long border - both land and riverine with this region that creates substantial potential for good connectivity (Study on Border Trade with India, IBTCI/UCIL, 2000).

8. Trade Opportunities Between Bangladesh and North Eastern States of India

The eight Indian states in India's east and north-eastern region are isolated by political geography from the rest of India. These states are connected with the rest of the country by long-winding and tortuous mountainous roads and also railways along the Siliguri corridor. These states are economically backward compared to other states but, rich as they are in natural resources, their economic development is of great importance to India. Some of these states are also of great strategic importance because of their common borders with countries such as Nepal, Bhutan, China, Bangladesh and Myanmar.

All these states are basically agricultural, producing a variety of food crops, cash crops and horticultural products. Industrially they are much behind than other Indian States, although some of them have drived towards industrialization. Most backward among these States are Mizoram, Nagaland, Tripura and Manipur.

These states are, however, rich in natural resources. Large reserves of coal, oil and gas, dolomite, limestone, graphite, marble, lead and zinc are found in Arunachal Pradesh; petroleum, natural gas, limestone and coal in Assam; coal, limestone and dolomite in Meghalaya; and natural gas in Tripura. Some of these states have also rich forest wealth with varieties of flora and fauna. States having deep forest cover and abundant forest resources are Assam, Tripura and Meghalaya.

The rich natural resource endowment of the region notwithstanding, its potential has remained unrealized because of highly under-developed physical infrastructure, poor connectivity with the rest of the country, distance from large markets, political unrest, and persistent law and order problems.

The road network is underdeveloped, a major portion of which is unsuitable for heavy traffic. Railway links except in the states of Assam are virtually non-existent. There are also difficulties in accessing the region for security reasons.

These states are not readily accessible because of deteriorating law and order conditions.

These states do not have an easy access to seaports at present. They have to transport their goods all the way to Kolkata Port for export purposes. Under transshipment arrangement, these states would be able to use the Chittagong and Mongla Ports more economically for international trade purposes. Bangladesh also will stand to gain in the process. The Chittagong Port is already too congested to meet even Bangladeshi's own needs. In order to be able to provide port facilities to meet the international trade needs of the Eastern and North-Eastern States, the capacity of Chittagong and Mongla Ports will need to be expanded significantly.

At present, the north-eastern states supply tea, petroleum products, limestone, gas, coal, wood to other parts of India, whilst receiving consumer goods and cereal. Traffic between Kolkata and Assam is mainly carried on rail and road links along the Siliguri Corridor. To transport goods to and from the north-east through this corridor a 25% transport subsidy has for many years been provided by the central government. The total amount of inward and outward movement is estimated at about 13.6 million tons a year (inflow to the region amounting to about 8.2 million tons while the outflow amounts to about 5.4 million tons) of which only a small proportion currently passes through Bangladesh, mostly by river transit.

Meghalaya exports mainly coal to Bangladesh through Dawki-Shillong road. Delegations from two countries exchanged many visits to explore possibilities of trade and economic co-operation between the business people in Bangladesh and the north eastern states of India. Although many opportunities were discussed little has so far been implemented in reality.

Mutually beneficial trade in consumer goods can be promoted between Bangladesh and the NER States. Bangladesh could provide a large market for many agro-based and mineral-based products of these Indian States, and in return these Indian States could import a lot of consumer goods more cheaply from Bangladesh than from the rest of India. The potential Bangladesh exports could be poultry, fish, vegetables, cosmetics, toiletries, pharmaceuticals, cement, ceramics, plastic and melamine products, and readymade garments. Likewise, the huge demand for electricity in Bangladesh could be met by setting up hydro power projects in the north-eastern Indian States. The natural gas and forest resources of Bangladesh and the Indian States of Assam and Meghalaya may be utilized as inputs in joint venture industries for the production of chemicals and fertilizers, paper and newsprint, and then for trade in the region. Even tourism could be made a profitable proposition in this part of the sub-continent by developing summer resorts in the north-east India and winter resorts in the beaches of the Bay of Bengal. Thorough studies should, however, be conducted to identify actual opportunities.

9. Conclusion

India and Bangladesh are two friendly countries sharing vast land and water bodies between them. Huge infrastructure facilities have been developed separately in these two countries that could initiate a close cooperation relating trade, socialization and other issues not only between two countries but also among other countries like Nepal and Bhutan. What is awaiting is an ignition. Hope, we are not too far to wait long to see India, Bangladesh, Nepal, Bhutan and other regional countries are linked to a well coordinated transport link for betterment of all. Following are few points that need to be considered for a better transport linkage between NER of India and Bangladesh to expedite the trade and cooperation through communication and enhance the socio-economic and cultural status and relationship:

- Development of infrastructure at the land customs stations is needed to facilitate trade. Infrastructure on the Indian side is in relatively better shape and is being developed further. Bangladesh needs to develop infrastructure on its side.
- Proper care should be taken to continue the normal maintenance, including any necessary upgrading of roads, bridges and culverts to keep them in good condition.
- While designing the transport linkage the concerned authority may draw lessons about the legal, administrative and logistical aspects of transshipment or transit transportation from various international conventions. These may also be used as a convenient discussion point in negotiations between Bangladesh and India on transport linkage matters.
- Modernization of the existing fleet capacity of road transport.
- Bangladesh should open visa offices in potential NER cities like Guwahati in addition to the one now existing in Agartala. Both Bangladesh and India should issue long-term multiple entry visa to business persons. This will facilitate easy flow of business persons between the two countries leading to enhancement of trade.
- Bangladesh has to negotiate with India to make her accept Bangladesh product standards and tests. If necessary, product standards and tests can be harmonized between two countries for facilitating trade.
- The current business world is information-intensive. Both exporters and importers should be aware of the Acts, Agreements, Rules governing trade between Bangladesh and India.

- The stakeholders from the two countries should meet at regular intervals to discuss issues relating to exports/ imports and try to resolve the issues in an atmosphere of mutual cooperation and understanding.
- Joint venture establishments in manufacturing by using the natural resources of Bangladesh and the adjoining NER States offer great opportunities for the two countries. Transport linkage will also benefit these Indian States by allowing them access to Bangladeshi Ports for international trade purposes.
- The existing trade volume between Bangladesh and Nepal and between Bangladesh and Bhutan is very small. The volume of trade can be expanded significantly if appropriate steps are taken in that regard and proper transport link is established.

REFERENCES

Gurudas Das and R K Purkayastha (eds), 2000, *Border Trade: North-East India and Neighboring Countries*, Akansha Publishing House, New Delhi.

Study on Border Trade with India, IBTCI/UCIL, 2000.

Study on Transshipment Agreement with India, IBTCI/UCIL, 2000.

Study on the Possibility of Market Access to Seven Sisters in India, IBTCI/UCIL, 2004.

NEDFI Databank website.

5

LACUNA IN TRADE FACILITATION AND INFORMALISATION OF TRADE: LESSON FROM INDIA-BANGLADESH TRADE

Sanjib Pohit

1. Introduction

Trade facilitation has currently become an issue of significant importance in the non-tariff barriers agenda, as tariff rates of protection have fallen after the Uruguay Round, along with the availability of advanced information technology that can speed cross-border goods transfer. Broadly speaking, trade facilitation is the other name for reduction in transaction cost for trading goods. According to a recent study by the OECD, the cost of poor border procedures could vary between 2% to 15% of the total transaction value. According to another study undertaken by the UNCTAD, direct and indirect transaction costs i.e. banking and insurance, custom, business information, transport and logistics etc. add up to 10 per cent of the total value of world trade. This highlights the wasteful costs involved considering that the average post-Uruguay tariffs on the industrial goods amounts to mere 3.8 per cent. Furthermore, trade facilitation can even become more important in today's world because of the following reasons:

- More and more industrial products sold throughout the world are assembled in one country from components manufactured in several others. As complexity in the supply chain increases, the delay and costs caused by slow and inefficient border procedures are multiplied.
- Increase reliance on just-in-time production and just-in-time delivery makes just-in-time custom clearance a major issue for business.
- Custom needs to modernize to manage the exponential growth in volumes of cross-border trade in goods
- Small and medium business particularly in developing countries, who as a whole stands to suffer more as the burden of cumbersome procedures tends to fall disproportionately on them.
- Cumbersome custom procedures pose a major impediment to trade liberalization and need to be overcome to fully realize the benefits of negotiated agreements.
- Most important for investment decision-makers are to ensure a reliable, low cost flow of raw materials and components into and out of a manufacturing facility. Efficient custom procedures have become a national competitive specially in terms of attracting foreign direct investment.

At the outset, it must be mentioned that the ambit of trade facilitation is very broad and touches upon several areas. The main indicators of trade facilitation are:

Port Logistics

- Cargo Dwell Time
- Warehousing facilities (including refrigerated warehouses for perishables)
- Rail and road links from hinterland to ports

Customs Procedures

- Electronic Data Interface (EDI)
- Signature less, Internet based process for filing customs related documents.
- Trust based systems
- Post clearance audit
- Pre-Shipment Inspection Agreements (PSI)
- Risk analysis and assessment

Standards Harmonization

- Reform of domestic Standards setting and monitoring authorities
- Moving towards regional and global convergence on standards
- Mutual Recognition Agreements on standards

Business Mobility

- Movement of Professionals and transparent visa systems
- Adequate financial systems including Banking, Insurance and Clearance mechanism

Trade Information and e-business Facilities

- Proper channels and access to market information, legal systems and standards and regulations
- Availability of information electronically through the internet
- e-Business infrastructure to enable business to business contacts

Administrative Transparency and Professionalism

- Simple and transparent procedures for export and import

- Non-discriminatory approach to enforcement based on risk assessment techniques
- Public/Private co-operation and information sharing to improve enforcement and compliance

India has problems in several of the above areas of trade facilitation leading to high transaction cost and thereby making India's exports non-competitive. While efforts have been made in recent years to reduce transaction costs, there is still a long way to go to match to the global standard in this area. At the India-Bangladesh border a consignment needs at least 22 documentation, more than 55 signatures, and minimum 116 copies for the final approval (RIS, 2004). Each country requires different documents, such as transit, export, and import declarations. Exporters must prepare separate documents at each side of the border. For Indian exporters, it of course, involves dealing with a multitude of government of India (GOI) agencies separately.

2. Trade Facilitation Bottlenecks of India-Bangladesh Border

In the previous section, we have emphasised the importance of trade facilitation measures in today's world to maximise the benefits from globalised world. However, if one examines the status of LCS between India and Bangladesh, one gets the impression that India is probably not too keen to expand trade with Bangladesh. The focus of our discussion would be on the LCS between West Bengal (India) and the corresponding ones in Bangladesh. Since most of the official trade is conducted through the LCS of West Bengal (India), it is expected that the condition of the LCS would be better than the LCS engaged in small volume of trade. However, this is not so as we see below.

2.1. Description of Border Crossing Logistics[1]

Three LCSs in West Bengal, namely Petrapole, Mahadipur

and Hilli are the most important gateways for trade with Bangladesh in terms of trade volume and value. For our understanding, Table 5.1 provides a summary picture of the physical infrastructure at these LCSs. As this table shows, parking lots in all the LCSs lack the basic amenities like drinking water and toilet. The approach roads to the LCSs are congested. The frequent power cuts coupled with low voltage at the LCSs adversely affect the efficiency of customs officials. Surprisingly, there is no government-bonded warehouse in these LCSs. Thefts from parking lots are common and corruption is rampant. Since the problems prevailing in the three LCSs are similar in nature, we have

TABLE 5.1

Bottlenecks in Physical Infrastructure and Procedural Hazards

Facility	*Hilli*	*Mahadipur*	*Petrapole*
Approach Road to LCS	- Single lane congested road	- Poor physical condition	- Passes through congested towns and places infested by hawkers.
Parking lot	- No sanitation facility and inadequate drinking facility. - Not secured - loss through theft - Prevalence of speed money	- Lack of basic amenities. - Highly discriminatory parking fees - Not secured - loss through theft - Prevalence of speed money	- No sanitation facility and inadequate drinking water facility. - Not secured - loss through theft - Prevalence of speed money
Warehouse	- No government bonded warehousing	- No government bonded warehousing	- No government bonded warehousing
Others	- Poor quality of power - Local clubs with political affiliations extort exporters for donations - Hilli not notified in Duty Entitlement Pass Book (DEPB) port registration – traders of DEPB items not getting the benefit.	- Poor quality of power affects efficiency of customs officials - Absence of bank collection centre - No office space for clearing & forwarding agents	- Irregular power supply with low voltage - Single gate for export, import and passengers - Frequent strikes delay official work - Electronic Data Interchange (EDI) ineffective due to lack of efficient operator

Source: Field Survey.

chosen Petrapole border for our in-depth study as it handles the highest trade (66% in value terms during 2001-2002) between India and Bangladesh.

Petrapole is located about 95 kilometres from Kolkata. The commodities that are traded through Petrapole LCS originate from all over India. Kolkata is the final transhipment area for most of these commodities and they are carried to the Petrapole border by trucks through the National Highway 35, formerly known as Jessore Road as it originates from Jessore in Bangladesh. The delay in this route is a normal phenomenon due to the heavy traffic, three railway crossings and five congested towns (Barasat, Dutta Pukur, Ashoknagar, Habra and Bongaon) en route, poor physical condition and narrow width of the road, and encroachments[2]. Another major hurdle in transportation is the narrow Naobhasa Bridge, which is located 3 kilometres prior to Petrapole. The bridge is so narrow that at a time only one truck can pass. Moreover, heavy trucks with carrying capacity of 15 to 18 tonnes or more cannot pass through this bridge due to its poor condition. This results in transhipment either in Kolkata or Bongaon incurring additional transportation cost and time.

Merchandise has to face substantial loss of time at the border. The delay takes place at the parking lot, in customs clearance and at the entry/exit point. It is mandatory for the trucks coming from Kolkata during daytime to park at Bongaon Municipality Parking instead of moving directly towards the Central Warehousing Corporation (CWC) parking lot which is situated near the border gate and adjacent to the Indian Customs House.

The existing custom clearance procedures at the border lead to significant costs and delays. The existing custom procedures and documentation are not transparent. As a result, all the exporters employ clearing agents on a commission basis to take up the responsibilities of all paper works at the border. Although, there is no official fees for paper work at customs office, exporters have to bear for overtime allowances of custom staffs if they want their consignment to be cleared on holidays or before/after the scheduled working hours. Recently, the government of India introduced the Electronic Data Information (EDI) system at custom office at Petrapole for streamlining the system. However, the system did not have smooth operation and so the manual clearing of papers is still the norm.

The entry point at the border has one single gate, which is used for exports, imports as well as for passenger movement. At a time, only one truck can pass through the gate. As a result, the entry point remains very congested. Big trees at the entry-exit point often become irritants to traffic flow. The Indian trucks after unloading at Benapole (in Bangladesh) are allowed to enter India only after 7 PM. or are allowed to return to India before the start of exports from India (i.e. 10 AM). This results in wastage of time together with payment of detention charges.

2.2. Framework, Methodology and Sampling Design

A trader/exporter incurs transaction costs in all the phases of the export process starting from obtaining information about market conditions in any given foreign market and ending with receipt of final payment. Our objective is to quantify these costs. The cost estimates in this paper are based on primary data collated through field survey. We have surveyed exporters and transporters engaged in India-Bangladesh trade. The survey of Indian exporters and transporters was conducted using structured questionnaires in towns adjoining to Petrapole including Kolkata during the months of July and August, 2002. The questionnaire solicited information from the exporters and transporters regarding time and cost of different phases of trade transaction. For clarity, the entire activities related to exports through the Petrapole-Benapole border have been divided into the following three distinct phases:

- Phase 1 - loading at Kolkata, unloading at Benapole in Bangladesh and crossing of border while returning from Bangladesh
- Phase 2 - transportation and
- Phase 3 - exports including parking, customs clearance and crossing of border during exports.

The questionnaires elicited information on several variables. The data was collected on transaction costs and time taken for transaction for each of these phases. Information was also solicited from the traders on transportation cost, cost of credit, incidence of bribes, delay in obtaining export remittances, duty refund and in respect of obtaining Import-export code. Besides these, traders were asked to provide money value (opportunity cost) to the time loss due to delay.

The information on transaction costs needs further clarifications. In our analysis, the transaction costs that are quantified are only those incurred by Indian exporters up to the point at which they leave their cargoes in Bangladesh. Transaction costs beyond this point in Bangladesh are not quantified, so the total transaction costs of India-Bangladesh trade are not quantified. To be specific, the present paper solely deals with the total additional transaction costs incurred by the Indian exporters. Even in quantifying the additional transaction costs of the Indian exporters, certain transaction costs are not picked up in the survey[3].

The population of the survey consisted of exporters and transporters, engaged in India-Bangladesh trade through the Petrapole-Benapole border. Once we established the scope of the population, we obtained a sampling frame – a list of population elements. The lists of 'major transporters' (25 in all) and 'major exporters' (155 in all) with commodity specifications were acquired from the respective federations in Kolkata. Before selection of samples, we held discussions with representatives from the different federations of exporters and transporters. The discussions revealed that the population was not heterogeneous enough to be critically worried about the sample size and sampling error. Hence, given the time and budget constraints, fifteen transporters were contacted and interviewed. Though information was solicited from 155 exporters, responses were obtained from 82 only.

2.3. Estimation of Cross Border Delay

Tables 5.2, 5.3, 5.4 and 5.5 summarise our survey findings regarding the loss of time incurred by traders in exporting goods to Bangladesh through Petrapole-Benapole route. In each table, the delay incurred in different phases of transaction is calculated using transporters' responses of actual time taken and his estimate of ideal time for the same transaction. In the questionnaire, the transporters were asked to indicate their perceptions about the ideal time for transporting consignments from Kolkata to Petrapole if the Jessore road were wider or in better condition. They were also asked to respond about the actual time of transportation given the poor state of the road. For the other phases of transaction, questions pertaining to ideal and actual time were asked in a similar manner.

Table 5.2 shows that unloading at Benapole in Bangladesh assumes highest extent of loss of time in absolute terms as well as in relation to perceived ideal time. The loss of time while unloading at Benapole is more than four times the perceived ideal time for unloading. Similarly, it is about three times the perceived ideal time for crossing of border while returning from Bangladesh.

TABLE 5.2

Loss of Time in Phase 1

	Ideal Time (in hrs)	*Loss of time (in hrs) time*	*Loss of time as % of ideal*	*Ideal Time (in hrs)*	*Loss of time (in hrs)*	*Loss of time as % of ideal time*	*Ideal Time (in hrs)*	*Loss of time (in hrs)*	*Loss of time as % of ideal time*
	Loading at Kolkata			*Unloading at Benapole in Bangladesh*			*Crossing of Border while returning from Bangladesh*		
Average	2.50	4.10 (40)	126.67	1.83	9.00 (43)	444.00	1.60	4.67 (8)	300.00
Std. Dev	2.07	10.16	152.21	2.04	11.87	314.25	0.51	1.91	126.77
Coef. of var	0.83	2.48	1.20	1.11	1.32	0.71	0.32	0.41	0.42

Source: Field Survey.

Note: The figures in the parenthesis represent the maximum loss of time

On the other hand, Table 5.3 shows that on an average there is a loss of more than 3 hours in transporting merchandise from Kolkata to Petrapole (95 kms). The loss of time is nearly 1.5 time the perceived ideal time for covering this 95 kilometres.

TABLE 5.3

Loss of Time in Phase 2

	Ideal Time (in hrs)	*Loss of time (in hrs)*	*Loss of time as % of ideal time*
		Transportation	
Average	2.40	3.20 (5)	146.19
Std. Dev	0.95	0.90	57.56
Coef. Of var	0.40	0.28	0.39

Source: Field Survey.

Note: The figure in the parenthesis represents the maximum loss of time.

Table 5.4 summarises our findings regarding the time loss incurred in exports including parking, custom clearance and crossing of border during exports. As this table shows, the average ideal time for exports is perceived to be slightly more than 21 hours. However, the actual time for exports is 99 hours resulting in loss of around 78 hours. The loss of time is estimated to be 3.75 times the perceived ideal time for exports.

TABLE 5.4

Loss of Time in Phase 3

	Ideal Time (in hrs)	*Loss of time (in hrs)*	*Loss of time as % of ideal time*
	Total Time for Exports Including Parking, Customs and Crossing of Border during Exports		
Average	21.33	78.07 (96)	375.67
Std. Dev	5.43	17.29	125.84
Coef. Of var	0.25	0.25	0.36

Source: Field Survey.

Note: The figures in the parenthesis represent the maximum loss of time.

In summary, the aggregate delay (loss of time) pertaining to all the three phases of exports turns out to be around 99 hours on an average (approximately 4 days) for a single shipment (see Table 5.5). The data suggests that the aggregate delay could be as high as 192 hours (8 days)

TABLE 5.5

Cumulative Loss of Time in Exports.

	Ideal time (hrs)	*Loss of time (hrs)*
Phase 1	5.9	17.8
Phase 2	2.4	3.2
Phase 3	21.3	78.1
Cumulative	29.6	99.1

Source: Field Survey

2.4. *Transaction Cost Vis-a-vis Shipment Value*

We have attempted to quantify the extent of this additional transaction cost in relation to the average value of shipment based on the perceptions of our sample exporters. By and large, exporters were found to be trading in multiple commodities. So the response of an individual exporter in the questionnaire regarding the transaction cost vis-à-vis shipment value pertains to an average figure taking into account all the commodities that he is engaged in trading. Thus our analysis fails to identify commodity specific results in this respect. The results are given in Table 5.6.

TABLE 5.6

Transaction Cost Vis-à-vis Shipment Value

Cost Elements	*% of Shipment Value*	
	Average	*Maximum*
Delay in customs clearance including Transport, parking and queue at border	5.73 (0.54)	18
Total bribes	2.50 (0.74)	10
Delay in obtaining export remittances	2.15 (1.33)	12
Total	10.38	

Source: Field Survey.

Note: Figures in the parenthesis indicate the coefficient of variation.

As Table 5.6 shows, the average financial implication of the loss of time in customs clearance and transportation including parking and queue at border turns out to be 5.73 per cent of value of shipment. The survey results indicate that the maximum perceived loss is 18 per cent. Similarly, the financial implications of bribes and delay in obtaining export remittances are 2.50 per cent and 2.15 per cent of the shipment value respectively (Table 5.6). The results of the survey reveal that majority of the exporters pay bribe which varies between 1 and 3 per cent of the shipment value; the maximum being 10 per cent. The maximum perceived loss due to delay in obtaining export remittances is 12 per cent of the shipment value.

Thus, it may be concluded that on an average an Indian exporter incurs in sum an additional transaction cost of about 10 per cent of the shipment value.

3. Informalisation of Trade

In recent years, India and Bangladesh have adopted not only unilateral trade policy reforms but have also undertaken liberalisation under Uruguay Round and successive rounds of South Asian Preferential Trading Arrangements (SAPTA). Despite these, recent works (Chaudhari, 1995; Taneja, 1999) indicate that India's informal trade with Bangladesh continues to thrive and shows no sign of decline.

To the extent that informal trade is taking place, due to high tariffs and non-tariff barriers in the region, it is reasonable to expect such trade to shift to legal channels with removal of trade barriers.

Illegal trade could also take place due to domestic policy distortions. For instance, a trader has the incentive to siphon off subsidised items from the public distribution system to the neighbouring countries if such commodities fetch higher prices across the border. Illegal trade of this kind can be checked only if domestic reforms address such policy distortions.

If there are factors other than trade and domestic policy barriers that determine informal trade, then a deeper understanding is essential. There could be several institutional and non-economic factors that influence informal trade. It may be possible that an efficient institutional arrangement exists, which supports informal trade. It is also possible that the informal channel has a better payments mechanism or a good marketing distribution network. These factors would attract traders to the informal channel.

By contrast, if the infrastructure supporting formal trade

is weak and costs of trading increase substantially with higher volumes, some of it may spill over into informal trading. In particular, the official machinery through which formal traders have to operate may be very cumbersome causing delays and thereby escalation in costs. Moreover, the rent-seeking activities of the public servants at each step of transactions may dissuade traders from using the official channel. Furthermore, a distinctive feature of the South Asian countries is the inadequate transit and transport systems (see Taneja, 1999). This often results in high transport costs in the region and creates a strong incentive for trade to take place through informal channels.

There are also other factors. It should be kept in mind that prior to the 1947, Bangladesh, Pakistan, and India were in fact a single country. While this traditional, historical, and ethnic links is an important factor both for formal and informal trade, this is more so in the case of informal trade since ethnic ties help in ensuring that payments are guaranteed. Under formal trade, contract is enforced by law. Another factor that could be an important determinant of informal trade flows is that traders with lower education may have lower access to formal channel.

To understand the mechanism and functioning of informal trading markets, a survey was conducted during 1999. Bangladesh has a long and porous border with India covering five of her states, namely West Bengal, Assam, Meghalaya, Mizoram and Tripura. However Chaudhari (1995) reported that nearly 95 per cent of illegal exports to Bangladesh goes from West Bengal. Consequently, sample of traders were drawn from the border districts of West Bengal in India and from the border regions of Khulna and Rajsahi divisions of Bangladesh, which span the border districts of West Bengal. Given the time and cost consideration, 200 traders consisting of 100 traders each in the formal and informal channel, split equally between the two countries, were covered.

The traditional argument is that informal trade takes place due to trade and domestic policy distortions. As and when such distortions are corrected informal trade would shift to the formal channel. However, our survey revealed that institutional factors were the most important factors encouraging informal trade between India and Bangladesh. The top four factors (viz, quick realization of payments, no paper work, no procedural delays and lower transportation costs) in Bangladesh or India are found to be factors giving rise to transaction costs (see Table 5.7). The inadequate transport systems that have been in existence between India and Bangladesh have led to high transportation costs. With respect to transit modalities, the survey has identified following bottlenecks: port congestion, excessive documentation, delays, slow movement of goods, transhipment and other indirect costs. While in India ethnic ties ranked fifth in importance, the presence of high duties in the official channel ranked fifth in Bangladesh.

It should be noted that third country goods does not appear to be a major factor influencing informal trade from Bangladesh to India. This is contrary to Chaudhari (1995) where it was indicated that this is the most important factor influencing informal trade flows from Bangladesh.

Since perceptions on factors influencing informal trade were sought from Bangladeshi as well as Indian traders, a Spearman's rank correlation was computed for the ranking of factors given by both kinds of respondents. It shows a high value of 0.77 indicating converging of views regarding the factors influencing informal trade. Formal traders in Bangladesh and India were also asked to give their perceptions on the factors that they considered important for informal trade. A Spearman's rank correlation for perception of factors between formal and informal traders in Bangladesh yields a high value of 0.75. The same for the Indian traders yields a value of 0.76. Thus, there is high degree of agreement among the traders regarding the relative importance of various factors.

TABLE 5.7

Reasons for Informal Trade (Percent of Respondents)

F Factors Influencing Informal trade	*Bangladesh*	*India*
Presence of high duties in official channel	50	18
Quantitative restrictions	34	22
Imported from third country into Bangladesh	18	6
Leakage of administered price goods	12	14
Absence/shortage of storage/warehousing facilities	24	6
Produced locally across border	40	22
Presence of haats/bazaar	22	20
Lower transportation cost	72	50
Lower time to reach destination for perishable commodities	36	42
Lower time to reach destination for non-perishable commodities	28	30
Absence of trading routes	0	10
No procedural delays	52	82
No paperwork	76	92
Quick realisation of payments	88	94
Lower bribes	26	38
Nexus between enforcement agencies and traders	46	30
Ethnic ties	24	42

Source: Field Survey

Note: Respondents had the option of ticking more than one factor.

As noted above, institutional factors dominate among the reasons put forward by the traders for existence of vibrant informal trade. Naturally, the question arises whether informal trade flourishes because of lower transaction cost in informal trading than in formal trading. In this context the survey instrument was used to arrive at the transactions costs that traders incur in the two channels. The sign-rank test suggests that transaction cost in formal in India as well as in Bangladesh is significantly higher than the informal counterpart. (see Table 5.8).

TABLE 5.8
Results of Wilcoxon's Signed-Ranked Test

Parameter	*Bangladesh Territory*		*Indian Territory*	
	Z statistics	*Inference*	*Z statistics*	*Inference*
Transaction Cost (TC)	4.84	Fo>If*	3.27	Fo>If

* Fo pertains to formal, If pertains to informal. The tests have been carried out at 5 % level of significance.

4. Summary and Conclusion

This chapter attempts to stress the importance of trade facilitation measures at the India-Bangladesh border for efficient movement of goods through the LCSs. We have also made an attempt here to quantify the cost implications of the informal trade barriers that impinge upon trade between the two countries through the land border. It has also been argued that lack of efficient system has led to the growth of informal trade between the two countries.

The primary survey reveals that the transaction costs in the informal channel are significantly lower than the formal channel in both the countries. This aspect was further highlighted when informal traders were asked about why they opted for the informal channel. The survey revealed that factors like quick realisation of payments, no paper work, and no procedural delays were instrumental in driving the traders towards informal channel.

One aspect that is usually not taken into account while undertaking trade liberalisation, either unilaterally or through free trade agreements (FTAs), is the welfare implications of the existing institutional barriers. In low income and transitional economies including India and Bangladesh, currently the real barrier to trade is quite often institutional taking the form of unreasonable customs delay accompanied by widespread demands for bribes to expedite the movements of goods. In this kind of regime, perishable commodities are obviously more adversely affected by delays than non-perishables. Tariff reductions have little or no impact on domestic prices due to the capacity constraint in processing imports. More queuing results in added real resource costs, rather than generating revenues, as is true with tariffs. Perishability considerations affect the costs of liberalisation through more product loss. However, the literature on trade liberalisation or cost and benefits of FTAs has rarely touched on this issue. The precise length of these delays and how they arise is, unfortunately, poorly documented, but their impact on trade is undeniable.

The crucial question is whether the institutional factors can marginalise or negate the India's gains from trade liberalization, either by unilateral route or through FTA route. Sadly, none of the past Indian studies quantifying the gains from FTAs or trade liberalization have accounted these factors in their analysis. In fact, similar studies for other countries are also silent on this account. The sole exception being the study for Russia by Edgar Cudmore and John Whalley (2003), which has shown that liberalization can be welfare worsening rather than welfare improving as is usually the case in conventional models if one incorporates border delays in the analysis. In the context of India-Bangladesh trade, this finding has immense relevance in emphasising the need to have a fresh look in improving the infrastructure in the LCSs. If the Bangladesh tariffs were reduced or abolished and capacity were not expanded, the resulting increase in congestion costs at the border could conceivably exceed the welfare gains from the reduced tariff.

Our estimation shows that the total delay (loss of time) in exporting a single shipment from India to Bangladesh is to the tune of four days (99 hours). Our analysis also shows that on an average an Indian exporter incurs in sum an auxiliary transaction cost of about 10 per cent of the shipment value; the maximum delay occurs in custom clearance including transport, parking and queue at border.

The approach roads towards the LCSs have to be widened. A Government bonded warehousing facility is mandatory in all the LCSs to promote an efficient system of handling exportables. Efforts should also be made to operationalise the EDI system round the year. Local administration with co-operation from exporters should take the responsibility to ensure supply of drinking water and proper sanitation facilities at the parking lots. In addition, the concerted effort by local administration and exporters should sort out the issues related to poor quality of power supply and strikes.

The negotiation is on for signing a FTA with Bangladesh. Our view is that the Government of India needs to focus more attention on administrative considerations, infrastructure development and border delays as far as Bangladesh exporters/Indian importers are concerned for realising the benefits of a FTA with Bangladesh. The present study has shown that improved infrastructure and administration at the border are essential for increasing volume of trade with Bangladesh through Land Customs Stations. It would be even more important to do this if trade is liberalised, because congestion costs will otherwise rise with the resulting increased demand for trade across the border.

NOTES

1. The finding of this section is drawn from Das and Pohit (2004).
2. The width of Jessore road is only 16 feet.
3. For example, theft in the border parking lots which presumably leads to increased insurance costs and the costs involved in pre-shipment inspection are not covered in this paper.
4. Transaction costs for informal traders include payments made to enforcement agencies, transportation costs, cost of credit and cost of curency exchange. For formal traders transaction costs include bribes paid at various stages to officials, transportation costs including insurance and cost of credit.

REFERENCES

Anderson, James E. and Wincoop, Eric Van, 2001, "Borders, Trade and Welfare", National Bureau of Economic Research, working paper # W8515, October.

Bougheas, Spiros, P.O. Demetrades, and E.L.W. Morgenroth, 1999, "Infrastructure, Costs and Trade". Journal of Development Economics 47.

Chaudhari, S.K., 1995, "Cross Border Trade between India and Bangladesh", National Council of Applied Economic Research (NCAER), New Delhi, working paper # 58.

Chow, Garland and J.J. McRae, 1989, "Nontariff Barriers and the Structure of the U.S.-Canadian (Transborder) Trucking Industry", Transportation Journal 30(2):4-21.

Cudmore, Edgar and Whalley, John, 2003, "Border Delays and Trade Liberalization," National Bureau of Economic Research, working paper # W9485, February.

Das, Samantak and Pohit, Sanjib, 2004, "Quantifying the Transport, Regulatory and Other Costs of Indian Overland Exports to Bangladesh," NCAER working paper.

Exim Bank of India, 1999, "Transaction Costs of Indian Exports: An Analysis", Working paper # 104.

Hummels, David, 2001, "Time as a Trade Barrier", Working paper, Purdue University, July 2001.

Lin, J.Y. and Nugent, J.B., 1995, "Institutions and Economic Development" in Handbook of Development Economics, Volume III, Edited by J. Behrman and T.N. Srinivasan.

Pohit, Sanjib and Taneja, Nisha, 2000, "India's Informal Trade with Bangladesh and Nepal: A Qualitative Assessment", Working Paper # 58, Indian Council for Research on International Economic Relations (ICRIER), New Delhi, July.

Subramanian, Uma and Arnold, John, 2001, "Forging Subregional Links in Transport and Logistics in South Asia", The World Bank, Washington, D.C., January.

Subramanian, Uma, 1999, "South Asia Transport: Issues and Options", Paper presented at the World Bank/ESCAP Regional Technical Workshop on Transport and Transit Facilitation, Bangkok, April.

6

DOING BUSINESS WITH BANGLADESH: A CUSTOM'S POINT OF VIEW

J.S.R. Khathing

The dynamics of Indo-Bangladesh relations are not confined to the arena of trade and commerce. A wide range of issues tend to influence the mindset and thinking of our policy-makers in determining our interests and priorities vis-a.-vis Dhaka. Some issues that concerns India are immigration, transshipment/transit facilities for the Northeast States and security concerns. From the Bangladeshi point of view, the issues are border security, border demarcation, trade imbalance and fair sharing of river water. The lists of contentious issues in Indo-Bangladesh relations are many. A reconciling of interests between these two neighbours appears to be daunting.

Border trade and economic development in border areas are interdependent, as border trade leads to economic development, which through secondary effects increases border trade, manifold. With an increasingly shrinking world, international borders are rapidly losing their rigidity, where there is interplay of global forces through dynamics brought about through trade, transport, and communication. How to gain from this development without losing control over our resources and how to promote reinvestment of profits within the region for social and economic development will be the challenge facing North East India in the new millennium. This issue has caught the imagination of our policy makers who are increasingly viewing cross border trade as a panacea for generating growth impulse in the stagnant economy of the region. -

The North East India is surrounded by Bangladesh, Myanmar, China and. Bhutan. It is connected with the mainland through what is known as *Chicken's Neck.* This strategic corridor, about 22 km wide, connects the Northeast region to the rest of India. Given this peculiar geo-political location, cross-border markets are likely to be more cost effective for North East India than distant national markets (Das:2000). Often, we have talked of the isolation of the North Eastern region, which has resulted in its economic backwardness and its alienation from the mainstream. Time has come to convert our geographical handicap into an opportunity. Our strength lies in the international borders and beyond; we should look outward towards neighboring countries rather than only viewing inward.

Indo-Bangladesh Trade in the North East

The North East Region of India is bounded by Bangladesh in the west and southwest with an international border of nearly 1500 km. The border, extending over hilly tracts, forested area and rivers, is porous, touching in its ambit, the States of Assam (350 km), Meghalaya (400 km), Tripura (400 km) and Mizoram (350 km).

The region has age-old socio-economic ties with Bangladesh. Although the partition has disrupted the structure of age-old flow of goods and services between these two areas, even then the communication channels are not completely abandoned. The old road links and waterways are still being

TABLE 6.1

Land Customs Stations along Indo-Bangladesh Border in the North Eastern Region

SI.No.	**Land Customs Stations in Assam**	Status
01	Karimgang Ferry & Steamerghat	Functional
02	Sutarkandi	-do-
03	Mahisasan Railway Station	Non-functional
04	Silchar RMS Office	-do-
05	Dhubri Steamer ghat	Functional
06	Golakganj	Non-functional
07	Mankachar	Functional
08	Guwahati Steamerghat	Non-functional
	Land Customs Stations in Meghalaya	
01	Dawki	Functional
02	Bholaganj	-do-
03	Borsora	-do-
04	Shellabazar	-do-
05	Ryngku	Non-functional
06	Baghmara	Functional
07	Dalu	-do-
08	Ghasuapara	-do-
09	Mahendraganj	-do-
10.	Balat	Newly notified
	Land Customs Stations in Tripura	
01	Agartala Land Customs Station	Functional
02	Srimantapur Land Customs Station	-do-
03	Muhurighat Land Customs Station	Non-functional
04	Khowaighat Land Customs Station	-do-
05	Dholaighat Land Customs Station	-do-
06	Old Raghna Bazar Land Customs Station	Functional
07	Manu Land Customs Station	-do-
	Land Customs Stations in Mizoram	
01	Demagiri Land Customs Stations	Non-functional

Source: Office of the Commissioner of Customs, Shillong.

used in many places for export-import trade between Bangladesh and the North East. In fact, the land borders between Bangladesh and the North Eastern Region are more accessible and cost effective than the borders with other neighboring countries such as China, Myanmar and Bhutan (Das: 2000).

TABLE 6.2

Value of Indo-Bangladesh Trade Through the Land Customs Stations of the North Eastern Region: Exports

	Total value of export		
	Entire North East Region (Rs.Crore)	*Across Indo-Bangladesh border (Rs.Crore)*	*% share of exports across Indo-Bangladesh border vis-à-vis entire NE Region*
2000-2001	404.07	151.23	37.42
2001-2002	379.15	185.89	49.02
2002-2003	410.12	202.70	49.42
2003-2004	435.02	240.01	55.17
2004-2005	422.67	190.42	48.57

Source: Office of the Commissioner of Customs, Shillong.

The average value of exports through the various export/import points of the entire North Eastern Region during the last five years (2000/2001-2004/2005) was Rs. 410.21 crore of which the share of exports across Indo-Bangladesh border was Rs. 194.05 crore, i.e. about 48 per cent.

The average value of imports through the various export/import points of the entire North Eastern Region during the last five years (2000/2001-2004/2005) was Rs. 24.04 Crore of which the share of imports from across Indo-Bangladesh border was Rs. 9.98 Crore, i.e. about 40 per cent.

TABLE 6.3

Value of Indo-Bangladesh Trade Through the Land Customs Stations of the North Eastern Region: Imports

	Total value of export		
	Entire North East Region (Rs. Crore)	*Across Indo-Bangladesh border (Rs. Crore)*	*% share of imports from across Indo-Bangladesh border vis-a-vis entire NE Region*
2000-2001	19.57	7.19	36.73
2001-2002	15.94	5.52	34.62
2002-2003	20.79	6.10	29.34
2003-2004	33.28	11.52	34.61
2004-2005	30.64	19.58	63.90

Source: Office of the Commissioner of Customs, Shillong.

TABLE 6.4

Items Exported from India to Bangladesh Through the Land Customs Stations of the North Eastern Region

	Value in Rs.Crore				
	2000-2001	*2001-2002*	*2002-2003*	*2003-2004*	*2004-2005*
Mineral products	148.01	182.49	197.39	235.58	185.05
Fish/Dry fish/other animal products like raw hides skin/ poultry feed etc.	0.11	0.16	0.004	0.18	0.35
Fruits	0.96	1.37	1.19	1.31	0.71
Agricultural and Forest produce	1.19	1.73	3.52	1.88	4.20
Other miscellaneous goods	0.96	0.14	0.60	1.06	0.11
Total	150.23	184.89	201.704	239.01	190.42

Source: Office of the Commissioner of Customs, Shillong.

Note: Minerals include coal, boulders, stone chips, sandstones and limestone, etc. Fruits include orange, pears, citrus fruit, grape, jackfruit etc. Agricultural and forest produce include vegetables, ginger, onion, turmeric, dry chilly, betel leaves, potato, bamboo, tomato etc. Other miscellaneous items include consumer goods like tape recorders, woolen garments, printed books, wall/table clock, machinery equipments, natural rubber, sanitary ware, stainless steel utensils, paper, marble slabs, handloom and handicraft, safety glass, umbrella and umbrella parts, tractor and motor parts, audio cassette, etc.

From the above, it would be evident that the balance of trade is in India's favour. While on an average about 48 per cent of exports from the North Eastern Region flows to Bangladesh, imports from Bangladesh to the region on an average constitute only about 40 per cent of total imports to the region.

As can be seen from the Table 6.4, Indian exports to Bangladesh from the North Eastern Region constitute mostly of minerals and raw materials like coal, limestone, boulders, stone-chips etc. The average value of exports to Bangladesh during the last five years (2000/2001-2004/2005) was Rs. 194.05 crore of which an overwhelming 82.45 per cent (about Rs. 160.00 crore) consisted of minerals such as coal, boulders, sandstones etc. These are all products that are used for developmental activity in the importing country i.e. Bangladesh. The contribution of manufacturing sector in the export basket over the last five years is pathetically low at about 0.20 per cent (about Rs. 0.57 crore). It may also be mentioned here that agricultural/horticultural products that are exported to Bangladesh are exported without any value addition.

In almost all the bilateral meetings involving trade and commerce, the Bangladesh side habitually raises issues of unfavorable balance of trade. Non tariff and Para-tariff barriers. However, a critical analysis of these from a broader perspective would reveal that the size of economy of Bangladesh and limited items in its 'export basket' leave our neighbour little space to manoeuver. As mentioned earlier, Bangladesh imports coal, boulder stone, limestone and other mineral and natural products from the North Eastern States. All these products are imported in bulk and hence involves huge amount. India on the other hand does not have to import any such commodity involving substantial amount of money and its imports are confined to consumer goods of daily necessity, cheaper cost being the main factor. As such it would be impracticable to try to balance the trade. All the mineral and natural extracts are used by Bangladesh for building their basic infrastructure and hence it is imperative that this issue is viewed beyond the scope of mere balance of trade.

The main reason for demand of mineral products is the complementarities between the resource base of the hills of North East and the plains of Bangladesh, which provide a firm basis of trade between them. The North Eastern Region, with a large reserve of minerals and congenial climatic condition for large-scale production of horticultural products coupled with traditional trade linkages between production and consumption centers across the border is a treasure house for Bangladesh. The cement factories, tea gardens and brick-manufacturing units of Bangladesh depend heavily on North Eastern Region for limestone and coal (Das:2000) .

As far as export of manufactured products is concerned, except for a few items, the North East itself has to procure them from the national market. The manufacturing sector of the region is yet to develop so as to complement the demand structure of manufactured goods in Bangladesh. However, the region has the potential resources to produce a few of these items. In fact, the long term gains from trade with Bangladesh will depend on the region's capacity to value addition instead of just marketing its raw materials.

Imports from Bangladesh

Almost all of the imports from Bangladesh to India consist of manufactured items and processed food items other than *hilsa* fish and dried fish. Most of the imports from Bangladesh to the North East take place through the State of Tripura and through Karimganj district of South Assam. This is probably because of the fact that compared to other States like Meghalaya and Brahmaputra Valley of Assam; the communication to Tripura and South Assam over land from other parts of India is far more expensive and time consuming. Tripura and South Assam, therefore, finds it more cost effective to import manufactured goods from Bangladesh rather than from mainland India.

Informal Trade with Bangladesh

Informal trade or unrecorded trade can be broadly defined as all trading activities between any two countries, which should be included in the national income but are not captured by official statistics.

Due to the vast stretch of mostly porous international border, coupled with large tracts of forested area and inhospitable terrain, there are many areas in this region vulnerable to smuggling along Indo-Bangladesh borders. Further, a large number of villages in the region are situated on the extreme border area with traditional road links. This makes the scope of smuggling of contraband or informal trade in this region enormous. However, because of the very nature of such trade, it is not possible to quantify the magnitude of informal trade, though available evidences suggest that informal trade is rampant and if such trade is brought within the official ambit a significant increase in export/ import can be witnessed.

Items of Illegal Trade

Main items of illegal export from North Eastern Region to Bangladesh are biris, sugar, pharmaceutical preparations like phensedyl cough syrup, betel nut & leaves, cattle, textiles such as sarees/lungis, kerosene/diesel, motor parts, agricultural products, alcoholic liquor, etc.

The main items of illegal import from Bangladesh are gold, pirated CDs and cassettes, potato chips, synthetic fabric, ready made garments, rape seed oil, fruit/synthetic drinks, GCI sheets, fish and dry fish, soaps, vegetable oil, cement, etc.

Though it is difficult to accurately quantify the magnitude of informal trade, studies conducted by various agencies/ NGOs reveal that of the informally traded goods brought into Bangladesh from North Eastern Region, spices constitute about 23 per cent, textiles 13 per cent, sugar 12 per cent, drugs/pharmaceutical products 10 per cent, processed food 9 per cent, cereals 8 per cent, fish 6 per cent and fruits 3 per ecnt. The rest 16 per cent consists of biris, motor parts, mineral oils etc. Of the informally traded goods that come to the North Eastern Region from Bangladesh, electronic items constitute 20 per cent, jute 15 per cent, plastic products 10 per cent, edible oil 7 per cent, spices 4 per cent, textiles 4 per cent and fish 4 per cent the rest 36 per cent consist of gold, currency etc.

Reasons for Informal Trade

Informal trade suggests the extent of potential trade that exists in the region. The reasons for informal trade is the various trade barriers, complexity of international trade norms, lack of infrastructure at Land Customs Stations, lack of good roads and other institutional factors like banking. Some of the main reasons responsible for inducing trade through illegal channels are discussed below:

(i) The Indian Perspective

a) *Delays in receiving reimbursement from Bangladesh:* Several banks in the North Eastern Region have pointed out that the banks in Bangladesh are late in their payment for exports. Most of these delays are attributed to various bottlenecks within the financial system.

b) *High transaction costs:* The traders of the North Eastern Region have often observed that the reimbursement costs for Letters of Credit *(L/C)* processing charge by certain banks in Bangladesh is very high. While costs of financial transaction with other countries were in the range of 0.2 per cent to 3 per cent of the amount, transaction between India and Bangladesh cost 10 per cent to 20 per cent of the transacted amount. This encourages informal trade where payments are received through unofficial channels at a much lower cost.

c) *Margin/collateral requirement on imports to North Eastern Region:* While banks in the North Eastern Region require a security of roughly 5-20 per cent for exports, many often insist upon 100-150 per cent margin for imports. This, it appears, is because the bank is liable to make payment to Bangladeshi exporter. The unwillingness of the bankers in the North Eastern Region to take any exposure in import financing acts as a disincentive to import trade.

(ii) The Bangladeshi Perspective

a) *No adequate control mechanism for the import of goods:* Bankers in Bangladesh are of the view that there is no quality control in terms of the goods that are imported from the North Eastern Region and that this leads to numerous problems in trade finance, ultimately causing delay in remittance of export proceeds. In many cases it has been seen that after the importer in Bangladesh realizes that the imported goods are deficient in terms of quality/quantity, he lodges a complaint with the local bank and tries to stop payment. Warehouse/storage facility at the Land Customs Stations in Bangladesh, where the importer can physically verify the quality before signing off for payments can mitigate this problem to a large extent.

b) *Problem of mail L/Cs:* Most of the L/Cs that are issued for importing goods from North Eastern Region are mail L/Cs. The widespread use of mail L/Cs has been identified as one of the causes of L/C forgery in trade between North Eastern Region and Bangladesh. In addition, signature verification causes delays in payments. Use of modern technology can mitigate this problem.

The above problems are further aggravated due to poor communication between the banks of the two countries.

Problems Due to Tariff and Non-tariff Barriers

As regard Non-tariff and Para tariff barriers, India has already relaxed the requirement of testing and BIS registration for products, which are important and major constituents of 'export basket' of Bangladesh. Some of these are detailed below.

(a) Import of goods under Chapter 72 mentioned vide Sl. Nos. 77 to 109 of Appendix III to Schedule 1 of ITC (HS) Classification have been exempted from adhering to Indian Quality Standards vide DGFT Notification No.21 (RE-2003)/2002-2007 dated 28.01.03.

(b) Textile and textile articles are not subjected to any testing if such import consignments are accompanied by a pre-shipment certificate from a nationally accredited agency of Bangladesh. Even when such import consignments are not accompanied by any pre-shipment certificate, such products are tested in notified laboratories of India and if such a consignment is found to conform the Indian standards of requirement, such a certificate stays valid for subsequent imports for further period of 6 (six) months provided the importer, supplier and the country of origin are same (DGFT Notification No. 29/9RE-2004)/2002-2007 dated 28.01.04).

(c) India made the process of BIS registration for import of cement from Bangladesh simpler. The standard of BIS for cement has already been conveyed to testing agencies in Bangladesh for the purpose and few manufacturers of cement of Bangladesh have already been registered under BIS under liberalized regime.

(d) Imports of Electronic Lamps, appliances and switches as mentioned vide SI.Nos. 69 to 76 of Appendix III to Schedule 1 of ITC (HS) Classification have been exempted from adhering to Indian Quality Standards (vide DGFT Notification No.13 (RE-2003)/2002-2007 dated 20.06.03). Except for 14 High Risk items as notified by DGFT by DGFT Policy Circular No. 37(RE-2003)/2002-2007 dated 14.06.2004, the requirement of 100% sampling for other food products has been dispensed with. Instead such products if found to conform to Indian Standards under PFA Acts and Rules when subjected to tests from first few consignments, are subjected random sampling and testing.

However, Indian exports to Bangladesh suffer higher tariff barriers since the customs duty structure in Bangladesh includes value added tax, advance income tax and infrastructure development charge in addition to basic customs duty. Most of the Indian products exported to Bangladesh do not enjoy concessional duty under SAPTA. The concession given by India to Bangladesh under SAPTA is very liberal. The concessions have been further liberalised vide Notification No.43/2004 dated 27.02.2004, in which SAPTA concession to products across the board have been increased by 10 per cent and above. Thus, Bangladesh has to reduce its tarrif barriers for increased trade through legal channels and curbing of informal trade.

It might be pertinent to add that both Bangladesh and India are signatories to SAFTA accord and the accord itself has adequate provisions for addressing any deserving concern of tariff and non tariff barriers. In the quest of free trade regime, the following simplification in customs procedure and harmonisation of trade documents can be accepted to curb informal trade:

(a) Identification of *highly traded items* and evolving uniformity in classification of all such items at 8 and 10 digit HS level with the same nomenclature. For this purpose, a working group of Customs may be formed, in which representatives of trade of both India and its South Asian neighbours may be invited.

(b) Evolve a procedure for valuation of goods identified as *commonly tradable* by a common group of Customs where representation from field experts and also trade may be present.

(c) Introduction of 'deferred duty payment scheme' without any interest for a short span - say 14 days- for the manufacturer-importer/exporter.

(d) Introduction of Audit based post clearance scrutiny for a class of importers/exporters mentioned above and also for exports undertaken by manufacturers through merchant exporters.

(e) Introduction of a system of release of goods even where documentation is not complete, *subject to adequate revenue safeguards.*

(f) Gradual removal of all NTB's as far as practicable, other than requirement of bio-security and sanitary-phyto sanitary import permit based on risk analysis of primary agricultural products which are included in the agreed terms of the WTO Agreement on the application of sanitary and phyto sanitary measures.

In these cases too, more reliance may be placed on certificates issued by bodies/organizations authorized by the exporting countries and also National Accreditation Councils that may be set up in all countries. For this purpose it would be imperative that the apex trade bodies of such country takes lead to ensure the individual manufacturers adhere to the minimum standards adopted by importing countries for specific sectors.

(g) Gradual introduction of 'risk assessment' based targeting techniques for physical examination.

(h) Exchange of signature of the customs officials posted on both sides of the trading points to facilitate authentication of customs documents.

(i) Installation of direct hotlines between the important Land Customs Stations on both sides of border.

It would, however, be imperative that Bangladesh reciprocates the trust reposed by all the above-mentioned simplification and does not dilute the standard specified under such special dispensation. These techniques can also be gradually implemented for all other items, including high risk items, presently under non tariff barriers if our neighbour is able to reciprocate to our faith placed on them.

Lack of Infrastructure: Transport and Transit System

The inadequate transport and transit systems that have been in existence in the North Eastern Region and between India and her neighbour have led to high transportation costs. It is seen that transport cost of export/import items in the North Eastern Region and Bangladesh is far higher than in other parts of the world. A large part of trade therefore takes place informally in order to curb cost. Further, lack of infrastructure in the Land Customs Stations aggravates the problem of smooth transaction of formal trade. Many of the Land Customs Stations in the North East do not even have basic amenities like safe drinking water, electrification and staff quarters. The border areas of the North East are mostly underdeveloped, remote and often difficult to access. Similarly, the levels of infrastructure available in the countries with which we have contiguous borders are also not upto the mark.

Road connectivity

Availability of cheap access to communication is a pre-requisite to both growth in international trade and also industrialization. Road connectivity in this block continues to be poor due to missing links and poor road conditions, most of which are still fair weather roads. To improve inter zonal and intra zonal road connectivity of this block, it would be imperative that we see a huge investment in roads in near future. The condition of the roads leading to the international borders from the production centers is a severe impediment to international trade. Roads need to be straightened and broadened so that heavy vehicles can carry larger tonnage in shorter time. These roads can be constructed under a *pay and use scheme* by collecting toll tax from users. For example, Shillong-Guwahati Road: Length 103 km. can be straightened, broadened and shortened to 60km. Advantage: larger loads carried in much shorter time. Calculating on an average traffic of 10,000 vehicles (both ways) per day @ Rs.500/- per vehicle will generate Rs. 183 crore per year, not to speak of savings on valuable fuel in the bargain.

What a good road connection can do to boost the trade can be seen from the experience of Sutarkandi L.C. Station. Simply by widening and black topping the 15 odd kilometers of road connecting the L.C. Station to Karimganj town has boosted the trade through this point by about 100% during the past five years. In 2001-02, before the road was made, the total volume of trade was Rs. 14.51 crore, whereas, by 2004–05, it rose to Rs. 28.12 crore.

Road Transit Through Bangladesh

Initiatives need to be taken to allow transshipment of goods from North Eastern Region to the mainland India and vice-versa through Bangladesh territory. The Customs Act, 1962 already has provision for transportation of goods from one part of India to another through a foreign territory under the Transportation of Goods (Through Foreign Territory) Regulations, 1965. India has already extended transit facility to goods imported by Bangladesh from Nepal and vice versa through Phulbari Land Customs Station under Darjeeling District of West Bengal. The Bangladesh Government too has allowed transit facility to goods, shipped from North East to our mainland and vice versa, by their riverine route under the Protocol on Inland Water Transit and Trade. However, this facility is yet to be extended by Bangladesh for transportation by land. Article 8 of the SAFTA (South Asian Free Trade Area) accord signed recently has specific provision for extending such facilities to the member countries to the accord. Since both India and Bangladesh are signatories to the accord, this issue is needed to be taken up by higher authorities at appropriate forum. The declared bus routes of Agartala-Dhaka and Dhaka-Kolkata already in use can be used for such transportation from North Eastern Region.

Rail Connectivity

Railways are the cheapest mode of transport. Intra zonal Rail connectivity still remains insufficient in this sector. Needless to say that this mode of transport is yet to reach any of the important Land Customs Stations of North East. Under the Asian Land Transport Infrastructure Development Project (AL TID), the ESCAP suggested development of the following two routes:

(a) Mughalsharai-Patna-Siliguri-Lumding-Silchar as a route of sub-regional significance;

(b) Attari-Amritsar-Delhi-Mughalsarai-Gede-Darshana-Jamtoli-Shabazpur- Mahishashan-Badarpur-Silchar-Jiribam-Tamu (Myanmar) as a route of international significance. This route touches all the three countries of Banglasdesh, India and Myanmar.

As such it would be necessary that these two routes are developed on a priority basis to make our industries and trade flourish. Similarly restoration of the railway links between other South East Asian countries should also be accorded top priority.

The development of road corridors and rail linkages will not only complement the sea trade but will also provide a shorter, faster and perhaps cheaper alternative to the sea route. It would, at the same time, open up a vast land locked area to the realms of international trade and faster economic growth. The issue for consideration would, however, be identification of the mutually (bilaterally or multi-laterally) accepted linkages and prioritization of the rail and road options. In all possibility, the establishment of road linkages will provide the requisite base for exploiting trade possibilities that are either already available or are likely to develop in the foreseeable future. The railway project, on the other hand represents trans-continental aspirations for building a whole gamut of system capable of speedy movement of large volumes of bulk and containerized goods over a long distance and could play an effective role only after trade linkages have been fairly developed/stabilized and enough confidence/ mutual trust has grown between the countries of the region.

Inland Water Transport

The Brahmaputra, having been declared as a National Waterway, by the Central Government can be developed as a major inland water trade and transport route, carrying people and goods as far south as Bangladesh or for that matter the main land India. Development of this gives export goods access to the seaports of Chittagong (Bangladesh), Calcutta and Haldia (West Bengal).

It may be mentioned here that it has been reported that the Asian Development Bank (ADB) has proposed $ 150 million assistance to develop night navigation system on the river Brahmaputra. This will give a fillip to the movement of heavy cargo like coal, cement etc. However, success of using the riverine route will largely depend on the Indo-Bangladesh protocol on inland water transit and trade over a long term. Presently, Bangladesh is extending this protocol to only a short period of time, i.e. only a few months. The cargo operators who find this protocol advantageous are not happy with the short term of extensions.

Air Connectivity

It cannot be denied that the North Eastern region has tremendous potential for production of horticultural products. While there exists a substantial market for fruits and vegetables in Europe, the cost of transportation from North East by air works out to be more than the cost of the goods. Though the Ministry of Commerce, through Agricultural and Processed Food Export Development Authority (APEDA) offers subsidy for transportation of horticultural products for the purpose of export, it would be a better idea to start a weekly dedicated cargo flight from Guwahati direct to foreign destinations (possibly, destinations in Bangladesh) for such exports instead of granting transport subsidy which is, more often than not, misused.

Conclusion

Under formal trading arrangements, the recourse to law defines contracts between two contracting parties. This ensures that goods move across borders and payments are guaranteed. On the other hand contracting parties in informal trade cannot resort to the law for violation of terms of contract. Consequently, it is reasonable to assume that individuals trading through informal channel have developed parallel institutional mechanisms for contract enforcement and dispute settlement. Also, the smooth functioning of such markets shows that traders have developed efficient mechanisms for obtaining information on quality/quantity of commodities to be traded and for mitigating risk that arises from the transacting environment.

Also, it is important to understand that the institutional structure that supports formal trade is affected by factors like administrative processes, government rules/regulations, infrastructural bottlenecks, banking scenario etc. Thus, if the institutional arrangement under informal trading is more efficient than the supporting structure for formal trade, traders will prefer to trade informally via illegal channels giving rise to apprehensions of criminal activities and rise in anti-national subversive activities. Hence, it is of utmost importance to the governments of both India and Bangladesh to reduce administrative and infrastructural bottlenecks for not only promoting legal trade but also for national security.

REFERENCES

Das, Gurudas, (2000), "Trade Between the North Eastern Region and Neighbouring Countries: Structures and Implications for Development", in Das, Gurudas and R K Purkayastha, (eds), *Border Trade: North East India and Neighbouring Countries*, Akansha Publishing House, New Delhi.

7

BORDERLESSNESS AS A KEY TO ECONOMIC GROWTH: PROSPECTS FOR NORTH-EASTERN INDIA IN AN INTERNATIONAL SERVICE ECONOMY

Sunandan Roy Chowdhury

The objective of this volume, so far as I understand, is to take stock of trade between Bangladesh, and the states of North-eastern India, and to explore ways and means of enhancing the trade to the advantage of the economy of the north-eastern states. I, however, ·choose to widen the geographical scope a bit further. It is true that the states of north east India share a long border with Bangladesh and that can be extremely useful for bilateral trade. But if we look at a map of Asia, and see countries that are quite close to India's north-east then we will find Bangladesh, Nepal, Bhutan, Burma, Cambodia, Laos, Thailand, Vietnam and China, all on that list.

There are reasons that prompt us to think of a zone consisting of these countries to be a target economic zone for India's north-east. This is particularly true for that part of the economy which we loosely term 'service sector.' In the area of manufacturing industries, trade between two countries requires the physical movement of goods. So if we are producing furniture in Nagaland and want to sell the products in Bangladesh, we would need to physically transport them. For that, we would usually require good transport links. Unfortunately, India as a whole, and north east India in particular, does not have a good, efficient road network. If we compare India's roads even with Bangladesh, one finds the roads in that country generally far better than India's roads. There is of course the possibility of air transport that is a costly alternative.

As opposed to manufacturing, if we were to run a service sector company – say a call centre like the ones that have now mushroomed in some of the big Indian cities, we would not have to rely on the road infrastructure. Of course, for call centres, we do need a telecom and power infrastructure, but India is a lot better in those areas of infrastructure than it is in the area of road transport. So if we run a call centre, or a business process outsourcing operation, we could sell our data-processing, research, clerical work and other services through telecom network, and there is no need for physical transportation.

Hence, the physical proximity – or the issue of having land borders – becomes less important. I would argue that for the service sector economy to grow in north east India we first need to think beyond Bangladesh, and incorporate all the nine countries into our planning frame.

There is a second reason why I argue for visualising this economic zone as the logical economic zone for the development of the seven states of north east India.. Economic links are not only about the movement of goods or services; it is also about the links between people, businessmen, professionals, and clients. One feels that there is a certain cultural proximity between the various peoples of north eastern India, and the even greater variety of peoples that inhabit mainland Indochina, and the provinces of southern China. To give just an example, the Assamese people, and the Thai people, are both said to be descendants of the Tai people coming from southern China about 800 to 1000 years ago, and still have recognisable linguistic and cultural similarities. Some linguists now believe that the languages of the Mon-Khmer group – prevalent in Cambodia and parts of Burma – are derived from Khasi, the language of the people here in Meghalaya, again highlighting historic cultural ties. Even during the colonial period, people of the north east region had, in some cases, stronger trade and social links with provinces of what is today Burma than with the main centres of India. I am told that that a privately owned, colonial-era travelling circus based in Manipur travelled through the north east and Burma in what it considered its natural circuit and audience base.

There is a third reason for considering this an integrated region, and that is the state of technology in the world today. From the time of the industrial revolution in England in the second half of the 18th century, we have seen the industrial landscape spread its wings far afield. The trend still continues. There are countries in the world which are industrialised, there are those that are somewhat industrialised, and there are those that are hardly industrialised. Without going into details in this issue, it is enough to note that the least industrialised countries or regions will continue industrialising at a slow, or at a fast pace. North-Eastern India, and may be even most of central and eastern India, can be seen as a least industrialised region. Now, to chart an economic development today, we can go for the more traditionally manufacturing industries, or we can go for the service sector companies.

One advantage of the service sector is that it is relatively 'green' in the sense that it does not pollute the environment.

But I think that more importantly for north-eastern India, with its physical infrastructure in not the best of shape, service sector should be seen as a major thrust area for growth. The present state of technology pushes us towards this. Take telecom, for instance, in a landline network, we needed a much larger physical infrastructure to support the system, whereas it is much less for mobile telephony. To set up businesses, like call centres, or back-up offices for accounting firms based in more developed economies, we need power, computers, office space, telephone lines, and people with some specific skills. With this kind of resource at our disposal, we can do business worldwide. We do not need to feel that we are in an isolated corner of the Indian landmass. Or for that matter, in terms of exports, we could look beyond Bangladesh.

But there is a key element of the service sector economy that needs to be appreciated. Skilled manpower is the single most important resource for the service sector. These skills are not only the skills of languages like those needed to run call centres, or the skills of a software engineers, but also the skills of doing business with people from other cultures and other political systems. So development of trained manpower is of utmost importance to the development of the service sector, and that is what I turn to now.

Higher Education: Wise Investment, Great Economics

Governments in India have tried to teach many a discipline to students in colleges and universities. One discipline which it almost did not try to teach – with some exceptions – was computer engineering, and various skills woven around the computer. Yet Indians have possibly made the greatest progress in a rather short period of time in this field. How did that happen? I would say that market-driven, private investment in this sector has been the force behind this rapid development. But there can be a role of governments too, and this we see in Karnataka. The world now knows Bangalore as one of the major global hubs for software firms, and development. But in the early 1980s, Bangalore was a sleepy, leafy town. There are a host of important factors that led to Bangalore's fantastic growth, but in my opinion, one of the key factors is the Karnataka state government's willingness to encourage private investment in certain sectors of higher education. As we all know, Karnataka allowed entrepreneurs to set up engineering and other professional colleges. This educational environment that emerged in the 1980s was the enabling infrastructure – in terms of human resources – for the software industry to take off.

Of course, there was another key strategic factor, and this was the end of the Cold War, which facilitated the opening up of Internet world. As state governments, or universities, or as small companies, we cannot bring an end to phenomenon like the Cold War, or stop an India-Pakistan War. However, we can make the arena of higher education more in tune with the requirements of economic development and plan the higher education sector in a way that it nurtures future economic growth.

What can we do in higher education so that north-eastern India can become a dynamic economic zone? We are creating call centres all across India, and in this business we are harnessing the spoken English skills of our graduates. We can use English in another important way, and this is to start teaching English to students from Bangladesh, Burma, Cambodia, Thailand or China. Now it is true that some form of learning English exists in all these countries. But the standard of English-education is much higher in India, and especially so in some good universities here in the north-east. So we can start short, medium, and long-term courses in English education. This has to be carefully structured, though. Some of the courses may even be run as distance education courses. In that way, you will be actually getting into trans-border education and more towards a borderless economy. But this educational effort can have another business prospect, and that is to send Indians from here as English language teachers to these countries. Thailand, for example, has already started recruiting teachers from India to teach English in regular Thai government schools. I would argue that Indian universities should take the initiative to set up programs to tap into this potential market for English education that exists in South East Asia and China. We can think of private public partnership in such efforts. And then there is of course the issue of promoting north-eastern India as a destination for higher education.

Let us turn to the specific case of Bangladesh. Bangladesh's population is around triple that of the seven states here. A substantial portion of this population has finished secondary school, and an important part of this group is going into some form of tertiary education. Bangladesh has developed its own public university and college system substantially in the 35 years of its independence, and there is also a mushroom growth of private colleges and universities, offering management, engineering, and other professional courses. But for the average Bangladeshi student, the aspiration of going abroad for higher education is higher today than ever before. One of the most favoured destinations, namely because of affordability and geographical proximity, is India. In the late 1990s, I was told by an Indian diplomat in Dhaka that there were 60,000 Bangladeshi students studying in India at any given point in time. I think that if Indian universities think of appropriate courses, and market themselves well, in major cities of Bangladesh this number can grow five-fold in a period of three to five years. But this requires a detailed plan, where I would argue a public-private partnership can do wonders. Among other things, one has to remember that

Bangladesh being a Muslim society, we should take particular care that students coming from there feel at home in a foreign country. That means ensuring they can continue with much of their food habits, dress, and religious practices. I would suggest a small planning group and an international education promotion cell be formed here in North Eastern Hill University to create an effective business plan, and appropriate courses, to attract Bangladesh students. In this context, it is important to remember that many of the courses that will be designed for Bangladeshi students will be equally applicable for students from Burma, Cambodia, Laos or China.

But as much as we should try to export our educational expertise, we should also start courses to facilitate the development of our young people in a way that they can be part of the international service economy that we are talking about. I am sure that various courses related to computer and the new economy is already being run here in the north-east. But to take advantage of the regions' location in the Asian landmass, we need people with language skills in Burmese, Chinese, Thai, Khmer, and various other languages of the countries that can be viewed in the economic zone defined earlier. I would recommend the establishment here in the north east of an academy of Asian languages and civilisations. We do not have such an institution in all of India. This will provide the much needed academic input into the Prime Minister's 'look east' policy. It is befitting that such an institution – which could emerge as a centre of real academic excellence for teaching, learning and research on historic and contemporary Asia - should be set up here in the north east, the region of India with the closest links to South East Asia. Again, there needs to be a working group of academics, and members of other professions, to chalk out a detailed plan for such an academy.

These developments in the field of education will not only create an educational services economy where the institutions in the north-east will cater to an international demand but also create links between the north-east and the countries of its natural economic zone. The students who will come to study here from Bangladesh, Burma, Cambodia or China will go back equipped with skills. At the same time they will go back hopefully, with positive impressions about the people of this part of India. They can in the future form the greatest assets for economic cooperation between north-east India and these countries.

I am sure some of them will start businesses which will link their respective countries to this region. Hence an investment in higher education will help create an educational business in the short term but will also pave way for other businesses in the medium and long terms.

Various Areas of Service Economy

Editorial and Design Services: Bangladesh, Thailand and many other countries have international organisations like the UN who have extensive operations in some of these countries. There is also a large number of domestic and international NGOs working in Bangladesh, Cambodia and Thailand. There is a need to edit and design texts and allied materials being produced by these organisations. Businesses providing editorial and design services can be set up may be again in public-private partnership to cater to this demand. There can be a business in translation services too. For example, lot of businesses and professionals in Bangladesh are getting into international connections. Many of them require effective high-quality translation services from Bengali to English or from other languages to Bengali.

Banking: In international trade, whether in goods or in services, one of the cornerstones is banking. Without a smooth and effective banking system we cannot have a rapid growth in trade between economies. Banking is also an important service sector industry. It is useful for international trade if we could induce banks from Bangladesh, Thailand or China to set up operations here in the north-east. Whatever trade we do, whether we import goods or export services, it will be a great help if a Thai importer of Assamese tea can do the banking transaction through a Thai bank. And, it will be a psychological boost to the parent in Chittagong that he can easily wire money to his son's account in the Shillong branch of Agrani Bank from his own neighbourhood branch of the same bank.

But that apart, foreign investment in banking here can also lead to greater international linking up of the economy. I think that there are banks in Bangladesh or Thailand that have some economic muscle to expand in foreign economies. They may not want to venture into Bombay because of heavy competition but Guwahati may be a better base for their entry into a new market. Plus banks from these economies can start tapping into the professional managers that India is producing through its management and business schools.

Health Services: Bangladesh has become a market of various health businesses in the region. Like some cities in India, the big cities in Bangladesh can no longer cope with the health-related requirements of its people. Bangladeshis who can afford are coming to India or going to Thailand for treatment. There is a private hospital in Bangkok which has marketed itself extremely well to Bangladeshi patients. They have, among other things, shown by a sign in each room which way is the west, and, this is to make sure that the Muslim patients from Bangladesh know which direction in the room they should be facing during their prayers. Earlier in the paper, I mentioned that it is important to acquire skills in dealing with people from other cultures. This, for instance, is an example of how important such skills can be. Of course, for the health services to be exported to Bangladesh or other countries, we first need to have first class facilities here in the north-east. The big tea companies, the oil and gas sector, the central government and the state governments can pool in resources to create some world class facilities here and that can then attract health tourists. It will be important, however, to provide logistical facilities alongside best medical care. But, the possibility is definitely there. Heart patients form probably the largest percentage of Bangladeshi patients going abroad. You can definitely market health facilities in north-east saying that they provide an added advantage of keeping the heart feel the clean air and green surroundings once the surgery is over. So, you offer recuperation after the surgery in a fantastic atmosphere.

Tourism: The north-east is fabled for its beauty and yet there is hardly any foreign tourist here. I am not sure of the statistics but it may be drawing as little as 2 per cent of foreign tourists coming to India. There is one major bottleneck in this. There is not enough flights out of Guwahati to international destinations. I think there was flight between Guwahati and Bangkok that started three years ago, I am not sure whether it's still running. There is possibly no flight linking it to Dhaka or to any city in Burma. I would say, this sector needs immediate inputs in a major way if the north-east has to be put on an international tourist map. And, this is as much important for tourism as also for business. We should explore how soon we can have air-links between Guwahati and Dhaka and Guwahati and a city in Burma. And, of course, to boost tourism in this sector, there needs to be sustained marketing in key markets like Bangladesh, Thailand and Singapore. The Andhra Pradesh government teamed up with Sri Lankan Airlines to promote Andhra Pradesh in Thailand. If Bangladesh Biman starts a flight to

Guwahati, it will make eminent sense to tie up with them in promoting Kaziranga or other destinations in South-East Asia or in China. But to tourism to take off in a major way, one should think of innovative packages like a scenic walk through tea gardens or a weekend with a little known tribe in Nagaland. Another very important sector to tap into is conference tourism. International academic and professional associations look out for venues of their conferences. Public-private partnership can boost this area. One Indian state has done a remarkable thing for the last ten years. Andhra Pradesh has hosted the International Children's Film Festival each year. This is not a huge affair but it does put Hyderabad on the map for some film makers and when they want to do a film in an inexpensive way they may choose Ramoji Film City as their base. That brings in money and creates jobs. One area that can be promoted is bringing Bangladeshi film producers to do the song and dance numbers in the scenic backdrop of the north-east. There is a substantial growth potential in north-east, however, it calls for sustained and concerted effort.

I have tried to put forward ideas of developing various areas of the service sector in the north-east. I would like to conclude by saying that intelligent use of technology, scientific and cultural, and a mental frame of borderlessness can possibly transform the north-east from economic backwaters of India to a vibrant zone linking India to South-East Asia and China.

PART II

INDO-BANGLADESH BORDER TRADE: WEST BENGAL-BANGLADESH SECTOR

8

INDIA-BANGLADESH BORDER TRADE: SOME ANALYTICAL ISSUES

Ajitava Raychaudhuri

Introduction

International trade is basically governed by the principle of static and dynamic comparative advantage. The problem arises when countries having similar factor endowments trade with each other. In this case, one may find the emergence of intra-industry trade whereby traded commodities belong to the same industry for the exporting and importing countries. The Indo-Bangladesh trade to certain extent suffers from this phenomenon. However, the trade between India and Bangladesh have two separate dimensions—one is the formal trade aspect and the other is the informal trade. The formal trade passes through all the regulations of the participating countries whereas the informal trade has a different dynamics of its own. The present chapter will concentrate on the formal trade aspect with occasional references to the informal trade component.

One of the reasons for concentrating on the formal trade aspect is rather obvious- the authenticated data are available easily from the Government of India designated source Directorate of Commercial Intelligence and Statistics (DGCI & S). The second one relates to the recent tendencies on the part of the countries in South Asia, among other countries in the developing world, to liberalise and simplify the export and import procedures. This has the obvious impact on the incentives to go for formal channel trade compared to the informal channels. Thus it is expected that the formal trade will pick up compared to the informal trade in future.

The most important objective of this chapter is to analyse the bilateral trade scenarios between India and Bangladesh and comment on the nature of such trade. More specifically, we would like to focus on the type of goods traded so that one can have some idea whether Indo-Bangladesh trade in general follow the comparative advantage principle. The second objective is to highlight the role of border trade in the whole process given the enormous scope of developing such trade between India and Bangladesh. The issue here is whether the border trade follows the same pattern of the overall trade between India and Bangladesh or it is governed by other considerations. In case of the latter, it is possible that the comparative advantage principle is overshadowed by some short-term mutually advantageous considerations. Finally, based on the findings, some concluding remarks will be made on the prospects of such border trade in the context of a generally flourishing trade between India and Bangladesh.

Nature of Trade between India and Bangladesh

As mentioned in the introduction, India's trade with Bangladesh is carried out both formally and informally. The informal trade flourished because of a long stretch of border between India and Bangladesh. The reasons for an extensive informal trade between India and Bangladesh, apart from the border advantage are several (Taneja, 2004). They are mainly two - (1) Trade Policy Distortions in the sense that high Tariff and Non-tariff barriers prompt small producers to go for informal trade channels and (2) High transaction costs in terms of bad infrastructure and poor governance led many producers to take the illegal route.

The important question that arises in this context is how far the formal and the informal trade between India and Bangladesh are complementary to each other? Further, one is interested to know how far the formal trade pattern between India and Bangladesh conform to the overall trade pattern of India and Bangladesh, so that both the parties may reap the benefits of comparative advantage. In addition, the issue of border trade is central to this chapter and will be given its due importance. Let us first look at the following data collected from various sources.

TABLE 8.1

India's Formal Trade with Bangladesh (In Indian Rs. Lacs)

Sl No.	*Items*	*1999-2000*	*2001-2002*	*2003-2004*
1.	EXPORT	275,728.38	477,957.97	799,897.63
2.	% Growth	54.92	40.55	
3.	% Share in India Total	1.73	2.29	2.73
4.	IMPORT	33,865.95	28,194.03	35,670.79
5.	% Growth		-23.24	18.79
6.	% Share in India Total	0.16	0.11	0.10
7.	India's Trade Balance	241,862,43	449,763.94	764.226.84

Source: Department of Commerce, Government of India, Export Import Data Bank.

TABLE 8.2

India's Share in Bangladesh's Trade

Sl No.	*Items*	*1995*	*2000*	*2003*
1.	% Share in Exports Total	1.1	1.0	0.7
2.	% Share in Imports Total	15.3	11.3	15.5

Source: Mohammed Mafizur Rahman, "Bangladesh-India Bilateral Trade: Causes of Imbalance and Measures for Improvement", Working Paper Econ 2005-1, School of Economics and Political Science, The University of Sydney.

TABLE 8.3

A Comparative Picture of India's Formal and Informal Trade with Bangladesh, 1992-93 (US Million Dollars)

Sl. No.	*Items*	*Formal*	*Informal*
1.	Exports	349.1	299.0
2.	Imports	7.8	14.0

Source: Taneja, "Informal and Free Trade Arrangements", South Asian Journal, 4th Issue, 2004, available at www.southasianmedia.net/Magazine/Journal/Informal_Freetrade.htm (Internet).

TABLE 8.4

Average Unweighted Tariff Rates in Bangladesh and India

Sl. No.	*Items*		*1991*	*1996*
1.	Consumer Goods	Bangladesh	124.4	8.3
		India	145.5	33.1
2.	Intermediate Goods	Bangladesh	79.0	22.2
		India	129.8	36.9
3.	Capital Goods	Bangladesh	72.0	15.0
		India	105.2	35.3

Source: Rahman, 2005, *op. cit.*

The above tables (8.1-8.4) more or less speak for themselves. Just to correlate them, we note that the trade favours India heavily. The percentage contribution of Bangladesh in India's total imports is steadily falling. On the other hand, percentage contribution of India in Bangladesh's total imports had some fluctuations but apparently shows signs of increase. At the same time, informal trade percentage, which was very close in magnitude to the formal trade in the early nineties, should have a tendency to fall given an all-round reduction in the tariff levels both in India and Bangladesh. However, the non-tariff barriers like transport delays and infrastructural bottlenecks are still playing a crucial role in hampering formal trade between India and Bangladesh (Das and Pohit, 2004).

Let us now look at the commodity composition of trade of the two countries, India and Bangladesh. This would give us some idea about the trade pattern of India and Bangladesh globally:

TABLE 8.5

Commodity Composition of Exports from Bangladesh, 2001-02

Sl. No.	*Items*	*% of Country Total*	*% of World*
1.	Men's outwear non-knit	22.06	3.25
2.	Under garments non-knit	14.94	6.89
3.	Women's outwear non-knit	14.63	1.52
4.	Under garments knitted	11.77	1.82
5.	Outer garments knit non-elastic	10.58	1.08
6.	Shell fish fresh, frozen	5.88	1.79
7.	Leather	4.38	1.30
8.	Textile	3.22	0.90
9.	Other woven textile fabric	1.64	0.97
10.	Textile Yarn	1.20	0.19
11.	Remainder	9.69	

Source: UNCTAD Handbook of Statistics, 2004.

TABLE 8.6

Commodity Composition of Exports from India, 2001-02

Sl. No.	*Items*	*% of Country Total*	*% of World*
1.	Pearl, precious and semi-precious stones	14.24	12.46
2.	Petroleum products, refined	4.80	1.58
3.	Women's outwear non-knit	3.89	3.82
4.	Textile Yarn	3.55	5.29
5.	Medicinal, Pharmaceutical prdcts	3.21	1.04
6.	Under garments knitted	2.86	4.18
7.	Gold, silver ware, jewellery	2.74	5.34
8.	Textile articles nes	2.44	6.46
9.	Shell fish fresh, frozen	2.11	6.07
10.	Remainder	60.16	

Source: UNCTAD Handbook of Statistics, 2004.

As is well known, the trade pattern is normally dictated by the principle of comparative advantage. However, the distortions in trade caused by tariff and non-tariff barriers cause deviations from this pattern. As one can find from the trade pattern of the Bangladesh, it is heavily concentrated on three items, namely garments and textiles, leather and frozen fish. Part of it is definitely on account of Multi-Fibre Agreements in textiles which gave Bangladesh access to a large market in the OECD countries. On the other hand, India's trade pattern is much more diversified although gems and jewelleries, textiles and garments, leather, frozen fish and lately petroleum products and medicines, occupy major percentages in India's trade. What we want to study is whether Indo-Bangladesh trade pattern is consistent with this overall trade pattern for world. Once this is studied, the border trade really falls into place and one knows exactly whether the border trade is similar to the general trade pattern with Bangladesh.

Table 8.7 throws some interesting observations. The items which have gone up significantly in India's formal export basket to Bangladesh are (1) cereals (2) vegetables (3) fruits (4) coal (5) some articles of iron and steel (6) colouring materials (7) organic compounds etc. Most notable items which have gone down in share are (1) cotton yarn (2) portland cement (3) mineral or chemical fertiliser (4) chassis fitted with engines (5) knitted or crocheted fabrics etc. How far this is entirely a fall from the angle of India's export or a switch to informal trade is difficult to gauge. We will comment on the similarity of this trade with India's overall export pattern in the concluding section.

TABLE 8.7

Major Commodity Exports from India to Bangladesh

(in Rs. Crores)

Sl. No.	*Item*	*1996-97***	*2003-04***	*Change*
1.	Fish Fresh or chilled	7.94	0.0005	Fall
2.	Fish Frozen excluding fish fillets	1.01	0.496	Fall*
3.	Onions, shallots, garlic etc.	36.52(1.2)	288.31(3.6)	Big Rise
4.	Dried Leguminous Vegetables	0.65(.02)	125.53(1.6)	Big Rise
5.	Dates Figs, Pineapples, Guavas etc.	3.52	42.09	Big Rise
6.	Citrus Fruit	16.73	54.35	Big Rise
7.	Pepper of Genus	0.68	49.78	Big Rise
8.	Wheat and Meslin	34.28(1.1)	900.10(11.3)	Big Rise
9.	Rice	145.31(4.7)	904.32(11.3)	Big Rise
10.	Cane/Beet sugar	16.62(0.5)	144.78(1.8)	Big Rise*
11.	Portland Cement	101.25(3.3)	65.12(0.8)	Big Fall*
12.	Coal Briquette	52.77(1.7)	248.01(3.1)	Big Rise
13.	Organic Compounds	18.29	75.71	Big Rise
14.	Medicaments	12.25	26.29	Rise*
15.	Mineral or Chemical Fertiliser	50.06(1.7)	NIL	Big Fall
16.	Synthetic Colouring Material	57.70	103.63	Big Rise
17.	New Pneumatic Tyres of Rubber	51.20	102.15	Big Rise
18.	Cotton Yarn	921.51(29.9)	439.18(5.5)	Big Fall
19.	Knitted or crocheted Fabrics	49.43(1.6)	1.77	Big Fall
20.	Flat Rolled Products of Iron and Steel	108.19(3.5)	159.66(2.0)	Rise(Fall)
21.	Unwrought Aluminium	36.25(1.2)	87.08(1.1)	Rise(Fall)
22.	Other Articles of Iron and Steel	1.15	260.95(3.3)	Big Rise
23.	Electrical Transformers	51.90	62.54	Rise
24.	Chassis fitted with Engines	131.23(4.25)	70.62(0.9)	Fall
25.	Motor Cycles	59.31	73.59	Rise*
26.	Parts and Accessories of Vehicles	16.89	37.36	Rise

Source: Department of Commerce, Government of India, Export Import Data Bank

* denotes fluctuations. **Brackets are percentages to the total.

Now let us look at the import pattern from Bangladesh in Table 8.8.

India's imports from Bangladesh are heavily concentrated on a few items. Notable change between 1996-97 and 2003-04 is very rapid growth of import of ammonia anhydrous used for fertiliser, which is accompanied by total washout of mineral or chemical fertiliser imports from Bangladesh. Jute import is fluctuating, although jute based woven fabrics have created a market in India. More important to note is the import of men's and boy's shirts from Bangladesh which was absent in 1996-97.

TABLE 8.8

Major Commodity Imports of India from Bangladesh

(In Rs. crores)

Sl No.	*Items*	*1996-97***	*2003-04***	*Change*
1.	Fish Fresh or Chilled	16.32(7.4)	23.04(6.46)	Rise/Fall
2.	Ammonia Anhydrous	40.03(18.1)	145.84(40.9)	Big Rise
3.	Mineral or chemical fertilisers	84.19(38.1)	NIL	Big Fall
4.	Jute & Other Textile fibers	72.00(32.6)	93.89(26.3)	Fall*
5.	Men's or Boy's shirts	NIL	20.27(5.7)	Big Rise
6.	Woven Fabrics of Jute	NIL	10.13(2.8)	Big Rise

Source: Department of Commerce, Government of India, Export-Import Data bank.

* Fluctuating, ** Figures in the bracket denote percentage to Total.

India-Bangladesh Border Trade and Its Pattern

As is well known, India and Bangladesh share a long border between them and it runs mainly along West Bengal and also partly along Meghalaya, Assam, Mizoram and Tripura. It is natural that border trade will flourish between the two countries, which additionally shares a common language and culture with West Bengal. Let us have a look at the shares of border trade as given by the important land and railway customs station in India and Bangladesh. The Eastern Railway, which carries a major portion of goods trade, has provided the map (Map 8.1) which clearly demarcates the geographical locations of some of the important border customs stations through which trade is carried out between India and Bangladesh.

TABLE 8.9

India's Exports through Major Ports

(Percentages)

Sl.No.	*Port*	*1996-97 **	*2003-04***
A. LAND (Road and Railways)			
1.	Petrapole (mainly Road)	56.6 (1)	36.2 (1)
2.	Ranaghat (Gede) (Rail)	5.2 (3)	11.5 (2)
3.	Radhikapur (Rail)	0.6 (-)	1.9 (-)
4.	Hili (Road)	2.9 (6)	5.9 (4)
5.	Kotwaligate (Mohedipur-Road)	4.3 (4)	6.9 (3)
B. SEA			
1.	Mumbai	9.3 (2)	1.3 (-)
2.	Nhava Seva	3.3 (5)	5.3 (5)
3.	Chennai	1.9 (7)	2.5 (7)
8.	Tuticorin	1.8 (8)	1.5 (-)
9.	Vishakapatnam	0.7 (-)	2.8 (6)
10.	Kakinada	0.9 (-)	2.5 (8)

Source: DGCIS, Ministry of Commerce, Government of India.

** Figures in the bracket are percentages to the total.

The above table clearly shows that Railways has gained the most over the years, while Land and Sea routes have not grown that highly. The reasons may be many, but the picture will be clear once one brings in the commodity composition of border trade in the next table.

Table 8.10 clearly shows that for some of the important items of exports, border trade plays an important role. The table only gives select border trade data for West Bengal land customs station only. However, Table 8.10 does not give details of the Ranaghat (or Gede) Rail checkpost, which carries a good deal of border trade also, especially in cement, wheat and sugar. Some of the important items which have grown in India's exports basket and are increasingly traded

Map 8.1
Indo-Bangladesh Railway Network

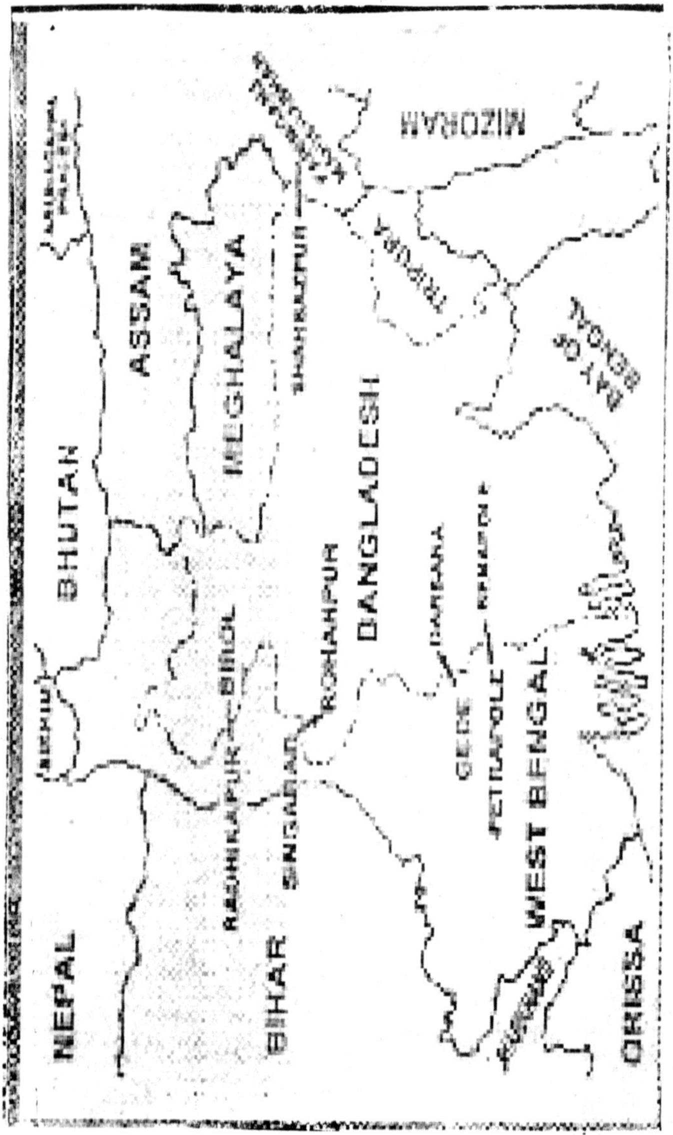

Source: Eastern Railway, Ministry of Railways, Government of IndiaTable 8.10.

through the land and rail transports are onions and garlic, rice, cotton woven articles (code 5209) which includes denims which are in high demand, synthetic organic colouring materials, unwrought aluminium, other materials of iron and steel, pneumatic tyres, chassis of cars with engines, radio receivers and video apparatus which includes monitors etc. One must note that almost all of these items have shown rising trends in India's export basket. Some of the important items which do not figure here are cement, sugar, cotton yarn, coal briquettes, wheat etc. However, most of these items did not show very rapid growth except perhaps wheat and coal briquettes. So apparently, the border trade played an important role in the items which have shown growth trends while non-border routes did not carry goods which had shown rising prospects over the years. So the importance of exports through the border cannot be undermined.

TABLE 8.10

Commodities Exported Through Select Borders

(Percentage of Total)

Sl. No.	*Ports*	*Commodities*	*1996-97*	*2003-24*	*Change*
1.	Hili and Petrapole	Onions and Garlic	57.3	44.6	Fall
2.	Hili and Petrapole	Oranges fresh & Dried	93.4	12.4	Fall
3.	Hili, Petrapole & Radhikapur	Rice	22.5	43.9	Rise
4.	Petrapole	Synthetic Orgnic Coloring Mat	100	100	Same
5.	Petrapole	New pneumatic tyres	53.7	86	Rise
6.	Petrapole	Woven Cotton (5209 code)	36.5	92	Rise
7.	Petrapole	Other articles of Iron & Steel	13	97.2	Rise
8.	Petrapole	Unwrought Aluminium	88	76.2	Fall
9.	Petrapole	Radio receivers, Video apparatus	95	97	Rise
10.	Petrapole	Chassis fitted with engine	99.5	95.3	Fall

Source: DGCIS, Department of Commerce, Government of India.

Let us have a quick look at the imports scenario of Bangladesh through some of the borders in West Bengal.

TABLE 8.11

Commodities Imported from Bangladesh Through Borders (Percentage of Total)

Sl. No.	*Ports Items*	*1996-97*	*2003-04*	*Change*
1.	Petrapole Hilsa and other fish	100	100	Same
2.	Petrapole Jute	100	100	Same
3.	Petrapole Betel Nuts	NIL	100	Rise

Source: DGCIS, Department of Commerce, Government of India.

Table 8.11 clearly shows that out of the three major commodities Bangladesh exports to India, two come entirely from land routes, namely, hilsa and other fish and raw jute. The other major item which Bangladesh exports is ammonia anhydrous or in aqueous solution. But this is more or less exported through the sea ports.

Concluding Remarks

From the above discussion, it is clear that India Bangladesh trade pattern does not follow strictly the principle of comparative advantage. The reason is that some of the goods are produced in common in both the countries due to similar factor endowments and factor intensities, like garments, leather etc. One must note garments is the major item of export for Bangladesh, followed by leather products and shell fish. India imports not really the shell fish but hilsa, which is primarily consumed in West Bengal due to cultural similarities.

Let us divide the commodities exported through the border in the following categories-

1. Vegetables – This is exported to Bangladesh mainly due to shortage of the same in Bangladesh and not really due to any great cost difference in the production.
2. Citrus fruits- India has a relative comparative

advantage and its exports through borders make sense as it is cheaper than the landed costs of say middle eastern fruits. However, globally, India is still not among the best producers due to technology factors.

3. Onions and Garlic- Again it is relative advantage which makes exports of this an advantage to Bangladesh.
4. Rice – This again is due to shortage of the same in Bangladesh and not really due to any great comparative advantage on part of India.
5. Iron and Steel and unwrought aluminium- India certainly has relative comparative advantage but again not globally. So this does not show areas of India's production strength at present, although in future, the scenario might change.
6. Chassis of Cars fitted with engine- Same story as above although India is fast becoming a major player in the automobile market.
7. Woven Cotton especially Denim Jeans- One has to make a detailed study regarding comparative advantage to come to a conclusion.

As pointed out by a recent World Bank Study (2005), corruption increases the transaction cost of production for many of the items of comparative advantage in Bangladesh, especially garments, leather, shell fish etc. Along with that poor infrastructure, especially electricity supply increases production costs tremendously. It is not that these problems are absent for India, but they seem to be more in case of Bangladesh.

Now coming to the problem of infrastructure as an obstacle in increasing the border trade between the two countries, one may mention the problem of road and rail infrastructure in this context. An ADB Document (2003) mentions the limited terminal and line capacity of Bangladesh Railways for the Darshana segment which is the link to Gede (Ranagahat) Rail station in the Nadia district of India. Gede carries the maximum rail traffic to Bangladesh. The document says only two trains are allowed to cross the border although the requirement is for five trains daily. The document says that the cement is the most important traffic through the Gede route. Similarly, as the paper by Das and Pohit (2004) mentions, the transaction cost in terms of waiting at the Petrapole checkpost for 4 days is exceedingly high. Widening of the road and fast computerizations are the need of the hour but the first will take much time due to congestion along the route from Petrapole to Kolkata.

This study did not go into the informal trade aspects. We did mention the magnitude of informal trade in the early nineties, which must have come down a little after reduction in the tariffs on both sides. But the high transaction costs in terms of waiting time and bribes at the checkposts still drive many exporters to go underground. In fact, we did not mention the service trade at all as one paper by Rahman (2000) clearly puts the informal trade in education and health services at a very high proportion.. Another important dimension not touched is the informal trade in cattle which may be still continuing unabated (Pramanik, 2004).

In conclusion, one may say that India Bangladesh trade promotes some activities which may be consistent with relative comparative advantage but not global. However, some of these may give impetus to the growth of some industries where a country may enjoy potential comparative advantage which might develop in future with suitable technological upgradation and government support towards this end. The imbalance of trade between India and Bangladesh may be addressed in this light whereby the two governments may try to encourage productions and exchange among goods where one country has genuine comparative advantage although due to similarities both produce the same. Border trade provides such an opportunity to make such coordinated efforts a success.

REFERENCES

ADB Document (2003) - Eastern South Asia Sub-region (ESAS) Cooperation in Transport & Communication.

Das, S. and S. Pohit (2004) - "Quantifying Transport, Regulatory and Other Costs for Indian Overland Exports to Banglades", Paper presented to the Annual Development Economics Conference, Jadavpur University.

Pramanik, B. (2004) - "Cattle Smuggling Across the Indo-Bangladesh Border- An Analysis", Dialogue, July-September, 2004.

Rahman, Mustafiz (2000) - "Bangladesh-India Bilateral Trade: An Investigation into Trade in Services", Paper prepared for SANEI, Dhaka: Centre for Policy Dialogue.

Rahman, M.M. (2005) - "Bangladesh-India Bilateral Trade: Causes of Imbalance and Measures for Improvement", Working Paper No. ECON2005-1, University of Sydney, School of Economics and Political Science.

Taneja, N. (2004) - "Informal and Free Trade Arrangements", South Asian Journal, 4th Issue, available on the internet at www.southasianmedia.net/magazine/journal/informal_freetrade.htm

World Bank (2005) - Bangladesh: Growth and Export Competitiveness. Report No. 31394-BD.

9

CROSS-BORDER TRADE BETWEEN INDIA AND BANGLADESH: A COMPARISON BETWEEN WEST BENGAL AND NORTH EASTERN REGION

Dilip Halder

Introduction

Border trade is a global phenomenon and it is conceptually narrower than international trade, in the sense, it takes place between the neighbouring countries only, sharing common international boundaries. Apart from the economic factors like price disparity and scarcity of commodities and complementarities of various nature, the distance or the geographical proximity of finished goods and factors of production mainly account for the present practice of cross border trade. The Eastern Region and North-Eastern Regions (ER and NER) share international boundaries with Nepal, China, Myanmar and Bangladesh. Movement of men, material and cattle takes place, legally or illegally, mainly under economic compulsion creating problems of economic, social, political, demographic and diplomatic nature. To size up the problems and to ease them out at a minimum social and private cost, to the mutual benefit of the trading nations, an indepth analysis of the ground reality with spatial dimension is essential.

Objective

Towards that objective the present chapter aims at analysing the commodity composition, volume and value of the cross border trade as well as the illegal component of it that could be seized in NER and comparing them with those of West Bengal (WB) border. Along with that an attempt has been made to assess the infrastructure facilities, rail, road and riverine, which might go a long way to facilitate vigilance to check illegal trade and help promote legal cross border trade between India and Bangladesh.

The Problem Area

The total length of Bangladesh border with India is 4185.00 km which is the longest of all borders that India shares with her neighbouring countries. Bangladesh is almost surrounded by Indian territory except a small stretch of about 200 kms, which she shares with Myanmar. The stretches that Bangladesh shares with Indian States are broken up in Table 9.1.

TABLE 9.1

The Statewise Break-up of India's Border with Bangladesh

	Name of the State	Length of Border (in kms)
1.	West Bengal	2,306.00 (land 2,216.00 kms + river 90 kms)
2.	Tripura	856.00
3.	Meghalaya	443.00
4.	Mizoram	318.00
5.	Assam	262.00

The longest stretch is claimed by West Bengal then comes in order Tripura, Meghalaya, Mizoram and Assam. The stretch of West Bengal alone is 2,306.00 kms and that of the rest four together is 1,879.00 kms which is less than the former.

Methodology and Database

The analysis of commodity composition has been made by constructing three tables showing (i) items of export and import common to both list of West Bengal (WB) and North Eastern Region (NER), (ii) items of export specifically from WB and NER border, and the (iii) items of import specifically to WB and NER from Bangladesh. This tabulation has been made by using the official data of last five years to bring out the characteristic difference, if any, in the composition of the traded commodities between these two regions.

Thereafter, the volume analysis has been made particularly of the traded commodities through the NER border. Following this an analysis of the values of exports and imports from these two regions have been made to compare them subsequently.

To have an idea about the illegal trade the official figure of value and commodity composition of the smuggled goods have also been used. But since they also cannot give the complete idea about the composition of commodity movement across the borders, data of other studies on the subject made in Bangladesh have also been used.

For suggesting improvement of cross border trade, the role of transport infrastructure development has been highlighted giving a description of the present status and perspective plan on the basis of secondary data.

Composition of Traded Commodity

To Bangladesh, India is an important source of imports so far as formal trade is concerned. More than 12 percent of total formal imports of Bangladesh comes from India. The total formal export to India from Bangladesh is 1 per cent of the total export of Bangladesh. In the composition of this import 8 per cent constitutes capital goods, 10 per cent intermediate goods, 13 per cent primary goods and 20 per cent consumer goods. The export-import ratio of Bangladesh is 1 : 10 (1 export against 10 import) (Rahman 2004), which perhaps includes informal component also. To reduce informal (or illegal) component and to boost up the volume of trade to the benefit of both the trading partners, it is urgent to analyse the commodity composition of border trade of India with Bangladesh.

The commodity composition has been divided into West Bengal border trade and NER border trade for comparison. The items of import and export that could be collected from official sources have been presented into three categories.

1. Common items of export and import from WB and NER to Bangladesh
2. Export items specifically from West Bengal and NER to Bangaldesh, and
3. Import items from Bangladesh specially to WB and NER.

TABLE 9.2

Common Items of Export and Import from West Bengal & NER to Bangladesh

Sl.No.	*ITEMS OF EXPORT*	*Sl.No.*	*ITEMS OF IMPORT*
01.	Coal	01.	Raw jute
02.	Boulder stone	02.	Hilsa fish
03.	Fruits	03.	Men's shirt
04.	Onion	04.	Cotton waste
05.	Rice (non-basmati)	05.	Soap
06.	Machinery	06.	Battery plates
07.	Printed books	07.	Fruit drinks
08.	Poultry feed	08.	Molasses

Source: Office of the Commissioner of Customs, Shillong and Kolkata.

Tables 9.2-9.4 have been constructed by making use of the information from land customs offices of Shillong and Kolkata to give an idea about the commodity composition in the above three categories.

TABLE 9.3

Export Items Specifically Through West Bengal and NER Border

WEST BENGAL	*NER*
Cotton fabric, Chemicals, Tyre & tubes, Two wheelers, Chassis, Writing Comm. Plywood, Wheat, Maize, Fly ash, Cereals, Phospho gypsum, Soybean extracts	Ballast stone, Lime stone, Citrus, fruits, Orange, Ginger, Parts of tractors, Betel leaf, Fresh fruits, paper etc, Paper, Marble stone, Marble slab/tiles, Crude marble, Bed sheet, Dry fish, Wall clock, Cloth, Rui fish, Chocolates, Jack fruit, Machinery, Wood apples, Poultry feed, Pine apples/pears, Tea, Stone chips, Sand stone, Crushed stone, Stone blast, Unpolished marble, Tamarind, Audio cassette recorder, Sugar confectionery, Woven fabrics, Other fabrics of painting & shirting, Tape recorder, Potato, Bicycle, Dry chilli, Raw hides and skins, Plywood Mooli bamboo, Umbrella, Motor parts, Synthetic sarees, Vegetable incl. Spices, Reconditioned vehicle, Colour printing paper, Dust variety coal, Oil & gas field equipment, Smoked sheets of rubber, Hides & skins of animals, Stainless steel, Handicrafts for display, Sanitary ware, Natural rubber latex, Coir mattress, Playing cards, Turmeric, Tezpata (leaves of cassia lingnea), Switch socket of plastic

Source: Office of the Commissioner of Customs, Shillong and Kolkata.

In the analysis of composition and volume of the traded commodities emphasis has been given to NER. And that is why the data on the volume of commodities to and from NER have been presented in the next section and those of WB have not been presented, though subsequently in the comparison of values of border trade between WB and NER the data of both the stretches have been used.

TABLE 9.4

Items of Import from Bangladesh Specifically Through West Bengal and NER Border

WEST BENGAL	NER
Jute bag, Packing cloth, Jamdani sarees, Readymade garments, Lead acid, Accumulators, Potato chips, Zinc flux, Zinc plates, Betel nuts, Snacks, Lead screw, Copper tube, Rly. Sleepers	Waffers, Jeans/short pants, Mosquito net, Chips, Chocolate, Brass product, Keya soap, Toilet soap, Bakery product, Metal wooden furniture, Biscuits, Aluminium products, Ferrous waste and scraps, R.C. Cola, Small fish, M.S. Rod, Bhujia, Cream milk, powder, Dry chilli, Dry fish, Waste of wool, Fruit juice, Flat rotted bar of iron, Pickle, Sauce, Mineral water, Old cake milk, Squash, Raw material of ONGC, Other waste of wool, Non-knitted syn. Fibre Pvc Sylco, brand pipe, UPs, Emergency light, P.P. Film, Food processing machine, Garlic, Pellets & Seasing, Prawn products, Malamine table ware, Cotton saree, Wall and floor tiles, Mini fruty, Gell & potato crackers, Fruit juice, Mango bar/Chana chur, Soya/mustard/veg. Oil, Masala/ toiletory soap, Aluminium profile, Pvc foam sheets/profile, Pvc plastic door, Tin sheets, Pellets and seasoning, Broken or crushed stone, Lay flat tube of plastic, Brick crusher machine, Glaze tiles, Scrap of cast iron, Water lemon, Mattress or rubber, Dry garlic, Ice cream, Accumulators/batt. Parts, Grey Portland, Cement, Plastic moulded chair, Ladies hand bag, Shawl, Cotton saree, Silk saree, Frying pan, Casserole, Pressure cooker, China ceramic table ware, Imitation jewllery, Bailey tops, Potato crackers, Tooth paste, Detergent, Fruit gel, Beverages, Polyurathene foam, Non-electric lamp, Inedible molasses, Carding machine, Lay flat tube, Building bricks, Unfinished tobacco, Manufactured hooka tobacco, Other non-knitted plastic fibre, Hand pump for water, Galvanized ridging, Chakka washing machine, Wireline logging and testing, Rope of jute, Lascha Semai, Deep fried crispy snack, Beauty soap, Aerated water, Fitter sets, Coriander, Cashew nut, Candy, Badam Bhujia, Babul gum, Animal feed, Resins.

Source: Office of the Commissioner of Customs, Shillong and Kolkata.

Exports

It may be observed that Indian exports to Bangladesh from NER constitute mainly the minerals and raw materials like coal, lime stone, boulders, stone chips etc. In fact, 97 per cent of all exports from NER constitute these items. These are all used for developmental activities in Bangladesh. The minerals and natural extracts are used by Bangladesh for building their infrastructure and hence these are essential

TABLE 9.5

Commodities Exported from NER To Bangladesh

Sl. No.	*Items*	*YEAR*				
		2000-2001	*2001-2002*	*2002-2003*	*2003-2004*	*2004-2005*
01.	Coal	744960.15 m.t.	898962.08 m.t	1048825.46 m.t	1225241.16 m.t	1349473.1 m.t
02.	Boulder stone	30056.60m.t	8587.1 m.t	2111.040 m.t	16637.00 m.t	4419 m.t
03.	Ballast stone	159165.00 c.f.t	259940.00 c.f.t	283000 c.f.t	-	382050 c.f.t
04.	Lime stone	230342.60 m.t.	265875.78 m.t.	234253.00 m.t	256357.00 m.t	88817 m.t
05.	Citrus fruits	410751 nos.	246222 nos.		1736458 nos	2232060 nos
06.	Orange		6489914 nos		7956806 nos	3889770 nos
07.	Ginger	957.988 m.t	104587.20 m.t	4135.055 m.t	1556.514 m.t	3119.899 m.t
08.	Parts of tractors	20 nos.				
09.	Betel leaf	11.199 m.t.	10.657 m.t	41.673 m.t	4.473 m.t	3.244 m.t
10.	Fresh fruits	12.448 m.t		44.00 m.t		
11.	Onion	12.660 m.t.	4028.100 m.t.	32.000 m.t		3 m.t
12.	Paper	357.556 m.t.		11.000 m.t		
13.	Marble tiles	3700 sq. mtr.	3322.11 sq. ft.	7000.00 m.t		
14.	Marble stone	1139.43 m.t.				
15.	Crude marble			11.000 m.t		
16.	Bed sheet	750 pcs.				
17.	Dry fish	50.850 m.t.	106.250		94.500 m.t	184.5 m.t
18.	Wall clock	1030 pcs			500 pcs	1500 pcs
19.	Cloth	900 pcs				
20.	Rui fish	12.000 m.t.				
21.	Chocolates	0.200 m.t.				

TABLE 9.5 (Contd.)

Commodities Exported from NER To Bangladesh

Sl. No.	*Items*	*YEAR*				
		2000-2001	*2001-2002*	*2002-2003*	*2003-2004*	*2004-2005*
22.	Jack fruit	2.000 m.t.	6842.00 m.t			
23.	Machinery	2 nos.				
24.	Wood apples	4.000 m.t.				
25.	Poultry feed	8.00 m.t.				
26.	Pine apples	17.000 m.t		7810.000 m.t		
27.	Pears			54168 kgs	15200 kg	
28.	Tea	3000 kgs				
29.	Stone chips		11108.50 m.t.			
30.	Sand stone		641 m.t		230.000m.t	
31.	Crushed stone		4660.00 m.t	15988.00 m.t	11819.000 m.t	8333 m.t
32.	Stone blast	159165 c.f.t	259940 m.t	283000.00 cft		532 m.t
33.	Tape recorder		78 nos			
34.	Confectionery		0.003 m.t		500.000 kgs	
35.	Printed books		592 nos			10 m.t
36.	Woven fabrics		840.00 m.t			
37.	Potato seeds				100.00 m.t	233.3 m.t
38.	Potato		100.00 m.t		80.000 m.t	
39.	Tomato		300 kgs		4.000 m.t	
40.	Tamarind		28.000 m.t			
41.	Bicycle		50 nos	40.123 m.t		
42.	Dry chilli		2000 m.t		20.275 m.t	62.55 m.t
43.	Plywood		413.000 m.t			

TABLE 9.5 (Contd.)

Commodities Exported from NER To Bangladesh

Sl. No.	*Items*	*YEAR*				
		2000-2001	*2001-2002*	*2002-2003*	*2003-2004*	*2004-2005*
44.	Mooli bamboo		1,00,000 nos.	200000 nos		50000 nos
45.	Umbrella		8000 nos.			
46.	Motor parts		2183 pcs	126 pkts	104 nos	
47.	Synthetic sarees		574 pcs			
48.	Vegetable,Spices			1222.00 kgs		8.176 m.t
49.	Reconditioned vehicle			04 nos		
50.	Oil & gas field equipment			02 nos		
51.	Smoked sheets of rubber			8000 m.t		
52.	Hides & skins		84 pcs	130 pcs	335 pcs	1725 pcs
53.	Ceramic wire					320 pcs
54.	Sanitary ware				204 ctns	100 pcs
55.	Natural rubber					15.96 mt
56.	Coir mattress					663 cft
57.	Playing cards					100 groos
58.	Turmeric					12.5 m.t
59.	Other fabrics					500 mtrs
60.	Tezpara					18.435 m.t
61.	Rice (non-bas)					77.692 m.t
62.	Stainless steel			01 set		
63.	Natural rubber				15.960 m.t	
64.	Switch socket					767.08 kg

Source: Office of the Commissioner of Customs, Shillong.

imports, which cannot be curtailed to improve the balance of trade position of Bangladesh.

In addition to these items, a few agricultural and horticultural products, like orange, peas, citrus fruit, vegetables, ginger, onion, turmeric, dry chilli, betel leaves, potato, bamboo, tomato etc. are exported to Bangladesh and that too without any value addition.

Among the manufactured goods machinery, equipment, natural rubber, sanitary ware, stainless steel materials, paper, marble slabs, handloom and handicraft, safety glass, umbrella and umbrella parts are mainly the items. It may be noticed that these items are sporadic in nature. The contribution of manufacturing sector in the export basket is very low and in terms of percentage, it is less than one percent in last five years.

Imports

Interestingly a sharp contrast may be observed in the nature of the import items from Bangladesh to India. Almost all the items of imports from Bangladesh to India are manufactured goods and processed items and also processed food items including *hilsa* fish and dry fish. Most of the imports from Bangladesh to the NER take place through the state of Tripura. This may be due to the fact that compared to other states like Meghalaya and Assam, communication to Tripura over land from other parts of India is far more expensive and time consuming. Tripura appears to be relatively more cost-effective to import manufactured goods from Bangladesh rather than the mainland India.

The Volume of Traded Commodities through NER

The volume of goods exported and imported through NER border over last five years have been listed in Table 9.5 and Table 9.6 respectively. The number of commodities

TABLE 9.6

Commodities Imported to North-East Region

Sl. No.	*Items*	*YEAR*				
		2000-2001	*2001-2002*	*2002-2003*	*2003-2004*	*2004-2005*
01.	Waffers	54 pkts				
02.	Hilsa fish	796.906 m.t.	619.900 m.t	339.800 m.t	850.575 m.t.	759.417 m.t
03.	Jeans/short pants	515 nos				
04.	Mosquito net	18600 nos.		238050mtrs	97000 mtrs	346145 mtrs
05.	Chips/potato chips	4496 pkts	1291 ctns		0.300 m.t	810 ctns
06.	Chocolate	12 pkts				
07.	Brass products	9.70 kgs				
08.	Soap and Talcom powder	10647 nos				95.215 m.t
09.	Keya soap		1124 ctns			25.776 m.t
10.	Toilet soap				14.256 m.t	1933 ctns.
11.	Bakery product					28.332 m.t
12.	Metal/wooden furniture					14.544 m.t
13.	Biscuits					8206.60 kgs
14.	Aluminium product	17.40 kgs.		1 ctn		
15.	Ferrous waste, scraps	49.000 m.t				
16.	R.C. Cola	600 ctns				
17.	Small fish	0.710 m.t				420.25 m.t
18.	M. S. Rod	3497.60 m.t		21.000 m.t		
19.	Bhujia	55 ctns				3481.32 m.t
20.	Cream milk powder	1000 ctns.				
21.	Cotton yarn waste	1.5 m.t		89.000 m.t		43 m.t
22.	Dry chilli	1.000 m.t	3.000 m.t			

TABLE 9.6 (Contd.)

Commodities Imported to North-East Region

Sl. No.	*Items*	*YEAR*				
		2000-2001	*2001-2002*	*2002-2003*	*2003-2004*	*2004-2005*
22.	Dry chilli	1.000 m.t	3.000 m.t			
23.	Dry fish	94.155 m.t	93.805 m.t	158.852 m.t	166.875 kgs	383.210 m.t
24.	Waste of wool	76.000 m.t	910300 m.t			
25.	Fruit juice					69.768
26.	Flat rotted bar of iron	2.000 m.t				
27.	Pickle	51 ctns				
28.	Sauce	23 ctns				
29.	Mineral water		5515 ctns	16485 ctns.		
30.	Squash	10 ctns				
31.	Other waste of wool					188.285 m.t
32.	Non-knitted syn. Fibre		17050 mtrs			120000 mtrs
33.	Pvc Sylco brand pipe		1565 mtrs			
34.	Ups/emergency lights		24 nos	214 nos		
35.	Emergency light		92 nos			
36.	P. P. Film		595 kgs	0.294 m.t		
37.	Food processing m/c		2 nos			
38.	Garlic		2.000 m.t			
39.	Pellets & Seasing		3.230 m.t			
40.	Prawn products		3000 m.t			
41.	Malamine table ware			26557 pcs	46486 pcs	
42.	Cotton saree			200 pcs	948 pcs	
43.	Wall and floor tiles			5 ctns		
44.	Mini fruty			100 ctns		

TABLE 9.6 (Contd.)

Commodities Imported to North-East Region

Sl. No.	*Items*	*YEAR*				
		2000-2001	*2001-2002*	*2002-2003*	*2003-2004*	*2004-2005*
45.	Gell & potatocrackers			13 ctns	3.190 m.t	
46.	Fruit juice			11 ctns		
47.	Mangobar/Chanachur			11 ctns		
48.	Soya/mustd/veg. Oil			23 ctns		
49.	Masala/toiletory soap			9 ctns		
50.	Alluminium profile			1 ctns		
51.	Pvc foam sheets/profile			4000.00 m.t		
52.	Pvc plastic door			15 nos.		
53.	Tin sheets			360 nos		
54.	Molasses			686.966		45 m.t
55.	Pellets and seasoning			6.463 m.t		
56.	Broken or crushed stone			2214.00 m.t		
57.	Lay flat tube			129.000 m.t		
58.	Brick crusher m/c			6 nos.		
59.	Glaze tiles			3785 ctns.		
60.	Scrap of cast iron		7.000 m.t	30.000 m.t		
61.	Water lemon			4.000 m.t		
62.	Raw jute			1132.037 m.t		
63.	Mattress or rubber			566 cft		
64.	Dry garlic			2.000 m.t		
65.	Ice cream		485 ctns	453 ctns		
66.	Accumulators/battery					

TABLE 9.6 (Contd.)

Commodities Imported to North-East Region

Sl. No.	Items	YEAR				
		2000-2001	2001-2002	2002-2003	2003-2004	2004-2005
67.	Grey Portland cement			1775.00 m.t		
68.	Plastic moulded chair			1000 pcs		
69.	Ladies hand bag				30 pcs	
70.	Shawl				320 nos	
71.	Silk saree				28 pcs	
72.	Frying pan				69 pcs	
73.	Casserole				25 pcs	
74.	Pressure cooker				24 pcs	
75.	Ceramic table ware				1257 pcs	
76.	Imitation jewllery				427 pcs	
77.	Shirt				50 pcs	
78.	Bailey tops				30 pcs	
79.	Potato chips			1.8 qtls		
80.	Potato crackers				7.090 m.t	
81.	Battery/Accumulators			6.000 m.t	20500pcs	
82.	Beverages				14.514 m.t	28.5 m.t
83.	Polyurathene foam				260 pcs	
84.	Non-electric lamp				6000 nos	
85.	Inedible molasses				165.000 m.t	
86.	Carding machine				1 no	
87.	Building bricks				9000 nos	
88.	Unfinished tobacco				6000 m.t	
89.	Mfg. hooka tobacco				4000 m.t	

TABLE 9.6 (Contd.)

Commodities Imported to North-East Region

Sl. No.	*Items*	*YEAR*				
		2000-2001	*2001-2002*	*2002-2003*	*2003-2004*	*2004-2005*
90.	Non-knitted plastic fibre				21500 mtr	
91.	Hand pump for water				100 pcs	
93.	Chakka washing m/c				12.630 m.t	
94.	Wireline logging				2 nos	
95.	Rope of jute				5.000 m.t	46.07 m.t
96.	Lascha Semai					2.4 m.t
97.	Aerated water					950 ctns
98.	Coriander					3.2 m.t
99.	Cashew nut					7 m.t
100.	Candy					925 ctns
101.	Badam bhaja					820 ctns
102.	Babul gum					125 ctns
103.	Resins					911 m.t
104.	Woven fabric		250 mtrs			
105.	Various small fish		1.110 m.t	0.540 m.t		
106.	Ginger		307.638 m.t			
107.	Mooli bamboo		50000 nos			
108.	Betel leaves		343.00 kgs			
109.	Citrus fruit		10575 nos			
110.	Motor parts		253 pkts			
111.	Salted hilsha fish				400 kgs	
112.	Different food items				682236 ctns	

Source: Office of the Commissioner of Customs, Shillong.

exported from NER are sixty four and those imported, being one hundred and twelve, outnumbered the export items.

One interesting point which becomes visible from these official lists of exports is that only five items namely, coal, boulder stone, line stone, ginger and betel leaf are found to be present in the list of items in all the five years. The volumes of coal in terms of quantity remain in the range of 744960.15 mt in 2001 and 1349473.1 mt in the year 2004-05. This quantity appears to be steadily increasing. The quantity of boulder stone ranges between 2111.04 mt (in 2002-03) and 30056.6 mt (in 2000-01). The quantity of limestone ranges between 88817 mt (in 2004-05) and 265875.78 mt (in 2001-02). The quantity of ginger ranges between 957.988 mt (in 2000-01) and 104587.20 mt in 2001-02. The quantity of betel leaf ranges between 3.244 mt (in 2004-05) to 41.673 (in 2002-03).

Apart from this five, there are six items which were exported four times, five items three times, thirteen items twice and thirty five items only once. A close look at Table 9.5 makes it clear that the stable items of export which were exported in all the five years constitute one fuel, four building materials and the rest are consumer goods of which two are non-vegetarian processed food and the rest are agricultural consumer goods.

The lesser stable items, which appear on the list of exported items twice or thrice in five years also constitute building materials and consumer goods. A large number of items which constitute more than half of the listed items appeared only once in last five years. They constitute a wide variety of durable and non-durable consumer goods. These items appear to be most unstable and sporadic so far as the official record is concerned. This does not, however, necessarily mean that their flow is actually unstable or sporadic because the actual flow might not have been recorded.

Now, turning to the analysis of volume of imports from Bangladesh to NER, we that items (Table 9.6) only two items out of 112 are stable in the sense they appear in all the five years. They are piscicultural products, to be precise, they are *hilsa* fish and dry fish. The quantity of hilsa fish imported ranges between 339.80 m.t. in 2002-03 and 850.58 m.t. in 2003-04. The quantity of dry fish ranges from 93.80 mt in 2001-02 to 116.88 m.t. in 2003-04. Following these two items, the less stable ones, defined on the basis of the frequency of their appearance on the list less than five times, two items appeared four times, one item three times, twenty three items appeared twice.

The most unstable or sporadic item which appear only once in five years are 85 in number which constitute seventy five percent of the listed items. The less stable items, whose frequency is less than five but more than one constitute consumer goods of various types which include cosmetics, confectionery, soft drinks and electrical gadgets etc. In the sporadic group, it may be found that, starting from consumer goods (durable and non-durable), garments, building materials etc., a wide variety of articles, appear.

In case of imported commodities also the same suspicion occurs, as did in case of export items in the official document, regarding their representativeness of the actual cross border movement of commodities. It is likely that the actual movements do not get registered, for various reasons, in the official documents. The strength of this suspicion may be fortified by the study results on this subject discussed subsequently in the section on informal trade.

A Comparison of Value of Trade between WB and NER

In terms of value of border trade with Bangladesh, West Bengal scores above NER. The land-custom-stationwise (LCS) export and import values of NER (Table 9.7) and those of

West Bengal (Table 9.8) over last five years, from 2000-01 to 2004-05, reveal that in terms of both export and import values West Bengal border scores much higher values than those of NER. It may be seen from Table 9.7 that the total export values of NER to Bangladesh range from Rs. 151.00 crores in 2000-01 to Rs. 238.11 in 2003-04 and the import values from Bangladesh to NER range from Rs. 07.19 crores in 2000-01 to Rs. 19.58 crores in 2004-05, which is steadily on the increase.

TABLE 9.7

LCS-wise Value of Export (NER)

(Rs. in Crore)

STATIONS	*2000-2001*	*2001-2002*	*2002-2003*	*2003-2004*	*2004-2005*
SHILLONG DIVN					
DWAKI	55.22	80.91	86.21	88.16	55.49
BORSORA	29.44	45.27	47.70	69.51	74.14
SHELLABAZAR	03.62	02.34	1.87	01.47	10.58
BHOLAGANJ	04.10	03.68	03.66	05.64	06.89
KARIMGANJ DIVN					
KARIMGANJSTEAMER AND FREEY STN	02.63	03.91	06.00	02.02	03.64
SUTAKANDI	18.01	13.78	22.87	46.16	21.34
MANU	—	00.0012	00.0012	—	00.02
OLD RANGA BAZAR	00.10	00.14	00.26	00.17	00.11
AGARTALA DIVN					
AGARTALA	00.52	01.07	01.06	01.00	00.96
SRIMANTAPUR	00.13	00.06	00.26	00.20	00.39
GUWAHATI DIVN					
GHASUAPARA	24.41	27.86	22.67	15.47	17.46
BAGHMARA	00.02	—	00.05	00.06	00.00
DALU	00.83	01.11	02.88	02.67	06.90
DHUBRI DIVN					
MANKACHAR	—	—	00.10	00.11	00.16
MAHENDRAGANJ	12.19	05.74	06.95	05.53	01.31
TOTAL	151.20	185.87	202.54	238.11	190.39

Source: Office of the Commissioner of Customs, Shillong.

TABLE 9.8

LCS-wise Value of Import (NER)

(Rs. in Crore)

STATIONS	*2000-2001*	*2001-2002*	*2002-2003*	*2003-2004*	*2004-2005*
SHILLONG DIVN					
DWAKI	00.0039	00.02	00.02	00.05	0.0087
BORSORA	—	—	—	—	—
SHELLABAZAR	—	—	—	—	—
BHOLAGANJ	—	—	—	—	—
KARIMGANJ DIVN					
KARIMGANJ STEAMER AND FREEY STN	00.01	00.33	00.13	00.005	00.08
SUTARKANDI	00.87	00.73	00.08	01.55	06.78
MANU	00.0021	—	—	—	—
OLD RANGA BAZAR	00.02	00.03	00.03	00.13	00.13
AGARTALA DIVN					
AGARTALA SRIMANTA PUR	06.16	04.39	05.79	09.14	01.18
GUWAHATI DIVN					
GHASUAPARA	—	—	—	—	—
BAGHMARA	—	—	—	—	—
DALU	—	—	—	—	—
DHUBRI DIVN MANKACHAR	—	—	—	—	—
MAHENDRAGANJ	—	—	00.04	00.21	00.33
TOTAL	07.19	05.50	06.09	11.52	19.58

Source: Office of the Commissioner of Customs, Shillong.

Whereas in case of West Bengal (Table 9.9 and Table 9.10) the relevant LCS wise export and import values over the corresponding last five years reveal that the total export values of West Bengal to Bangladesh range from Rs. 3079.93 crores in 2001-02 to Rs. 6516.73 crores in 2004-05 which is also on the upward trend (Table 9.9).

TABLE 9.9

LCS-wise Value of Export (W.B)

(Rs. in Crore)

STATION	*2000-2001*	*2001-2002*	*2002-2003*	*2003-2004*	*2004-2005*
PETRAPOLE	2389.89	1668.25	2077.42	2733.27	3639.60
CHANGRABANDA	378.68	116.81	57.38	163.84	281.18
HILLI	482.84	300.75	228.38	462.96	637.14
MADHIPUR	429.97	509.59	416.39	561.14	556.22
GHOGADANGA	36.75	75.83	92.29	169.17	227.43
RANAGHAT	325.56	889.74	782.55	891.86	873.67
T.T SHED	11.42	26.16	97.64	49.89	56.29
SINGABAD	40.81	91.93	159.60	155.82	195.95
RADHIKAPUR	-	30.87	18.59	42.05	49.25
TOTAL	4095.92	3709.93	3930.24	5230.00	6516.73

Source: Office of the Commissioner of Customs, Kolkata.

TABLE 9.10

LCS-wise Value of Import (W.B)

(Rs. in Crore)

STATION	*2000-2001*	*2001-2002*	*2002-2003*	*2003-2004*	*2004-2005*
PETRAPOLE	186.97	158.27	194.03	187.33	254.24
CHANGRABANDA	32.99	13.93	2.83	5.50	10.74
HILLI	0.06	0.59	2.75	0.08	0.62
MADHIPUR	0.07	1.65	10.19	2.39	1.7 3
GHOGADANGA	1.37	2.42	2.92	4.96	8.07
RANAGHAT	—	—	—	—	—
T.T SHED	—	—		—	8.49
SINGABAD	—	—	—	—	3.49
RADHIKAPUR	—	—	—	—	—
TOTAL	221.46	176.86	212.72	205.53	287.38

Source: Office of the Commissioner of Customs, Kolkata.

It should be mentioned here that there are 90 LCSs on the India-Bangladesh border (West Bengal 56 plus NER 34) but all of them are not operative (Appendix). The legal trading activities are carried on through 24 LCSs, 15 in NER and 9 in West Bengal.

There are two apparent reasons behind this inoperativeness of these LCSs. One, physical and the other financial. The lack of adequate physical infrastructure like rail, road etc. may be one reason. The other reason may be inadequate flow of goods, which does not make maintenance cost of LCS, breakeven.

However, further analysis of the export-import data will throw up interesting results which will make the comparison more meaningful.

TABLE 9.11

Value of Export / Import of NER With Bangladesh

YEARS	*EXPORT (E) (Rs. in Crore)*	*IMPORT (I) (Rs. in Crore)*	*E : I*	*E – I*	*E – I/E*
(1)	(2)	(3)	(4)	(5)	(6)
2000-2001	151.23	7.19	1 : 0.047	144.04	0.95245623
2001-2002	184.78	5.52	1 : 0.029	179.26	0.97012664
2002-2003	202.55	6.10	1 : 0.030	196.55	0.96988398
2003-2004	238.19	11.52	1 : 0.048	226.67	0.95163525
2004-2005	190.42	19.51	1 : 0.012	173.91	0.89754228

Source: Office of the Commissioner of Customs, Shillong.

The striking feature of Table 9.11 is the values of trade surplus (E – I) in column 5 which is very high over last five years. This feature has been reflected in the ratios E : I in column 4 and in relativity E – I/E in column 6. The fluctuations in trade surplus have also been captured in these figures showing significant drop in the current year's figure.

TABLE 9.12

Values of Export / Import of WB with Bangladesh

YEARS	*EXPORT (E) (Rs. in Crore)*	*IMPORT (I) (Rs. in Crore)*	*E : I*	*E – I*	*E – I / E*
(1)	(2)	(3)	(4)	(5)	(6)
2000-2001	4095.92	221.46	1 : 0.054	3874.46	0.94593616
2001-2002	3709.93	176.86	1 : 0.047	3533.18	0.95232794
2002-2003	3930.24	212.72	1 : 0.054	3717.52	0.94587607
2003-2004	5230.00	205.53	1 : 0.039	5024.47	0.96071720
2004-2005	6516.73	287.38	1 : 0.044	6228.93	0.95590120

Source: Office of the Commissioner of Customs, Kolkata.

The same striking features have also been displayed in Table 9.12 with much higher values to the advantage of India. The trade surplus values (E – I) in column 5 assumes much higher values than those of NER. This fact has been reflected by the values in columns 4, and 6.

This phenomenon makes worthwhile a comparison between NER and WB in so far as trade surplus is concerned. A comparison has been attempted in Table 9.13 by calculating ratios to show how many times the values of exports, imports and trade surpluses WB are over those of NER.

TABLE 9.13

A Comparison of the Values of Export / Import and Trade Surplus of NER and WB

YEAR	E_{WB}/E_{NER}	I_{WB}/I_{NER}	$(E\text{-}I)_{WB}/(E\text{-}I)_{NER}$
(1)	(2)	(3)	(4)
2000-2001	27.08	30.80	29.590
2001-2002	20.08	32.04	19.710
2002-2003	19.40	34.87	18.913
2003-2004	21.96	17.84	22.166
2004-2005	34.22	14.73	36.446

Source: Office of the Commissioner of Customs, Kolkata and Shillong (calculated).

It may be seen from Table 9.13 that the legal trade performance of WB has always been several times better in terms of value over last 5 years, though the number of operative LCSs is less (9) than those of NER (15). The values of export of WB are found to be more than 19 to 34 times (Column 2 Table 9.13) and imports more than 14 to 30 times (Column 3) and trade surplus more than 19 to 36 times (Column 4), than those of NER during last five years. This relative position of WB and NER might not hold good if items, which did not feature in the composition of the officially traded commodities, were taken into account. For instance, some important items namely, cows, bullocks and buffaloes for which Bangladesh is heavily dependent on India, are not found in the official list of export of WB and NER.

Informal Trade

The informal component of the border trade between India and Bangladesh is substantial. It is very difficult to estimate this component and to add that to the total volume of trade. Informal or illegal trade takes place not only through regular routes but through other routes as well, which escapes the notice of the BSF and Customs personnel. In spite of present arrangements of surveillance and vigil the international border in this region is highly porous.

It is said that the illegal imports and exports are as large as their formal counterparts (Rahman 2004). In another estimate the ratio of legal to illegal import from India stands to 1: 1.5. Still another estimate (Bakht 1996) of informal exports to India may have been at least 6 times higher than legal exports.

"Compared to illegal import, Bangladesh provides only a limited number of items as illegal exports to India. Gold is the most important item of illegal export from Bangladesh to India. As high as Tk 721 million worth of gold might have been exported through only three centres (Shibgonj, Daulatpur and Karimganj) during 1988" (Rahman :2004).

Notwithstanding the fact that illegal volume of trade is very high, the doubt about the accuracy of the estimates cannot be ruled out. The official figure of illegal trade, which may be known from the record of seizure, though an underestimate of the ground reality, is also substantial. They do not suffer from the error of estimate. The following are the figures of illegal trade reflected in seizure figure (Table 9.14).

TABLE 9.14

Indo-Bangladesh Seizure Figure of NER

Year	*Case*	*Value (Rs. in Lakh)*
2000-2001	6828	528.17
2001-2002	7274	892.18
2002-2003	7405	969.83
2003-2004	7687	581.90
2004-2005	7789	813.27

Source: Office of the Commissioner of Customs, Shillong.

From Table 9.14 we find that total number of seizure cases during last five years is 36,983 and the total value works out to be Rs. 37.85 crores. If we compare this with the corresponding figures of West Bengal border, which are 24475 and Rs. 22.94 crores, we find that number of cases of seizure and their values in NER are more than those of West Bengal border. In addition, it is interesting to note that the value of seizure per case in WB is Rs. 9,373 and that of NER is Rs. 10,235 which is more. The possible reason behind this higher value may be due to the fact that very high value goods get smuggled in or out through the NER border. It may, however, be relevant in this context to know from government source the main items of smuggled goods across Indo-Bangladesh border in NER (Table 9.15).

TABLE 9.15

Main Items of Smuggling across Indo-Bangladesh Border

1. Shillong Sector (Khasi & Jaintia Hills of Meghalaya

Items illegally exported	*Items illegally imported*
Bidi	Gold
Sugar	Currency
Motor parts	Pirated CDs
Betel leaves & nuts	Audio cassette
Ganja	Cheap cosmetics
Phensedyl	Cigarettes
Liquor	Potato chips
Timber	Dry fish
Boulder stone	

2. Agartala Sector (State of Tripura other than North Tripura):

Items illegally exported	*Items illegally imported*
Cotton Sarees	Rape seed oil
Metal Scrap	Ready made garments
Phensedyl	Old Garments (wind cheater, jackets)
Sugar	Synthetic Fabrics
Bidi	Garlic of Chinese origin
Ganja	Dried peas
	Fruit drinks
	Fish
	GCI Sheets

3. Karimganj Sector (Districts of Southern Assam and North Tripura bordering Bangladesh):

Items illegally exported	*Items illegally imported*
Bidi	Ready made garment
Cattle	Vegetable oil
Electrical Items	Gas lighters
Motor Parts	Synthetic fabrics
Sugar	Soap
Kerosene oil	Potato chips
Diesel	

4. Dhubri Sector (Garo Hills region of Meghalaya and Dhubri/Goalpara Districts of Assam):

Items illegally exported	*Items illegally imported*
Ganja	Readymade garments
Sugar	Fish
Betel nuts	Dry Fish
Betel leaves	CDs
Diesel	
Livestock	
Liquor	

Source: Office of the Commissioner of Customs, Shillong.

TABLE 9.16

List of Items according to Perceived Change in Volume Traded

Significant Increase :	Imports : Cows and bullocks, buffaloes, ruhi fish, pulses, salt, sugar, powder milk, satellite receiver, blade, matches, fishing net, pesticides.
	Exports : Hilsha fish
Moderate Increase :	Imports : Shrimp, hides & skins, betel leaf, grapes, oranges, potatoes, onion, garlic, cardamom, timber, bidi, cotton saree, medicine, glass, bicycle tyre, fertilizer.
	Exports : Copper, brass and bell metals, gold.
Moderate Decrease :	Imports : Cigarettes, Non-Indian bedsheets and Towels, thaan cloth, warm clothing, hair oil, ceramic-ware, stainless steel utensils, table fan, misc. electrical fittings, diesel, kerosene.
	Exports : Used cloth
Significant Decrease :	Imports : Toilet soap, VCP, TV, yarn
	Exports: Synthetic textiles, urea, C.I. sheet, VCP.

Bakht, Zaid (1996), "Cross Border Illegal Trade in Bangladesh: Composition, Trends and Policy Issues", BIDS.

Doubt occurs about the exhaustiveness of the list of illegally traded or smuggled goods given by the government agencies, if we look at the increase and decrease of illegal inflow and outflow of goods into and out of Bangladesh in first three years of the 1990s. According to the perceptions of majority of respondents in a study (Bakht :1996) "there has been a significant increase in inflow of illegal imports into Bangladesh and a considerable decline in the outflow of illegal exports out of Bangladesh.....".

There is no apparent reason behind reversal of this perception even today. If it is so, then surely the official statements of composition and volume of traded commodities, legal and illegal, suffer from errors of omission and/or commission willy-nilly.

A close look at the smuggled items across Indo-Bangladesh border (Table 9.15) makes it evident that the goods smuggled include high value materials like gold, prohibited articles like narcotics, drugs, liquor, ganja etc and also goods produced in countries outside India and Bangladesh. Besides that the items which appear in the list of officially imported and exported items like boulders stone, betel leaf and nuts, dry fish, readymade garments, synthetic fabrics, motor parts, fruit drinks, fish electrical items, potato chips also are smuggled. This may be because of prohibitive tariff, non-tariff barrier like high cost of documentation, wide variation of the method of assessment of duties, failure of SAPTA negotiation etc. In addition to that lack of adequate physical infrastructure at the border check-post and lack of transit rights also account for the indulgence in smuggling across the border (Rahman: 2004).

Infrastructure to facilitate Cross Border Trade

From the above discussion three important points, among others, have come out without any scope for doubt. One, the steadily increasing trade balance in favour of India has run adverse to Bangladesh economy; two, the contingent of illegal trade is on the increase to the detriment of both the economies, and, in India, illegal trade volume and value is relatively more in NER than WB, and three, there are valid reasons to hypothesize that scope exists for increasing the volume of formal and reducing the volume of illegal trade to the benefit of both the nations. In the sense that the absolute volume of trade and value of both the nations might increase and the balance of trade of Bangladesh might also increase having overall favourable impact on Bangladesh economy.

One of the important factors for bringing about these favourable changes is to improve the infrastructure facilities of both the nations having bearing on the connectivity needed for smooth border trade activities. This will not only create condition favourable for international trade but intra-national trade as well. Improvement in rail, road and riverine transport infrastructure will immensely benefit both the nations (Halder: 1997).

There are ample scope for improvement of all these systems, and if they are adequately developed, much of the illegal traffic will be reduced, as more efficient patrolling and control may be exercised in the border areas and, the infrastructure bottlenecks being removed, the smooth movement of commodities on the either side will be possible boosting up the volume in response to demands generated in both the countries (Bera, Konar, and Halder: 2003).

The historical factor should also be kept in mind in so far as planning and construction of infrastructure of the said type is concerned. What is necessary is a coordinated effort of both the nations toward the success of such a project. The historical factor is that the rail, road, riverine and coastal shipping connections that already existed before partition, are still there upto the border. They are also operative to a certain extent on both the sides. The marginal expenditure to restore that connectivity will yield a very high social productivity to be shared by both the nations.

With the advancement of technology in the era of liberalised socio economic ethos – as both the nations are wedded to the principles of LPG – much greater benefit can be reaped in terms of economic gain, improvement of man to man relation, and reduction of diplomatic complications and social tensions.

Railway Link

Right at this moment, India has five railway links with Bangladesh, three of them have broad gauge and two meter gauge

The Broad Gauge lines are:

1. Gede-Darshana
2. Rohanpur-Singabad
3. Petrapole-Benapole

The meter gauge lines are:

1. Radhikapur-Biral, and
2. Mahisasan-Sahabajpur.

The full advantage of these railway linkages could be taken by Bangaldesh if the Jumuna Bridge (Bangabandhu Setu, commissioned in 1991) is made open to Indian Railways so as to make the container movement possible. If it is done, the advantage to Bangladesh economy would be many fold more in terms of cost and time saving. A simple example can be cited in this regard. A twenty ton container, from, say, Ludhiana or Delhi to Dhaka, at present takes a round about way, first to Columbo and then to Dhaka via Chittagong costing more than $1000, which could be reduced to its half or even less if it could be carried through Jamuna Bridge. Therefore, improvement of railway link from Indian side is not good enough if it is not complemented by similar improvement from Bangladesh side.

Map 9.1
Indo-Bangladesh Rail Link

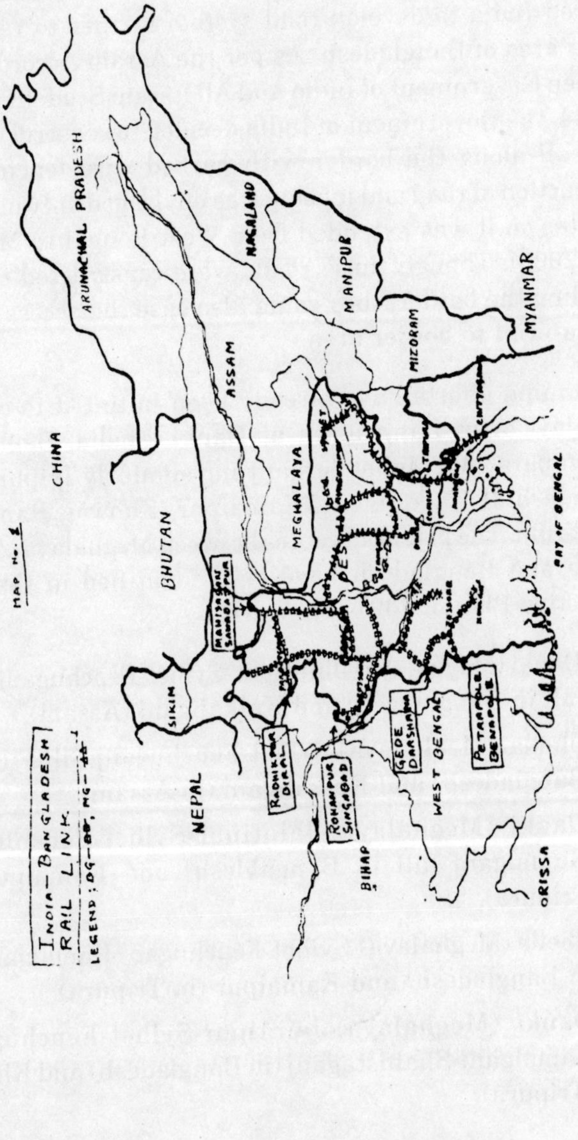

Road Network

The other infrastructure is the road network connecting Bangladesh with India. It is already reasonably developed on Indian side and recent realisation of its necessity has inspired India to develop road system further to reach the border area of Bangladesh. As per the Assam Accord signed between Government of India and All Assam Students' Union in 1984, the Government of India decided to construct border roads all along the border with barbed wire fencing. The construction of road and fencing was envisaged only in Assam but later on it was extended from West Bengal to Mizoram (Deb. 2005). Though these roads were constructed only for patrolling the border, they could also ease the access of men and material to border area.

Planning efforts have already been initiated to connect Meghalaya with Bangladesh at Dauki, Shella, Baghmara, Burengapara, and Mahenderganj and similarly Tripura with Bangladesh at Kalkalighat, Kamalpur, Khowai, Ranibazar and Sabrum. The potential routes between Meghalaya, Assam, Tripura and Bangladesh have been identified in the NER Perspective Plan of 2021. They are:

"1. Dauki (Meghalaya)-Jaintipur-Sylhet-Fenchuganj-Silua (all in Bangladesh) and Kalkaliganj (Assam).
2. Shella (Meghalaya)-Sylhet-Fenchuganj-Silua (all in Bangladesh) and Kalkaliganj (in Assam).
3. Dauki (Meghalaya)-Jaintipur-Sylhet-Fenchuganj-Kamalganj (all in Bangaldesh) and Kamalpur (in Tripura).
4. Shella (Meghalaya)-Sylhet-Fenchuganj-Kamalganj (all in Bangladesh) and Kamalpur (in Tripura).
5. Dauki (Meghalaya)-Jaintipur-Sylhet-Fenchuganj-Kamalganj-Shahistaganj (in Bangladesh) and Khowai (Tripura).

6. Shella (Meghalaya)-Sylhet-Fenchuganj-Kamlaganj-Shahistaganj (in Bangladesh)-Khowai (Tripura).
7. Dauki (Meghalaya)-Sylhet-Habiganj-Shahistaganj (in Bangladesh)-Khowai (in Tripura).
8. Shella (Meghalaya)-Sylhet-Habiganj-Shahistaganj (in Bangladesh)-Khowai (Tripura).
9. Baghmara (in Meghalaya)-Durgapur-Jaria Jhanjali-Shamganj-Bhairab Bazar-Comilla, Ramgarh (in Bangladesh) and Sabrum (in Tripura).
10. Burengapara (in Meghalaya)- Piarpur-Begunbari-Dhaka-Comilla-Ramgarh (all in Bangladesh) and Sabrum (in Tripura)
11. Mehendergarh(Meghalaya)-Nandina-Piarpur-Begunbari-Dhaka-Comilla-Ramgarh (all in Bangadesh) and Sabrum (in Tripura).

By linking Mizoram at Tiabung with Bangladesh a shorter route between Mizoram and Tripura (at Sabrum) can be developed. Apart from this, alternate routes between Mizoram and Meghalaya can be developed through Bangladesh via Chittagong and Dhaka (Ranganathan and Rajeev Sapra: 2005).

Initiative from the Bangladesh side should also be there to take advantage of this road infrastructure development on Indian side. For instance, the road links between Kolkata upto Dhaka and from Dhaka to Tripura already exist. If a corridor from West Bengal through Dhaka is allowed to reach Agartala by road, it will become highly advantageous both for India and Bangladesh in so far as trade and commerce is concerned. The advantage of India would be in terms of reduction of distance from, say, Kolkata to Agartala, which is about 1738 kilometers and 1680 kilometers by railway road at present, gets reduced to about 450 kilometers which is about 1/4th of the present distance. This will encourage

Map 9.2
Kolkata-Agartala Road Link Via Dhaka

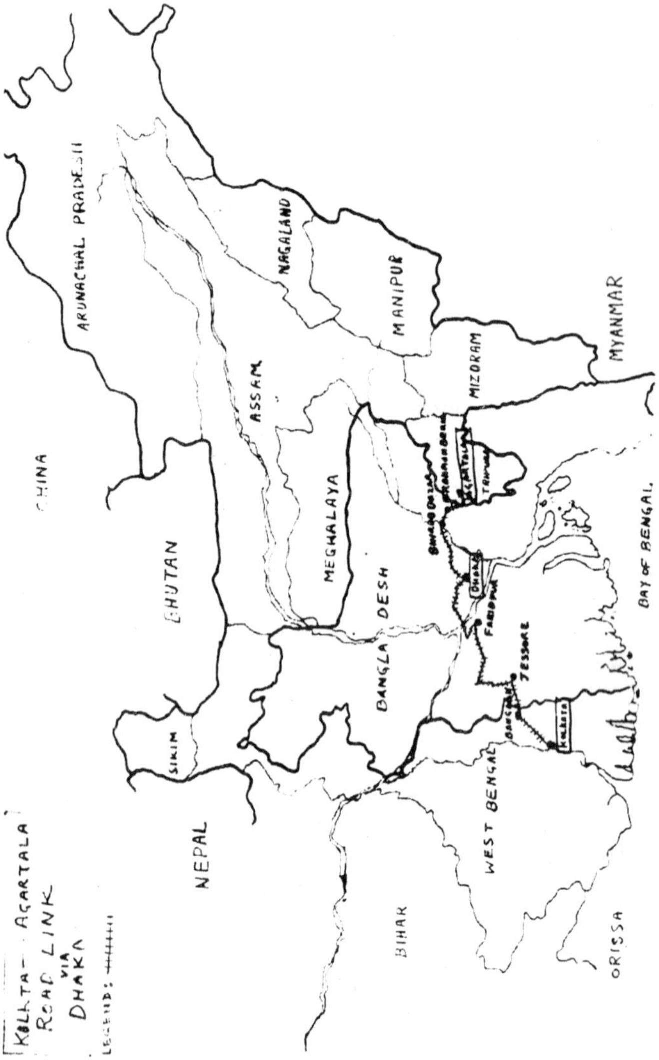

trade between India and Bangladesh, within Bangladesh and between one part of India with the other. This will not only help international but intranational trade of India and Bangladesh.

River System

Besides rail and road connections, river routes from Kolkata and Haldia on Indian side right up to Silchar through Khulna, Barishal, Bhairab Bazar, Sylhet and Karimganj is possible. Again, from the same origin in India by the same river route movement is possible up to Chandpur and therefrom taking a left turn through Padma and Jamuna, riverine transport can go up to Dhubri in Assam and can proceed along Brahmaputra river right up to Rashighat through Dibrugarh, even further up. At present two routes, from Kolkata through Bangladesh destined to Guwahati and Karimganj, are operative. But it takes 7 to 8 days to cover this distance because night journey is not possible due to lack of visibility. Proper lighting arrangement would have reduced this transit time to half. Besides, earlier the permit to move across Bangladesh used to be given for three years at a stretch, now it has come down to one month only. That means every month the permit has to be obtained without any guarantee that it would be available in the next month which exposes the users and operators of river transport systems to extreme uncertainty. These riverine routes would obviously be much more cost effective and echo-friendly to the advantage of both India and Bangladesh, which is universally accepted. Development of this system depends upon the mutual understanding and good intention to have well orchestrated programme of action to the mutual benefits of the two nations.

Concluding Observations

1. Indo-Bangladesh border is the longest of all the borders that India shares with her neighbouring nations, stretching

Map 9.3
India-Bangladesh River Link

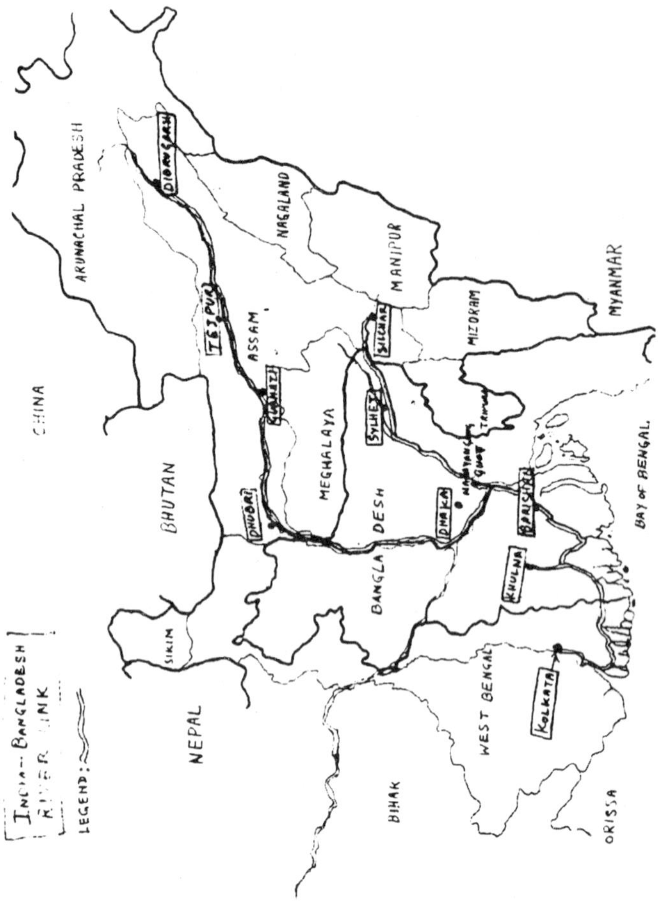

over 4,184 kms. Naturally the commodity composition of cross-border trade will be most diverse and the problems associated with border trade are likely to commensurate. It is difficult to maintain and manage this long border, as this boundary is not a natural one. As such it is highly porous making cross border movement of men, material, animals and criminals easier.

2. Bangladesh, being literally surrounded by land on all sides except a small land window of 200 kms, which she shares with Myanmar at the south-eastern corner of her territory, cannot but utilize the landmass of India for movement of men and material across the border. Hence the lion's share of border trade on land has to be transacted with India, making India a natural trade partner.

3. The location of industrial and agricultural activity conditioned by geophysical situation and natural endowments of undivided Bengal, which created an economic complementarity between East-Bengal and West Bengal, and as a result, almost all the industries got located in West Bengal and agricultural activities in East Bengal. That complementarity still exits long after the Partition creating the compulsion for cross border trade, which is felt much more intensely by Bangladesh.

4. The more intensely felt compulsion of cross border trade by Bangladesh got reflected in her commodity composition, volume and values of import and export which have been analysed in the preceding sections. It has been observed by analysing the data on commodities exported and imported both by India and Bangladesh through NER border and West Bengal border, that large variety of commodities are exported and imported officially from the operative LCSs of WB and NER to Bangladesh.

5. It has also been found out that 97 per cent of exports from NER constitute minerals and raw materials like coal, lime stone, boulders, stone chips etc. Besides that, consumer goods – agricultural and industrial, manufactured goods like machinery, equipments, paper, marble stones etc are also exported. One of the important items for which Bangladesh depends heavily on India belongs to cows, bullocks, and buffaloes do not feature in the official records of LCS.

6. In the analysis of the official data on composition and value of the exported commodities though NER, five items out of 64 are found to be stable over last five years and the rest are not so stable and thirty-five items were exported only once in five years. In the list of imported goods through NER only two items hilsa fish and dry fish have their presence in the basket of imported commodities in all the five years and the rest are not stable.

7. This raises suspicion about the correctness about the composition and volume of the commodity flow records at the disposal of the Government. This suspicion is heightened by a study made in Bangladesh on cross border illegal trade (Bakht: 1996).

8. A list of seizure is available from the Government source which gives a picture of the smuggled goods across the border of both the sides. This list also does not give a complete picture. A close scrutiny of the list of smuggled goods and their values give an idea of the nature of smuggled goods, in which it has been found that the goods imported illegally constitute precious metal like gold, and many of the prohibited articles like narcotic drugs, liquor, ganja etc. and also the goods which are permissible by official channel. But some important items like, cows, bullocks and buffaloes do not feature in the list.

9. The analysis of the value of trade surplus shows that India is gaining over time and Bangladesh is loosing. To correct this imbalance, initiative should be taken by Bangladesh by improving infrastructure facilities and good neighbourly relationship with India.

10. A comparative analysis of the formal cross border trade of NER and West Bengal gives a much higher value of the trade surplus of West Bengal border. As a matter of fact it is several times more than that of NER which ranges between 18.9 to 36.4 times. It raises the suspicion that NER is more vulnerable to illegal trade and smuggling

11. Looking at the value of Indo-Bangladesh seizure figure it appears that illegal trade is more in NER than in West Bengal border and the average value per case is higher in NER than West Bengal.

12. Infrastructure development has an important role to boost up official cross border trade and to reduce illegal trade by facilitating vigilance and control.

13. There is ample scope for improving connectivity between India and Bangladesh in terms of rail, road, and riverine transport system though the existing infrastructure on Indian side is more or less reasonably developed.

14. Corresponding development of infrastructure on Bangladesh side in an orchestrated manner might go a long way to increase return from cross border trade to be shared by both the nations.

15. From Indian side there are several road and rail development projects to improve connectivity with the border areas. If corresponding projects are completed at the Bangaldesh side, the cross-border trade will get a boost.

16. The acceptance of the proposal to open up Bangabadnhu Bridge to Indian rail system and road connectivity between Kolkata and Agartala through Bangladesh might benefit both the trading partners by improving cross-border trade and man-to-man relations.

APPENDIX

TABLE 9.17A

Land Frontiers and Land Custom Stations (LCSs) of WB and NER

Sl. No.	*Land Frontiers (Districts)*	*Sl. No.*	*Land Customs Station (LCS)*
	WEST BENGAL		
1.	Calcutta and Howrah	1.	Armenion and Kulpighat Steamer Station
		2.	Baghbazar Rly. Station
		3.	Baja Ghat
		4.	Bandhaghat and Moraporaghat
		5.	Bengal River Service Godown next to Nimatolaghat
		6.	Calcutta Jetties No. 4 & 6
		7.	Chitpur Railway Station and Dhanighat River Station
		8.	Cossipore Railway Station and Cossipore Hydralic Press Ghat
		9.	Government Salt Gola Salkia
		10.	Hanuman Jute Press Ghat and Panditghat.
		11.	Howrah Coal Depot.
		12.	Howrah Railway Station
		13.	Jagannath Ghat Steamer Station and Rajaghat
		14.	Kantapukur Rly. Station
		15.	Nimtala Rly. Station and Katgolaghat
		16.	Outramghat
		17.	Pathuriaghat
		18.	Rajabazar Dock Yard
		19.	Rathcola Rly. Stn
		20.	Sahebbazar Rly Stn.

District	Location
	21. Sealdah Railway Stn
	22. Shalimar Coal Depot
	23. Surinamghat
	24. *T T Shed (Kidderpur)
	25. Ultadanga Rly. Stn.
	26. Union South Jute Mill Shed
2. Cooch Behar	27. Bamanhat Rly. Stn.
	28. Changrabandha
	29. *Chandrabandh Rly. Stn
	30. Gitaldah Rly. Stn
	31. Gitaldah River
	32. Gitalda Road
	33. Haldibari Rly. Stn.
	34. Hassimara Rly. Stn.
3. Darjeeling	35. Phulbari
4. Malda	36. *Kotawalighat (Mohedipur
	37. *Singabad Rly Stn
5. Murshidabad	38. Dhulion
	39. Gede Rly Stn.
	40. Khanduaghat
	41. Lalgola Town
	42. *Ranaghat Rly. Stn
	43. Tungi
6. 24 Parganas	44. Bangaon Rly. Stn
	45. Budge Budge
	46. *Ghojadanga
	47. Hingalganj
	48. Jalalpur
	49. Naihati
	50. Namkhana
	51. Orient Jute Mill Jetty
	52. *Petrapole Rly Stn.
	53. Petrapole Road
7. West Dinajpur	54. Dangi
	55. *Hilli (West)
	56. Kukrahaha
	57. *Radhikapur Rly. Stn.
8. Purnia	58. Katihar Rly. Stn

	ASSAM		
1.	Cachar	1.	*Karimganj Ferry Stn
		2.	Karimganj Rly. Stn
		3.	Karimganj Steamerghat
		4.	Latu Bazar
		5.	Mahisasan Rly. Stn
		6.	Silchar R.M.S. Office
		7.	Silchar Steamerghat
		8.	Sutarkandi
2.	Darang	9.	Tejpur Steamerghat
3.	Goalpara	10.	*Dhubri Steamerghat
		11.	Golakganj Rly St.
		12.	*Manikarchar
4.	Kamrup	13.	Guahati Steamerghat
5.	Sibsagar	14.	Neamati Steamer Ghat
	MEGHALAYA		
1.	Garo Hills	15.	*Baghmara
		16.	*Dalu
		17.	*Ghasuapara
		18.	*Mahendraganj
2.	Jaintia Hills	19.	*Dawki
3.	Khasi Hills	20.	Balet
		21.	Bolanganj
		22.	*Borsora
		23.	Ryngku
		24.	*Shella Bazar
	MIZORAM		
1.	Lungili	25.	Demagiri
	TRIPURA		
1.	Tripura North	26.	Dhalighat
		27.	Manu (Kailasahar) Sub-Stn
2.	Tripura South	28.	Muhurighat
		29.	Sabrum
3.	Tripura West	30.	*Agartala
		31.	Khowaighat
		32.	*Srimantapur

The asterisks (*) indicate operative LCS.

Source: Office of the Commissioner of Customs, Kolkata and Shillong.

REFERENCES

Bakht, Zaid (1996), *Cross Border Illegal Trade in Bangladesh: Composition, Trends and Policy Issues,* BIDS.

Bera, Debasis; Konar, Dhirendra Nath and Dilip Halder (2003), "Road Infrastructure and its Role on Economic Cooperation between West Bengal and Bangladesh", *Artha Beekshan*, Vol. 13, No 3, December.

Deb, Pankaj Kumar (ed.) (2005), *Past the Chicken's Neck: A Study of Transportation in North Eastern India,* New Joykali Press, Kolkata.

Halder, Dilip (1997), "Technoeconomic Cooperation and Bilateral Trade Prospects between India and Bangaldesh", in B. K. Jahangir and Jayanta Kumar Roy, (eds) *India Bangladesh Cooperation Brodening Measures*, K. P. Bagchi & Company, Calcutta.

Rahman, Atier (2004), "Bangladesh-India Economic Relations: Potential and Imperatives", *Artha Beekshan*, Journal of Bangiya Arthaniti Parishad (Bengal Economic Association), Vol. 13, No. 3, December.

Ranganathan N.P., Rajeev Sapra (2005), "Development of Transport Network in North East India to Promote India's International Trade with China and Other Countries", in Jayanta Kumar Roy and Prabir De, (eds), *India and China in an Era of Globalisation: Essays On Economic Cooperation*, Bookwell, New Delhi.

[Acknowledgement: Author is indebted to Mr. J.S.R. Khathing, Chief Commissioner, Central Excise & Customs, Mr. Arabinda Dutta, Mr J.N. Dutta, Mr. Swarup Gupta, IRTS (Rtd.), Mr. Debasis Bera, Mr. Debjyoti Bhattacharyya and Mr. Tapan Chakraborty for their kind help and cooperation in writing this paper.]

10

THE NATURE OF INDO-BANGLADESH BORDER TRADE: A CASE STUDY OF MALDA DISTRICT OF WEST BENGAL

Pankaj Kundu

Introduction

Bangladesh has a long-standing relationship with India due to its historical position, geographical contiguity and cultural heritage. Heavy population pressure-3 percent average annual growth rate of labour force (1990-99) (World Bank: 2001) coupled with poor industrial base and failure in agricultural sector have made the country dependent on other countries for food and other commodities. The malaise of underdevelopment in Bangladesh compels her to go for international trade, mainly to import. Geographically, most part of Bangladesh is surrounded by India except a smaller southeastern part touching with Myanmar. Within India, West Bengal has the most convenient international border with Bangladesh. As a result Bangladesh finds it most convenient to make trade with India through international border points of West Bengal.

It is commonly known that international trade between two countries depends on various tariff and non-tariff barriers. However, after the Uruguay Round of WTO talk, which ensures the lowering of tariff protection regime, the non-tariff barriers have assumed a special significance for international trade. Trade between India and Bangladesh is carried out as per the Indo-Bangladesh trade agreement which provides "Most Favoured Nation" treatment to goods and services of both countries .The prospects of border trade between India and Bangladesh may get a substantial boost after the South Asian Free Trade Area (SAFTA) agreement among the South Asian countries comes into effect from 1st January 2006.

Indo-Bangladesh trade flows through two channels: official or formal and unofficial or informal. Official trade flows through the Land Customs Stations (LCSs)/ customs check posts along the international border points between India and Bangladesh. West Bengal has a number of LCSs at different places of nine bordering districts. Lion's share of India's official international trade with Bangladesh is carried out through these LCSs of West Bengal. Among the nine bordering districts of West Bengal, Malda district is unique due to its location. This particular border district is situated almost at the middle of the western bordering part of Bangladesh. Since Malda is situated at the mid point of Bangladesh, the benefit of international trade can well be percolated throughout Bangladesh at the minimum of transportation cost. Perhaps, due to Malda's geographical proximity with Bangladesh the headquarters of Malda Divisional Customs office has been established in this district. The Malda customs division comprises two bordering districts, namely Malda and South Dinajpur with three LCSs. While South Dinajpur has only one LCS, Hilli, connected by road, Malda has two LCSs, viz., Mahadipur-connected by road and Singabad LCS linked by rail for trading. Malda district has the distinction of having both road and rail transportation facilities for carrying international freight through LCSs.

The pattern of imports of Bangladesh shown in Table 10.1 represents the contemporary demand structure of that country. All food items along with agricultural raw materials constitute 33.20 percent of total imports of Bangladesh.

TABLE 10.1

Imports of Bangladesh: 1991

Commodity Group	*Percentage Share of Total Imports*
All food items	29.90
Agricultural raw materials	3.30
Fuels	13.70
Ores and Minerals	2.50
Manufactured goods	50.20
Unallocated	0.40
Total	100.00

Source: The Least Development Countries 1995 Reports, UNCTAD, UN

Bangladesh imports host of goods through the two LCSs of Malda. The Malda route is mainly used for the export of agricultural commodities to Bangladesh. The local agricultural products have had some contribution in evolving out this kind of trade through this route. The economic viability of the Indo-Bangladesh trade route in Malda can well be attributed to the factors, namely, communication facilities of Malda with the rest of the country, the locational advantage of Malda District with Bangladesh and the demand pattern of Bangladesh.

Objectives

The present chapter attempts to analyse the nature of Indo-Bangladesh border trade carried out through the LCSs. As we have already mentioned in the previous section that non-tariff barriers play a crucial role in border trade, this paper also attempts to identify the physical barriers, which ultimately enhance transaction cost of trading. Finally, an attempt is made to point out the issues in order to over come the physical bottlenecks of trade. Our analysis is confined mainly to formal trade with few passing remarks to informal trade.

Data Base and Methodology

The study is basically based on secondary data. The secondary data have been collected from the different official sources. Some information were elicited from the exporters / importers as well as the government officials through personal interviews. Simple tabular presentations have been made for the analysis of secondary data.

Importance of the LCS of Malda

The importance of the LCS of Malda can be judged on three major considerations, the total value of export, the total value of import and the total revenue earned by the government of India.

TABLE 10.2

Value of Export Through the LCSs of Malda

(Rs. in Crore)

Year	*Mahadipur LCS*	*Singabad LCS*	*Total*
2000-2001	430.36	41.20	471.56
2001-2002	508.82	91.53	600.35
2002-2003	418.54	159.52	578.06
2003-2004	561.95	152.52	714.47
2004-2005	572.92	196.16	769.08
Total	2492.59	640.93	3133.52

Source: Office of the Superintendent, Mahadipur LCS & Singabad LCS, Malda.

TABLE 10.3

Value of Import Through the LCSs of Malda

(Rs. in Crore)

Year	*Mahadipur LCS*	*Singabad LCS*	*Total*
2000-2001	0.08	—	0.08
2001-2002	1.65	—	1.65
2002-2003	9.87	—	9.87
2003-2004	2.67	4.42	7.09
2004-2005	1.94	3.49	5.43
Total	16.21	7.91	24.12

Source: Office of the Superintendent, Mahadipur LCS & Singabad LCS, Malda.

Table 10.2 reveals that the average value of exports per year for the last five years from 2000-01 to 2004-05 through the LCSs of Malda is Rs. 626.70 crores .It means that on an average LCSs of Malda carry 13 per cent of total official border trade done through the 9 operational LCSs of West Bengal. A clear rising trend of the value of exports through both the LCSs of the district is observed from Table 10. 2 .The value of imports has also exhibited an increasing trend (Table 10.3), however, the total value of import compared to total value of export is very negligible.

TABLE 10.4

Government Revenue Earning from the LCSs of Malda, 2003-04

(Rs. In Lakh)

Name of The LCS	*Export cess*	*Import Duty*	*M.O.T.& other*	*Total Revenue*
Mahadipur	171.32	118.96	13.92	304.20
Singabad	45.96	144.33	-	190.29
Total	217.28	263.29	13.92	494.49

Source: Office of the Superintendent, Mahadipur LCS & Singabad LCS, Malda.

Revenue earned by the government from these two LCSs has been presented in Table 10.4-10.5. The average revenue earning per year from these two LCSs together stood Rs. 4.65 Crore.

Export cess is collected from the exportable agricultural commodities and this rate is very minimal. Despite the minimal rate, export cess collection exceeds to Rs. 2 crores in each year. On the other hand, import duty collection is quite significant, although the total value of imports as percentage of total value of border trade is negligible. This high value of total import duty arises due to high rate of import duty. The collection under the head of M.O.T & others, i.e. Merchant Over Time & other is an indicator of pressure of trade at the LCS.

TABLE 10.5

Government Revenue from the LCSs of Malda, 2004-05

(Rs. In Lakh)

Name of The LCS	*Export cess*	*Import Duty*	*M.O.T.& other*	*Total Revenue*
Mahadipur	171.32	118.96	13.92	304.20
Mahadipur	174.96	62.45	3.04	240.45
Singabad	54.33	141.25	—	195.58
Total	229.29	203.70	3.04	436.03

Source: Office of the Superintendent, Mahadipur LCS & Singabad LCS, Malda.

The Mahadipur LCS collected Rs. 13.92 lakh in 2003-04 on this account. Assessment of export / import applications are not undertaken on Sunday and government holidays. If the exporters / importers under compulsion request the customs officials to assess the application during these days, the M.O.T. is charged from the exporters / importers on hourly basis for overtime allowances of customs staffs. It is observed that the M.O.T. collection is higher at Mahadipur

LCS as perishable agricultural commodities are exported through this port.

Thus, considering the importance of the LCSs of Malda, it would be appropriate to analyse the nature of the border trade through the LCSs of Malda which may throw some light about the growing importance of trade between India and Bangladesh.

Nature of Trade Through the LCSs of Malda

The flow of trade through the LCSs of Malda has increased significantly for the last couple of years. Earlier maximum volume of trade in Malda customs division was carried out through Hilli LCS but presently it flows through the two LCSs of Malda. However, apart from the growing importance of Malda as a viable LCS, the choice of Bangladesh importer is another definite reason for the shift of trade route from one port to another. The two other reasons may also explain the increasing volume of Indo-Bangladesh border trade through the LCSs of Malda district. First, Bangladesh is of high demand of boulders and stone-chips, wheat and maize. While boulders and stone chips are available in plenty in Rajmahal Hills of Jharkhand and wheat and maize are produced in abundance in Bihar. Contiguity of Bihar and Jharkhand with Malda facilitates the exports of these items through LCSs of Malda at a lesser cost. Another factor that may have caused the growth of trade through Malda LCSs is the shifting of informal trade to formal trade channels. A considerable volume of unofficial or informal trade may have been shifted to formal channel due to border fencing operations. The Malda customs division has total 421 kms. of bordering area with Bangladesh. The border fencing has been completed nearly 75 percent of the total area. The border fencing has checked the smuggling of goods to a great extent except cattle smuggling (Pramanik: 2004).

Personal interviews with the villagers residing near the border as well as with the government officials reveal that smuggling of bulk consignment of commodities is now thing of the past in those areas where border fencing has been completed. All these factors may have caused to rise in the volume of trade through the LCSs of Malda.

In order to analyse the nature of trade, it is essential to know the composition of commodities traded. Despite our best effort to collect the commodity composition for the last five years, we have been successful to procure only for two years, i.e., 2003-04 and 2004-05 data. Notwithstanding, the data limitation has not influenced the result of our analysis, as these two years are very normal years (devoid of anything unusual like flood, drought, war etc.) for both India and Bangladesh. Indian exports to Bangladesh through Mahadipur and Singabad LCSs shown in tables 10.6-10.9 for both years of 2003-04 and 2004-05 depict more than 84 percent of total export flow to Bangladesh involves agricultural commodities only.

TABLE 10.6

Indian Exports to Bangladesh Through Mahadipur LCS: 2003-04

Commodity Group	*Value (Rs. in Crore)*	*% To Total*
Agricultural Commodities	489.56	87.12
Manufactured goods and others	72.39	12.88
Total	561.95	100.00

Source: Office of the superintendent, Mahadipur LCS, Malda.

TABLE 10.7

Indian Exports to Bangladesh Through Mahadipur LCS: 2004-05

Commodity Group	*Value (Rs. in Crore)*	*% To Total*
Agricultural Commodities	523.21	91.32
Manufactured goods and others	49.71	8.68
Total	572.92	100.00

Source: Office of the superintendent, Mahadipur LCS, Malda.

The major elements of agricultural commodities include non-basmaṭi rice, pulses, wheat, maize, fresh-fruits, fresh vegetables, onions, spices etc. The local agricultural products like non-basmati rice, pulses, fresh-fruits, fresh vegetables of the district find a good market in Bangladesh. The fly ash from Farakka Thermal Project and boulders and stone-chips from Jharkhand constitute the major elements of manufactured goods and others through the LCS of Malda.

TABLE 10.8

Indian Exports to Bangladesh Through Singabad LCS: 2003-04

Commodity Group	*Value (Rs. in Crore)*	*% To Total*
Agricultural Commodities	128.20	84.05
Manufactured goods and others	24.32	15.95
Total	152.52	100.00

Source: Office of the superintendent, Singabad LCS, Malda.

TABLE 10.9

Indian Exports to Bangladesh Through Singabad LCS: 2004-05

Commodity Group	*Value (Rs. in Crore)*	*% To Total*
Agricultural Commodities	173.60	88.50
Manufactured goods and others	22.56	11.50
Total	196.16	100.00

Source: Office of the superintendent, Singabad LCS, Malda.

As the flow of agricultural commodities export to Bangladesh through Mahadipur LCS and Singabad LCS is very high attention may be paid to the weightage of individual items in the agricultural commodity basket. As many as 38 agricultural commodities have been exported through Mahadipur LCS in 2003-04 and 2004-05. However, tables 10.10 and 10.11 show only six.

TABLE 10.10

Agricultural Commodities Item-wise Indian Exports to Bangladesh Through Mahadipur LCS: 2003-04

Agricultural Commodity	*Value (Rs. in crore)*	*% To Total*
Non-Basmati rice	134.00	27.37
Onion	109.00	22.27
Wheat	66.34	13.55
Pulses	52.24	10.67
Fresh Fruits	78.40	16.01
Maize	20.61	4.21
Others	28.97	5.92
TOTAL	489.56	100.00

Source: Office of the superintendent, Mahadipur LCS, Malda.

These items constitute 94 percent and 88 percent of total agricultural commodities export in 2003-04 and 2004-05 respectively. It is also observed that just two items, non-basmati rice and onion together share nearly 50 percent and 42 percent of total agricultural commodities export for the years 2003-04 and 2004-05 respectively. Fresh fruits account at 15 percent of total export of agricultural commodities per year. Limited number of purely non-perishable agricultural commodities are exported through Singabad LCS. In 2003-04 and 2004-05, only items like non-basmati rice, wheat, maize, tobacco stem and soybean extraction have been exported through Singabad LCS. In terms of value non-basmati rice and wheat constitute the major portion of the export trade carried out by rail at Singabad LCS.

However, imports from Bangladesh through the LCSs of Malda are, by and large, very negligible and confined to only four or five items of intermediate goods, such as zinc plate, brass and metal scrap, cotton waste etc. Besides these, few railway machineries of third country origin are also imported through the Singabad LCS. It is, therefore, evident that

Indo-Bangladesh trade through these two LCSs is almost unidirectional exports to Bangladesh.

TABLE 10.11

Agricultural Commodities Item-wise Indian Exports to Bangladesh Through Mahadipur LCS: 2004-05

Agricultural Commodity	*Value (Rs. in crore)*	*% To Total*
Non-Basmati rice	137.70	26.32
Onion	80.34	15.36
Wheat	89.15	17.04
Pulses	49.28	9.42
Fresh Fruits	73.77	14.09
Maize	29.16	5.57
Others	63.81	12.20
Total	523.21	100.00

Source: Office of the superintendent, Mahadipur LCS, Malda.

Facilities at the LCSs

India's share to Bangladesh's total imports have gone up from 7 percent in 1991 to 16 percent in 1997 (Bakshi: 2000). Therefore, it signifies that the importance of border trade between the countries through the LCSs is rising. The most relevant question arises, thus, whether our LCSs are capable to cope up with the increasing demand of the border trade.

The quantum of export has increased rapidly but there has not been any corresponding improvement in the infrastructural facilities. Weak infrastructure is responsible for corrupt practices in border trade. Customs officials at the LCS are at the receiving end to contain the malpractices which have taken roots manifold. In this section an attempt is made to assess the existing infrastructures at the Mahadipur LCS and Singabad LCS.

The facilities available at the LCSs of Malda are as follows:

Connecting Road

Mahadipur LCS is 15 km. away from the national Highway-34 passing through Malda town. This 15 km long stretch is supervised by the PWD of Govrnment of West Bengal. But the sorry state of this important connector makes the transporters totally helpless. Moreover, the road is narrow and full of potholes. During rainy season, the innumerable potholes on this road put the driver of the heavy vehicle in a difficult situation to negotiate with the road, which often proves costlier to the exporter.

Railway Track

Singabad Railway Station where the Singabad LCS is located is 27 km. away from Malda Town railway station and it is connected by a single track. Track constraint is felt severely at the Singabad Station, which has only four tracks. Usually one rake consists of 30-40 wagons but the nearest railway station of Bangladesh, Rohonpur, has the capacity of taking only 25 wagons at a time causing great hardship for both the countries. Adequate railway tracks in either side of the border can only lessen the heavy load of consignments.

Authorised Truck Terminal

At Mahadipur LCS, there is no authorized truck terminal at present. The vehicles loaded with export cargo are parked in queue on the road leading to 'Zero Point' thereby causing traffic congestion, law and order problem and creating hindrance in smooth running of export / import cargo.

Storage Facility

It is needed especially for the imported goods, which is to be examined at the LCS. Neither of our two LCS have any godown for storage of imported goods. Unless imported goods are checked thoroughly at the LCS, possibility of entering contraband goods cannot be ruled out. LCS may be the heaven for trading of contraband goods devoid of any storage facility.

Checking Area

Separate checking area is almost indispensable in this strategic zone for the border trade by road. However, trade by rail does not specifically require checking area as such. In case of trading by road, trucks are required to be checked thoroughly in a separate checking area. If the checking is done on the road it creates traffic snarl. Mohadipur LCS doesn't have the facility of separate checking area resulting different malpractices in trading. The long queue of heavy vehicles loaded with export cargo is a common picture. The cumulative effect of all such maladies leads to incurring of huge revenue losses.

Checking Gadget

Neither of the two LCSs of Malda has installed any modern checking gadgets. None have X-Ray machine to check cargo. The process of chemical testing is quite cumbersome. Collected sample is sent to Kolkata for laboratory testing, which is time consuming. Such innate constraint makes the whole border trade vulnerable as contraband goods may have the easy access to either side of the border.

Weight Measurement

Surprisingly the Mahadipur LCS lacks a basic ingredient like weighbridge for measuring the cargo. The customs officials, thus, have no option to verify the weight of the cargo of their own but to remain content with the papers collected from private agencies by the exporters / importers.

The customs officials are aware that private weigh bridge owners' manipulate the actual weight of the cargo in exchange of money. The non-availability of weight measurement facility at the LCS gives the exporter / importer, very often, a chance to send excess cargo than stipulated in the appraisement paper.

The situation at Singabad LCS is not as bad as in the Mahadipur LCS, although Singabad LCS also has no local weight measurement facility. Indian Railways has its own weight measurement machinery. Hence the customs officials depend on the weight measurement certificate issued by the Indian railways. Therefore, in case of trade by rail, the formality of weight measurement lies with the railways.

Banking Facility

International trade usually involves huge amount of money. Therefore, local banking facility is needed by the exporters / importers. However, the Mahadipur LCS had no banking facility from the very beginning. Only very recently the Central Bank of India, Mahadipur Branch which is one and half km. away from the LCS has authorised by the Reserve Bank of India to accept government revenue. Singabad LCS still has no banking facility in its vicinity. The exporters / importer avail the banking facility at Malda town which is 29 km. away from the Singabad LCS. This involves an extra cost..

Office Accommodation

None of the LCS in Malda district has well furnished office accommodation. The office accommodation is a matter of serious concern for Singabad LCS. Neither it has proper accommodation nor it has skeleton of furniture to keep the office record in safe custody. This facility is not that poor at Mahadipur LCS. But space shortage is a serious problem at Mahadipur.

Security

Security is essential both for export / import cargo and

the customs officials. However, adequate security arrangements is awfully missing in these two LCSs. Often law and order problems erupt at the drop of a hat. The customs officials at the border point always feel threatened from many visible and invisible forces and often succumb to the pressure.

Staff Shortage

Both the LCSs of Malda are understaffed. It seriously hampers the day-to-day work of the LCSs and most importantly reduces the flow of cargo movement.

The immediate fall out of these inadequate facilities at the LCSs has been the indiscriminate rise of an unscrupulous trade through the LCSs. It has been seen that border fencing has almost checked the cross border smuggling of commodities of every day use but lack of basic facilities at LCSs gives birth to various malpractices. One instance is exporting or importing more quantity than stipulated in the Letter of Credit. In other words overloading of commodities has been a feature in this zone. Repeated cargo despatch against a single paper is another way to duping the government revenue. These unfair practices obliterate free competition, and the corrupt exporters / importers get an edge in trading over others and build an unholy nexus with the vested interests.

The infrastructural constraints of the LCS adversely affect the border trade in another way. In the absence of proper verification of the market prices of the trading commodities, the official trade, very often, takes place at a price below the market price. The gap between the market price and the officially traded price is compensated to the exporter through illegal channels, which has serious adverse implications on the domestic economy. First the government gets lesser revenue due to under pricing deal between the two parties and secondly, it boosts the flow of unaccounted money in the domestic economy. What is worse is that if any importer refuses to make illegal payment to the exporter the latter is left with no option but to bite his nail.

It is therefore evident that physical barriers come in a big way as impediment to carry out border trade with Bangladesh through the two LCSs of Malda. If transhipment cost of goods is taken into consideration along with other costs, the total transaction cost of trade will appear to be much higher.The quantification of actual transaction cost of trade may throw light on the economic advantage of using a particular LCS route for border trading.

Having analysed in detail the nature of Indo-Bangladesh border trade through the LCSs of Malda district, the major findings can be summed up here. These are:

(a) The importers of Bangladesh have clear preference to import commodities through the Mahadipur LCS and Singabad LCS of Malda district.

(b) Mostly agricultural commodities are exported through the LCSs of Malda.

(c) Despite the severe limitations of infrastructural facilities, Mahadipur LCS carries out huge volume of export to Bangladesh.

(d) Major agricultural commodities exported to Bangladesh through the LCSs of Malda are non-basmati rice, onion, wheat, pulses, fresh-fruits and maize.

(e) The major items exported through these routes are collected by the exporters either locally or from the nearby states.

(f) Bulk of non-perishable agricultural items passes through Singabad LCS. Perishable agricultural items are not exported through rail linked LCS of Singabad.

(g) One of the possible reasons of increasing flow of export through the LCSs of Malda is the checking of illegal trade due to border fencing.

(h) A special kind of unofficial border trade within the official channel of LCS has emerged. This unofficial border trade has become possible with the help of enforcement personnel by exporting excess quantity over the stipulated quantity marked in the Letter of Credit.

(i) The unlawful border trade using the official channel causes serious concern for the domestic economy. It increases the flow of unaccounted money as well as it evades the revenue to the government.

(j) The Indo-Bangladesh trade through the LCSs of Malda is characterised by almost unidirectional flow of exports from India to Bangladesh.

Concluding Remarks

Indo-Bangladesh trade is being suffered mostly due to non-tariff barriers like low quality of infrastructure, under developed transport and logistic services, and very peculiar lengthy bureaucratic procedures dealing with trade .The experience of border trade over the years through the LCSs of Malda district suggests that proper infrastructure development is essential for trade facilitation, which in turn can make the border trade competitive. The policy of trade liberalization is not the sole issue for cross border trade. The infrastructure development synergy by both India and Bangladesh may usher in the new vistas of border trade. The local economy in which the LCSs are located can get a boost from the increasing of border trade.

REFERENCES

Bakshi, S.R., (ed, 2000), *Bangladesh Gazetteer*, Vol -I, 2000, Cosmo, New Delhi.

Chaudhari, S.K. (1995), *Cross Border Trade between India and Bangladesh,* working paper No. 58, NCAER, New Delhi.

Das, G and Pusakaystha, R. K. (eds.) (2000), *Border Trade: North East India and Neighboring Countries,* Akansha, New Delhi

Das, G (2001), "Trade between NER and Bangladesh: Nature Trends and Implications for Development Co-operation", Dialogue, April- June.

Pramanik, Bimal (2004), Cattle Smuggling Across the Indo-Bangladesh Border - An Analysis, Dialogue, July - Sept.

UNCTAD, (1995), The *Least Development Countries Reports*, UN.

World Bank, *World Development Report 2000 -2001*, Oxford.

11

INDO-BANGLADESH BORDER TRADE: A CASE STUDY OF CHANGRABANDHA-BURIMARI TRADE ROUTE

Sadhan Chandra Kar
Surya Narayan Ray

Introduction

The geographical area, which is known as Bangladesh, was a part of the Bengal Province of undivided India before 1947. On the 14th of August, 1947, this area emerged as a part of Pakistan and was known as East Pakistan and subsequently in 1971; this geographical area became an independent country. Historically, the demarcation between India and Pakistan and that of India and Bangladesh was the product of a sloppy surgery made by an Englishman, Cyril Radcliffe, the then head of the Boundary Commission appointed by the British Viceroy of India (Banerjee: 2001). It is known from the writings of Leonard Mosley that Radcliffe had arrived in India in the July of 1947 and done that gigantic work of determination of the Demarcation Line within a month, even without a right map of the region and without knowing the socio-cultural heritage of the area. Mitra (1951) and Roy (1961) reported that Radcliffe's sloppy surgery was done on the basis of Report of the Revenue Officers.

One unfortunate outcome of that demarcation was the emergence of enclaves mainly along the southern part of the district of Cooch Behar. Enclaves, mainly known as 'Chitmahals', are the villages or pockets of land physically located in one country, but occupied by the citizens of other country. India has 130 such enclaves with the total area of 20957 acres in the territory of Bangladesh and Bangladesh has 95 such enclaves with a total area of 12289 acres in the territory of India. Obviously, a large number of Indian citizens are residing in the 'Chitmahals', surrounded by the Bangladesh land and Bangladesh citizens and vice-versa. The social-economic and political conditions of these dry islands on both sides are rather inhumane due to the lack of proper administrative network and the existence of smugglers-touts regime. The exchange of these enclaves, as it is, remains as a prolonged pending job on the part of Bangladesh and India and perhaps, the only pending example in the world. Another unfortunate outcome of the sloppy surgery is the dysfunction of the demarcation due to natural turbulent flow of the rivers. The length of such riverine border is about 536 kms. The natural change in the course of the turbulent river flow gives another impetus to the ongoing problems of the border. Again, that sloppy surgery had been made in many areas, through the villages, schools, hats and even through the households and thus made the demarcation a cruelty. Thus, despite the brave efforts made by the BSF and the BDR jawans, the problem of the dysfunction of the Demarcation Line persists. Thus, the rational (?) reformation of political map appears, in many places, as irrational and has created many unwanted problems along the vicinity of the porous border.

We have observed that the children and women,

particularly those belonging to the below poverty line category, residing in the vicinity of the border, act merely as pawns in the hands of the smugglers and the touts in the very dangerous game of smuggling. Again, the smuggler-burecracy-political leader nexus in both sides of the borders makes the situation more complex. Thus, in spite of the mutual trust that exists between the two neighbouring countries and the long standing trading relation among them, we still remain marooned in a broken boat.

TABLE 11.1

Indo-Bangladesh Border

(in kms)

State	*Land*	*Land P.C.*	*Riverine*	*Riverine P.C.*	*Total*	*P.C. of Total*
Assam	160	4.38	103	19.22	263	6.28
Meghalaya	443	12.14	-	-	443	10.58
Mizoram	58	1.59	260	48.51	318	7.60
Tripura	773	21.18	83	15.48	856	20.45
West Bengal	2216	60.71	90	16.79	2306	55.09
Total	3650	100.00	536	100.00	4186	100.00

Source: Government of India Records (Approx).

Data and the Design of the Study

For the purpose of the present study, we have selected the Changrabandha-Burimari Trade Route, the only trade route in the district of Cooch Behar under the jurisdiction of the Changrabandha Land Custom Station (LCS). This LCS is one of the nine operating LCS along the West Bengal–Bangladesh border and is located 90 kms away from the district headquarters and 20 kms away from the National Highway No. 31. Though the trade route was opened in 1986 for cross border trade (CBT) between India and Bangladesh, but for the purpose of our present study, we have considered the time period from 1994-95 up to 2003-04. Accordingly, we have collected the time series data for that period. We have also collected the cross-section data on commodity composition of exports and imports for the years 1996-97, 2000-01 and 2003-04. Side by side, we have also collected information regarding illegal cross border trade (ICBT) from the official records of the LCS and through personal interviews with competent authorities and some inhabitants residing in the vicinity of the border.

In the second section, we have analysed the nature and extent of legal cross border trade (LCBT) with the help of time series and cross-section data. Our third section deals with the ICBT with the help of time-series data and personal interviews. Trade facilitation forms the fourth section of our study. The final section covers the findings and conclusions.

II

The Nature of Export

At the outset, an account of the commodity composition of our export is in order. We have observed some sort of differences in the commodity composition of our export. If we consider the period from 1994-95 to 1999-00, we see that the major export items, according to the order of importance were coals, stone boulders, fresh fruits, onions, commercial plywood, anarzite chips, dry chili, sanitary goods, machinery parts etc. On the other hand, if we consider the time period from 2000-01 to 2003-04, then export items as per order of importance are coals, stone boulders, fresh fruits, onions, rice, wheat, anarzite chips, commercial plywood, etc. . Thus, the demand for dry chili, sanitary goods and machinery parts has rather disappeared in the later period. However, this changing trend of commodity composition certainly brings the opportunity to increase the production of rice and wheat in the region adjacent to the Indo-Bangladesh border. We have presented the volume of export in Table 11.3.

TABLE 11.2

Volume of Export

(in million U.S. dollars)

Year	*Volume of export*	*Percentage to Total*	*Increase Rate.*
1994-1995	15.46	4.00	——
1995-1996	69.44	18.04	3.50
1996-1997	17.65	4.57	-0.74
1997-1998	28.27	7.32	0.60
1998-1999	57.16	14.94	1.04
1999-2000	36.84	9.54	-0.36
2000-2001	24.34	6.31	-0.34
2001-2002	12.21	3.16	-0.49
2002-2003	55.13	14.30	3.52
2003-2004	68.80	17.80	0.25
Total	386.00	100.00	——

Mean= 38.6 & S.D.= 21.20.

Source: Changrabandha Custom Office.

One can see from Table 11.2 that the volume of export during the period of our consideration stands at 386 million U.S. dollars, i.e., 38.6 million U.S. Dollar annually. Out of these ten export years, the highest performance year was 1995-96, while the lowest performance year was 2001-02. If we define the good export year on the basis of the periodic average figure of export, then we see that half of the selected period may be termed as good export year. Again, if we consider the rate of increase, then it is revealed that four years have recorded as negative increase. Thus, export years are not uniform as per the volume of export. To find out the smooth export line, we use the simple least square method. Under this method we consider the equation X= a + b T. Here X is the volume of export in value term and T stands for time .We have calculated 'a' and 'b' on the basis of the date given in Table 11.3 and the two values are 38.6 and 0.96 respectively. Thus our fitted trend equation becomes X=

38.6 + 0.96 T. The actual Trend Line and the Fitted Trend Line of export are given in Figure 11.1.

Figure 11.1
Export (in US$ Million)

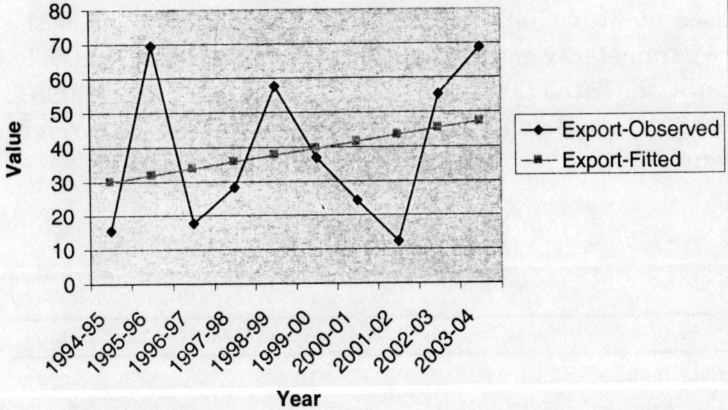

Nature of Import

Like the exported items, the imported items are not uniform over time. If we consider the period of 1994-95 to 1999-2000, then we can see that the major imported items are hilsha fish, jute, juice, snacks and soaps, while the major imported items of the rest of the period are cotton waste, readymade garments, mosquito net, soaps etc. Thus, the shifting of demand from one commodity to another commodity is an important phenomenon of import as observed from the sample study.

We have presented the volume of import in value terms in Table 11.3. The total volume of import in value terms during the reference period stands at 11.32 million U.S. Dollars, which is as much as 34 times lesser than the volume of export. What we observe is that, except the change in rate of import for the year 2000-01, both the export and import years have been faced with negative change rate. This implies that both exports and imports closely follow the same pattern of change. To determine a rather smooth import trend, we apply the least square method here also. Under this method, equation to be considered is M = c + d T, where M is the volume of import in value terms and T stands for time. Based on Table 11.4, we have calculated the values of the two parameters c and d. These are 1.13 and 0.098 respectively. Hence, the fitted trend equation becomes M = 1.13 + 0.098T. Both the actual and fitted trend lines of import are given in Figure 11.2.

TABLE 11.3

Volume of Import

(In Million U.S. Dollars)

Year	*Value of Import*	*Percentage to Total*	*Change Rate*
1994-1995	0.21	1.86	—
1995-1996	0.92	8.13	3.38
1996-1997	0.23	2.03	0.75
1997-1998	0.70	6.18	2.04
1998-1999	1.01	8.92	0.44
1999-2000	0.83	7.33	0.18
2000-2001	2.90	25.62	2.49
2001-2002	0.60	5.30	0.79
2002-2003	1.42	12.54	1.37
2003-2004	2.50	22.08	0.76
Total	11.32	100.00	—

Mean = 1.132 S.D. = 0.85.

Source: Changrabandha Custom Office.

Balance of Trade

Balance of Trade (BOT) is simply the absolute difference between the volume of export and import in money terms during a specified period of time. From Table 11.4, it is clear

Figure 11.2

Import (in US$Million)

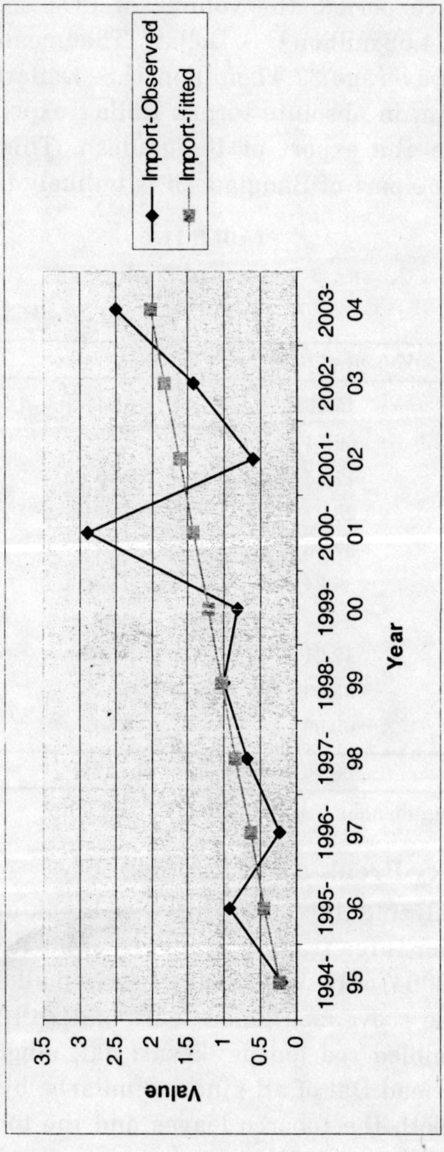

that the BOT has all along gone against Bangladesh. During the reference period, the volume of BOT in value terms stands at 374.68 million U.S. Dollars. That means Bangladesh pays on an average 37.47 million U.S. Dollars annually to India. Again, in absolute terms, India's export is 34 times larger than the export of Bangladesh. This, huge trade deficit on the part of Bangladesh is unlikely to sustain.

TABLE 11.4

Balance of Trade

(In Million U.S. Dollars)

Year	*Volume of Export*	*Volume of Import*	*Trade Balance*
1994-1995	15.46	0.21	-15.25
1995-1996	69.64	0.92	-68.72
1996-1997	17.65	0.23	-17.42
1997-1998	28.27	0.70	-27.57
1998-1999	57.66	1.01	-56.65
1999-2000	36.84	0.83	-36.01
2000-2001	24.34	2.90	-21.44
2001-2002	12.21	0.60	-11.61
2002-2003	55.13	1.42	-53.71
2003-2004	68.80	2.50	-66.30
TOTAL	386.00	11.32	-374.68

Source: Changrabandha Custom Office

Commodity Break-up of Exports

For analyzing the commodity wise break-up of export we just consider three trading years viz. 1996-1997, 2000-2001 and 2003-2004, only. We have categorized all the exportable items in the above mentioned years under thirty heads. We have assembled red lentils, kesari dal, mugdal and gram under the head Dal of all kinds. Similarly, by Tobacco etc., we mean both the tobacco leaves and the tobacco stumps, though the share of tobacco stump is major in this group. Our Textile head includes items like cotton T-shirt, silk

TABLE 11.5

Commodity Composition of Exports from India

(in US $)

Sl.No.	Items of Export	1996-1997	2000-2001	2003-2004
1.	Rice	2325504	1255804	11658204
2.	Wheat	214001	248000	18773752
3.	Maize	684789	775820	2493538
4.	Onion	2788885	5956815	12144396
5.	Vegetables	14320	Nil	Nil
6.	Dal of all kinds	205938	123650	8536983
7.	Dry chili	Nil	26730	3680747
8.	Oilcakes, etc.	2304	86100	1184675
9.	Cumin seeds	274438	56100	262041
10.	Sunflower oil	314960	Nil	Nil
11.	Poultry feed	2194404	144100	Nil
12.	Fresh fruit	734210	770378	1425226
13.	Dry feed	24500	Nil	Nil
14.	Processed food	56474	49020	1485029
15.	Tobacco, etc.	776048	381740	Nil
16.	Commercial plywood	116346	601850	1084069
17.	Stone Boulders, etc.	763886	1189978	1060617
18.	Machinery parts, etc.	116610	130536	7945
19.	Chemicals	1233934	749580	Nil
20.	Cullet, etc.	20536	17650	4900
21.	Coal (Meghalaya)	4470087	4665220	3429801
22.	Textiles	39090	3475028	Nil
23.	Cosmetics, etc.	243320	414199	32100
24.	Ball point pen	Nil	2695050	Nil
25.	Ginger, etc.	37720	224741	1388168
26.	Trip rubber plastic, etc.	Nil	305107	Nil
27.	Playing card	Nil	Nil	39349
28.	Anis seed, etc.	Nil	Nil	49909
29.	Soya bean extraction	Nil	Nil	41625
30.	Others	Nil	Nil	21275
	Total	17652304	24343196	68804349

Source: Changrabandha Custom Office.

fabric, polyester yarn, etc. Under the head ginger etc., we have assembled ginger, cardamoms, garlic and turmeric. The items under processed foods are biscuits, milk powder, isobgul, etc. Finally, the items under the head cosmetics are talcum powder, alum, hair remover, kali mehandi and kutch. Commodity-wise break-up of exports is given in Table 11.5.

Table 11.5 shows that the number of commodities whose demand have increased over the years under reference is eleven. They are rice, wheat, maize, onion, dal of all kinds, dry chili, fresh fruits, commercial plywood and ginger. The commodities, whose demands have declined, are cumin seeds, stone boulders, machine parts, culets, coal, and cosmetics. Again, the number of items whose demands have disappeared are vegetables, sunflower oils, poultry feeds, dry fish, chemicals, textiles and ball point pens; while the new items included are four in number. On the other hand the number of stable items, that is the items which appear in all the reference years are 16 in number. Out of these 16 items, the number of items, whose demands have increased over time, is 10 in number. Again, if we have a look at the total volume of exports, then we see that the percentage increase in the volume of export between 1996-97 and 200-01 stands at 37.90%.

Locally produced commodities in the export basket are vegetables, tobacco and tobacco stumps, commercial plywood, cullet and oilcakes. In case of rice and wheat, as reported by the custom personnel, the share of local products stands at around 30 per cent. If we widen the area to the North Bengal division of West Bengal, then the items like fresh fruits, stone boulders, ginger, etc. will be added to the list of the local products. Thus, the value of local products exported to Bangladesh becomes 3.72 million US $ in the year 2000-01 and 16.05 million US $ in the year 2003-04. Now the point is that if we are able to supply the full amount of the items like rice, wheat and onions, which is quite possible, then the value of exportable items produced locally becomes 4.78 million US $ and 37.36 million US $, during the last two reference years. Thus, strengthening the local resource and trade linkages will, no doubt, enhance economic growth of North Bengal in terms of higher production, employment, income and standard of living.

Commodity Break-up of Imports

The commodity composition of imports for the year 2003-04 is presented in Table 11.6. It has been observed that the volume, value and commodity composition of imports from Bangladesh through this border post are much lesser than their export.

TABLE 11.6

Commodity Composition of Imports

(in US Dollars)

SL. No.	*Items*	*2003-2004*
1.	Cotton/Yarn Waste	1249806
2.	Ready Made Garments	600543
3.	Mosquito Nets	257234
4.	Lead Acid Accumulator	131132
5.	Saree	99951
6.	Beauty Soap	99155
7.	Toilet Soap	14880
8.	Lay Flat Tube	17600
9.	Biscuits	12168
10.	Synthetic Fabric Waste	8100
11.	Lead Acid Lithartage	6000
12.	Carding Machine	4200
13.	Hilsha Fish	1950
14.	Ceramic Tiles	1469
15.	Steel Furniture	923
TOTAL		2500111

Source: Changrabandha Custom Office.

III

Illegal Cross-Border Trade (ICBT)

In this section, we have tried to assess the extent and nature of ICBT. For this, we have to depend on the data on seizure made by custom personnel, B.S.F. personnel and police personnel within the jurisdiction of Changrabandha Custom Station. Side by side, we have also made a quick visit to the vicinity of the border of the Indian part to acquire some knowledge about the ICBT. We have observed that our national family planning schemes have been more or less ineffective among the inhabitants in the vicinity of the border. What is more surprising is that, the smugglers and touts are the promoters of the philosophy of large family. They have injected very carefully, the more child more income slogan among the inhabitants of the border region. Further, it has been noticed that the B.S.F. jawans are, to some extent, sympathetic towards the BPL children. Making use of this opportunity, the smugglers and touts are generally using

TABLE 11.7

Export and Import Seizure

Year	*No. of Cases*	*Percentage*	*Amount (in lakhs of Rs.)*	*Percentage*
1994-1995	326	6.54	4.14	4.31
1995-1996	537	10.77	4.90	5.10
1996-1997	710	14.24	10.35	10.78
1997-1998	660	13.23	9.05	9.43
1998-1999	727	14.58	7.00	7.29
1999-2000	658	13.19	7.64	7.96
2000-2001	339	6.79	13.07	13.62
2001-2002	386	7.74	13.53	14.10
2002-2003	358	7.19	9.51	9.91
2003-2004	286	5.73	16.79	17.50
Total	4987	100.00	95.98	100.00

Source: Changrabandha Custom Office.

these BPL children as mere pawns in the dangerous game of smuggling. Among the BPL adults, the female adults are engaged more in numbers in smuggling activities than their male counterparts. Table 11.7 presents export and import seizures at the sample trading post.

The illegal export items as recorded in the seizure list are cattle, sugar, salt, fertilizers, onions, etc., while the illegally imported items are Bangladesh currencies, raw hides, goats, jute and gold. It can be observed from Table 11.7 that the annual average seizure is amounting to nearly 10 lakhs. But, what is really cause for concern is that the trend of smuggling is increasing at an alarming rate over the period, despite the fence lodged in the border to fend off ICBT. Needless to say that these figures on illegal smuggling are only the mere tip of the iceberg. According to our presumption, the volume of ICBT is almost equal to the volume of LCBT.

IV

Trade Facilitation

With the decrease in tariff walls following the Uruguay Round, the Non-Tariff Barriers (NTBs) assumed increasing importance in CBT. NTBs give rise to high transaction cost of trading goods. Poor border maintenance procedures contributes up to 15 per cent of the total transaction cost as revealed from the recent OECD study. Trade facilitation depends mainly on three types of infrastructure- Physical Infrastructure (PI), Financial Infrastructures (FI) and Social Infrastructure (SI). By PI, we mean transportation facilities via roadways, railways and airways, housing, electrification, water supply and sanitation, tele-communication, truck terminal and government warehouse with refrigeration facility. By FI we mean the financial and insurance services including currency exchange facilities provided by the banks, insurance companies, C&F agents and their sub-agents. By SI we mean, better ways of human resource development in terms of education, health, recreation, skilled personnel manning the LCS and Zero Point.

On examination of the PI of the Changrabandha LCS, the focus of our study, the following points have been noted:

(i) The LCS is very well connected by both railways and roadways. Though the railway routes have been kept suspended since last year, the scope is there for providing a better railway transportation system and it can be done conveniently with a minimum cost, just by transforming the Meter Gauge Line into a Broad Gauge Line. Further, the Changrabandha railway station is very near to the Zero Point (ZP), so the transshipment of the Indian goods to the Burimari dry ports of Bangladesh will become very easy and it can be done even with the help of the hand-driven push cart. Again, this type of transshipment will open up new avenues of employment among the local inhabitants and lead to income generation. Further, this type of transshipment will further reduce the loading and unloading time, which is incurred in the cargo transportation system.

From the point of view of roadways, it is seen that the LCS is very well connected with the national Highway No. 31. The distance is only 20 kms and the road condition is very good. The breadth of the connecting road is about 5 metres and maintained well by the Public Works Department of the Government of West Bengal. This connecting road is known as Mekhliganj-Siliguri Road. However, the approach road from the Mekhliganj-Siliguri Road to the ZP is under construction and locally known as the SAARC Road with a length of about 1.5 kms. The breadth of the SAARC road is about 6 metres. But, the condition of the approach to the LCS is in a very poor condition. This appalling condition has been persisting for the last 4 to 5 years. There is no proper airways or waterways connecting the LCS. The only nearest working airport is situated at Bagdogra which is 90 kms away from the LCS.

(ii) Housing is the fundamental input of any LCS. In the LCS under study, the condition of housing is rather poor, particularly the conditions of the rooms meant for official works. This is an old model tin-roofed-bricked-wall and cemented floor accommodation with a total carpet area of about 216 sq. feet. What is more surprising is that this small room is further separated in four portions by giving the length-wise and breadth-wise partitions. The first two relatively bigger portions are meant for the Superintendents and Custom Inspectors. The two other small portions are used for wireless and official works. In the periphery of the LCS, there are two other rooms, which are used as dwelling purpose by the custom personnel. The conditions of these two rooms also demand immediate renovation. The LCS has no satisfactory drinking water facilities. All the custom personnel usually use hand-tube well water for drinking. But, what is more unhygienic is that the LCS is running without proper sanitary facilities. However, the electricity connection is there.

(iii) In this era of satellite communication, this particular LCS is connected with the outside world, only through the Telephone and Fax. There is no Electronic Data Interface System which is very essential to reduce the time delay for filling up and processing customs related documents.

(iv) Another important infrastructural drawback of this LCS is the absence of a well furnished Truck Terminal, equipped with Cargo handling equipment. This LCS was opened to CBT in the year 1986, but it still remains a prolonged pending job. We have observed only a foundation stone in a low land area of about 10 acres for the proposed Cargo–Terminals. As a result of which most of the loaded trucks coming from different parts of the country and also from Bhutan are using the roadside as parking place.

(v) What is more alarming is that this LCS has not a single bonded warehouse. But across the border this facility has already been provided by the Bangladesh government. Thus the cargos coming from Bangladesh use the ground of the LCS (area about 0.33 acres) as a terminal point for custom related activities and after complying with all the custom formalities (for ordinary commodities), those cargos use privately owned godowns for unloading the commodities in the presence of the custom officials. But the commodities, which require some sort of chemical test for clearance, the cargos of those commodities generally use the private godowns, after paying higher rents for detention for the time consuming chemical tests.

(vi) The LCS area has two branches of financial institutions, one of which is the branch of the State Bank of India and the other is the branch of the Uttar Banga Khetriya Gramin Bank. However, the private agents run the foreign exchange market. At ZP, we have noticed six such small stalls where foreign exchange transcations are conducted. The services rendered by these agents are far from satisfactory. There is a common tendency among them to by pass the official exchange rates and fix up the value of US $ on the basis of the demand for conversion.

(vii) The nexus of Carry and Forward(C & F) agents and

their sub agents are also not satisfactory from the point of view of transparency. In this LCS there are nine C& F agents, who have their offices at Siliguri, Kolkata and Delhi. Under each C & F agent, there are five sub-agents, who have setup makeshift offices in the vicinity of the LCS. These sub-agents have an unwritten agreement between them as to the category of goods each of them will cater to. Sometimes this leads to unnecessary friction between them as to who will dominate whom. The C&F sub-agents escort the exports from LCS up to ZP. Moreover, the 2 P.M. deadline at the ill-equipped LCS, for submitting tenders is an obstacle for efficient and free flow of exports. If the export related documents are not submitted within the 2 P.M. deadline, then the trucks carrying the related cargo will unnecessarily have to be delayed for another 15 to 20 hours. This further adds some additional cost.

(viii) There is a lack of clerical staff at the LCS. There are two Superintendents, six Custom Inspectors but only one Wireless Operator and one Clerical Staff. For an important LCS handling a large volume of CBT, there should be more clerical staff. This dearth of support staff creates an unnecessary logistic problem. The behavior of the LCS staff towards the truck drivers and C&F agents is appalling. The high handedness of the custom is a detrimental factor for higher export.

V

Conclusion

The study shows that the trade between India and Bangladesh is very much lopsided in nature. Bangladesh suffers from a huge trade deficit throughout the period of our consideration and it is rather an uphill task for Bangladesh to improve her trade deficit with the help of the existing commodity trading system. The Most Favoured Nation Clause of the WTO treaty (Article XXIV, 1994) provides both nations enough opportunities to work towards the free trade regime. But, the ground reality is that for long, following the formation of SAARC and SAFTA, we have remained mired in trivial political debate, which in turn makes the already delicate situation even more fragile. We must endeavor to improve the trade, commodity as well as service, for the better utilization of resources keeping aside the petty political squabbles.

Geographically, Bangladesh is in an advantageous position in respect of trade and communication. She can easily improve her service sectors through the riverine traffic routes and through the use of her ports and rail-routes. India can take this opportunity to send her commodities to North- East India via Bangladesh. The roadway distance between Kolkata and Agartala is about 2000 kms. The distance reduces to about one third if we avail of the sea route from Kolkata or Haldia to Chittagong and, then onwards, from Chittagang to Agartala, through the rail road. A rough estimation indicates that the above distance becomes merely 600 kms. History tells us that before 1965, there existed a riverine traffic route between Kolkata and Assam through Bangladesh. The experts are of the view that the traffic route remains navigable from Kolkata to Ashuganj, a river port of Meghna, throughout the year. Again the land route distance between Ashuganj and Agartala is merely 40 kms. Bangladesh can earn a handsome royalty from India by offering her routes and services to India and at the same time, India will be able to supply different commodities to the people of North-East India, and then onwards from the North-East India to other countries, at a very low transport cost.

Finally, we have observed that the trend of ICBT is rather alarming and both the countries suffer from huge revenue losses that hampers the growth and development of both. Simultaneously, the nexus of smuggling activities supporting the ICBT creates a negative impact on the socio-economic-cultural fabric of the society, residing in the vicinity of the porous border. If proper measures are adopted, the LCBT of both the countries will improve in leaps and bounds, thereby stimulating the synergic growth and development of this Indian sub-continent.

REFERENCES

Banerjee, S, 2001, "Indo-Bangladesh Border: Radcliffe's Ghost", EPW, XXXVI, NO. 18.

Mitra, A., 1951, District *Hand Book Cooch Behar*, Saraswati Press, Calcutta.

Roy, B., 1961, *District Census Hand Book*; Cooch Behar, Government of India Publication, Calcutta.

PART III

INDO-BANGLADESH BORDER TRADE: NORTH EASTERN REGION-BANGLADESH SECTOR

12

BILATERAL TRADE BETWEEN NER AND BANGLADESH: CHALLENGES AND PROSPECTS

D.K. Sarma

Introduction

A rapid process of liberalization and proliferation of the norms of bilateral trade characterize the regional trading environment. While Bangladesh has proficiently recognized the market in NERI (North Eastern Region of India), the traders from the region have also shown considerable interest in doing business with Bangladesh. This is evident from large number of participants in seminars, conferences on bilateral trade/border trade in various places in NERI.

Apart from Bangladesh, the NERI has international border with Myanmar, Bhutan and China. Nonetheless, due to the obvious fact and reality, business prospects of NERI and Bangladesh are far brighter and more realistic than with other bordering countries. The North Eastern Region of India (NERI) is surrounded by Bangladesh in the west and southwest with an international border of nearly 1800 km. Strategic geographic location coupled with supportive natural advantages, complementary resources and modest infrastructural facilities of Bangladesh have all the potential to help accelerate the economic progress of NERI vis-à-vis of its own. The NERI is not only the next door neigbours of Bangladesh, but also shares a close cultural, emotional and historical heritage and tradition. There are lot of complementarities between the economics of Bangladesh and NERI, and as such, it is very important to have a common platform for the co-operation and collaboration for the betterment and economic development of both the region.

The NERI is bestowed with huge resources like minerals, quarry, forestry, horticulture, crops, plantation and others. Despite these resources galore, this landlocked region is distantly connected with the rest of India only through a narrow Siliguri corridor. In fact all the state capitals of this landlocked region are at a distance varying from 1080 km to 1680 km from the nearest mainland port city of Kolkata. Moreover due to undulating topography and innate difficulties, this region is underdeveloped with poor infrastructure, transportation system and other logistic facilities. As a result, transportation cost of goods to and from this region to rest of India and within the region is exorbitantly higher than that of any strategic parts of Bangladesh. This fact postulates the efficacy of developing a good trade and investment relation between the NERI and Bangladesh. There are very good prospects for Indian entrepreneurs to invest in Bangladesh either in joint venture or wholly owned for using the abundant raw materials of this landlocked region to meet the local demand and export to other countries particularly where Bangladesh enjoys preferential market access due to its better positional advantage to connect the SAARC and ASEAN countries, the two vibrant economic blocks of the world through the air, sea, land and rail route.

Indo-Bangladesh Trade

Border trade and economic development in border areas are interdependent, as border trade leads to economic development, which through secondary effects increases border trade, in manifold. The North Eastern Region of India (NERI) has prolonged socio-economic ties with Bangladesh. Although the partition has disrupted the structure of age-old flow of goods and services between these two areas, even then the communication channels are not completely abandoned. The old road links and waterways are still being used in many places for export-import trade between Bangladesh and the North East. In fact, the land borders between Bangladesh and the North Eastern Region are more accessible and cost effective than the borders with other neighboring countries such as China, Myanmar and Bhutan (Das: 2000).

Value of Indo-Bangladesh Trade through the Land Customs Stations

The average value of exports through the various export/import points of the entire North Eastern Region during the last five years (1999-2000 to 2003-2004) was Rs. 404.85 crore of which the share of exports across Indo-Bangladesh border was Rs. 189.93 crore, i.e. about 47 per cent. On the other hand, the average value of imports through the various export/import points of the entire North Eastern Region during the last five years (1999-2000 to 2003-2004) was Rs. 21.63 crore of which the share of imports from across Indo-Bangladesh border was Rs. 7.95 crore, i.e. about 37 per cent. During the current financial year (up to November, 2004) total export and import trade across Indo-Bangladesh border in the North Eastern Region was Rs. 95.73 crore of which about 88 per cent (i.e. Rs. 83.95 crore) constituted exports from India while just 12 per cent (i.e. Rs. 11.78 crore) constituted imports from Bangladesh.

Indian exports to Bangladesh from the North Eastern Region constitute mostly of minerals and raw materials like coal, limestone, boulders, stone-chips etc. The average value of exports to Bangladesh during the last five years (1999-

2000 to 2003-2004) was Rs. 189.93 crore of which an overwhelming 98 per cent (about Rs. 186 crore) consisted of minerals such as coal, boulders, sandstones etc. These are all products that are used for developmental activity in the importing country i.e. Bangladesh. The contribution of manufacturing sector in the export basket over the last five years is pathetically low at about 0.33 per cent (about Rs. 0.63 crore). It may also be mentioned here that agricultural/horticultural products that are exported to Bangladesh are exported without any value addition.

TABLE 12.1

Volume and Value of Export from NERI to Bangladesh: 2002-04

Sl No.	*Items*	*2003-04*		*2002-03*	
		Quantity	*Value*	*Quantity*	*Value*
1.	Coal	1225241.16(MT)	2271345682	1046396.5(MT)	1886066116.8
2.	Lime Stone	256358 (MT)	74554959	234253.7(MT)	63293680.08
3.	Ginger	1556.51 (MT)	11622531	4145.03	32177128
4.	Dry Fish	94.5 (MT)	1724920.00	1.2 (MT)	23280.00
5.	Dry Chilli	20.28 (MT)	746177	40.13(MT)	1185344
6.	Boulder Stone	16637 (MT)	2122999.5	2111.04	641468.75
7.	Betel Leaves	4.48 (MT)	166099	41.69	562181
8.	Tea	21369733 kgs	1848530899	22180179 Kgs	2007287731
9.	Edible Buffalo Offal	1188.9 MT	41083465	487.72 MT	17529745
10.	Motor Parts	104 Pkts	131946.00	126 (Pkts)	98200.00
11.	Crushed Stone	11819 (MT)	7760128	15988 (MT)	11161924
12.	Rectified Spirit	229300 (Lt)	14864000	208000 (Lt)	1483400
13.	Soya Bari	531.31 (MT)	14371703	511.28 (MT)	12797635
14.	Cumin Seed	45.5 (MT)	4550000	95.75 (MT)	19070300
15.	Bamboo	—	—	200000 Nos.	1104357
16.	Pineapple	—	—	7800.00 (MT)	17944

Source: Office of the Commissioner of Customs, Shillong.

Note: Divisions include Shillong, Dhubri, Agartala, Karimganj, Imphal and Guwahati.

Figure 12.1

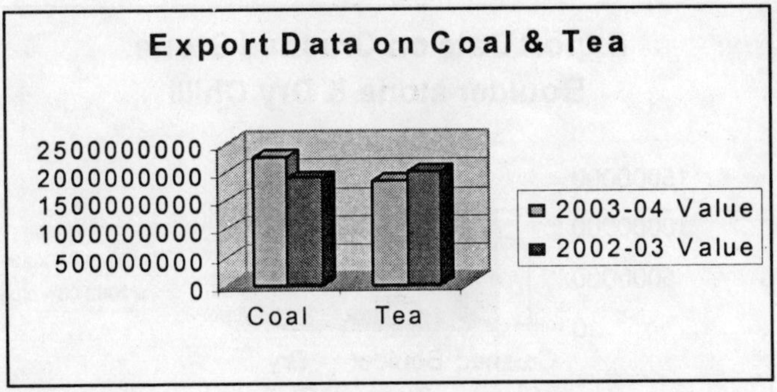

Figure 12.2

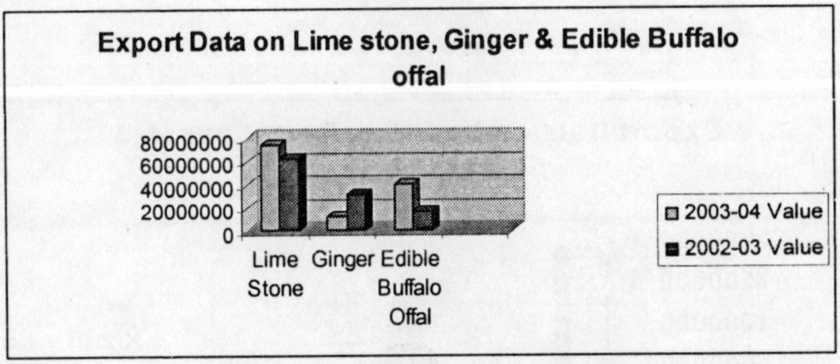

Figure 12.3

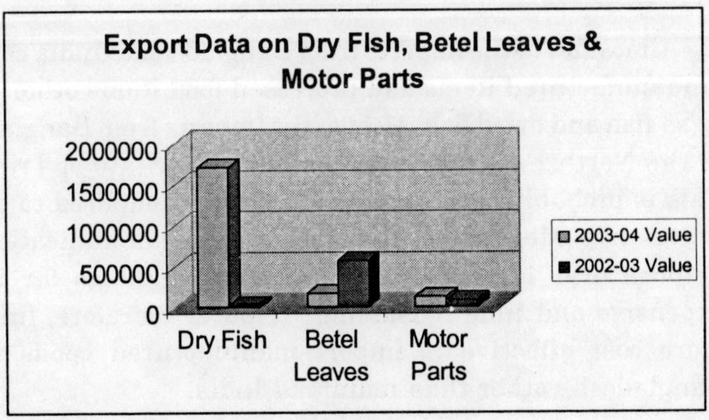

Figure 12.4

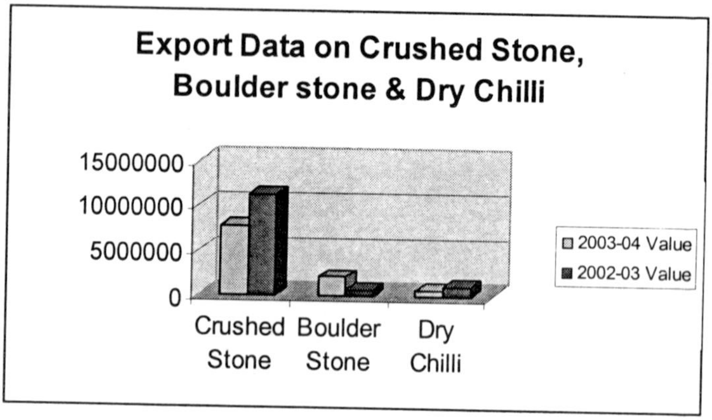

Figure 12.5

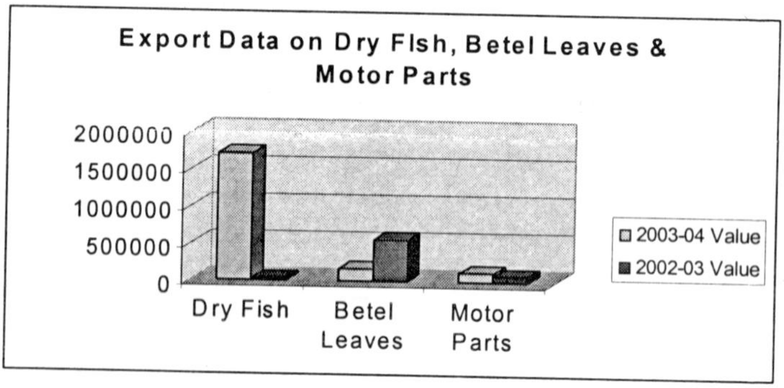

Almost all of the imports from Bangladesh to India consist of manufactured items and processed food items other than *hilsa* fish and dried fish. Most of the imports from Bangladesh to the North East take place through the State of Tripura. This is probably because of the fact that compared to other States like Meghalaya and Assam; the communication to Tripura over land from other parts of India is far more expensive and time consuming. Tripura, therefore, finds it more cost effective to import manufactured goods from Bangladesh rather than mainland India.

TABLE 12.2

Value of Export from NERI to Bangladesh: 2000-2005

(Value in Rs. Crore)

	2000-2001	2001-2002	2002-2003	2003-2004	2004-2005
Mineral Products	165.29	148.01	182.49	197.39	235.58
Fish/Dry fish/other animal products like raw hides skin/poultry feed etc.	0.95	0.11	0.16	0.004	0.18
Fruits	0.56	0.96	1.37	1.19	1.31
Agricultural and Forest produce	2.64	1.19	1.73	3.52	1.88
Other miscellaneous goods	0.38	0.96	0.14	0.60	1.06
Total	168.82	150.23	184.89	201.704	239.01

Source: Office of the Commissioner or of Customs, Shillong.

Note 1. Minerals include coal, boulders, stone chips, sandstones and limestone, etc.

2. Fruits include Orange, pears, citrus fruit, grape, jackfruit etc.
3. Agricultural and forest produce include vegetables, ginger, onion, turmeric, dry chilly, betel leaves, potato, bamboo, tomato etc.
4. Other miscellaneous items include consumer goods like tape recorders, woolen garments printed books, wall/table clock, machinery equipments, natural rubber, sanitary ware, stainless steel utensils, paper, marble slabs, handloom and handicraft, safety glass, umbrella and umbrella parts, tractor and motor parts, audio cassette, etc.

Figure 12.6

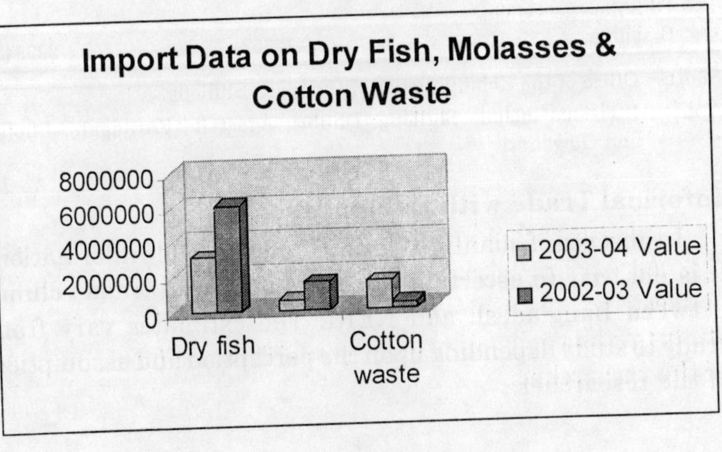

TABLE 12.3

Volume and Value of Imports from Bangladesh to NERI: 2002-04

Sl. No.	*Items*	*2003-04*		*2002-03*	
		Quantity	*Value*	*Quantity*	*Value*
1.	Malamine Table Ware	46486 (Pcs)	89345	26557	32773.7
2.	Dry fish	—	3124121	158.85 (MT)	6105639
3.	Biscuits	—	1951498	—	378828.3
4.	Mosquito Net	—	460302	—	450065
5.	Accumutars/Battery Parts	30000 (Pcs)	139100	—	219275
6.	Imitation Jwellery	—	886087	—	—
7.	Fruit Juice/ Mineral Water etc.	—	11387388	—	1806544
8.	Cellular Phone and Accessories	—	1612317	—	796467
9.	Garments/ Handloom and handicrafts items	—	354365	—	135807
10.	Cotton waste	416.9 (MT)	1621288	89 (MT)	405885
11.	Soap/Detergent	—	1650506	—	17340
12.	Hilsa fish/Small fish	—	41268099	—	24888765
13.	Molasses	—	612002	—	1627310
14.	Tiles	—	56812	—	2733554
15.	Ice Cream	—	13432	—	23980.00
16.	UPS/Emergencylight/ Stabilizer	—	272652	—	229943

Source: Office of the Commissioner of Customs, Shillong.

Note: Divisions include Shillong, Dhubri, Agartala, Karimganj, Imphal and Guwahati.

Informal Trade with Bangladesh

In absence of quantitative data and verifiable information, it is not easy to ascertain the exact unofficial trade volume between Bangladesh and NERI. The estimates vary from study to study depending upon the perception and assumption of the researcher.

Figure 12.7

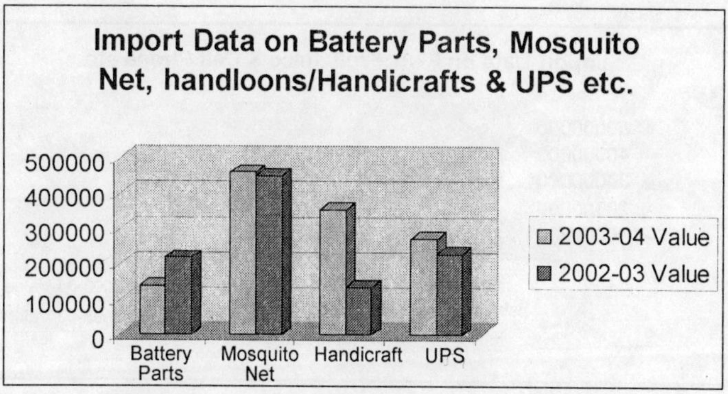

Figure 12.8

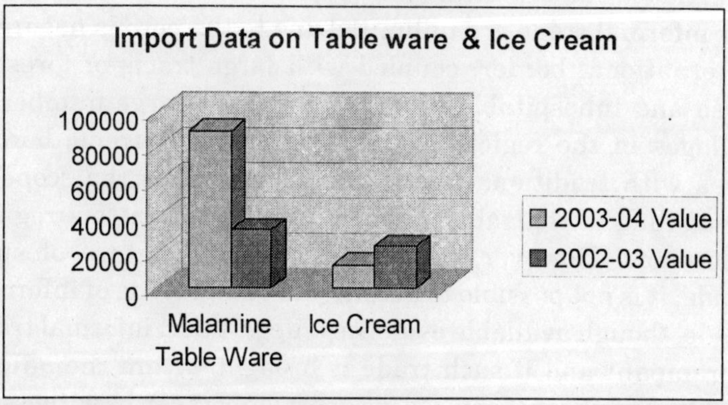

Figure 12.9

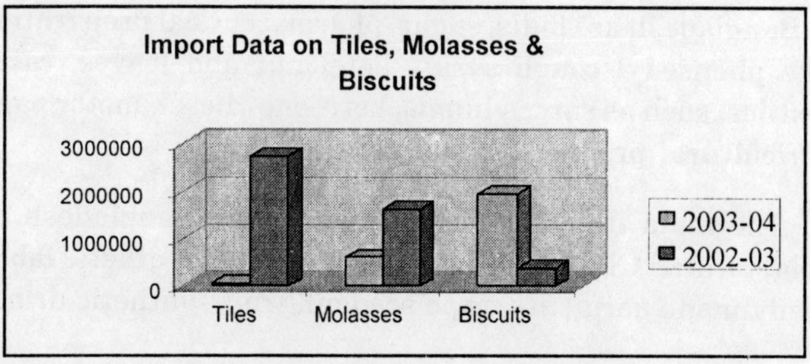

Figure 12.10

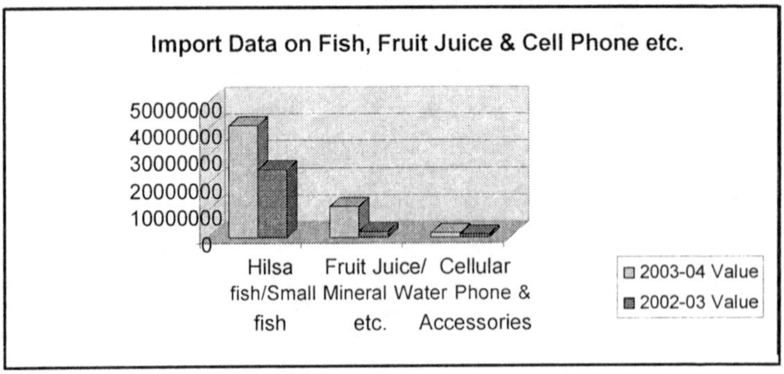

Though routes and channels for formal trade between Bangladesh and India are limited, but the routs and channels for informal trade are unlimited due to the porous nature of international border, coupled with large tracts of forested area and inhospitable terrain. Further, a large number of villages in the region are situated on the extreme border area with traditional road links. This makes the scope of smuggling of contrabands or informal trade in this region, enormous. However, because of the very nature of such trade, it is not possible to quantify the magnitude of informal trade, though available evidences suggest that informal trade is rampant and if such trade is brought within the official ambit a significant increase in export /import can be witnessed.

Main items of illegal export from North Eastern Region to Bangladesh are bidis, sugar, pharmaceutical preparations like phensedyl cough syrup, betel nut and leaves, cattle, textiles, such as sarees/lungis, kerosene /diesel, motor parts, agricultural products, liquor etc.

The main items of illegal import from Bangladesh are gold, pirated CDs & cassettes, potato chips, synthetic fabric, ready made garments, rape seed oil, fruit/synthetic drinks,

GCI sheets, fish and dry fish, soaps, vegetable oil, cement etc.

It is also learnt that goods traded between the two countries through unofficial channels contribute over 70 per cent of the total informal trade volume. Though it is difficult to accurately quantify the magnitude of informal trade, studies conducted by various agencies /NGOs reveal that of the informally traded goods brought into Bangladesh from North Eastern Region, mainly spices constitute about 23 per cent, textiles 13 per cent, sugar 12 per cent, drugs/pharmaceutical products 10 per cent, processed food 9 per cent, cereals 8 per cent, fish 6 per cent, and fruits 3 per cent. Of the informally traded goods that come to the North Eastern Region from Bangladesh, primarily electronic items constitute 20 per cent, jute 15 per cent, plastic products 10 per ccnt, palm oil 7 per cent, spices 4 per cent, textiles 4 per cent and fish 4 per ecnt.

In fact there is almost no informal trade through recognized and functional Land Custom Station as the vigilance of different law enforcing agencies of both the countries is strong there. But there are lot of informal trade routes between Bangladesh and Northeast India at the adjoining areas of all these functional LC stations. There are a good number of organized syndicates engaged in unofficial trade in the frontiers of both the countries. Some of these syndicates are very strong and responsible for most of the informal trade. Smuggling also occurs through non-functional LCS and some of these are considered as safe and secure routes by the organized syndicates as there is no customs office. In these non-functional LCS, smuggling is done without disturbance in connivance with the law enforcing agencies across the borders. Besides these, there are many outlets through which informal trade flows too. Informal trade suggests the extent of potential trade that exists in the region. The reasons for informal trade are many. Some of them include: communication gap between the local businessman and the manufacturers of exportable products or items at distant area, complexity of international trade norms, lack of infrastructure at Land Customs Stations, lack of good road communication, insurgency problem, lack of corporate culture, and institutional factors like banking and other service facilities.

Trade Prospects of Bangladesh and North East Region of India

While India is growing fast, its growth has not been uniform. The northeast region has always been in the shadows and known to be a slow growth market with natural and man-made calamities. Annual flooding of the Brahmaputra Valley restricts investment in the key sectors, while extortion and extremism cause security problems to the agents of economic change. In such a climate trade with Bangladesh has tremendous importance. Some of the dimensions of the trade prospects between the NERI and Bangladesh are discussed below.

- The increased formal trade between Bangladesh and NERI will reduce informal trade and increase government revenue as well as contribute immensely to reduce persistent poverty in the region. The goods exported from NERI to Bangladesh are mainly coal, rice, ginger, onion, dry chili, orange, apple, boulder stone, poultry feed, dry fish, motor parts betel leaves, bamboo, pulse etc. and the goods imported from Bangladesh to NERI is ready-made garments, fruit juice, chips, confectionery items, plastic footwear, plastic table, plastic kitchenware, PVC pipes, UPS, emergency light, cements etc.
- It is also learnt that goods traded between the two

countries through unofficial channels contribute over 70 per cent of the total volume of bilateral trade.

- The business prospects of NERI and Bangladesh are far brighter and more realistic than that with other bordering countries due to the strategic geographic location coupled with supportive natural advantages, complementary resources and modest infrastructural facilities.
- Due to its strategic geographical location, Bangladesh is the bridgehead point of SAARC and ASEAN. It means that Bangladesh has better positional advantage to connect these two vibrant economic blocks of the world through the air, sea, land and rail route. This situational advantage of Bangladesh also opens a bright prospect for the resourceful landlocked NERI in harnessing these opportunities by collectively undertaking economic cooperation and collaboration with Bangladesh.
- There are very good prospects for Indian entrepreneurs to invest in Bangladesh either in joint venture or wholly owned for using the abundant raw materials of this landlocked region to meet the local demand and export to other countries particularly where Bangladesh enjoys preferential market access. Buyback arrangements for the said landlocked region and rest of India can also be a very good option for the Indian visitors.

Trade Challenges between Bangladesh and North East Region of India

- Communication gap between the local businessmen and the manufacturers of exportable goods at distant area also appears as a hindrance in promoting trade between the two countries.

- Lack of knowledge of the local businessmen about export/import procedures and lucrative export/import incentives offered by the government acts as a major impediment in promoting export and import through the LCS of Bangladesh–NERI border despite having enormous potential.
- The businessmen of NERI lack proper knowledge about the products and services that can be procured from Bangladesh at very competitive price and vice-versa. This information gap hinders the prospect of bilateral trade and investment between the two countries.
- The absence of close relationship and cooperation between the business community of Bangladesh and that of NERI also stands on the way of cross border trade and investment.
- Inadequate transport and transit systems between NERI and Bangladesh have led to high transportation costs. It is seen that transport cost of export/import items in NERI-Bangladesh trade is far higher compared to other parts of the world. A large portion of trade, therefore, takes place informally to save cost. Further, lack of infrastructure in the Land Customs Stations aggravates the problem of smooth transaction of formal trade. Many of the Land Customs Stations in the North East do not even have basic amenities like safe drinking water, electrification, and staff quarters. The border areas of the North East are mostly underdeveloped, remote and often difficult to access. Similarly, the levels of infrastructure available across the border are also not upto the mark.
- Insurgency problem poses a security threat towards the trade between the two countries.
- The L/C opening in Meghalaya, Mizoram and Tripura for exporting/importing goods is a cumbersome and

protracted procedure. All the cities and LCS do not have banks with international banking facility to open L/C. As a result, cross border trade between the two regions is hampered to a great extent.

- Most of the L/Cs that are issued for importing goods from North Eastern Region are mail L/Cs. The widespread use of mail L/Cs has been identified as one of the causes of L/C forgery in trade between North Eastern Region and Bangladesh. In addition signature verification causes delays in payments. Use of modern technology can mitigate this problem.
- Policies, rules and regulations adopted by the government with regards to export, import and investment are quite dispersed and not easily available. On the other hand, almost all the government officials responsible for promoting investment and export tremendously lack expertise, professional outlook and responsive attitude to help the entrepreneurs in this regard.
- Bankers in Bangladesh are of the view that there is no quality control in terms of the goods that are imported from the North Eastern Region and this leads to numerous problems in trade finance, ultimately causing delay in remittance of export proceeds. In many cases, it has been seen that after the importer in Bangladesh realizes that the imported goods are deficient in terms of quality /quantity, he lodges a complaint with the local bank and tries to stop payment. Warehouse /storage facility at the Land Customs Stations in Bangladesh, where the importer can physically verify the quality before signing off for payments can mitigate this problem to a large extent.
- Banking infrastructure at NERI for international and border trade is quite inadequate. The bank functioning

at NERI does not have direct arrangements with banks in Bangladesh. This tremendously hampers the bilateral trade between Bangladesh and NERI.

- Availability of cost effective access to communication is a pre-requisite to the growth of cross border trade. Road connectivity across the border continues to be poor due to missing links and poor road conditions, most of which are still fair weather roads. To improve road connectivity, it would be imperative to undertake a huge investment in roads. The condition of the roads leading to the international borders from the production centers is a severe impediment to cross border trade. Roads need to be straightened and broadened so that heavy vehicles can carry larger tonnage in shorter time. These roads can be constructed under a pay and use scheme by collecting toll tax from users. Railways are the cheapest mode of transport. Needless to say that this mode of transport is yet to reach any of the important Land Customs Stations of North East.

Action Plan for Promoting Bilateral Trade between NERI and Bangladesh

The challenges listed above can be overcome if the following measures are adopted.

- Efforts should be made to create a win-win situation between the two countries through a two way trade mission to identify opportunities of trade and investment.
- There is an urgent need to address the information gap that exists between the business communities of our two nations. In fact setting up of a joint interactive portal where business leaders can connect in cyber space and exchange information on business needs and opportunities.

- A joint study group can be constituted which will study the focus areas for business development such as agri business, infrastructure, textile and garments, gems and jewellerys, technology transfer, and services like IT, health care, tourism, education and entertainment.
- People to people contact needs to be intensified to strengthen the partnership.
- While trade history of many developing countries has witnessed a revolutionary change with the emergence of free trade regime, Bangladesh and India are yet to gear up to face the challenge of dynamic bilateral trade between the two countries. Despite the natural geographical proximity to boost trade, non resolution of non-economic issues has barred the utilization of full trade potentials. Most of the products produced in one country having demand in the other country find their way through third country market or through informal routes.
- A platform should be created for the exchange of views, ideas, experiences between the businessmen of both the countries particularly in the service sector for the mutual benefit and promotion of economic cooperation.
- Providing transit facilities to each other could be another area of possible cooperation.
- In order to capture the new markets in South East Asian countries, setting up of joint ventures could be useful.
- The frequent exchange programmes of officials, intellectuals, writers, businessmen, chambers of commerce officials, social workers, celebrities and trade delegation on reciprocal basis could improve people to people contact.

- Direct trade between NERI and Bangladesh makes better economic sense. Increased mutual and international trust, therefore, should be built.
- Capacity building for greater trade creation should be taken up jointly by both the countries for making bilateral trade smooth and sustained.
- In addition to land routes, water transport should be developed with night navigation facilities through river Brahmaputra. The initiatives taken by Inland Waterways Authority of India, Central Water Transport Corporation Ltd., a Government of India undertaking, Inland Waterways Transport Department, Government of Assam should be supported and encouraged by both the countries for transportation of goods to and fro.
- Improvement and development of infrastructural facilities at the existing land customs stations of both the countries should be expedited.
- Air connectivity with visa offices between Dhaka and Guwahati is essential for promotion of bilateral trade.
- Setting up of trade centers of international standard at Guwahati to facilitate regular meeting between buyers and sellers with facilities for exhibition of products should be taken up.
- Both India and Bangladesh should bring down the tariff rate on items having mutual interest for both Bangladesh and NERI.The restriction of RBI in obtaining foreign currency transaction right for banks in NERI should be eased so that at least one bank in every district headquarter of all the states of NERI has foreign currency retention and transaction right.
- India and Bangladesh should also eliminate all sorts of para tariff and non-tariff barriers, which are heavily impeding the acceleration of bilateral trade between Bangladesh & NERI.

- Northeast India has enormous resources like minerals, quarry, forestry, horticulture, crops, plantation and many others which are not economically feasible to carry to mainland India either in the form of raw material or finished products. It is rather feasible and pragmatic to set up industries in Bangladesh based on those raw materials and then re-export to Northeast and other parts of India. Against this backdrop, Indian entrepreneurs can set up joint venture industries in Bangladesh for meeting the local demand as well as send those to India again as buyback arrangement. The joint venture industry will have scope to export to other countries also. Both Bangladesh and Indian Governments should workout a joint action plan in this regard.
- Banks in Northeast India having foreign currency transaction and retention right should be allowed to make direct correspondence with the banks in Bangladesh instead of through any other bank branches elsewhere.

Conclusion

Prospects of bilateral trade between Bangladesh and India are bright. There are many areas where the two countries can join hands and enhance trade, but non-resolution of non-economic issues makes the trading between the two countries difficult. While the many countries have witnessed revolutionary changes following the emergence of free trade regime, India and Bangladesh are yet to gear up to the realities of bilateral trade. One of the instruments that can be utilized for achieving the potentials of bilateral trade between the two countries is Free Trade Agreements (FTAs). There is a wide spread belief among the trading communities of the two countries that with the introduction of FTA trading between India and Bangladesh would get a boost. The sooner the governments of the two countries understand the pulse of the trading communities will be better.

REFERENCES

Das, Gurudas, (2000), "Trade Between the North Eastern Region and Neighbouring Countries: Structures and Implications for Development", in Das, Gurudas and R K Purkayastha, (eds), *Border Trade: North East India and Neighbouring Countries*, Akansha Publishing House, New Delhi.

13

INDO-BANGLADESH TRADE THROUGH KARIMGANJ: PROBLEMS AND PROSPECTS

Niranjan Roy

Introduction

The Barak Valley region constituting three districts, namely, Cachar, Karimganj and Hailakandi forms the southern most part of the state of Assam. The valley is bounded by the North Cachar Hills district of Assam and the state of Mizoram in the north and south respectively. The principal river Barak flows in from Manipur in the east reached Badarpur town in the Karimganj district. From Badarpur to Haritikar, it provides the boundary between the Karimganj district and the Bangladesh. At Haritikar, the river is divided into two branches, namely, surma and kushiara. The later branch entered Bangladesh while the former entered Karimganj town and continues to form the frontier of Barak Valley region with Bangladesh. The economy of the region is predominantly agricultural with more than 70 percent of the work force being engaged in agriculture and other primary activities. Though the region is not devoid of manufacturing units, its geographical isolation handicaps it for a programme of large-scale industrialization (Roy and Bezbaruah, 2000). The prospect of economic development of the region therefore depends critically on the growth of agriculture and allied activities linking with cross border trade.

The Karimganj district of the Barak valley region shares one hundred kilometer border with Bangladesh. A large volume of border trade of the north eastern region with Bangladesh takes place through the two border transit points, namely, Sutarkandi Land Custom Station and Karimganj Steamerghat Land Custom Station (reverine route), both located in the Karimganj district.

Objective

The present chapter attempts to analyse the prospects of bilateral trade between India and Bangladesh in the backdrop of SAFTA and the flaws associated with it. Karimganj being an important border trade transit point between India and Bangladesh, the study aims to analyse the issues related to cross border trade in that trade point. Both formal and informal trade have been taken up for analysis.

Database and Methodology

The study is based on both primary and secondary data. Secondary data have been collected from the Department of Customs, Karimganj and from other publications. For collection of primary data, simple random sampling method has been used. For analysis of both secondary and primary data simple tabular representation is used.

Historical Perspective

Trade between India and Bangladesh in north eastern region takes place mainly with three states, namely, Meghalaya, Assam and Tripura. Karimganj is the only border trade point in South Assam between India and Bangladesh. Karimganj with an area of 1839 sq. kms is a district of Assam in its southern periphery bordering Bangladesh in the north-west side and the state of Tripura on the southwest, Mizoram in the south and Cachar and Hailakandi districts in the eastern side. This part of Assam had a unique history of its own. "Untill 1874, Sylhet formed an integral part of Bengal, being included in the Dacca division, but in that year by proclamation dated 12th September, it was transferred to the newly created province of Assam together with the adjoining district of Cachar" (Hunter, 1879). Originally, an integral part of Sylhet district which was tagged with Assam in 1874 from the Dacca division of the then Bengal in order to make Assam a viable state, at the moment of partition of India, a referendum was inflicted on Sylhet district, to be or not to be within the Indian union. The referendum opted in favour of joining East Pakistan and the entire district of Sylhet became a part of East Pakistan. As a result of the Radcliffe Boundary Commission Award, making the Kushiara river as the natural boundary between Assam and East Pakistan, three and half thanas of Karimganj sub-division of the Sylhet district, viz, Ratabari, Patharkandi, Badarpur and half of Karimganj came back to Assam on 17th August, 1947. This part is what now constitutes Karimganj district which till 1st July, 1983 was a sub-division of Cachar district (Nath, 1995).

The post independence period is divided in to two parts, (a) the East Pakistan period, from 14th August, 1947 till December, 1971, the emergence of Bangladesh as an independent country, and (b) the Bangladesh period. From trans-border trade point of view, the East Pakistan period is from 14 October, 1952, the day passport system was made effective to the beginning of the Indo-Pak war of 1965. There was trade holiday for six years, 1965-71. It is to be noted that before the emergence of Bangladesh, that is, before 1965, Karimganj border had four Land Custom Stations (LCS), namely, the Mohissason LCS (rail route), Sutarkandi LCS (land route), Karimganj Steamerghat LCS (reverine) and Karimganj Ferryghat LCS (land route). After 1965, the reverine route via East Pakistan was closed. So Karimganj Steamerghat LCS was amalgamated with Karimganj Ferryghat LCS. The Mohissason LCS has also become virtually defunct with the closure of bitumen import from Chittagong refinery of Bangladesh. During the East Pakistan period there were three categories of trans-border trade, namely, (1) OGL, open to all under export finance rules that had been in force from time to time (2) Licensing control and (3) Reserved for government agencies like Department of Agriculture and State Trading Corporations of both Central and State governments. The articles of formal export were quite large. These included rice, salt, chilli, ginger, black pepper, betelnut, citrus, pineapple, orange, readymade garments, cosmetics, motorparts, electrical goods, kerosene, sugar, coal, cement etc. Non-formal or illegal items were hashish, India made foreign liquor, bidi, cattle, heroine, gold and foreign exchange. Formal import items were fresh fish, dry fish, chita molasses, bitumen etc. Informal articles smuggled were mostly foreign goods which were not imported to India, namely, powder milk, calculator, pens, tape recorder, TV sets, camera, gold, narcotic drugs, foreign exchange and unskilled labour. There have been some changes in importance of traded goods and a little addition during the Bangladesh period (Dass, 1999).

Formal Trade

With the SAARC initiative the volume of trade with Bangladesh has increased since 1990s. Due to the logistic advantage, traditionally trade with Bangladesh was mainly informal (Dutta and Roy, 2000). Things have changed during the past couple of years due to the liberalization in trade restrictions amongst the SAARC countries. As a result volume of trade and balance of payments have improved. In keeping with the overall Indo-Bangladesh trade trend, the Karimganj LCS also confirms favourable balance of trade and improving terms of trade. Data collected from the Customs Department,

Karimganj about export and import are presented in table-13.1

TABLE-13.1

Value of Export and Import Through Karimganj LCS

(Rs. in crores)

Year	*Sutarkandi LCS*		*Steamerghat LCS*		*Total*	*Trade*
	Export	*Import*	*Export*	*Import*	*Export* *Import*	*Balance*
1996-97	21.67	4.70	4.29	0.0008	25.96 4.7008	+21.26
1997-98	33.76	4.56	9.48	nil	4.56 42.24	+38.68
1998-99	28.63	5.30	22.62	0.05	5.35 51.25	+45.9
1999-00	35.38	3.93	2.12	nil	37.5 3.93	+33.57
2000-01	18.38	1.68	2.63	0.01	22.01 1.69	+19.32
2001-02	13.79	00.73	3.91	00.33	17.70 1.06	+16.64
2002-03	22.87	00.08	6.00	00.13	28.87 00.21	+28.66
2003-04	48.14	1.63	2.03	0.004	50.77 1.637	+49.133
2004-05	21.34	6.61	3.64	0.07	24.98 7.67	+17.31

Source: Department of Customs, Karimganj.

As per the statistics available from the department of Customs, Karimganj, the total amount of both export and import trade at the two transit points of Karimganj fluctuated during the period under study. Export trade reached a peak level during 1998-99, while that of imports in 2004-05. However, after 1998-99 exports declined substantially. The reason being the worst road condition between Karimgamj and Sutarkandi. During 2001 efforts have been made by the Government of India to improve this border road and it was declared as National Highway 151. The construction work of this road has been carried out by the Border Roads Organisation. There has been an increasing trend of exports from India with the improvement of road conditions. The balance of trade situation is favourable to India.

The major export items are coal, non-basmati rice, fresh ginger, dry chillies, citrus (local variety called Hatkada), fresh vegetables, jackfruit, banana, grapes, pineapple, fresh orange, betel leaves and nuts, mango, peas, raw cotton, soyabean, onion, garlic, turmeric, rohu fish (Andhra variety), grain sorghum, tubelight, readymade dress materials, parts and accessories of tractors and motor vehicles, umbrella parts, soap, aluminium and brass products, poultry feed etc., while imports consisted mainly of hilsa fish, chita molasses, dhakai sari, fruit juice, cold drinks etc.

While coal comes from neighbouring state of Meghalaya, fresh vegetables and fresh fruits originate from Mizoram and Manipur and other industrial products come from the heartlands. It is to be noted that the demand for agricultural commodities like fresh vegetables and fruits in Bandgladesh has increased manifold over the years. The entire north eastern region can take the advantage of this growing demand for agricultural commodities in Bangladesh. The region possesses tremendous potentials for production of ginger, citrus, pineapple, orange etc.

Informal trade and under invoicing are major irritants which hamper growth of formal trade notwithstanding trade liberalization measures. It is estimated that during the winter, about 200 truckloads of coal move to Bangladesh everyday carrying at least seven tones of coal instead of five tones permissible limit. Cess per tonne coal varies between Rs.700/- to Rs.800/-. The loss in the collection of cess, thus, amounts to in the range of Rs.2.8 lakh and Rs.3.2 lakh a day (Dass, 1999).

Informal Trade

Detail statistics on the volume of trans-border informal trade with Bangladesh via Karimganj is not available. However, Research and Information System (RIS), New-Delhi, had undertaken a study in 1996 on informal border trade in India with select neighbouring countries. Table-13.2 presents data relating to informal border trade with Bangladesh via north eastern region.

TABLE-13.2

Volume of Transborder Informal Trade with Bangladesh Via North Eastern States: 1996

(Rs. in Lakh)

Country	*Value of Export from North East India*	*Value of Import to North East India*
Via Mizoram	1862	268
Via Tripura	36236	5956
Via Meghalaya	1362	758
Via Assam	2550	6180
Total	42010	768

Source: Research and Information System (1996), India's Border Trade with select Neighbouring Countries, New-Delhi.

There is, however, some limitations of the data published by the RIS survey like under valuation of traded goods by the respondent traders, non-quantification of volume of barter trade etc. Nevertheless, these data provide some indications of the volume of informal transborder trade with Bangladesh through the north eastern region. The data also exibit favourable balance of trade for the region.

There were strict restrictions of both passenger traffic and goods during 1952-65. With Bangladesh becoming a SAARC member, trade restrictions have been substantially liberalized. As a result, volume of trade has increased. Total revenue earning has also gone up even though customs duty earning is nominal. However, seizure value now compensates for the loss of custom duty due to liberalization in the wake of SAARC agreements. Interestingly, the seizure value now a days is higher than formal duty revenue. Goods are seized for violation of the Import Export Control Act, the Customs Act, 1962 and allied Trade Control rules and orders. Disposal of seized goods assumes importance because it is an important source of income. The Customs Act 1962 authorises the BSF and Assam police to seize any goods that might be apprehended during illegal cross-border transit. Such goods are to be handed over to the Custom's authority at the earliest for final disposal. Seized goods, claimed or unclaimed, are disposed of by the Custom authority under district adjudication procedure (Dass, 1999). Table 13.3 shows the revenue earned by Karimganj Custom Division from duty plus seizure value.

TABLE 13.3

Income from Duty Plus Seizure Value at Karimganj Customs Division

(Rs.in lakhs)

Year	*Duty*	*Seizure Value*	*Total*
1996-97	27.0	31.0	58.0
1997-98	18.0	37.0	55.0
1998-99	10.0	95.0	105.0
1999-00	6.97	30.37	37.34
2000-01	6.86	17.71	24.57
2001-02	13.16	17.49	30.65
2002-03	6.39	39.82	46.1
2003-04	22.28	21.04	43.32
2004-05	63.05	27.97	91.02

Source: Department of Customs, Karimganj Division.

Table13.3 shows that since 1996-97, the seizure value is higher than the income earned from duty. The data during the pre-liberalisation era are not available. However, it can be assumed that the revenue loss due to liberalization in customs duty are now being compensated by income from seizure value. It is to be mentioned here that the figures presented in Table 13.3 are also not exhaustive. This is because it does not take in to account the value of the precious articles confiscated, namely, gold and silver, foreign currency etc. As per the provision of the Customs Act some seized articles, gold, foreign currency, silver etc are confiscated and deposited to the Reserve Bank of India, Alipur mint and the Ministry of Finance, Government of India.

To examine the position of informal border trade as compared to RIS study in 1996 (in which the present author was associated with survey work), a random sample from 50 traders of different categories has been drawn from the Karimganj town. The purpose of this sample study has been to assess the current informal trade status in this border trade point. Most of the traders involve in informal trade are found to have their formal trading activities as well. They informed that traders from Bangladesh easily cross the border at some points and purchase goods from them under the disguise of an ordinary customer of the town. Since there is cultural and linguistic homogeneity of the people of the town and their counterparts across the border, the middlemen utilize this advantage without any risk. They usually pay in Indian currency, which can be acquired at a small commission from the border agents. The goods are transported by road as well as by country boats or even by porters on foot. Data collected on informal border trade from the sample survey are presented in Table 13.4.

TABLE 13.4

Export/Import Data of Informal Trade with Bangladesh Via Karimganj during 2004-05.

(Rs. in Lakh)

Name of commodities	Value of Exports	Value of Imports
Motor parts (used)	12.84	—
Cattle	3.02	—
Rohu fish (Andhra variety)	9.8	—
Hilsa fish	—	10.1
Foreign liquor (India made)	8. 7	
Bidi	7.6	—
Gold and silver	—	19.76
Rice	27.9	10.5
Grocery items	29.3	—
Foreign exchange	—	11.12
Total	99.16	51.48

Source: Field Survey.

Data presented in Table 13.4 are in conformity with the results of the study conducted by RIS, New-Delhi in 1996. It may be noted that some of the items like rohu fish, hilsa fish etc. are common in both formal and informal category of trade. A substantial part of informal trade in fish is done through under invoicing. Interestingly, used motor parts are of high demand in Bangladesh than that of fresh ones. It is informed that the used motor parts are generally re-used in motorboats and in other vehicle making in Bangladesh. The grocery items are also in high demand in Bangladesh. These are mainly demanded by the people residing in the adjoining areas of border. In Sutarkandi area even the border crosses in between residential plots of the inhabitants of that area. There is also informal trade in manual labour. Very often the labourers from Bangladesh cross over to India in the morning to work as rickshaw puller, hand thela puller or wage labourer and return in the evening. No reliable data is available to estimate the income outflows associated with informal trade in manual labour. However, from personal experience and informal discussions with some rickshaw pullers and daily labourers, it is known that there is influx of Bangladeshi daily labourers in the town. These daily labourers are demanded mainly in construction works because of their cheaper wage rate. It is roughly estimated that about three to four hundred such labourers cross the border at Karimganj daily.

Need for Closer Ties

Recognising the need to enhance border trade between India and Bangladesh, US Consul General in Kolkata George N Sibley has said that a transit route through Bangladesh, connecting Tripura with Kolkata, should be worked out to explore "untapped resources" of the northeastern state. The geography has brought Bangladesh and northeastern region of India closer. There is a huge potential for border trade between the two countries and "land-locked" north east can be connected with Kolkata with a transit route through Bangladesh. The Indian and Bangladeshi governments should work out a policy for border trade and transit route between the two countries. There are massive "untapped resources" in north eastern region which can be explored by attracting expertise and investors from outside and there can also be gas-based industries because of the huge recoverable reserve of natural gas. The abundance of pineapple which can be used as a raw material in several industries can be a boon. North Eastern Region's handicraft products can find a market anywhere in the world (Indian Express, 2004).

Indo-Bangladesh economic relations have been affected by the legacy of history. Bangladesh, after all, was a part of Pakistan for more than two decades when Pakistan fought two wars with India. History has not ceased casting its long shadow. The mindset and preconceptions inherited from the past linger on in both countries. Moreover, in the post-independence period, the ebb and flow in political relationships have affected economic relations as well. In inter-country relationships, economic and political relations are intertwined. There is no reason to expect any exception in this case. Close or strong economic relationships, including trade and economic cooperation between countries, have often been propelled by the prevailing close political relations or by a desire to strengthen future political relations.The Indian economy is not only much larger and more diversified but also is more advanced in terms of industry, services and technology. The asymmetry in economic size and population has implications for the distribution of possible gains from economic cooperation. However, while India's gain in relation to her economy as a whole may be marginal, it could be sizeable if it is judged in relation to the economy of the neighbouring states of West Bengal and the North-Eastern Region (Islam, 2004).

TABLE 13.5

Taka-Rupee, Rupee-Taka Market Exchange Rate (Batta-Rate)

	Taka to Rupee 'Upor Batta'		*Rupee to Taka 'Tol Batta'*	
Year	*Taka*	*Rupee*	*Rupee*	*Taka*
1968	1.64	Rs.1	Rs.1	1.61
1978	1.52	Rs.1	Rs.1	1.50
1988	1.22	Rs1	Rs.1	1.19
1997	1.17	Rs.1	Rs.1	1.14
1998	1.18	Rs.1	Rs.1	1.16
1999	1.20	Rs.1	Rs.1	1.17

Source: Dass, 1999.

Infact Bangladesh economy today is much stable than it had been in the past. It is a fast growing economy in South Asia despite problems of over population and riddled with poverty. Its growth rate today is better. According to the World development report, its per capita income has increased from $130 in 1986 to $240 in 1996 to $344 in 1995-96 and then to $444 in 2003-04. Another indigenous but empirically reliable indicator is the market exchange rate taka to rupee (called 'Upor batta') and rupee to taka (called 'Tol batta'). The changes of this rate over time as collected from 'Battadars' in Karimganj are shown in Table 13.5.

The data in Table 13.5 indicate Bangladesh's better economic performance in terms of appreciation of the value of her currency. This increases the scope for cross-border formal trade. The Bangladesh market is now much bigger and has been expanding. Dhaka and Chittagong (the country's chief port) are the principal industrial centers where clothing and cotton textiles, jute products, processed food, steel, and chemical fertilizers are manufactured. In addition to clothing, textiles, jute, and jute products, exports include tea, leather, fish, and shrimp. Remittances from several million Bangladeshis working abroad are the second largest source of foreign income. Since the country is unable to feed itself, the most important import of Bangladesh is food. Capital goods, petroleum, and textiles are other major imports. Western Europe, the United States, India, and China are the main trading partners. The country's economy is based on agriculture. Rice, jute, tea, sugarcane, tobacco, and wheat are the chief crops. Bangladesh is the world's largest producer of jute. Fishing is also an important economic activity, and beef, dairy products, and poultry are also produced. Except for natural gas (found along its eastern border), limited quantities of oil (in the Bay of Bengal), coal, and some uranium, Bangladesh possesses few minerals (Islam, 2004).

Since Bangladesh is the only SAARC member having border with North Eastern Region of India, there is a necessity for closer bilateral trade relationship with Bangladesh. The Bangladesh market is now much bigger and has been expanding. The major export items going from the region to

Bangladesh consist of minerals, agricultural and agro-products. As such the region has potential to tap this expanded market since the region produces a number of agricultural and allied goods, which have high demand in Bangladesh. The entire region has abundant labour force and rich natural resources which could provide a good basis for export oriented manufacturing sector, particularly in the areas of medicinal product, rubber, handloom products, handicrafts, bamboo and cane products etc. The geo-climatic conditions of the region are favourable to large scale production of pineapples, orange and banana. Of the total production in India, the region produces 50 percent of pineapples, 13 percent of oranges and 6 percent of bananas. If their marketing and processing could be developed, it could open up a wide scope of marketable surplus in the region (Choudhury, 2003).

The initiative taken by the North Eastern Federation of International Trade (NEFIT), Chambers of Commerce and Industry of Sylhet and Chittagong of Bangladesh to jointly promote bilateral trade and investment between the states of North Eastern Region and Bangladesh is a step towards right direction. A Memorandum of Understanding has already been signed between the Chambers of Commerce across the border.

Prospects of Karimganj Border Trade Post

It is to be noted that Karimganj is the only border point in the North Eastern Region, which is connected with Bangladesh by all the three popular transport modes, namely, roadways, waterways and railways. But this unique transportation potential is not utilized fully. Misperception exists among some sections in Bangladesh about India's intention for more cooperation in transport sector. It is evident from the observations made by M. Rahmatullah, Bangladesh Transport and Infrastructure Programme Director that lack of awareness among Bangladesh's civil society about real benefit of co-operation, lack of trust and lack of political will are proving as stumbling blocks in transport co-operation between India and Bangladesh. Even when the world is increasingly becoming a global village, people in Bangladesh still apprehend that any cooperation in the field of transport would benefit only India and not to Bangladesh.

South Asia accounts for only four per cent of the world trade and transportation bottlenecks appears to be the prime cause for this poor performance. There is the prospective short-cut Asian Highway link through Sylhet-Sutarkandi-Karimganj-Imphal-Tamu. Since Bangladesh has a highway from Seola (opposite side of Sutarkandi) which connects Dhaka via Sylhet, the NH 151 via Karimganj town is a very good link between two countries. There are some long pending issues that need to be addressed for harmonizing the transport system between the two countries. For harmonizing the railway network between the two countries, coupling and braking system need to be standardized. Similarly for harmonizing road transport, standardisation need to be done at the earliest as axle load in India is 10 tons compared to 8 tons in Bangladesh which will add to cost constraints. Bangladesh roads are of high standard but have high non-motor traffic. Considering average distance from North East India, Rail and Inland Water Transport could be cost effective (Indian Express, 2004). Despite the protocol since 1980 for inter-country transit traffic, Inland Water Transport has not been used to the fullest extent There are lot of problems such as lack of round the year navigation and night navigation, lack of sufficient port of call, slow traffic speed at 50 kilometres per day which need to be addressed. Although Karimganj inland water port was constructed in the late 1980s by the Inland Water Transport Corporation of India, it was hardly used all these years. Recently, it has been brought to life again on since July, 1999. Presently coals are being exported to Bangladesh by steamer services. It is to be mentioned that before the partition, water routes used to be an important mode of transport of goods between Barak Valley and the rest of the world through the rivers in East Bengal. These waterways continued to be active till the Indo-Pak war of 1965. But subsequently volume of transport through these waterways had declined considerably. Whatever transportation by steamer takes place between Karimganj in Barak Valley and Calcutta Port on the Bay of Bengal through this traditional waterway is restricted only in the summer season (Roy and Bezbaruah, 2003).

Infact Karimganj was a hot spot for smuggling activities even in the late 1990s. This had also an effect on socio-economic environment of the town as reflected in the frequent occurrences of anti-social activities (Dutta and Roy, 2000). However, after trade liberalization the situation has improved and there is a declining trend of crimes in the town. Smuggling of earlier days has been transformed in to legal trading activities to a large extent. There are about 180 individual members of the two exporter-importer associations in the town. The Sutarkandi has been declared as SEZs. The Ministry of Commerce, Government of India, has also undertaken infrastructure development at Sutarkandi. Thus, this border point has immense potential to carry out cross border trade between North Eastern Region and Bangladesh.

REFERENCES

Choudhury, Rabindra Kumar (2003) "Economic and Industrial Base of North East", Assam Tribune, Saturday, July, 12.

Dass, Susanta (1999), "Trans-Border Trade via Karimganj, 1947-98", The North East Twilight, Silchar, 30th September.

Dutta, P.C and Niranjan Roy (2000), 'The Impact of Cross- Border Human Traffic: A case study of Karimganj district' in Gurudas Das and R.K. Purkayastha, (eds), *Border Trade: North East India and Neighbouring Countries,* Akansha Publishing House, New- Delhi.

Roy, Niranjan and M.P. Bezbaruah (2000), "Performance of Agriculture in the Barak Valley region of Assam from mid-1970s to mid-1990s", Indian Journal of Regional Science, Vol. 32, No. 1.

Roy, Niranjan and Bezbaruah, (2003), *Agricultural Growth and Regional Economic Development,* Mittal Publication, New-Delhi.

Koshy, Perumal (2002), "Regional Cooperation and the Need to Accelerate Intra SAARC Trade", http://www.boloji.com/analysis/052.htm, November 10.

Hunter, W.W. (1879), *A Statistical Account of Assam,* Vol. II, Trubner & Co., London, p. 259.

Nath, Sudarshan (1995), Impact of Technology on Green Revolution in Karimganj District, Assam, Gauhati University (unpublished thesis).

Islam, Nurul (2004) "Indo-Bangladesh Economic Relations- Some Thoughts", Economic and Political Weekly, September 4-10, Vol. XXXIX, No. 36.

Indian Express, 27th May, 2004.

14

TRADE AND TRADE ROUTES: HISTORICAL PERSPECTIVE

Sanjeeb Kakoty

Historical Backdrop

Meghalaya has a border of 423 kilometres with Bangladesh. All throughout history, the hill people have maintained extensive trade relations with the plains of Bangladesh. Most British writers have noted this trade and Robinson writing in 1841 said "A considerable trade in cotton, iron ore, wax, ivory, betel leaf and cloths, is carried on between the plains and the hills and Jaintiapore, the capital, is the great *entreport,* in which all commercial dealings are transacted." (Robinson 1841):[1]

W.W. Hunter, in his *Statistical Account of Assam* (1879) noted that

> *the external commerce of the Khasi and Jaintia Hills is chiefly conducted on the southern boundary, through the district of Sylhet. The total value is more considerable than might be expected, owing to the fact that these Hills practically possess the monopoly of supplying Bengal with lime, potatoes and oranges. Other important articles of export are raw cotton, stick-lac, betel-nut and pan leaves, and bay leaves or tezpat. The exportation of iron, which was once large, has now almost ceased.*[2]

Trade was carried out in markets known as *hats*. During the year 1876-77, it was estimated that the total import to the Khasi and Jaintia Hills was worth Rs 1,576,483, with rice being the major commodity with an import of 205,800 *maunds* and a value of Rs 720,300, and fish and dry fish imports worth Rs 215,400 and cloth imports totalling Rs 1,58,000 and the other major commodities being salt, tobacco, tea and coffee, bras pots and pans, liquor, country soap etc., while the value of total exports was estimated at Rs 1,603,530 with potatoes being the chief export commodity with an export value of Rs 501,250 and consisting of 200,500 *maunds*, limestone exports were next in value with an export of Rs 480,000, cotton Rs 216,000, stick lac Rs 100,000, betel nut and leaf Rs 95,600 and Oranges Rs 37,600 [3] Thus, it is amply clear that there existed a vibrant trade between the Khasi and Jaintia hills and the plains of Bengal, especially Sylhet. However, with the redrawing of political boundaries in the region and the emergence of new nation states, the centuries old border trade received a severe blow.

The Implications of the Modern State System

There is no denying of the fact that in the modern world, national boundaries have emerged as "sacrosanct symbols of sovereignty"[4]. But at the same time for people who routinely move to and fro over such boundaries, the existence of such artificial and man made borderlines represent mere obstacles to mobility! "This experience reflects a much older reality than national maps, because for most of human history, states had little power to regulate mobility across borders. For many centuries, social and cultural boundaries marked the supremacy of specific groups in particular places, without imposing restrictions on geographical mobility. Pre-modern territorial boundaries resembled island shores or edges of forest clearings more than gated city walls."[5]

Perhaps, it is our orientation about borders being the

sacrosanct symbols of sovereignty that predisposes us to view the inviolable nature of state boundaries. This in spite of the fact that often, as in the case of India's north east and present day Bangladesh, a shared history, ethnic affinity and economic symbiosis, ridicules the arbitrary drawing of the sovereign boundaries in this region. No doubt, political compulsions, skewed as they may be, have prompted successive governments to persist with the arbitrary border lines and promote an agenda of mutual exclusiveness. No matter that such a policy of mutual exclusion goes against the tide of the natural flow of history and economic ground realities.

The Border Commission and Demarcation of the Boundary

The mandate of the Boundary commission was simple and stated that the Boundary Commission is instructed to demarcate the boundaries of the two parts of the Punjab [or of Bengal] on the basis of ascertaining the contiguous majority areas of Muslims and non-Muslims. In doing so it will also take into account other factors.

What those other factors could be remained ambiguous and succeeded in opening another area for dispute.

The Partition of India and the Logic of Demarcation

As has been rightly pointed out "unlike much boundary-making in the colonial world, the Border between East Pakistan (Bangladesh) and India owed little to "modern" concepts of spatial rationality...the exact location of the new border itself became a bone of contention. Despite international mediation and several treaties, important parts of the border remain contested, undemarcated and volatile even today."[6] If one were to contrast the difference in what Congress in politically conscious Bengal had sought and what they actually received during partition, the politically less organized and conscious Khasis, could have hardly made their voices heard.

For instance, "the Congress had claimed for West Bengal about fifty nine percent of the area and forty six percent of the population of the province. Under the Radcliffle Award, only thirty six percent of the area and thirty five percent of the population were assigned to West Bengal. Of the total Muslim population of Bengal only sixteen percent came under West Bengal, while as many as forty two percent of non-Muslims remained in East Bengal."[7]

Partition dealt a severe blow to small communites living in the newly demarcated border areas. For instance, one may take the case of those villages of the United Khasi and Jaintia Hills which had secured the permission to pay their land revenue at the nearest tehsil which happened to be Sylhet, a few minutes downstream from their places of habitation. But administratively, they were under the the jurisdiction of Shillong or Jowai which were a considerable distance away. Though racially and linguistically they belong to the Khasi group, unfortunately for these villages, the boundary commission clubbed all villages remitting their revenue in Sylhet under Pakistan!

The Implication for the Khasis

Mr M.F. Ryngksai, the headman of Dawki and also the president of the Federal Council of Warmihngi and War Jaintia explained:

> *The demarcation of the border between India and Bangladesh was not done properly. It was not based on facts. As a result the Khasis lost a lot of land. At times the border was put plum in the middle of orchards or fields. The fields and orchards that fell to the Bangla side were destroyed. Understandably so, as they were not the owners of the orchards and "bagans" they had no love for them. They plucked the betel nuts and chopped the timber trees and ravaged the carefully*

> *nurtured orchards! It was thought, and very wrongly, that the Khasis only lived in the hills and hence the plains were a part of Bangla. So the hills remained with us and we lost the plains. But even today we have about one lakh Khasis still living in Bangladesh. It is another matter that many of them are thinking of moving over and are acquiring property in India with the help of their relatives here.*[8]

Similar sentiments were expressed by Mr John F. Kharshiing, Adviser and Spokesperson of the Federation of 25 Khasi States. He said that

> *the drawing of the boundary between India and East Pakistan during partition was not done in a fair manner. The way in which the boundary pillars have been placed seems to reinforce the assumption that the Hillmen or the Khasis lived only in the hills and they had no land or property in the plains. But this was simply not true. However, it appears that the survey team for the demarcation of the boundary too worked with this basic assumption in place. Hence, the demarcation was wrong and has not found acceptance even today....*[9]

What Does History Say?

Though it is common to ascribe the erroneous demarcation of the international boundary being the root cause that led to the alienation of much Khasi land in the plains of Bangladesh[10] and the fact that in present day Bangladesh there are roughly about one lakh Khasis, yet, the genesis of the process of land alienation among the Khasis in the plain areas of present day Bangladesh probably began in the Moghul times. David Ludden in an extremely well researched paper[11] has delved into this aspect very well. I have liberally drawn from his paper to highlight this neglected area of history:

In 1612, Mughal armies created the first system of state authority in the region called the Sylhet Sarkar ... advanced their supremacy by promoting agriculture, clearing jungle, and conquering, assimilating, and expelling jungle people. The Mughals pursued this mission extensively, because farms, not jungle, provided state revenue, and farmers, not jungle people, bowed to Mughal authority. When the English East India Company took Bengal from the nawabs, in 1757, the old northeastern frontiers of Mughal Bengal posed many problems. Khasis held most land north of the Surma and ruled mountains above. Jaintia Khasi rajas held mountains and lowlands north and east of Sylhet town...In the lowlands, the English increased taxation as much as they could, but Sylhet district remained poor revenue territory, covered with forest...In the 1780s, natural calamity made the jungles between Pandua and Sunamganj more attractive for lowland farmers and investors. Massive floods in 1784 and 1787 disrupted life drastically in the plains and mountains, and famines ensued. More investors focused their attention on land above the flood line, covered with jungle, even as merchant activity expanded along routes to the mountains. Pressed for funds to finance imperial wars, the English became more willing to use force to increase tax revenues. As a result, a motley, violent and chaotic mixture of British imperialism and Bengali enterprise invaded the land north of the Surma, where prime land for new farms lay in forests filled with people who never submitted to the Mughals, Nawabs or British. In November 1791, the 35th Sepoy Battalion left Sylhet, its mission only half-accomplished. The new state boundary drawn between British Bengal and mountain Khasi domains became a reality based on Khasi victories in the mountains and British victories below. The new border ran along the base of the mountains and bisected the route from Sunamganj to Pandua. It marked the northern limit of British Bengal, which only then extended indisputably to the mountains, and equally indisputably, did not include Pandua.

Marking boundaries firmly was not normal imperial practice at the time, so it required extensive justification... the English drew this boundary to restrict mobility by defining the northern mountains as independent Khasi territory. Henceforth, mountain Khasis officially became aliens in the plains, where all the land became Bengali territory... Government auctions of Khasi land began in 1792, and a year later, the collector reported that he had completed sales of all land expropriated from rebellious Khasi and Bengali villagers, except a "trifling remainder of Cosseah land." The old Mughal northeastern frontiers witnessed a rapid increase in privately owned landed property. In 1789, 4000 Sylhet taxpayers had owned land under Company law; in 1795, the number was 26,000, and a year later, it rose to 27,000...[12]

The Border Hats and Informal Trade

In the lands where borders were demarcated without reason and fences sought to be erected sans logic, familes and communities are separated by imagined lines. So too can livelihoods be as easily robbed, by considerations of sovereign boundaries! But thanks to human ingenuity and the overwhelming desire to survive, people in these areas continue to trade and to barter, exchanging things that they have for goods that they require. This finds reflection in the petty border *hats* and vibrant informal trade that these border areas have.

A plaintive call to regularize such informal markets can

be read in a memorandum[13] submitted to the President of India by the representatives of the Indigenous Khasi people on 20th march 2001:

> *We seek Constitutional recognition to our simple Hat Markets for our open barter trade of our perishable items with Bangladesh which has been existing since time immemorial which would resolve the genuine difficulties faced by our people in exchanging our "perishable items" such as Arecanut, Papaya, Citrust Fruit, Jack Fruit, Broomstick, Tejpatta, Oranges, Beatle Leaves, (sic) Rice and Pulses; and other Seasonal Fruits, also damaged and rotten vegetables and other perishable items in exchange for Fish, Eggs and Vegetables and other Seasonal Fruits not available on our side. The Central Agencies manning the Borders are helpless, and restrictions are imposed on the age old custom of barter trade in the Local Hats (Traditional Border Markets) due to the present Acts and Laws of the Country concerning International trade which were adopted without taking our Syiems, Sirdars, Dolois & Nokmas (Rulers) into confidence and without seeking their opinion, resulting in our traditional rights being deprived due to Constitutional legalities.*
>
> *The present system of declaring an area as an export and import route will not solve the problem of the thousands of poor people as they are not in a position to involve themselves in the intricacies of export and import as the majority are illiterate. They are just thousands of poor people who want to barter one or two baskets of their perishable items in exchange for fish etc., in their Hats (Traditional border markets).*
>
> *We submit and draw your attention to the following facts that there are more or less 30-35 local markets*

(Hats) all along the International Borders of the 25 Khasi States, Jaintia Hills and Garo Hills. The Local Hats (Traditional Border Markets) where barter trade has been going on since time immemorial are as follows:

Federation of Ri-War Mihngi Local Durbars;

Name of Market	*State (Hima) / Sirdarship*	*No of villages involved*	*Distance from Main Market*
01. *Hat* Nongjri	Nongjri Sirdarship	35	85 Kms
02. *Hat* Dearbally	Umnui -Tmar, Sirdarship	45	87 Kms
03. *Hat* Thymmai	Raid Nongskhen.Khyrim State	35	83 Kms
04. *Hat* Lyngkhat	Raid Lyngkhat, Khyrinn State	43	82 Kms
05. *Hat* Shimaw	Tynriang Sirdarship	12	85 Kms

Federation of Five Border Khasi States

Name of Market	*State (Hima) / Sirdarship*	*No of villages involved*	*Distance from Main Market*
06. *Hat* Mawdon	Mawdon state	35	78 kms
07. *Hat* Balat	Maharam state	45	91 kms
08. *Hat* Danger	Bhowal state	40	102 kms
09. *Hat* Sunatola	Dwaranontynrem	40	96 kms
10. *Hat* Ryngku	Dwaranontynrem sidarship	35	92 kms
11. *Hat* Shella	Shella state	35	105 kms
12. *Hat*Tyllap	Mawlong state	35	110 kms
13. *Hat* Ishamati	Mawlong state	40	115 kms
14. *Hat* Kyrdoh	Nonglait Sardarship	35	80 kms
15. *Hat* Parkan	Shella state	45	110kms
16. *Hat* Majai	Sohra state	50	112 kms
17. *Hat* Tharia	Mawlong state	45	110 kms
18. *Hat* Bholaganj	Mawlong state	50	105 kms
19. *Hat* Ranikor	Langrin state	55	110 kms
20. *Hat* Borkhat			
22.(sic) *Hat* Muktapur			
23. *Hat* kalaicherra			
24. *Hat* Rajara			
25. *Hat* Dawki			
26. *Hat* Dalu			
27. *Hat* Mahendraganj			
28. *Hat* Baghmara and many more.			

The above Border Hats (Traditional Border Markets) are situated 80 to 110 kms away and takes more than four / five hours to travel to the main market, further these Hats (Traditional Markets) are held every four days and they are the lifeline to the poor people of these surrounding villages as indicated above. Dislocating their markets and not allowing these very simple ancient activities is against all humanitarian considerations.

This memorandum, probably sums up, the entire sentiment behind the demand for the re-opening of the border *hats*. Interestingly a number of these border *hats* namely at Lyngkhat, Thymmai, Dierbali, Shimaw,Tshang (Nongjri), Dawki, Bakur and Muktapur, continued to function even after partition, and people mainly traded in foodstuff and other perishable items and temporary passes were also issued to facilitate cross border movements of people for the purpose of trade. However, following the war of Liberation in Bangladesh, the *Hats had been* closed and trade had been suspended.[14]

Though officially trade remains suspended, business goes on. As Mr M.F. Ryngksai headman of Dawki puts it:

It was out of compulsion that the people are forced to engage in what is termed as unofficial trade. When it was not possible to trade through authorised routes, people were forced to take the unauthorised route. You must realise that petty trade through jungle routes are for survival. If you want to be an exporter through Tamabil, you will need a minimum of ten lakh rupees. How many people have that amount? But for the petty unauthorised trader, even Rs 5000/- will do. That too, the transaction will be concluded hand to hand. No waiting. No uncertainty. You give me goods worth 5000/-, I give you Rs 5500/- This is a matter of

> *settlement of accounts immediately. Take the case of the pan leaves. Since it cannot be sent through authorised routes, it is sent through unauthorised routes. While a bundle of pan leaves here would fetch Rs 5/- across the border it can be sold for Rs 10/- which means that per basket the difference would be Rs 400/- But since Pan cannot be officially exported to Bangladesh because of the opposition from the pan growers there. For if Khasi pan were to go in freely, the price of pan there would drop. But if there is no supply from India, the price goes up. The government of Bangladesh gives permits to their traders to go and buy pan from the Khasi areas of Bangladesh such as Jaflong hat and Jaintiapur bazaar. After purchasing the pan from these areas they sell it in the mainland Bangla markets for a good profit. Moreover, unless one has a permit, one cannot go and indulge in the pan business. Interestingly, most of the pan sold in these markets is from India, supplied through the unofficial routes! If you want to stop unofficial trade, then border hats have to be reopened. By this, I am 100 per cent sure that unofficial trade will get reduced immediately.*[15]

According to a study conducted by the Indian Institute of Entrepreneurship[16], the total volume of illegal trade in the Indo-Bangladesh border is to the tune of 106.14 crores annually. Thus legalising the trade does appear to be an option that cannot be delayed for too long. Interestingly, the border people do not seem to favour the opening of unregulated and open border *hats*. This sentiment was made amply clear by a *Sirdar* of ten Khasi village, Mr F.Kongwang, who said that the *hats* should function on pre-determined days of the week in a designated place, preferably in the zero line. After the days trading was over, the people would return to their respective countries. This, he felt would prevent possible complications.

Mr M.F. Ryngksai was more candid when he opined that he is not in favour of free opening of border hats. He opined that what is required is the need to allow people here to trade the items that are in excess and purchase the items that are required here. The idea is to allow free passage of goods, not of people. How one can allow the opening of a border *hat*, say at Dawki, without a corresponding *hat* on the other side of the border, Ryngksai wondered. In that case their people can come and purchase whatever they need without us being able to go over to buy our necessities. Trade should mean that you are able to take whatever you need from us at our price and we take whatever we need from you at your price. So, the solution is to have identical *hats* on both sides or at the zero line on a particular day. It will be a common meeting ground, a common *hat*.

Fences or Bridges?

At a time when India is seeking to integrate itself with the world economy and there is talk of increasing cooperation with India's neighbours such as Bangladesh as well as developing regional and sub-regional cooperation, certain disagreements and irritants do hamper bilateral relations. One such issue that has cast a long shadow over the normalisation of relations between the two countries is the Indian decision to fence the border with Bangladesh. While India sees it as a necessary step to prevent the infiltration of migrants to its soil, and also check the flow of insurgents, and illegal trade, Bangladesh sees it as a patently unfriendly act and has opposed it strongly. There has been frequent instances of cross border skirmishes between the border troops of both the countries and the loss of lives of both civilians and troopers, over the issue of erection of the fence. In the heat and the din of the sabre rattling of both countries, it is a fact that the sentiments of the people in the border areas are studiously ignored.

Interestingly, the haste of the Indian decision to fence the border has led to wide spread protests even in the Indian side, as it is felt that the fence would not only lead to fossilisation of historical wrongs but also exacerbate the process of loss of Khasi lands. Bah Mit Ryngksai, Headman of Dawki was very foreceful when he said:

> *The original demarcation was wrong. But now, even that demarcation is being greatly altered...after the devastating floods in the 1970s, many of the boundary pillars got washed away. Subsequently, these were re-erected at safer places, so that they would be safe from the floods. Safer meant higher land, and higher land inevitably meant our hills. If one pillar is placed wrongly, the subsequent pillars are also wrong. So the entire border pillars of that sector are questionable. Now there is talk of erecting a border fence based on those pillars! The fence would be located 150 meters away from the zero line. In effect it would mean that we again stand to lose 150 meters of prime cultivable land. This is not acceptable. Can anyone tell me what will happen to the farmer whose field runs for some 500 meters adjacent to pillar 1277/4S. As of today, like his ancestors, he is cultivating on both sides of that pillar. What will happen to him when the fence is erected?*[17]

The sentiments echoed by him do not reflect only his personal views, because all through our visits to the border areas, people were unequivocally venting similar sentiments.[18] Meetings were being called, and the public were beginning to rally themselves. The decision to fence the border had certainly opened up a Pandora's Box!

Moreover, if the sentiments of Mr M.F. Ryngkshai are taken as being the unsubstantiated allegations of a person who does not hold any position of constitutional authority, let us have a look at a letter written by an Honourable Member of Parliament.

The letter in question was written on 21st January 2002 by Mr P.R.Kyndiah, then, an MP from Meghalaya and an important minister in the Union Cabinet today. He had written to the then Home Minister L.K.Advani stating that:

> *During my recent tour to the Indo-Bangla border of Meghalaya our people complained about the difficulties and hardship that they are facing as portions of their land falling under Indian Territory are now in the no man's land (beyond the fenced area) open to illegal activities of Bangladeshis for timber logging as well as cutting and taking away of paddies. This has come about as a result of fencing; the cultivable land is now beyond the fenced .area, which is very much within Indian Territory.*
>
> *I visited the Shella-Bholaganj sector on 18th of this month and was shocked to see that our Post Office, Customs Office, Public Health Centre, Traditional Dorbar House and even the State Police Outpost in Bholaganj bordering Bangladesh are on the other side of the fenced ared, in such a situation I feel that untill and unless there, is a proper demarcation of the boundary we stand to loose a lot of our productive land which is now in the so-called no man's land, which is benefiting the Bangladeshis as a result of fencing carried out without proper demarcation.*
>
> *Minister Border Area Development, Government of Meghalaya informed me that the Border Road Organization has started fencing along the border from Nongjri Sector in East Khasi Hills to Dawki Sector in Jaintia Hills where the disputed area between*

the two countries is yet to be settled. As it has happened in Shella Sector to Bholaganj a good portion of the Indian Territory are now beyond the fenced area and a similar fate awaits the villages in the sector referred to above, You may recall the national outrage when BDR and Bangladesh armed personnel intruded into Pyrdiwah and even occupied it for a while, but thanks to the bravery of our jawans we could retrieve the territory. If today border fencing continues, it would lead to slicing up the entire territory, which belongs to India. It is therefore imperative that fencing in this sector is kept in abeyance.

I therefore request you to use your good office to see that fencing undertaken by the Border Road Organisation is stopped till the territorial dispute is resolved and proper demarcation is done in the interest of the people living in the borders with Bangladesh.

To this letter, the then Home Minister Advani replied through letter no. L271/HMP/02, dated 6th February 2002, that he was having the matter looked into. But unfortunately, nothing further is known about what that "looking into" has resulted in!

A review of some of the correspondence that transpired within the state government and between the Government of Meghalaya and the Government of India also shows that the issue of the erecting a border fence without properly demarcating the Indo-Bangladesh border had given rise to a raging controversy and had the potential of snowballing into a major issue with wide ramifications.

For instance, Mr. K.K.Dkhar, Minister in charge of Border Areas and Trade, Government of Meghalaya, writing to his Chief Minister, on January 18th 2002 said:

> *I would like to bring to your kind attention that the Border Road Organisation has recently started fencing work along the international boundary with Bangladesh from Nongjri sector in East Khasi Hills District, where the disputed areas between the two countries is yet to be settled. These disputed areas and villages will naturally be located behind the fencing (i.e. within Bangladesh side) if the same is erected....It is also requested that the Government of India be apprised of the situation and joint survey and demarcation of the disputed areas between the two countries be conducted and settled once and for all early before the fencing is erected.*

Then again Mr G.P. Wahlang, Commissioner and Secretary to the Government of Meghalaya, writing to the Commissioner Borders, Ministry of Home Affairs, Government of India, on 15th February 2002 wrote "You are therefore requested not to go ahead with the survey and construction of a fencing along the above sector or other stretches of the border over which a final settlement with Bangladesh Government is yet to be arrived at".

To gain a wider perspective on the matter, one may also refer to the numerous appeals and memorandums submitted by organizations based on the border, to the state and central government on the issue. For instance, a memorandum submitted to the Deputy Commissioner of Jaintia Hills District by the organization called *The Federal Council of War Mhingi and War Jaintia* on 4.6.2004 appealed that

> *the Border Road Organisation has recently started surveying and erecting the fencing works along the International boundary with Bangladesh from Riwar Mihngi Area in the East Khasi Hills District to War Jaintia in the Jaintia Hills District and the Survey*

> *works had been done without the consent and knowledge of the respective Sordars, Dollois, Rangbah Shnong and Land Owners, which is very illegal and against the local interest. Moreover, the area mentioned above is still under dispute and still not settled. We, therefore, oppose to the survey and erection of any fencing until and unless the Border dispute is resolved. We further demand a fresh survey between India and Bangladesh in the presence of the Syiems, Sordars, Dollois, Rangbah Shnong, Land Owners and official of the District Councils and State Government Officil so as to enable us to exercise our rights over our ancestral lands and properties.*

A View from Dhaka

Imtiaz Ahmed, Professor of International Relations in the University of Dhaka,[19] when asked by this researcher to articulate what Bangladesh felt about the Indian decision to fence the border, made no bones about the fact that Bangladesh viewed it as an unfriendly act. He felt that for most people in Bangladesh, the equation that Indian goods would continue to flood the Bangladeshi market while at the same time India seeking to prohibit migrations of people, who are in search of livelihoods or security, seemed ridiculous! Perhaps, the hundreds of millions the Indian government proposed to spend on fencing the border could be better utilised by setting up industries in the border areas of Bangladesh or border areas of India could effectively pre-empt the whole necessity for migration.

Prof. Ahmed also wondered how the migration from Bangladesh could be termed illegal, as there was no mechanism in place which allows legal migrations. If a process of legal migration had been in place, say for the temporary purpose of work, then people not coming in through the legal route could be termed illegal. Unfortunately, till date no mechanism for legal migration exists hence all migrations are termed as illegal, which does not seem right.

Asked about how Bangladesh viewed the north east, Imtiaz Ahmed opined that an average person in Bangladesh had a soft corner for the region in terms of shared history and empathy for its problems and underdevelopment. When questioned about whether Bangladesh would be interested in giving transit facilities, as through the port of Chittagong, and how would their country gain out of it, Ahmed felt Bangladesh would be amenable to providing transit facilities as it would lead to the growth of the service sector in Bangladesh. In addition, transit facilities would also mean a tremendous development of communication including roads, which would certainly benefit their country.

Mohammed Rahmatullah, Director of the Centre for Policy Dialogue, Dhaka,[20] illustrating the irony of the situation showed how the demarcation of the border had ensured that almost all the natural resources were placed on the Indian side, whereas the larger chunk of the population as well as the transport infrastructure remained with Bangladesh. Without a healthy co-operation between the two countries which would bring about a healthy synergy of the assets of both the countries, development of this undeveloped region would continue to be a pipe dream. Probably putting in place proper transport infrastructure would be the first step to bringing about economic development of the region.

From Fencing to Stepping Stone

It certainly seems an irony that when the talk is of Looking East, Opening up, and greater economic cooperation, the ground reality is that of erecting fences and engaging in border skirmishes.

Probably the Berlin Wall which separated the two

Germanys was the best guarded frontier ever. Today, the border between the USA and Mexico is one of the best guarded frontiers. Nonetheless, none of these have succeeded in completely preventing the cross border movement of people. What have been found more effective are modern methods of surveillance, and a system of a proper identification of citizens. But, planners in this part of the world still seem to believe in the workability of physical barriers!

Probably, instead of border fences, what both countries need to do is to economically empower their people and bring about tangible development of the region as a whole. History has showed us how the hills and the plains have always maintained a symbiotic relationship. Though today, political compulsions seek to deny such shared history. Yet, economic compulsions and the need of a better tomorrow, should force our planners to realise that the days of isolated growth are well and truly over. If Bangladesh opens their gates to Northeast India to reach the rest of the world and in turn is allowed easy access to markets and provided support for their economic development, there will be no losers. In fact, such cooperation could truly transform the entire region. The question is, can we rise to the occasion!

NOTES

1. As quoted in Choudhury J.N., (1998), *The Khasi Canvas,* Shillong, p. 69.
2. Hunter, W.W., (1998), reprint, *A Statistical Account of Assam* (Vol. 2), p. 236.
3. *Ibid.,* pp. 238-239.
4. David Ludden, (2003), "Political Maps and Cultural Territories" in *Himal South Asian*, Internet edition, July.
5. *Ibid.*
6. Willem Van Schendel (2002), "Stateless in South Asia: The

Making of the India Bangladesh Enclaves" in *The Journal of Asian Studies* 61, No.1, (Feb., pp. 120-21.

7. V.P. Menon, (1981), *The Transfer of Power in India*, Orient Longman, New Delhi, p. 402.
8. Recorded Interview at Mawkhar, Shillong on 8.8.2004.
9. Series of interviews during 2004-2005 in Shillong.
10. Interviews with John F. Kharshiing, Spokesperson of Khasi Traditional Institutions, M.F. Ryngsai, Headman of Dawki and Secretary of the War Jaintias.
11. David Ludden, *op.cit.*
12. *Ibid*.
13. Joint Memorandum to the President of India, through the governor of Meghalaya, on 20.3.2001 by the Representatives of the Indigenous Khasi People under: The Federation of RiwarMihngi Local Dorbars under Syiem of Khyriem State, The Federation of Five Border Khasi States and Adjoining Areas Inhabiting the Khasi Hills on the North East of India at present attached to the State of Meghalaya.
14. Memorandum to the DC Jaintia Hills District by the Federation of RiWarMihngi and War Jaintia on 4.6.2004.
15. M.F. Ryngksai, *op.cit.*
16. Indian Institute of Entrepreneurship, Guwahati, "Prospect of Border Trade with Myanmar and Bangladesh Pre-Investment Feasibility Report", pp. 111-112.
17. Interview at Dawki on 7.7.04.
18. Visits in the entire stretch of the Indo-Bangla border in the Khasi-Jaintia Hills sector undertaken during 2004.
19. From a wide ranging discussion by researcher with Prof. Imtiaz Ahmed at Sanjoy Hazarika's home in Shillong on 7.9.2004.
20. Discussions held in Guwahati, in a Seminar "Towards a New Asia" organized by CENISEAS, 10-11.9.2004.

15

STATUS AND PROSPECT OF LIMESTONE QUARRYING IN MEGHALAYA AND ITS TRADE WITH BANGLADESH

Utpal Kumar De
R.D.H. Kharlukhi

Introduction

According to the standard trade theory, a country/region is expected to have comparative advantage in producing and exporting commodities, whose primary inputs are abundant in that particular country/region. On the other hand, the region is expected to import such commodities from outside, which are primarily based on some inputs scarce in that region. This can be drawn in line with the famous Heckscher-Ohlin model of comparative advantage (Heckscher, 1919 and Ohlin, 1933; Sodersten and Reed 1994, p. 59). Through exchange the country/region can optimize the use of its available resources and thus reach maximum achievable welfare with its resource constraint.

However, in some cases it is observed that due to some economic and non-economic constraints, industries have not been developed for which resources are plenty and rich in quality. The reasons may include infrastructure, size of market, uncertainty of growth, cost of transportation, etc. Whereas, in such cases, it may be convenient to transfer raw materials from the source region to elsewhere for the use in the industries there that has a better access to market and other prospects and earn secured revenue.

Meghalaya is a state in North-East India, whose economy is primarily agricultural. In spite of having rich mineral and other resources, growth of related industries are very limited. Most of the industries are of small scale and cottage type. Rather, these resources are mined and directly exported to the industries of other region of India and a major part to the neighbouring Bangladesh. Because of vicinity and long common border with Bangladesh, people on both sides of the border are engaged in trade of different commodities at different scales and earn their livelihood in the absence of suitable alternative opportunities. Whatever be the use (whether used in indigenous industries or exported), availability of resources always plays an important role in shaping the economy of a region. Thus, to quote W. A. Lewis, "The extent of a country's resources is quite obviously a limit on the amount and type of development which it can undergo" (Lewis, W. A., 1955, p. 52). Or following Fisher "Usually have to begin with and concentrate on the development of locally available natural resources as an initial condition for lifting local levels of living and purchasing power, for obtaining foreign exchange with which to purchase capital equipment, and setting in motion the development process" (Fisher, J.I. 1964, p 32).

After independence and partition, what was India's internal regional trade between Eastern Bengal and other parts of the country became its external trade with present day Bangladesh (erstwhile East Pakistan). Due to partition and socio-political tension and disturbances; trade between India's North-East and Bangladesh has been severely affected for long time. After the reopening of trade links, it has been growing continuously and now we observe a sizable quantity of transactions through the border. Because of the long common border, easy access of the people on either side of the border and comparatively lower transportation cost than that with the main land markets of the country; border trade with Bangladesh has been gaining importance in the socio-economic life of the people of the region.

Nature of the border trade here are of two types. Formal trade, that takes place through the land custom stations and informal or illegal trade that takes place through the porous borders. Because of poverty, unemployment (more so generated after the partition) many people on both sides of the border survive on these activities. In the absence of licensing authority for the small importers and exporters, they are compelled to follow such illegal practices, which is more convenient to them than going through the formal way.

At present 10 land custom stations operating in Meghalaya-Bangladesh border. These are Baghmara, Mahendraganj, Dalu, Ghasuapara in Garo Hills Districts, Shella Bazar, Bholaganj, Borsara, Balat and Ryngku in Khasi Hills Districts and Dawki in Jaintia Hills District.

Major export items to Bangladesh are coal, limestone, boulder-stone, crushed-stone and stone chips. Some quantity of cement is also exported occasionally. Among others are some horticultural and agricultural products. Some of the minerals, horticultural and forest products are also exported informally. Import items from Bangladesh to Meghalaya are very few. Mainly a few third country origin electronic items, textile goods and also hilsa fish through other border areas of Assam and Tripura are imported every year and most of them come informally.

Limestone Trade of Meghalaya

Limestone is the second most important mineral of Meghalaya after coal. In terms of export it brings second most export earning at present. Every year the quantity of export and earning from limestone has been increasing. However the data from 1998-99 show that though the quantity of export and gross earning from it has been increasing, but compared to other exports its growth has been lagging behind, which is clear from the decline in share of limestone in total export. Moreover, the growth of export earning is not consistent. It fluctuates significantly over the years. This is primarily due to heavy fluctuation of price of limestone, which is clear from table15.1. Though export of raw limestone has been declining insignificantly, percentage of limestone export to total production of Meghalaya has been declining significantly from 68.92 in 1998-99 to 36.54 in 2002-03.

TABLE 15.1

Export of limestone from Meghalaya to Bangladesh Since 1998-99

	1998-99	*1999-00*	*2000-01*	*2001-02*	*2002-03*
Quantity (000'MT)	268.11	250.02	230.34	256.88	234.25
Value (Rs Crore)	6.62	29.73	80.38	13.75	63.29
Share of Total Export	9.36	25.33	6.19	8.235	3.36
Total Export (Rs Crore)	70.73	117.33	129.83	166.93	171.99
Export to total production (percentage)	68.92	51.13	46.07	43.91	36.54

Source: Customs Department, Government of India.

Note: In the export figures the quantity goes to Chattak Cement Plant of Bangladesh is not considered. It has been getting limestone due to contract through the conveyer belt from the Kommorah Limestone Mining Company Ltd of Meghalaya. It will be more or less constant if production in that industry remains same.

Limestone occurs in an extensive belt (approximately 200 km long) along the southern border of Meghalaya. The quality of limestone found here varies from cement grade to chemical grade. Therefore the limestone of Meghalaya can be extensively used in different industries like steel, fertiliser, cement, lime and hydrated lime, precipitated and activated calcium carbonate, calcium carbide, bleaching powder, acetylene black and other chemical industries. It is most suitable for the manufacturing of cement, lime, precipitated calcium carbonate, etc. Table 15.2 shows the limestone reserve in Northeast India and it is found that most of the reserve occurs in the state of Meghalaya. Though Geological Survey of India estimates the total reserve so far as 4147 Mn tonnes, according to directorate of mineral resources inference it would be around 12000 Mn tonnes *(DMR, Information 2005).*

Figures show that Meghalaya has more than 91 per cent of total possible reserves of limestone in North-East India. Thus, there is the potential of investment in and development of limestone based industries in Meghalaya and the export of related products. Table 15.3 shows that the distribution of deposit is skewed towards Khasi and Jaintia Hills.

TABLE 15.2

Estimate of Limestone Reserves in North East India (Mn Tonnes)

State	*Reserve (Mn.t)*	*Percentage of total Reserve*
Assam	463	8.69 (3.51)*
Meghalaya	4147 (12000)*	77.82 (91.03)*
Manipur	6.40	0.12 (0.048)*
Mizoram	5.202	0.098 (0.039)*
Arunachal	350	6.57 (2.65)*
Nagaland	357	6.70 (2.70)*
Total	5328.602 (13181.602)*	100

Source: NEDFi, 2002.

Note: * Recent estimate of possible Limestone reserve in Meghalaya is 12000 Mn Tonnes. So terms in the parentheses in the last column show the percentage corresponding to latest estimate of Meghalaya's deposit.

TABLE 15.3

Spatial Distribution of Limestone Reserves in Meghalaya

Hills	*Quantity (in mn tones)*	*Areas where found*
Khashi Hills	2537	Cherrapunjee, Laitryngew, Mawlong, Ishamati, Komorrah, Shella, Borsora
Jaintia Hills	1050	Lumshnong, Sutunga, Nongkhlieh, Lakadong, Syndai, Nongtalang
Garo Hills	560	Darrang-Ear-Aning, Sigu-Artheka, Chokpot
Total	4147	All the above

Source: Geological Survey of India, Shillong.

Note: However present Geological estimate is 12000 Mn Tonnes in Meghalaya (DMR, Meghalaya).

In spite of having huge limestone reserves, till now limited number of limestone based industries have been developed in and around the state. Cement is the major manufacturing industry that consumes most of the limestone extracted. Cement and lime products are essential components of human environment that supports the modern lifestyle we enjoy today. Cement holds together much of our infrastructure: from roads to houses; dams to water treatment systems and schools to hospitals. It is hard to think of a safe and healthy society without it. There are 159 cement and cement based industries and 73 lime making industries in Meghalaya. But most of them are small and marginal in terms of production and intake of limestone. At present there are only seven major cement industries in Meghalaya with total investment of around Rs 37.14 crore that consume major portions of limestone. The total installed capacity of those units is 1575 MT per day and those are in operation for about 200 days a year, which makes total approximate production 3.15 lakhs tonne per annum. These information are presented in Table

15.4. The intake capacity of these industries together (4.41 lakhs tonne of limestone, considering the approximate requirement of 1.4 tonne for the production of a tonne of cement) is such that they cannot fully utilise the total limestone extracted in the state over the years.

TABLE 15.4

Cement Industries in Meghalaya

Name of the Plant	*Installed Capacity (Tonne per day)*	*Investment in Plant & machineries (Rs Crore)*
M/s R.K.B Cements (P) Ltd	100	1.8745
M/s H.M Cements (P) Ltd	330	5.00
M/S Mawmluh Cherra Cements Ltd	640	20.00
M/s AMS Cements (P) Ltd	35	0.628
M/s Jaintia Cements (P) Ltd	100	2.99
M/s Bomber Cements (P) Ltd	100	1.65
M/s Virgo Cements Ltd	270	5.00
Total Annual capacity*	1575 *200 = 315000 MT or 3.15 lakhs ton	37.1425

Source: Directorate of Industries, Government of Meghalaya.

Note: * Approximately those industries carryout production for about 200 days per year.

As Mawmluh Cherra Cements Ltd (MCCL) manufactures cement with their own extracted limestone; it is approximated by multiplying 1.4 with their total annual production. Also we have calculated the approximate intake of Chattak Cement Plant of Bangladesh in the same way considering the 70 per cent of its installed capacity is operated and it has been getting limestone through conveyer belt from the Kommorah Limestone Mining Company Ltd of Meghalaya. These two are added to the production figure (as those are not shown in the published data of extraction) to get the aggregate quantity of extraction. Adding those with the annual extraction figure we find total approximate extraction of limestone during

2003-04 was 11.656 lakh tonne. Thus cement industries in Meghalaya utilise 37.83 per cent of total limestone harvested.

Because of better access, limited availability of limestone in Bangladesh and better advantage of transporting, a huge amount of it is exported to Bangladesh every year. As mentioned earlier, instead of producing and exporting limestone-based product (like cement), a major part of raw limestone is directly exported and in return some other things are imported. Also this trade has huge importance for the generation of income and employment of inhabitants of both sides of the border and thus for the economy of Meghalaya as well. But Meghalaya's limestone and cement still could not capture a major part of their market in Bangladesh. Every year Bangladesh imports cement and clinker even from China, Indonesia, Singapur etc (because of comparatively lower price) though their transportation cost is high and quality degrades due to transportation from far off places. The present chapter tries to explore the nature of limestone quarrying and the status and prospect of Meghalaya's limestone trade with Bangladesh.

The plan of the chapter is as follows. In the next section, a brief method of enquiry will be incorporated. Thereafter the status of extraction of limestone, its growth and its sustainability/life cycle will be examined. It will be followed by the estimation of size of market and demand for limestone in Bangladesh and thus the scope and prospects of export from Meghalaya will be analysed. Then the advantages and disadvantages of Meghalaya in the production and export of limestone will be discussed. The final section will incorporate the conclusions and policy implications of the whole study.

Data and Methodology

For the purpose of analyses, data on deposit of limestone in Meghalaya, extraction of limestone, industries related to limestone especially the cement industries in Meghalaya and Bangladesh, their capacities of production, consumption and demand for limestone etc have been collected from the NEDFi Report 2002, Directorate of Mineral Resources, Government of Meghalaya; Directorate of Industries, Government of Meghalaya. The export figures have been collected from the Customs Department, Government of India. After careful examination of the scatter diagram of the extraction figures since 1960-61 in Meghalaya (presented in Appendix 15.1), an equation of the form $\text{Ln } Y_t = a + b.t$ is fitted by regression method to estimate the growth of cumulative extraction. Where Y_t is the cumulative total extraction up to time t i.e., $\sum_{k=0}^{t} Y_k$ and a, b are the two parameters. Here b represents the annual exponential rate of growth of cumulative extraction. After estimating a and b and putting Y_t equals to total possible reserves the equation is solved for t which gives the estimated number of years after which the total extractable stock is expected to exhaust unless new reserves are found.

Thereafter the number of industries in Meghalaya, especially the cement industries and their capacity utilisation is considered. By multiplying 1.4 with the capacity utilisation of the cement industries, we approximate the demand for limestone in Meghalaya. It is to be noted that one unit of cement production requires 1.4 unit of limestone (as informed by the Director of MCCL, Meghalaya). Moreover though cement utilises the major part of limestone quarried, it is also used in some other industries but at a lower scale. Also limestone from Meghalaya may be used in the industries in the neighbouring states in India, which is very less as per the information available so far. Those are not considered due to paucity and unreliability of the information available in this regard. It, thus, gives the lower bound of the demand for limestone in Meghalaya. Subtracting internal demand from the total extraction, surplus and exportable quantity of limestone is approximated. Following the same way, the demand for limestone and possible import demand is calculated for Bangladesh as there is no economically extractable limestone deposit in Bangladesh. The amount of actual export to Bangladesh has already been presented for some recent years. Therefore, the percentage of Bangladesh's market for limestone is known (by comparing with calculated demand) and can be compared with the surplus production in Meghalaya, which is the nearest possible exporter. Considering the same along with the facts of advantages and disadvantages of Meghalaya in limestone, clinker and cement production and export and other implications, the conclusion is drawn.

Results and Discussion

Limestone Extraction and Market in Meghalaya

The extraction of limestone has increased from 1.05 lakh tonnes in 1960-61 to 7.218 lakh tonnes in 2003-04. The figures exclude the quantity used by MCCL, Meghalaya and Chhatak Cement Factory of Bangladesh. Annual exponential rate of growth of extraction is around 5.57 per cent, which is highly significant. This is estimated through the regression equation $\ln E_t = 3.8945 + 0.05565\,t$, where E_t is the annual extraction in the year t. Now we also observe no significant changes in the rate of growth of extraction. It is clear from the sub-period regression of first and last 22 years data. The two equations are $\ln E_t = 3.92649 + 0.05278\,t$ and $\ln E_t = 5.09355 + 0.0579\,t$ respectively. So the annual exponential growth rate during 1960-61 to 1981-82 was around 5.278 per cent and during 1982-83 to 2003-04 was around 5.795 per cent. The growth rate is increasing but insignificantly.

The cumulative extraction follows almost an exponential

trend i.e., its log values follow a linear trend. The regressed equation is $\ln Y_t = 5.568 + 0.089\,t$, where Y_t is the cumulative extraction as defined earlier. Considering 4147 Mn tonnes of total reserve in Meghalaya, the total stock is expected to exhaust in around 110 years. This is minimum estimated years and as there is a small upward bias, it would linger a few more years. If the 12000 Mn tonnes can be harvested economically, it would last some more years (120-130 years as the growth may decelerate after reaching some peak level, when population will stabilize). As more than 40 years have already been elapsed, we can expect the sector to grow by another 65-75 years and thereafter, unless the alternatives to limestone is available, the situation may become critical.

Potential Market for Limestone in Bangladesh and Scope of Export from Meghalaya

Potential market for limestone is derived mainly from the potential demand for cement and the growth of the cement plant in Bangladesh. The following points can be mentioned from the Security and Exchange Commission Report of Bangladesh in this regard.

1. Long term growth of demand for cement is expected to be 8 per cent per annum.
2. Cement consumption in Bangladesh during 1999-2000 financial year was about 4.79 Million MT. Whereas total capacity of production was around 3.43 Million MT.
3. About 75 per cent of its consumption was met from the production of one cement industry and 14 other clinker grinding plants.

At present we see that there are 23 cement plants in Bangladesh with installed production capacity of 7.48 Million MT annually (but all of them are not in operation) and five units are under implementation with installed capacity of 4.25 million MT.

Projected demand, production and import of cement in Bangladesh are presented in Table 15.5.

TABLE 15.5

Demand, Production and Import of Cement in Bangladesh

Year	*Demand (Mn MT)*	*Total Installed Capacity (Mn MT)*	*Actual Production (Mn MT)*	*Share of Internal Production (%)*	*Import (Mn MT)*
1999	4.79	5.21	3.59	75	1.20
2001	5.185	5.21	3.647	70	1.54
2002	5.656	5.21	3.647	64	2.01
2003	6.182	7.06	4.942	81	1.19
2004	6.656	8.26	5.782	87	0.87

Source: Security Exchange Commission, Bangladesh.

Bangladesh meets its internal demand for cement from three sources.

1. One Integrated Cement plant with a production capacity of 0.27 Million MT per year produces cement by using limestone available in small quantities in the north of the country and mostly from Kommorah Limestone Mining Company Ltd of Meghalaya.
2. Fifteen clinker grinding plants located all over the country, mostly run by imported clinker with capacity of 4.9 Million Tonnes per year with an average capacity utilization of 70 per cent and above. Clinker is imported from Indonesia, Thailand, Malayasia, China and sometimes from India.
3. The rest of the cement is imported mainly from China, India and now even Indonesia has captured some portion of the market.

The number of plants has however recently increased to 23 (as mentioned earlier) and five more units are under implementation to increase the capacity to 8.68 Mn MT by the end of 2005. If that is materialized the country would have a little surplus and can become a net exporter of cement. But for limestone or clinker it will have to totally depend upon the imports.

The Lafarge Surma Cement Ltd (with 1.2 Mn MT proposed clinker capacity) has already started their venture to capture the cement and clinker market of Bangladesh, which will start operation soon by directly mining limestone in Meghalaya. So there is a fear of the existing suppliers of Meghalaya of loosing a potential market.

The estimated capacity of utilization of the existing 23 units including Chhatak Cement Factory in 2005 would be 5.6 Mn MT, which would require 7.8 Mn MT of limestone. Whereas Meghalaya's annual limestone production in 2003-04 was 1.166 Mn MT and Meghalaya's cement sector could use only 0.441 Mn MT. The surplus production of limestone was around 0.725 Mn MT, which is around 9.3 per cent of total requirement of Bangladesh. Around 56 per cent of surplus production was exported in that year. The rest can be assumed to have used by other industries in Meghalaya or by the neighbouring states or might have remained as inventory.

The analysis reveals that there is a potential market for limestone or clinker and Meghalaya can compete for its share as it has some natural locational advantages.

Advantages and Disadvantages of Meghalaya in the Production and Export of Raw Limestone, Clinker and Cement

1. Meghalaya has plenty of limestone reserves. Even if

the current trend of extraction continues, there is no fear of exhaustibility of resource at least in the short run.

2. Due to the geographical contiguity with Bangladesh and already established road connectivity it is convenient to export to Bangladesh than to export to other regions of India.

3. Till now, major part of the excess demand for cement in Bangladesh has been met by China. But due to long transportation time the quality of the cement degrades. As raw material is plenty in Meghalaya, if the production is done with improved technology and exported, then Meghalaya's manufacturers would have a natural advantage in Bangladesh market. Even if the production capacity of the proposed plants in Bangladesh materialize and meets the internal demand, the market for limestone can always be captured by Meghalaya.

4. Already conveyer belts are in use for the transport of raw limestone (Kommorah Limestone Mining Company Ltd has been exporting limestone to Chattak Cement Company Ltd of Bangladesh since 1973). It has produced over Rs 51 lakhs during 2001-02. Now Lafarge Surma has also an agreement to start such activities in their proposed Bangladesh Unit using 150 km conveyer belt from Nongtrai village, which alone will earn Rs 348.75 lakhs per annum for the economy of the Meghalaya.

The same process can also be followed to transport the cement from Meghalaya after proper packing and thus more cement plants can come up.

6. Electricity consumption is naturally less for exporting through rope way as the materials move down the hills from Meghalaya to Bangladesh plains.

7. The quality of limestone in Meghalaya varies from cement grade to chemical grade. Therefore the limestone from Meghalaya would be widely utilised not only in cement industries but also in fertilizer, steel and paper mills and similar other industries in Bangladesh.

Conclusions

It appears that there is ample scope for the development of limestone quarrying and limestone based industries (especially cement, which is the principal limestone based industry) in Meghalaya. There is huge potential market in Bangladesh for such products that can be accessed. Instead of directly exporting raw materials if it is processed and final output is exported it would generate more revenue and employment in the state. It appears that non-economic factors play some crucial role for not considering the region in general and the state of Meghalaya in particular as investment destination. Big firms are interested in the extraction of the state's raw materials but not in the establishment of manufacturing units. This is presumably due to insecurity arising out of the insurgent activities in the region as well as non-market control of land. If these threat perceptions could be removed, Meghalaya has all the potential to become an industrial hub in the region.

REFERENCES

Fisher, J.I. (1964), *The Role of Natural Resources in Economic Development: Principles and Patterns,* Williamson and Buttrick.

Geological Survey of India NER NEWS, Vol. 13, March 2001, Shillong, p. 6.

Heckscher, E.F. (1919), "Utrikeshandelns Verkan På inkomstfödelningen", *Ekonomisk Tidskrift,* Vol. 21, pp. 1-32.

Lewis, W.A. (1955), *The Theory of Economic Growth*, Allen and Unwin.

NEDFi Databank quarterly Report 2002.

Ohlin, B. (1933), *Interregional and International Trade*, Harvard University Press.

Securities and Exchange Commission, Bangladesh, *Prospectus*, downloaded from www.secbd.org/prospeldob.html.

Sodersten, B. and G. Reed, (1994), *International Economics*, Macmillan Press Ltd., London.

APPENDIX 15.1

Extraction of Limestone in Meghalaya during 1961-62 to 2003-04

Year	*Quantity (Thousand tonnes)*
1960-61	105
1961-62	79
1962-63	84
1963-64	79
1964-65	49
1965-66	30
1966-67	51
1967-68	66
1968-69	66
1969-70	65
1970-71	87
1971-72	74
1972-73	115
1973-74	145
1974-75	164
1975-76	113
1976-77	49
1977-78	156
1978-79	176
1979-80	181
1980-81	234
1981-82	156
1982-83	188
1983-84	211
1984-85	236
1985-86	249
1986-87	244
1987-88	237
1988-89	227
1989-90	273
1990-91	235
1991-92	188
1992-93	209
1993-94	380
1994-95	152
1995-96	439.8
1996-97	540.9

1997-98	396
1998-99	389
1999-00	489
2000-01	500
2001-02	585
2002-03	641
2003-04	721.8

Source: Directorate of Mineral Resources, Government of Meghalaya.

Graph 15.1

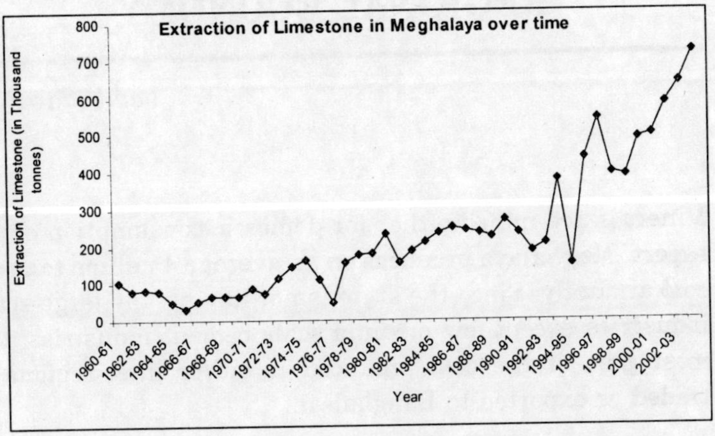

Graph 15.2

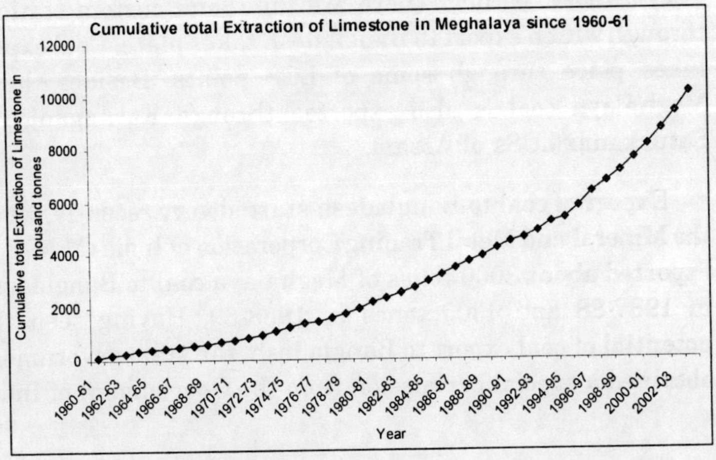

16

MEGHALAYA'S COAL EXPORT TO BANGLADESH AND ITS IMPACT ON REGIONAL ECONOMY

Lambodar Rout

Minerals are mined either for domestic consumption or for export. Meghalaya produces on an average 4 million tones of coal annually. Since the state is not having any large scale industries except few medium scale cement industries; the most part of the coal produced is either inter-regionally traded or exported to Bangladesh.

Bangladesh and Meghalaya share around 423 km international border. There are nine land custom stations through which export to Bangladesh takes place. Coal export takes place through some of LCS points. Besides these, Meghalaya coal is also exported through Karimganj and Saturkandi LCSs of Assam.

Export of coal to Bangladesh started very recently, when the Mineral and Metal Trading Corporation of India (M.M.T.C) exported about 3000 tones of Meghalaya coal to Bangladesh in 1987-88 and 4300 tones in 1988-89. Having seen the potential of coal export to Bangladesh, the state government obtained a special permission from the Government of India and in 1989-90 permited export of Meghalaya coal to Bangladesh by the state owned Meghalaya Mineral Development Corporation. At the same time, state government succeeded to persuade Government of India to delegate the power of transit paper clearance to the custom's office at Tamabil, Dawki. Subsequently, custom offices were opened at Borsora, West Khasi Hills; Ghasuapara of South Garo Hills and the like. Coal became black gold for Meghalaya.

With the passage of time, private international exporters came into the picture. They also formed their union like MITA (Meghalaya International Traders Association) in 1987. At present, Meghalaya coal is exported to Bangladesh through different land custom stations located both in Meghalaya and Assam. Table 16.1 presents the amount of coal being exported to Bangladesh through different land custom stations in different years.

TABLE: 16.1

Meghalaya's Coal Export Through Different LCS

(in '000 tonnes)

Name of the LCS	*1998-99*	*1999-00*	*2000-01*	*2001-02*	*2002-03*
Dawki	341862.121	222426.457	420622.418	304061.751	494966.534
Borsora	69793.200	166804.735	233758.200	169211.830	242577.500
Mohendraganj	Nil	61290.47	17133.000	Nil	23515.000
Ghasuapara	56684.500	92597.9	129386.200	122577.100	109012.406
Dalu	861.000	1007.5	5087.000	4089.700	14548.800
Baghmara	Nil	Nil	Nil	100.000	250.000
Karimganj	Nil	Nil	11740.000	8851.760	12594.000
Saturkandi	82655.364	202328.206	79057.323	92953.785	148441.165
Total export	551856.185	653857.368	817726.818	701845.926	1045905.459

Source: Custom's Office, Shillong.

TABLE 16.2

Total Export to Bangladesh as Percentage to Total Production of Coal in Meghalaya

(in 000 tones)

Year	*Export to Bangladesh*	*Total coal production*	*Percentage of coal export to total production*
1998-99	551.856	4237.06	13.02
1999-00	653.857	4060.1	16.10
2000-01	817.726	4064.9	20.11
2001-02	701.845	5149.3	13.62
2002-03	1045.905	4396.2	23.79

From Table 16.1 and 16.2, it is evident that there are three important land custom stations, that is, Dawki, Ghasuapara and Borsora through which Meghalaya's coal is mainly exported to Bangladesh. It is also found that coal export constitutes 10 to 25 per cent of the total production of coal in Meghalaya. Export performance shows a steady growth over the years, that is, from 13.02 per cent in 1998-99 to 23.79 per cent in 2002-03.

Export Procedure

The international exporters carry out export to Bangladesh. Each international exporter maintains an office comprising one manager and one assistant manager. Field study reveals that each international exporter spends around Rs. 15000.00 towards the maintenance of the management structure. Managers and Assistant Managers look after the procedural formalities of export. First, Letters of Credit are collected from international importers showing the demand for coal export. This LCs are produced in the DMR office and challans are obtained for the export of coal by paying a royalty to the tune of Rs. 165 per tone. Secondly, Meghalaya International Exporters Chamber of Commerce issues pre-shipment certificate recognized by Ministry of Commerce by charging

Rs. 3 per ton. After the completion of all these formalities, coal is exported to Bangladesh.

Coal Export to Bangladesh and its Impact on NSDP of Meghalaya

Export of coal has a modest impact on the Net State Domestic Product of Meghalaya. Table 16.3 presents the contribution of coal export to Bangladesh to the NSDP of Meghalaya.

TABLE: 16.3

Export of Coal and Its Impact (Rs in Crore)

Year	*NSDP at constant prices (1993-94)*	*Value of coal exported to Bangladesh*	*Percentage contribution of coal export to NSDP*
1998-99	1843.89	82.77	4.48
1999-00	2000.39	98.07	4.90
2000-01	2150.38	122.65	5.70
2001-02	2228.23	105.27	4.72
2002-03	2338.29	156.88	6.70

Source: Directorate of Mineral Resources, Meghalaya.

From Table 16.3, it is evident that the coal export to Bangladesh contributes 4-7 per cent of the NSDP of the state of Meghalaya.

Contribution of Coal Export to Government Revenue

The Government of Meghalaya presently charges Rs. 165 per ton as royalty for the export of coal. The revenue that comes from coal royalty goes to the state exchequer. Table 16.4 and 16.5 present coal royalty receipts from coal export to Bangladesh and its percentage to the state revenue receipts. It is evident that royalty earned by state government from coal export constitutes 1.5-3.5 per cent of the total internal revenue receipts of the state.

TABLE: 16.4

Export of Coal to Bangladesh and Royalty Receipts

Year	*Coal export to Bangladesh in '000' tonnes*	*Royalty receipts of the Government of Meghalaya (in Lakh)*	*Foreign Exchange Receipt (in lakh)*
1998-99	551.856	662.22	$ 226.26
1999-00	653.857	784.62	$ 261.54
2000-01	817.726	981.27	$ 327.09
2001-02	701.845	842.21	$ 280.73
2002-03	1045.905	1255.08	$ 418.36

Source: Directorate of Mineral Resources, Meghalaya.

TABLE 16.5

Coal Export Royalty and its Percentage Share to Total Revenue Receipts (in Lakh)

Year	*Total internal revenue receipts*	*Coal export royalty*	*Percentage to revenue receipts*
1998-99	40034.00	662.22	1.65
1999-00	48473.00	784.62	1.61
2000-01	32010.00	981.27	3.06
2001-02	42905.93	842.21	1.96
2002-03	51312.00	1255.08	2.44

Source: Directorate of Mineral Resources, Meghalaya.

Impact of Coal Export on Local Employment

Coal export related activities generate both direct and indirect employment. Since secondary data are not available on employment generation due to coal mining and export, field survey of production and trade outlets have been undertaken to generate primary data on both direct an indirect employment.

It is known from the field survey that if 290 workers are employed in a day, they can produce 100 metric tones of coal. Taking working season as 180 days, it is calculated that there are 73269 workers and miners working in the coal industry of Meghalaya. Figures released by the DMR shows that daily production is 24423.3 metric tones. It is calculated that 42.82 days of production of coal is exported to Bangladesh. Field experience indicates that there are approximately 200 international exporters operating in Meghalaya out of which 135 are operating in Dawki. Similarly, from exporters, it is known that approximately 1000 middlemen traders are also involved in the coal export.

If we take 180 working days for export activities, then 5810.58 mts of coal is exported daily to Bangladesh. If a truck carries 15 tones on an average, approximately 380 trucks are passing the border daily. That means 380 drivers and 380 handymen are getting employment everyday.

It is calculated that Meghalaya's coal export to Bangladesh generates 30, 33125.83 man days of employment for labourers and miners taken together. Besides exporters, managers, middlemen, drivers and handymen, a sizeable section of people are also employed as loaders. In order to load one S-Model truck, Rs. 600 is given to a group of 6 workers. Field survey of coal depots reveals that more than 3000 workers are engaged in Meghalaya in this activity. Besides direct employment, an odd number of services that require to support coal export activities have also engaged a sizeable section of local people indirectly. For example, a case study of Dawki land custom station reveals that there are twenty tea stalls run by Khasi/Pnar/War kongs (women) to provide tea, light refreshment, lunch, kwai (betel leaf and betel nut) ,etc to the workforce engaged in coal export.

The Process of Value Addition in Production and Export of Coal for 100mt

Stage-1: Rs 36000 is the labour value of coal.

Stage-2: Rs 5000 is the value added to the coal by the coalmine owner in his/her capacity as the owner of the land.

Stage-3: Rs 2000 is the value added to the coal by the coal agents who supply coal to the coal depots.

Stage-4: Rs 4000 is the value added by the labourers by way of loading coal to Shaktimans.

Stage-5: Rs 30000 is the value added by the truck (Shaktiman) owners when coal is transported from quarry to the road side dumping place.

Stage-6: Rs. 3000 is the value added by the coal depot agents when coal is sold to the middlemen traders.

Stage-7: Rs 9400 is the value addition by the middlemen traders when the coal is supplied by him/her to the international exporters.

Stage-8: Rs. 4000 is the value addition by the labourers when coal is loaded in S- Model truck for export destination.

Stage-9: Rs. 46600 is the value added by the truck owners when coal is transported to the trade outlet.

Stage-10: Rs. 13700 is the value added by the international exporters when coal is exported to Bangladeshi importer.

Stage-11: Rs. 16500 is the value added by Government of Meghalaya by way of royalty at the rate of Rs 165 per ton.

Stage-12: Rs. 1500 is the value added by the bank for LC advising.

Stage-13: Rs. 300 is the value added by the Meghalaya International Exporters' Chamber of Commerce for pre-shipment certificate.

Summing up all these stages gives the total value of Rs 172000.00 for 100 mt. The value per ton so arrived is equal to the international price of coal per ton.

17

INDO-BANGLADESH BORDER TRADE: THE GARO HILLS DIMENSION

Ajanta Deb Kar

Introduction

Garo Hills is a part of the Purvanchal mountain system, separated from the Himalayan ranges by narrow elevations known as ridges. These are not so high as the Himalayas and are sometimes called the Highlands. Garo Hills is one such highland along with the Khasi and Jaintia Hills, which are ridges thrown off in east-west directions.

East, West and South Garo Hills districts are the three components of Garo hills region of the state of Meghalaya, located in the north-eastern part of India. West and South Garo Hills share an international border on the south and west with Bangladesh. In this chapter, only two districts of Garo Hills, viz, West and South Garo hills are taken into consideration, excluding East Garo hills as it does not share any border with Bangladesh.

West and South Garo hills have a total area of 3677 sq. km and 1887 sq. km with a total population of 515813 and 99105 respectively (2001); number of villages in the two districts are 1481 and 595 respectively (Economic Census:1998); with one town each, the two districts have 8 and 4 community development blocks (2002) respectively. Percentage of literacy is the lowest in West Garo hills district at 51.03 whereas South Garo hills features 3rd lowest at 55.82 (2001). Medical facilities are also inadequate as West Garo hills district has only 3 hospitals and 9 dispensaries (1998-99) and South Garo hills enjoys the services of 5 dispensaries (1998-99) only. Number of doctors and nurses in these two districts are 61, 55 and 8, 7 respectively (1998-99). For the rural areas, services of PHC, CHC and family welfare centers are available. All the villages have their own source of drinking water, but few receive potable water from water treatment plants. Garo hills face bottlenecks in the fast development of postal communication particularly because of its hilly terrain and dense forests. Only 3.71 per cent of the villages of West Garo hills are connected with postal communication. Analyzing the available data, we grasp the fact that these two districts are comparatively backward among others in the state.

Garo hills are mostly hilly, interspersed with patches of plain lands. The hills rise sharply from the plain of Bangladesh on the south. These hills attain their highest elevation in Tura and Arbella ranges, slope down towards the Brahmaputra on the north. The plains are criss-crossed by a large number of rivers and streams. The main river is the Simsang (Someswari) which rises in the north of Tura hill. It flows eastward throughout the west Khasi hills border and then takes a turn to the south to fall into the Kangsa river in Mymensing district of Bangladesh.

Brief Economic Biography of Garo Hills

The economy of Garohills is basically agrarian in nature; though more than 80% of the indigenous population depends on agriculture, the net cropped area in West Garo hills is about 63377 hectare of the total geographical area of 371400 hectare and in South Garo hills, it is 18324 hectare out of a total geographical area of 185000 hectare (2001-02).In percentage term, it is only 17.06 per cent for West Garo hills and 9.9 per cent for South Garo hills. Forest cover in West Garo hills is 167650 hectare, and in South Garo hills it is 101796 hectare, which is 45.14per cent and 55.02 per cent of the total geographical area in West and South Garo hills respectively. Sal, Teak, Plywood are the major forest products of Garo hills; among the foodgrains, rice is the most important crop followed by maise, and wheat. Among the oilseeds, rapeseed, mustard and seasamum are important; of the fibre crops, mesta, jute and cotton are prominent. Garo hills are famous for its production of ginger; apart from ginger, it also produces turmeric, black pepper, chillies, bay leaf and areca nut. It also produces tapioca. Besides these, Garo hills is the homeland of many citrus fruits; Pineapple, papaya, oranges, jackfruit, banana, cashew kernel are the other important horticultural products of this region, which desperately look for better markets and improved marketing facilities.

Coal, limestone and clay are the three most important mineral resources found in Garo hills. The chief coalfields of Garo hills are

- West Darrangre
- East Darrangre group
- Siju
- Baljong-Doggreng-Hansapal
- Rongrengre

Limestone deposits in Garo hills are found along the southern slope of the Tura range. The high quality limestone found here is an essential component in the production of cement.

Historical Perspective of Border Trade in Garo Hills

Border trade in Garo hills is a century old practice. The Garos of the Southern hills along the Mymensing border of Bangladesh were in the habit of trading in all the markets of Sherpur and Susang areas of the Mymensing district .Capt. Pamberton, in his report on the Eastern Frontier (1809) stated that the total trade to be of the order of about 40 lakhs rupees. A.J.M Mills had observed in 1853 that 'the value of the trade was about Rs.50,00,000. The trade with the Garos in cotton, aghur, elephants and manufactured articles, was so lucrative that each estate holder established a string of weekly markets at all important passes in their respective estates. Besides the weekly markets, Mr. Elliot observed that there were fairs held only once or twice a year after due notice had been given in order that a considerable benefit may be derived at a time.

Cotton was the staple article of internal trade in Eastern India, tea not having been discovered before 1826.The Garos were the largest producers of cotton in Eastern India. In order to establish monopoly of trade interest with the Garos, the estates holders in their respective areas used to appoint estate-police and burkandazes to guard and maintain their hats at all principal passes, collect taxes levied by the estate holders on all Garos and non-Garo traders. They were also in charge of security of the border with Garoland. The low country businessmen would meet their tax burden from their enormous profits in their dealings with the Garos.

The prominent estate holders were those of Mechapara, Aurangabad, Kalumalupara and Karaibari in old Rangpur of Sherpur and Susang in Mymensing, now in Bangladesh, of Sidly and Bijni in Eastern Duars, now in Goalpara district of Assam. All of them existed during the period of British contact with the upland Garos.

Border Trade (Formal) in Garo Hills: Present Scenario

Garo hills enjoy the services of 5 land custom stations. These LCSs have been established by the Custom Department in Dalu, Gasuapara, Mahendraganj, Hallidayganj and Baghmara to facilitate border trade with Bangladesh and also movement of people of both the countries across the border. The bilateral trade between India and Bangladesh has been increasing, though tension prevails over several issues that need be addressed politically. The trade balance is significantly in favour of India. Focussing on the Garo hills component of the border trade in India, we find that Mahendraganj is the only LCS through which India imports some commodities from Bangladesh. All the other LCSs viz, Dalu, Gasuapara and Baghmara are involed in export of goods without any corresponding import of any kind.

TABLE 17.1

Composition of Export Through Dalu LCS in Garo Hills: 1999-2006

Year	*Commodity*	*Volume*	*Value (USD)*	*Rupee*
1999-2000	Coal	1367 MT	60160	2590000
2000-01	Coal	3650 MT	159551	7380724
	Boulders and crushed stones	80 MT	1770	78752
2002-03	Coal	12200 MT	512400	22033200
2003-04	Coal	33080 MT	1393560	63011047
2004-05	Coal Lime stone,	48315 MT	2093111	8905050
	Boulders and Crushed	1300 MT	8600	0374540
	stone Ginger	48 MT	7200	3,06,720
2005-06 (up-	Coal	1850 MT	80195	3496502
to May 2005)	Lime stone	400 MT	2400	102240

Source: Customs Department

Nothing has been formally imported through Dalu LCS over all these years.

Table 17.2 shows export of coal through Gasuapara LCS over the last three years where import from Bangladesh does not figure at all.

TABLE 17.2

Coal Export Through Gasuapara LCS in Garo Hills: 2002-05

Year	*Quantity*	*Value (USD)*	*Rupee*
2002-03	120525 MT	48,21,000	21,21,24,000
2003-04	78900 MT	32,34,900	14,23,35,600
2004-05	100200 MT	4208400	18,34,86,240

Source: Customs Department

TABLE 17.3

Composition of Export/Import Through Mahendraganj LCS in Garo Hills: 2004-05

Year	*Export*	*Value*	*Import (in Rs)*	*Value (in Rs)*	*Trade Balance (X-M)*	*Total Trade (X+M)*
2004-05	Coal, crushed stone, boulder stone, ginger	1,05,39,000	Mosquito net, cotton waste	29,99,250	75,39,750	1,35,38,250

Source: Customs Department.

Baghmara LCS is of less significance because formal trade here is mostly seasonal in nature and takes place only for few months. The only commodity exported through Baghmara is coal.

LCS in Hallidyganj is basically operating to prevent informal trade as this station is bereft of any formal trade.

Land custom station in Dalu bears a tremendous potential in terms of future growth of export, when compared to Mahendraganj or Gasuapara LCS because:

- Firstly, it is the nearest LCS for Chokpot coal fields.
- Secondly, Chokpot and Dalu are connected through a good road that helps in reducing transport cost.

- Thirdly, Dalu is the only LCS through which coal is exported to Bangladesh, directly from the Chokpot coalfield. It is cost effective since there is no dumping expense involved here.
- Fourthly, Chokpot coal is yet to find a local market in India and it is best suited to our interest to export it directly from the coalfield to Bangladesh.

Informal Trade

As per the information gathered from Garo hills border trade points, the major commodities exported informally from Garo hills to Bangladesh include cash crops, horticultural and agricultural products, valuable wood, salt and sugar. Cattle from Assam and interior Garo hills are smuggled out which is a significant component of informal trade across the border. Ginger, betelnut, greenchilli, orange, pineapple, jackfruit, banana, foreign liquor (wine) are some of the other items usually traded informally.

Salt and sugar are other important items exported to Bangladesh through Hallidyganj. These are procured from Dhubri in Assam and transported through the river Brahmaputra-Gingiram with the help of country-boats. Occasional seizure of these items by Hallidyganj LCS (usually 10 to 15 per cent of the total) brings about 4 to 5 lakhs annually to the Customs Department.

Seizure of valuable wood, viz, Sal, Teak, Gamari etc, by the B.S.F is quite common here. These are handed over to the Customs Department, which through the process of auction, raises 4 to 10 lakhs annually from these seizured treasure which is 5 to 6 times less than what these wood could have commanded in the open market.

Narcotics, mainly ganja goes to Bangladesh in large quantity, mostly through Hallidyganj. About 40 to 50 kg of ganja is seized annually which costs around Rs.40,000 to 50,000. This was coming mainly from Goalpara, Krishnai and Dudhnai of Assam. In the last two years, of course, there has not been a single incidence of seizure of narcotics.

Informal import from Bangladesh consists of palm oil, melamine dishes, crokeries, ready-made garments, mosquito nets, dry fish, salted hilsa, kerosin, disel and electronic goods, though the informal import of electronic goods is on the decline. Custom officials admit that there is not much informal import of hilsa from across the border as it was in the past. The informal channel is particularly attractive for exports of mass consumer goods. The inadequate transport and transit systems that have been in existence between India and Bangladesh have been a major constraint in enhancing trade through formal channels. Unless infrastructure development is undertaken on an urgent basis, unofficial trade will continue to be more attractive. India and Bangladesh will have to make a concerted effort towards synchronizing both trade and domestic policies in order to convert informal trade flows to formal ones.

TABLE 17.4

Informal Trade through Dalu Border (Custom Seizure)

Year	*Number of Cases*	*Value (in Rs)*	*Revenue(in Rs)*
1999-2000	40	45221	58,338
2000-01	55	110230	122468
20001-02	57	95335	104414
2002-03	50	74450	117631
2003-04	36	84492	127593
2004-05	40	51200	163670
2005-06 (Upto May 2005)	10	5000	22500

Source: Customs Department.

Conclusion

Garo Hills is rich in resources. It is important to use them for value addition first and then to export. Present Indo-Bangladesh border trade that flows across the Garo Hills border is characterized by export of raw materials from Garo Hills to Bangladesh. Income earned from the coal export is hardly invested in the local economy. For sustainable growth, this income needs to be invested in order to develop alternative source of income so that once coal reserve is exhausted people can fall back on those alternative avenues for livelihood.

ACKNOWLEDGEMENT

I take this opportunity to express my heartfelt gratitude and thanks to Mr. Uttam Das, Superintendent, Department of Customs and Excise, Ms. Gunme Marak, BADO, Ampati, and Mr. S.K. Verma, S.P.A., NEHU, Tura Campus, Mr. S. Bhattacharjee, Retd. Headmaster, Town Higher Secondary School, Tura. It will be unfair if I do not thank my family members, particularly my sister Ms. Rupa Kar Purkayastha, District Informatics Officer, NIC without whose constant support this chapter would not have been possible.

18

INDO-BANGLADESH BORDER TRADE: TRIPURA'S PERSPECTIVES

Kiran Sankar Chakraborty

Introduction

The geographical location of North East India (NEI) has a special significance to border trade. The region shares a longer border with neighbours like China, Bangladesh, Bhutan and Myanmar than mainland. Perhaps this is the reason why NEI takes interest in these countries for establishing trade relations. The poor infrastructure of the region coupled with transportation bottlenecks is the main reason of region's underdevelopment. Hence, NEI can take advantage of border trade and generate economic activities because of her close proximity to these countries.

NEI shares 1880 km. border with Bangladesh wherein 1439 km. is land border and 446 km. is riverine tract. Assam, Mizoram, Meghalaya and Tripura are the four of the NEI states, which share their borders with Bangladesh. Assam has a total of 263 km., Mizoram 318 km, Meghalaya 443 km. and Tripura 856 km. of border area (both land & riverine) . As can be seen from Table 18.1, Tripura has the lions share of border area with 773 km. of land border and 83 km. riverine border which accounts for 45.53 per cent of the total border area of our country with Bangladesh. So far as Indo-Bangla land border is concerned, Tripura shares 53.72 per cent of total land border. It is also to be noted that Tripura and Bangladesh have always shared close racial, lingual, ethnic and cultural affinity. The importance of border trade between the two regions, therefore, cannot be ignored but requires special attention. The present chapter focuses upon the issues associated with Indo-Bangla trade relation from the point of view of the state of Tripura. This chapter has five sections including the present one. Section two deals with the present status of trade between Bangladesh and Tripura; section three deals with the potential areas for developing trade between Tripura and Bangladesh. Impediments in the trade relation and strategies for developing trade between the two regions are dealt in sections four and five respectively.

TABLE 18.1

Indo-Bangla Border

(in km)

NE State	*Riverine*	*Land Border*	*Total*	*% of Total*
Tripura	83	773	856	45.53
Meghalaya	—	443	443	23.56
Mizoram	260	58	318	16.91
Assam	103	160	263	13.99
Total	446	1439	1880	100

Source: Govt. of India website.

SECTION II

Present Status of Trade

Bilateral trade between India and Bangladesh has been increasing rapidly since the last two decades. However, it is also noted that the balance of trade between the two countries considerably tilts towards India. This may be due to the fact that India's imports from Bangladesh are extremely skewed, limited to only a few commodities, as compared to its exports to Bangladesh. Indo-Bangla trade is currently close to $2 billion. The Indian exports to Bangladesh are nearly $1.8 billion. Hence NEI in general and Tripura in particular with its close proximity to Bangladesh can obviously play a distinct role in this bilateral trade. Let's take a glance at the present status of Tripura's import and export scenario with Bangladesh in comparison to NEI.

TABLE 18.2

Status of Value of Imports from Bangladesh to Tripura and NEI

Year	*Value of Imports to Tripura (Rs. in crores)*	*Value of Imports to NEI (Rs. in crores)*	*Share of Tripura in total value of imports to NEI (Percentage)*
1999-2000	7.44	9.43	78.89
2000-2001	7.19	9.69	74.20
2001-2002	4.38	5.52	79.35
2002-2003	5.47	6.10	89.67
2003-2004	10.18	11.52	88.37

Source: Office of the Central Excise & Land Custom, Govt. of India, Agartala.

TABLE 18.3

Status of Value of Exports from Tripura & NEI to Bangladesh

Year	*Value of Exports from Tripura (Rs.in crores)*	*Value of Exports from NEI (Rs. in crores)*	*Share of Tripura in total value of exports from NEI (Percentage)*
1999-2000	1.74	169.82	1.02
2000-2001	0.81	151.23	0.53
2001-2002	1.27	85.89	1.48
2002-2003	1.57	202.70	0.77
2003-2004	1.38	240.01	0.57

Source: Office of the Central Excise & Land Custom, Govt. of India, Agartala

TABLE 18.4

Status of Trade between Bangladesh and Tripura /NEI

Year	*Total value of Trade between Tripura and Bangladesh (Rs. in crores)*	*Total value of Trade Between NEI and Bangladesh (Rs. in crores)*	*Share of Tripura in Total value of Trade Between NEI and Bangladesh (in %)*
1999-2000	9.18	179.25	5.12
2000-2001	8.00	158.42	5.05
2001-2002	5.65	191.41	2.95
2002-2003	7.04	208.80	3.39
2003-2004	11.56	251.53	4.59

Source: Office of the Central Excise & Land Custom, Govt. of India, Agartala.

It is observed from Table 18.2 that value of imports from Bangladesh to Tripura is quite high in comparison to NEI. The total value of imports from Bangladesh to Tripura has increased from Rs. 7.44 crores in 1999-2000 to Rs.10.18 crores in the year 2003-04 .While the value of imports from Bangladesh to NEI has increased from Rs. 9.43 crores to Rs. 11.52 crores during the same period .The share of Tripura in the total imports of NEI during 2003-04 is 88.37 per cent.

Table 18.3 shows the value of exports to Bangladesh from Tripura and NEI during the period 1999-2000 and 2003-04. Here the picture is reverse. The value of exports from Tripura during the reported years is meager in comparison to exports from NEI. The value of exports to Bangladesh from Tripura has declined from Rs. 1.74 crores in the year 1999-2000 to Rs. 1.38 crores in 2003-04. On the other hand value of exports from NEI has increased from Rs. 169.82 crores to Rs. 240.01 crores during the same period. The percentage of Tripura's share in total exports of NEI is negligible.

The total value of trade during the period 1999-2000 and 2003-04 is shown in Table 18.4. It reveals that the Tripura's trade with Bangladesh has declined from Rs. 9.18 crores in

1999-2000 to Rs. 5.65 crores in 2001-02 but increased to Rs. 7.04 crores in 2002-03 and Rs. 11.56 crores in 2003-04. The total value of trade between NEI and Bangladesh, on the other hand, has increased from Rs. 179.25 crores in 1999-2000 to Rs. 251.53 crores in 2003-04. The share of Tripura in total value of trade between NEI and Bangladesh in the year 2003-04 was only 4.59 per cent.

Hence it is quite clear that though there is an immense potential, the Indo-Bangla trade has really not developed through Tripura. Out of the seven Land Custom Stations – Agartala, Srimantapur, Muhurighat, Khowai, Dhalaighat, Manughat, Ragnabazar, only 3 stations i.e. Agartala, Srimantapur, Muhurighat are functional as far as formal trade transactions are concerned .

NEI's share of imports are not quite large but regarding exports the states sharing borders with Bangladesh seem to enjoy an upper hand .The large reserves of minerals, production of horticultural products and a congenial trade atmosphere through border routes seem to help bilateral trade. Limestone and coal of NEI are exported to Bangladesh; hence the balance of trade is in favour of the North East with its value of exports much higher than the imports over the same period of time

Trade between India and Bangladesh has grown in the last 2 to 3 decades unprecedentedly. The major items of exports from NEI are coal, limestone, fruits, ginger, boulder stone, marble stone, paper, auto parts, bamboo, betel leaf etc. and major items of import from Bangladesh consist of fish, molasses, dry fish, jute, tiles, cotton waste, juice, mineral water, snacks and bakery items etc. The items of import from Bangladesh to Tripura are fruit juices, potato crackers, mineral water, soaps, cashew nut, mustard oil, soyabean oil, PVC pipes and tubes, synthetic fiber, stone chips etc. which seem to help the small and medium enterprises actively . Tripura exports ginger, betel leaves, fresh fruits, chilies, playing cards, natural rubber etc. Perhaps a lack of industrial infrastructure and a backward economy of the state may account for the fact that imports have remained constantly higher than exports in Tripura. Tripura is Bangladesh's gateway to the NEI. The nearest rail station on Bangladesh side from Agartala is Akhaura (8 km from Agartala, 125 km. from Chittagang port).

SECTION III

Potential Areas of Trade

Tripura lags behind in economic development due to her poor infrastructural facilities. However, Tripura has immense reserves of gas which can generate power so essential for industrial, agricultural and commercial development. The state is endowed with natural gas reserves of 588 billion cu.m. which has huge potentiality to generate power in excess of Tripura's requirement. Recently the North Eastern Electric Power Corporation (NEEPCO) and other organizations have initiated setting up of gas based power projects with 500 MW capacity .If the target is achieved, Tripura will have a surplus in power generation .In the absence of any industrial base in the state, Tripura can easily export the excess power to Bangladesh and neighbouring regions.

The agro-climatic condition of Tripura is suitable for development of tea plantation. The soil is generally fertile, without any major problems of toxicity or deficiency. The average annual rainfall is about 2100 mm, with a fairly even distribution over the year. Tripura has a history of tea plantations that dates back to 1916. In fact, Tripura is categorized as a traditional tea-growing state – with around 60 Tea Estates and 3,000 small tea growers, producing about 7.5 million kg. of tea every year . This makes Tripura the 5th

largest, among the 14 tea producing states, after Assam, West Bengal, Tamilnadu and Kerala . There is a considerable scope to increase the area under tea plantation as well as productivity. The tea currently produced in Tripura is recognized for its good blending qualities. Some plantation estates in the state are going for organic production of tea. There is considerable scope for the entrepreneurs of Bangladesh and Tripura. Tea produced in the state is at present sent to Guwahati or Calcutta for marketing. It can as well be marketed through Bangladesh.

In natural rubber production, Tripura ranks second only to Kerala in the country. More and more plantations are reaching yielding stage and the productivity levels are also encouraging. In view of the area under plantations together with the growth potential and rubber production trends, the state has been identified as the second rubber capital of the country. There is a vast potential for setting up of rubber-based industries in the state. The rubber produced in the state is also of high quality which faces trading problems in the absence of any rubber based industry in the state. In 2002-03 an area of about 17,701 hectare land was under natural rubber plantation in the state. Total rubber production was 17,849 MT and total value of rubber production was Rs. 69.42 crores in 2002-03. The raw rubber now produced is being sent out to the neighbouring states for further value addition. Internal trade in India takes a long route through the narrow corridor in Assam which is both time consuming as well as expensive. If exported to Bangladesh or to other countries through Bangladesh port, it will easily reduce the related expenses as well as increase foreign exchange earnings considerably.

Fruit processing is another potential area wherein bilateral trade between the two regions may be embarked upon .The agro-climatic condition of Tripura is favourable for growing various fruit and horticultural crops. The products of Tripura are well known- both in raw as well as processed forms. There is scope for expansion of area under any specific variety, if required. A modern Food Processing Technology Park is being set up near Agartala, to give a fillip to this sector. An Agri Export Zone for Pineapple is also being developed. There is a vast potential for setting up of food processing units in the state. Seasonal fruits such as pineapples, jackfruits, oranges, litchis etc. are grown in large quantities. These can be exported to Bangladesh for value addition. At present large quantities of these are informally traded with Bangladesh. Other food products, e.g., cashew nuts, vegetables and spices like pepper etc. too are commercially grown in Tripura . These products may be exported to Bangladesh instead of sending them to mainland India and facing the problems of transportation.

Tripura cane and bamboo handicrafts are considered to be among the best in the country for the exquisite designs, wide range of products and artistic appeal. This industry has a great export potential as well. Steps have been taken to develop this industry on modern lines. Not only that, in view of availability of large bamboo resources in the State, industrial products like bamboo tiles, laminated products, ply boards, corrugated sheets etc. can be produced, which can be used as building materials and furniture manufacture etc. Studies have shown that bamboo is a very effective substitute for timber and is, in fact, better in many respects.

Tourism is perhaps one of the most important sectors contributing to present day economic development of a nation. Tourism can build transnational communities as people can interact with each other and develop a deeper sense of appreciation, cooperation and ultimately remove all narrow barriers and develop friendship between the two countries. Tripura is an attractive tourist destination. The state has a rich cultural heritage. The state also has rich flora and fauna. There is also great potential for development of tourist circuits, involving all the NE states and if possible, Bangladesh as well. All these offer attractive opportunities for the growth of Hospitality Industry. Tripura and Bangladesh have always shared a special bond culturally, linguistically, ethnically since the princely regime. Partition has cut across the land and separated families as well as blurred the memories of the old days. Bilateral cooperation may be boosted if tourism is given special attention.This will be possible if people on the either side are allowed to cross over freely. An attempt to relax visa rules, substituting passport entry by permit rules, encouraging package tours and allowing private tour operators on both sides will perhaps lead to open border system. Reuniting families, creating a sense of oneness, preserving heritage monuments will no doubt boost up the border trade.

Transit route through Bangladesh is another important area of cooperation between two regions from Tripura's perspective. Due to its peculiar geographical location, the state is like an island and people of the state want a corridor to reach the mainland, which will be less expensive as well as less time taking. Recently Agartala-Kolkata via Dhaka bus service has been launched and is running with high hopes. If transhipment facility through Bangladesh is allowed, it would be beneficial for both the regions. According to an estimate by the Tripura Chamber of Commerce, every day more than 1,000 trucks could be utilized for transhipment of Indian goods and Bangladesh can earn about Rs.2,000 crores per annum and Tripura can become the gateway to NEI.

The higher education sector in Tripura has deepened and widened over the period. Some significant changes have also taken place in higher education sector of the state in tune with new economic policies. Privatization has already started shaping this sector in Tripura. One university and two technology and science colleges have been established in the private sector. A few more private universities and medical colleges are in the pipeline. In view of this, the state can explore the opportunity of catering to the demand for higher educational services of the students of Bangladesh. At present very few students from the adjacent areas of Bangladesh come to Agartala for higher education. The computer oriented courses are much sought after by the learners from Bangladesh.

Tripura can also explore the opportunity to cater the health care services to the Bangladeshi people residing in the adjoining areas across the border. It is a known fact that 20-30 per cent of the indoor and outdoor patients of the government hospitals and private nursing homes in Tripura are residents of Bangladesh . Most of them come illegally to this side of the border for better treatment. Relaxing visa rules or introducing permit system or even simply allowing them for a few hours for medical consultations could of immense benefit for the border population.

SECTION IV

Impediments

A major barrier to develop the trade between Tripura and Bangladesh is the lack of adequate infrastructure in both sides of the border. Among the major infrastructural constraints on Tripura's side which impede the development of trade are inadequate rail and road transport network in the state, poor road conditions, lack of cargo handling facilities, inadequate banking facilities as well as poor telecommunications, postal services etc.

It has been seen that of the seven land custom stations, only three stations are functional. Even these stations lack in basic amenities necessary for carrying out brisk trade. Firstly, there is no warehousing facility in the LCS. Since a major share of trade involves perishable items, traders face mounting challenges to carry out their business. Secondly, there is no proper parking bay for trucks. Thirdly, banking facilities exclusively to promote border-trade are almost non-existent. Fourthly, the documentation process in the custom stations is lengthy and even cumbersome which fails to attract traders to carry out trading formally. Fifthly, the stations lack in adequate staff strength too. Sixthly, it has noted that these stations even lack in basic civic amenities. Finally, there are no sales counters, shops, retailers near the custom stations, which can cater to the needs of the traders.

Transportation bottlenecks are the most important problems of trade in Tripura.. Tripura is linked with mainland by a narrow corridor which passes through Siliguri. Thus, goods, cargo transports from Delhi/Kolkata have to take a much longer route and involve more cost to reach the state. For example, it takes 3-4 days for the goods to reach Agartala from Kolkata. This increases the total cost of the traders at Agartala, the prices of essentials shoot up, even goods disappear from markets due to hoarding by unscrupulous traders and all these become more problematic when the roads are blocked due to landslides. The closed border, visa-permit regulations deter the two governments from allowing cargo/passengers through Bangladesh.

The communication system of the state is very poor. It requires upgradation. The communication system comprises of postal service, telegraph service, telephone service, internet service etc. Communication facilities in the state have been growing slowly. Insurgency problem in the state is one of the main reasons for such slow development. The postal and telecommunication facilities should be expanded to the remotest area of the state so that border trade gets an impetus.

One of the major impediments, which obstruct the formal trade between Tripura and Bangladesh, is the thriving informal trade. Needless to mention that there is considerable flow of informal trade between India and Bangladesh. This is largely due to cost difference between formal and informal trade arising out from both infrastructural and procedural bottlenecks. The value of informal exports from India to Bangladesh is reported in the range of US $350 to US $500 million every year (India Bangladesh Infrastructure Summit: 2000). Informal trade between NEI and Bangladesh is estimated at US $ 36 million in the year 2002 (Northeast India Bangladesh Initiative Map: 2004). Large volume of illegal trade between Tripura and Bangladesh flows, as the cost of trading in the informal channel is significantly lower than its formal counterparts. Earlier studies reveal that informal traders have developed efficient mechanism for the flow of information and contract enforcement. Although the volume of informal trade cannot be ascertained, figures available for seized goods are astounding. The value of goods seized from Indo-Bangla border in Tripura is Rs. 2.94 crores in 2003-04 and Rs. 4.35 crores in 2002-03.

There are also weekly markets operating in the border areas where agricultural products, household articles, bare necessities are exchanged among those living in close proximity. The value of such transactions is never brought into consideration.

India enjoyed a rail transit through erstwhile East Pakistan till 1965 but this was stopped after the Indo-Pak war. The nearest rail station from Tripura is, on the Bangladesh side, Akhaura—which is only 8 km from Agartala and 125 km. from the Chittagong port. The snapping of rail route has affected the economy of Tripura and also encouraged informal trade. Though there is an agreement on Inland Water Transit and Trade, 1972, it was renewed on 22nd August 1995 and effective from 4th October 1995 for a period of 2 years only. Under this protocol 8 river routes have been identified for cargo transit purposes but there is no point on the river route touching Tripura.

Another impediment is the lack of information with the traders/entrepreneurs of Tripura about the rules, regulations, documentation processes of formal cross border trade.

Corruption and bribery among the government officials in connection with procurement of passport, visa and customs and excise clearance is another important impediment in the flow of trade between the two regions .Corruption in all these departments has been institutionalized to a noticeable extent. Without bribery it is simply impossible to get the work done in due time.

SECTION V

Strategies for Improvement

The strategy for the promotion of border trade should focus on the removal of the above mentioned impediments. Tripura Chamber of Commerce, TIDC, banks and financial institutions, export promotion council, customs department—all need to be involved in framing the trade promotion strategy. It should aim at the following:

(a) Development of infrastructure at land custom stations. Modernization and upgradation of infrastructure at the LCSs should get immediate attention.

(b) More number of Land Custom Stations in the state need to be made functional.

(c) Banking facilities need to be extended to all LCSs.

(d) Negotiations need to be expedited with Bangladesh for providing goods transit facilities.

(e) Railway link between Agartala and Akhaura may be established.

(f) Initiative may be taken for the establishment of joint venture enterprise in the areas of rubber, fruit processing, tea and gas based power sector.

(g) Textile industry is quite developed in Bangladesh especially readymade garments sector. India has a strong primary textile industry with ample raw material supply. If the two countries collaborate in this sector, it will provide a win-win situation and even allow them to become globally competitive. Tripura may join in if an office operates from here.

(h) Travel operators may be encouraged to conduct package tours in both the regions to boost tourism.

(i) An export promotion council may be established in Tripura.

(j) Traders may be encouraged to use the waterways. Tripura's south district is barely 15 km. away from the Bay of Bengal through Feni river. Though there is no canal or sluiced gate that can be used as an outlet to the sea, attempt may be made to avail of waterways through Chittagong to Paradeep or even further down West Coast.

(k) Roads, riverine tracts need to be improved.

(l) Cargo gate for entry / exit needs to be separated from the passenger gates.

(m) Procedural mechanism and documentation need to be standardized and simplified.

REFERENCES

Bangladesh–India Chamber of Commerce and Industries (2000): India.

Bangladesh Infrastructure Summit, December 21, 2000, Calcutta. (www. saarcnet. com/ newsaarcnet /publications/summit.html)

Bhattacharya, Jayanta (2001): Tripura – Bangla: From History to Future, paper presented at the third dialogue on interaction with Indian Bordering States, organized by the Bangladesh Institute of International and Strategic Studies, Dhaka, August 21-23, 2001.

Bhattacharya, Pallab: Indo-Bangla Trade, PTI Feature. (www. sentinelassam.com/sentinel_en/archives/aug1704/ editorial.htm)

Chakraborty, Kiran Sankar and Das, B.C. (2002): An inside into the development of SSI in Tripura, *Southern Economist,* Volume-41, No-8, Bangalore.

Dahiya, L.N. (2004): India's International Trade in Higher Education, the Indian Journal of Commerce, Vol. 57, No. 3.

Das, Gangadhar (2004):Fruits and Vegetables Production in North Eastern Region: Export potential, The *Indian Journal of Commerce,* Vol. 57, No. 3.

Das, B.C. (2004): Health Care Facilities in Tripura, paper presented in the national Seminar organized by the Department of Economics, Tripura University and ESSOT, Agartala on 18th –19th September 2004 at Agartala.

Government of Tripura (2000): Speech of Minister, Industries and Commerce, Government of Tripura in 'First National Conference of Small Scale Industries,' Vigyan Bhavan, New Delhi 30th August, 2000.

Government of Tripura, Department of Industries and Commerce (2004): Tripura–The Land of Opportunities, Agartala.

Government of Tripura, Department of Industries and Commerce (2002): Speech of Chief Minister, Tripura, in the seminar on 'Promotion of Trade and Investment Between Tripura and Bangladesh', 31st May 2002.

Government of Tripura, Department of Industries and Commerce and Tripura Chamber of Commerce (2002): Proceedings of seminar on 'Promotion of Trade and Investment Between Tripura and Bangladesh', 31st May 2002

Jalil Altaf (2004): Northeast India-Bangladesh Initiatives Map, Bangladesh Enterprise Institute, Dhaka.

Verghese, B.G. (2002): Tripura Eyes Bangladesh, *The Statesman*, 22nd June 2002

19

SECURITY ISSUES IN INDO-BANGLADESH BORDER TRADE: A CASE STUDY OF TRIPURA

Tusharbindu Chakraborti

The security of a nation, as defined by Morton Berkowitz and Booke (1968), is 'the ability of a nation to protect internal values from external threat. Threat means the political instability, gross economic disparities, regional imbalances and, cultural, linguistic and ethnic antagonisms'. Therefore a nation can be said to have assured its own security when it is economically and technologically developed, politically stable and socio-culturally cohesive. According to Robert McNamara (1968) security is not only military hardware. Security is development and without development there is no security. Subrahmanyam, an Indian specialist on Security and Defence Studies elucidates that 'National security dose not merely mean safeguarding territorial integrity. It also means that the countries industrialize rapidly and have a cohesive egalitarian and technological society. Anything which comes in the way of this development internally and externally is a threat to national security'. Traditionally security meant threats from other countries. However, the external security environment for third world countries is substantially different from that faced by the developed world.

Economic development is essentially needed for the establishment of economic security of a particular state. Because the economic role of security is also vital due to its extensive spill over effects on other national values such as social harmony or political stability. Thus along with political and territorial security, other areas such as the economic and social security also play an important role in the national security. So economic development through trade is an essential part of the security build up of a country. On the other hand, well-developed security arrangements ensure peace and stability of a nation, resulting favourable impact on foreign trade.

Border trade between India and Bangladesh through Tripura may be of immense benefit for the state. Cross-border trade is, however, directly linked with the existing security environment between these two regions. Unless a favourable security environment is created, no spectacular growth in trade could be achieved. In fact India's relations with Bangladesh are an essential factor for the development of cross border trade between Tripura and Bangladesh. The present chapter is an attempt to focus upon the various security issues related to Indo-Bangla border trade through Tripura sector.

Border disputes between India and Bangladesh along the Tripura sector is one of the major hindrances towards the growth of vibrant cross border trade. Tripura shares about 856 km border with Bangladesh. The state is surrounded by Bangladesh and only a narrow neck links it to the mainland through Siliguri. The border between Tripura and Bangladesh is not well demarcated and guarded. This has not only encouraged illegal immigration and cross border human trafficking but also created a conducive environment for cross border terrorism, smuggling and trafficking of small arms, drugs and narcotics. The border disputes over many frontier places like Muhuri Char in the south district of Tripura (about 1.5 km) are no doubt the consequence of the legacy of ill-demarcation of Indo-Bangla border. Owing to these border disputes, Bangladesh often resorts to unprovoked firing that threatens the security of the state of Tripura. Border disputes have also paralyzed the work of barbed wire fencing in this sector.

Cross border terrorism is another issue that hinders the flow of trade between Tripura and Bangladesh. It is believed that Bangladesh plays a crucial role in helping cross border terrorism in the North Rastern Region in general and Tripura in particular. Bangladesh is believed to have tacit support in importing arms by the various insurgent groups to their bases in India through Cox Bazar port and to their camps in its territory surrounding Tripura. It is also reported that some top insurgent leaders from the region continue to live in Bangladesh. Bangladesh is reported to have allowed the insurgent groups of the North Eastern Region of India to use its territories surrounding Tripura for the purpose of the establishment of their transit camps, base camps and training camps. The gravity of the situation can be assessed from the fact that a total of 79 camps are at present in operation with active co-operation of ISI and Bangladesh army in the said areas. Details of the camps of insurgents disclosed by BSF on 4th July, 2005 are shown in Table 19.1. It is evident that NLFT (BM) has the highest number of camps, i.e., 42 in Bangladesh, followed by ATTF and PLA. NLFT (BM) has also highest number of training camps and transit camps among all the insurgent groups. Having a strategic interest in maintaining close relationship with the insurgent groups, it was reported that Bangladesh has moved a sizeable segment of its defence and security establishment in Chittagong Hill Tracts by setting up of 3 full fledged cantonments, 1 naval base at Dhalyachari, 1 school of jungle warfare at Mahalchari, 43 army camps, 30 Bangladesh Rifles camps, 33 Bangladesh

Armed Police camps, 49 Bangladesh Reserve police camps besides 28 police stations.

TABLE 19.1

Camps of the Insurgent Groups from North East India in Bangladesh

Name of group	*Training Camps*	*Transit Camps*	*HQ/ Base Camp*	*Rest Camp*	*Safe House*	*Hide-out*	*Launching Det*	*Total*
ATTF	02	04	03	01	03	—	—	13
NLFT (BM)	06	24	07	02	02	—	01	42
NLFT (NB)	01	02	01	—	—	—	01	05
NLFT (JASUA)	02	02	01	—	—	—	—	05
HNLC	01	01	—	—	—	—	—	02
PLA	03	08	01	—	—	—	—	12
TOTAL	15	41	13	03	05	—	02	79

Source: Frontiers Head Quarters, BSF, Agartala.

Insurgency is continuously bleeding the economy of the state. Huge security related expenditure is eating away the fund which otherwise could have been used for developmental activities. It has been roughly estimated that about 65 security personnel are employed for every insurgent in Tripura. The involvement of huge men, material and money for the purpose of counter-insurgency operations and their low success rate are bound to have an adverse impact on state economy. In such circumstances, cross border trade could hardly grow as these groups often stake claim on the gains from trade.

The intensity of cross boarder terrorism in Tripura can be gauged from the number of arms and ammunitions seized from the Tripura-Bangladesh border. The arms and ammunitions seized from the border areas of the state during the period 2000 and 2005 are shown in Table 19.2. The cache includes all types of ammunitions right from country made gun to AK-47. The figures, however, exclude the arms and ammunitions seized during counter-insurgency operations in hideouts of insurgents in the state.

TABLE 19.2

Seizure of Arms and Ammunitions Through Tripura-Bangla Border

Sl. No.	*Particulars*	*2000*	*2001*	*2002*	*2003*	*2004*	*2005 (upto August)*	*Total*
1.	Factory made Gun	—	12	06	06	25	08	57
2.	Country made Gun	08	15	14	13	19	04	73
3.	Ammunitions all types	07	2059	1360	167	10.763	388	14744
4.	Improvised Explosive Detonators	—	—	10	—	—	01	11
5.	Country made bomb	02	01	02	—	03	01	09
6.	Chinese Grenade	—	67	04	02	12	03	88
7.	Detonator	—	07	07	—	—	01	15
8.	Magazine all types	—	16	07	02	27	15	67
9.	Bayonet AK 47	—	—	10	—	—	—	10
10.	Explosive (in gms)	—	0.050	0.600	1.560	9.925	—	12.135
11.	Telescope	—	02	—	—	—	—	02
12.	H.E. Bomb	—	—	—	—	03	—	03
13.	Remote Control	—	—	—	—	01	—	01

Sources: Frontiers Head Quarter, B.S.F, Agartala.

Illegal immigration and cross border human trafficking from Bangladesh to India remains a bone of contention in Indo-Bangladesh relation. The illegal crossing of borders by the Bangladeshi nationals with a view to secure a settlement in Indian territory continues to plague the economy of the state. Further, this cross border human trafficking mostly of daily labourers has adverse effects on the plight of the workers in the state. Indian employers prefer labourers from Bangladesh, as they are not only cheap in comparison to Indian labour, but also are more efficient than their Indian counterparts.

It may be reminded that this continuous flow of illegal immigrants from Bangladesh is at the root of the feeling of insecurity among the indigenous people of the state who have already reduced to minorities in their own land. The fear of being swamped and loosing identity has led to the socio-political unrest among the autochthons that has almost paralyzed the law and order situation in the state. As a result of this, the people of the state have developed suspicion in their minds about the consequences of Tripura-Bangladesh border trade.

TABLE 19.3

Decadal Growth rate of Population

Year	*Tripura*	*NER Region*	*India*
1951	25.87	19.80	13.31
1961	76.86	40.44	21.51
1971	36.28	35.04	24.80
1981	31.92	26.40	24.66
1991	34.30	27.46	23.85
2001	15.74	—	21.34

Source: Census of India, 1951, 1961, 1971, 1981, 1991, 2001.

Informal trade, smuggling of small arms, drugs and narcotics trafficking and supply of fake currency are some other major security concerns which need to be addressed for the development of Tripura-Bangladesh border trade. The international drug and narcotic trafficking network and arms smuggling activities have a firm base in Bangladesh. Several intelligence reports including the report of Interpol reveal that the Bangladesh has become a sanctuary for drug trafficking and terrorist activities. The two notorious routes of drug trafficking and smuggling in this region are through Mayanmer and North-East India leading to the rest of the country; and through Cox Bazar port in Bangladesh to West Bengal and North-East India. The dangerous network of fake currency manufactured by the anti-India elements in Bangladesh also poses a direct threat to the state economy. Therefore, illegal trade, smuggling of small arms, drug and narcotic trafficking are endangering the security environment of Indo-Bangladesh border trade.

TABLE 19. 4

Seizure of Contraband Goods

Year	*Incoming Rs.*	*Outgoing Rs.*	*Total Rs.*
2000	79,49,376	4,57,99,807	5,36,49,184
2001	63,29,022	5,33,33,700	5,96,62,722
2002	66,57,437	6,00,42,965	6,67,00,402
2003	78,22,428	3,34,80,829	4,13,03,257
2004	1,77,48,035	3,79,48,016	5,56,96,051
2005	96,27,345	1,49,59,612	2,45,86,957
Total	5,60,33,645	24,55,64,930	30,15,98,576

Source: Frontiers Head Quarter B.S.F, Agartala.

TABLE 19.5

Particulars of Cross Border Smuggling Through Tripura-Bangladesh Border

Year	*No. cases*	*Seizure Value*
2000-2001	4101	Rs. 2,04,97,742.00
2001-2002	4413	Rs. 3,38,97,785.00
2002-2003	4223	Rs. 4,34,87,877.00
2003-2004	4104	Rs. 7,29,26,977.00
2004-2005	4021	Rs. 4,80,71,320.00

Source: Custom Division, Agartala, Government of India.

TABLE 19.6

Seizure of Drug & Narcotics along Tripura–Bangladesh Border

Sl. No.	*Year*	*No. of Cases*	*Value in Lakhs*
1.	2000-2001	01	.007
2.	2001-2002	03	2.90
3.	2002-2003	04	3.32
4.	2003-2004	—	—
5.	2004-2005	22	73.55

Source: Custom Division, Agartala, Government of India.

The amount of contraband goods seized during the period

2000 and 2005 is shown in Table 19.4 The total amount of seizure of contraband goods along Tripura-Bangladesh border was more than 30 crores. Out of which incoming goods seized was about 6 crores and outgoing seized Rs 24 crores.

The particulars of cross border smuggling is shown in Table 19.5. Seizure of smuggled goods to the tune of about 5 crores has been reported during 2000-05.

It is observed that smuggling in contraband goods like drugs and narcotics is on the rise in recent times along Tripura-Bangladesh border.

Thus, any border trade promotion policy needs to device some mechanism in order to eliminate these negative impacts of trade.

Conclusion

It is needless to mention that proper management of border can put a check on cross border terrorism, smuggling and illegal human trafficking. Encouraging the small border huts along the Tripura–Bangla border line and adequate steps for the socio-economic development of the people residing along the border can go a long way in improving the social environment across the border.

Proper border management is a sine qua non for the promotion of border trade. Security concerns of both India and Bangladesh should be factored into the framework of border management.

In view of the above discussion, there is a great need of comprehensive bilateral relations between India and Bangladesh in order to minimise these security threats for ensuring better environment for Tripura-Bangla border trade. The transit facilities through Bangladesh to the rest of

India, transborder tourism and access to the port in Chittagong end the isolation of Tripura.

BIBLIOGRAPHY

Ahmed; S. *Bangladesh-Past and Present*, APH Publishing Coporation, New Delhi, 2004.

Berkowitz, M and P.G. Booke, (1968), "National Security," in Sills, David, L., (ed.) *International Encyclopedia of Social Sciences,* Vol. II, London.

Bhattacharjee, K.K. *Northeast India–A Study*, Cosmo Publications, New Delhi, 1983.

Bhattacharya, S.B. and Das, R. *Perspectives on India's Northeast*, Bibhasa, Calcutta, 1998.

Bhattacharjee, S.R. *Tribal Insurgency in Tripura;* Inter-India Publications, New Delhi, 1989.

Bhowmik, S. *Insurgent Cross Fire in North-East India*, Lancer Publishers Pvt. Ltd., New Delhi 1996.

Chakraborti, T. "Insurgency in Tripura and India's Security," Published in the Proceedings of the XVth National Congress for Defence Studies, Nasik, 2002.

Chaube, S.K. *Hill Politics in Northeast India,* Orient Longman Limited, New Delhi, 1973.

Das, Gurudas and RK Purkayastha. *Border Trade North-East India and Neighbouring Countries*, Akansha Publishing House, New Delhi, 2000.

Ghosh, K. *Tribal Insurgency in Tripura, Booklinks Corporation,* Hyderabad, 1984.

Jayapalan, N. *India and her Neighbours,* Atlantic Publishers and Distributors, Delhi, 2000.

Jayaramu, P.S. *India's National Security and Foreign Policy,* ABC Publishing House, New Delhi, 1987.

Joint Declaration of the Indo-Bangladesh Coordination on 9th January,2004 in New Delhi.

McNarmara, Robert, 1968, *The Essence of Security,* London.

Narahari, Lt. Gen. N.S. *Security Threats to North-East India: The Socio-Ethnic Tensions,* Manas Publications, New Delhi, 2002.

Prabhakar, P.W. *Wars, Proxy-Wars and Terrorism – Post Independent India*, Mittal Publications, New Delhi, 2003.

Proceedings of the Meeting held between BSF and BDR, Frontiers Head Quarter, BSF, Agartala.

Ray; Syamal Kr. *India's North-East & the Travails of Tripura*, Minerva Associates Publications Pvt. Ltd., Kolkata,2003.

Reports of the Central Excise & Land Custom Department, Agartala Division, Govt. of India.

Reports of the Police Department, Agartala, Govt. Of Tripura.

Sengupta; D. and Sing, S.K. *Insurgency in North-East India—The Role of Bangladesh,* Authorpress, Delhi, 2004.

Some Basic Statistics of Tripura, Directorate of Economics and Statistics, Govt. of Tripura, Agartala, 2001.

Subrahmanyam, K, 1972, *Our National Secuirty,* Delhi.

Tripura Legislative Assembly Debates on 22-09-2003.

United Nations Commission on Human Rights. Regional Arrangements for the Promotion and Protection of Human Rights in the South Asian Region, 1989.

20

RESUMING A FORGOTTEN CORRIDOR: AN ASSESSMENT OF MIZORAM-BANGLADESH BORDER TRADE POSSIBILITY

Santanu Ray

National Perspective and Regional Need

The efforts towards integration of global economy by the famous trinity – the World Bank, the International Monetary Fund and the World Trade Organization claim to create an environment that will enable international trade to prosper in a new direction, propagated as Multilateralism. The world-wide wave of multilateralism received a serious set back in Seattle negotiations in December 1999. Following the fiasco in Seattle, the experiment of mutual cooperation among the nations sharing identical regional identities—Regionalism caught a special attention. The positive impact the regionalism has on international integration needs to be recognized. At least there is little disagreement about the coexistence of regionalism and multilateralism in future (Fisch G: 2001). The State-Centric approach of regionalism in the war-stricken world of 1940s, commonly labeled as Old Regionalism in recent literature, was dominated by politcs. However, notwithstanding the hegemony of globalization and resultant anti-globalization, regionalism constitutes a set of middle-level alternatives in policy and practice. In the post bi-polar world of 1990s, regionalism is not confined simply to formal inter-state regional organization and institution. The renewed and world wide trend of regionalism – often termed as New Regionalism—is characterized by its multidimensionality, complexity, fluidity and non-conformity (Sorderbaum F. and T.M. Shaw: 2003).In new millennium, the regional trade agreements have shown a strong commitment to open up markets and promote competition which contrast sharply with the inward-orientation of import-substitution practiced during 1950s and 1960s. The new agreements on border trade which by definition being a part of standard Exim policy have opened a scope to create additional avenues to border areas of the nations.

India's integration into global economy as well as into neighboring economies is only at a nascent stage. By any standard, it can hardly be called a strong globalizer. Two indicators, that show to what extent an economy is affected by the process of globalization, are salience of trade and that of investment. Neither the salience of trade – exports and imports relative to GDP—nor the salience of investment – inward and outward investment relative to gross fixed capital formation—exibits any indication of strong globalization. However, Indian policy of inward orientation had taken a new turn in the mid 1980s through the reduction of tariff and loosening of licensing requirement. Till early 1990s, India used to be considered as the most autarkic non-communist country in the world. The result was the steep decline in India's share in world exports from over 2.21 per cent in 1948 to a low of 0.4 per cent in the early 1980 and 0.5 per cent in 1990 (Srinivasan T.N.: 2003). The formal reform process, following the macro economic and balance of payment crisis, was introduced in 1991 and since then all successive

Union Governments had been serious and systematic with extensive trade liberalization and considerable relaxation of the restrictions of foreign capital inflow and direct investment. The positive impact of structural adjustment programme, adopted by the world's second largest populous nation, has been systematically propagated in World Bank 2005: '.... private investment as share of GDP nearly doubled....per capita GDP in India almost quadrupled....' during the period from 1980 to 2002. India '....experienced dramatic reduction in poverty....' Share of Indian population below poverty line ($ 1 per day) is reported to fall from 54 per cent in 1980 to 35 per cent in 2000.

Again, the surveys on Indian states clearly indicate that the process of reform, investment climate and their consequences on direct investment, income growth as well as on poverty reduction vary significantly across the states. Investors prefer Maharasthra, Karnataka, Gujarat, Tamilnadu and Andhra Pradesh as better places to produce than Delhi, whereas Punjab, Kerala, West Bengal and Uttar Pradesh are perceived to be worse (Stern N.: 2002). The post reform economic scenario of the country, judged by international agencies as well as Indian scholars also reveal that there has been an uneven income growth across the states. Several attempts have been made to explain this phenomenon under the purview of so called framework of regional disparities. It has almost become a fashion in post-reform Indian literature to argue that Indian states with better infrastructure and political influence could achieve a goal of better investment climate and states having disadvantageous position would decelerate. BIMARU and NE states are often categorized in the latter group, trapped into regional disparities. For the economic deceleration of BIMARU states, the ineffective governance that persists in concerned state is being questioned, however, in case of NE states the indifference attitude of the

Centre in removing socio-economic disadvantages of the region is fashionably blameworthy. Whatever may be the reasons of deceleration; efforts to accelerate reform process and to improve investment climate if not adapted by individual state with proper fiscal responsibility, diverging rather than converging trend of regional disparities is more likely in future.

Indian's northeast shares about 98 per cent of its total boundary with neighboring nations of China, Bhutan, Myanmar and Bangladesh. This unique geographical location of the region has so far been viewed as a serious disadvantage for its economic development. A new approach towards cooperation among the neighboring nations can turn the challenges into prospects. The world-wide phenomenon of renewed regionalism in post-bipolar world of 1990s and India's Look East Policy have certainly opened up a new set of opportunities for hitherto backward region in expanding trade relations with neighboring countries and in rescuing the region from the present trap of so-called regional disparities. The task ahead to achieve this goal, however, may not be as simple as it looks. The entire region has been suffering from a serious aid-addiction syndrome which has its far-reaching consequences on macroeconomic, mesoeconomic and most concernedly on socioeconomic fields. In most of the states, the governance has been highly exclusionary in nature characterized by anti-people features of elite domination and rent seeking. The ethnicity-based political character of the region has added an additional dimension to make it unproductive and to deprive people at large. In this chapter, taking the case of Mizoram economy, we examine the factors that are likely to come on the way of achieving a gainful alternative from mutual cooperation and trade relations across the border.

II

Mizoram: A Historical Note

Mizoram, the 23rd State of the Republic of India had traveled a long way to be counted as a federal unit. Lushai Hills District of Assam was formed by the colonial rulers in 1898 amalgamating two districts of two neighboring provinces: North Lushai Hills District and South Lushai Hills District under the then Assam and Bengal administration respectively.

TABLE 20.1

Border of Mizoram

(Figures in Kilometers)

Border	State / Country	Rural Development Block (District)
National (284)	Assam (123)	Zawlnuam (Mamit)
		Thingdawl (Kolasib)
		Darlawn (Aizawl)
	Tripura (66)	Zawlnuam (Mamit)
	Manipur (95)	Darlawn (Aizawl)
		Phullen (Aizawl)
		Ngopa (Champhai)
International (722)	Myanmar (404)	East Lungdar (Serchhip)
		Ngopa (Champhai)
		Khawzawl (Champhai)
		Khawbung (Champhai)
		Hnahthial (Lunglei)
		Sangau (Saiha)
		Tuipang (Saiha)
	Bangladesh (318)	West Phalleng (Mamit)
		Lungsen (Lunglei)
		Bungmum (Lunglei)
		Chawngte (Lawngtlai)
		Lawngtlai (Lawngtlai)
		Tuipang (Saiha)
Total	(1006)	

Source: Block Level Statistics, Directorate of Economics & Statistics, 2004.

However, in independent India the name of the district was changed to Mizo Hills District and continued to be a part of Assam until it was declared as Union Territory in 1972. Following about two-decade long armed revolution, it attained statehood in 1987. The state of Mizoram is the remotest and landlocked one among all the states in the country which has serious consequences on economic and social life of the people.

Over 70 per cent (722 km.) of total boundary length (1006 km.) of the state forms international border. The southern part which comprises at least twelve rural development blocks of six districts with about 60 per cent of total geographical area is typically landlocked by two neighboring nations: Myanmar and Bangladesh. Border length with these countries (Table 20.1) is 404 km. and 318 km. respectively. In places, the east-west length of the state reduces even to below 45 km. Bangladesh border with Mizoram, however, has an unique feature that over 80 per cent is riverine. The bordering river Kawrpui Lui (Thegakhal) which tears down the districts of Lunglei and Lawngtlai of Mizoram and hilly areas of Bangladesh is navigable during rainy season.

Trade referent of Mizoram has been traditionally the Surma Valley and Sylhet – both are part of Bangladesh since partition. Considerable trade flourished across the river Tlang (Dhaleshwari) which merges into Barak near Badarpur in Assam and glides into Bangladesh. The main trade centre in the then North Lushai Hills District of Assam was Sairang about 30 km. away from Aizawl (on NH 54). At this point, the traders from Sylhet and Silchar had their depots. Goods of all types—food grains, salt, clothing, stationary, fancy items used to be brought on head loads to Aizawl. Trade in South Lushai Hills District under Bengal administration was carried along different riverine routes. Traders from East Bengal (separated from India in 1947) would reach via Tlabung (Demagiri) through the river Tuilianpui (Karnaphuli) which was navigable. The traditional Karnaphuli riverine route was the life line for the district in accessing the rest of the country. River Tlang, navigable up to Lunglei, tears down the hills to meet Barak that steers through Bangladesh. This river called Surma in Sylhet and in some places Kalni had been deep and broad enough to receive steamers. Ultimately it meets Bramhaputra in south of Dhaka and called Meghna which meets Padma and empties in Bay of Bengal. Through the ages Barak water had been the mode of transport. Aizawl–Lunglei road was a bridle path till 1950 when a jeepable fair weather road was constructed.

The incidence of partition had been a crucial turning point not only for trade referent of Mizoram but also for the sudden changes in routes and channels that existed for other purposes. Scant attention had been paid by British rulers to develop agriculture, trade and commerce, education, medical facilities and in general level of living of the people at large. However, the imposition of several restrictive regulations separated the people of the area from mainland, both physically and psychologically and stood on the way of utilization of the development potential.

III

Economy and Governance

Among the small states in the country, Mizoram has attracted immense attention for its high social development coupled with very low level expansion in economic opportunities which sometimes create typical confusion in understanding the social reality. The logical consequence of low economic growth and high achievement in education has been the rise in the number of educated unemployed.

However, according to Census 2001, Mizoram ranks first among all the federal units of the country in terms of working population (Main and Marginal) relative to total population. The total employment in the state, as per census, was about 40.83 per cent as main workers (against the national average of 30.55 per cent) and 11.87 per cent as marginal workers (against the national average of 8.71 per cent). The dependency ratio (non-worker per worker) at less than unity (0.89) against the national average of 1.55 and NE average of 1.63.

Indian Census 1981 registered working population of Mizoram as 45.44 per cent relative to total population. During the period from 1981 to 2001, total workers (main plus marginal) grew at 3.76 per cent p.a. as compared to population growth of about 3 per cent p.a. However, the growth of main workers, having employment for at least 180 days in a year, registered at 2.88 per cent p.a. marginally lesser than the rate at which population grew. The growth of marginal workers, having employment for less than 180 days, had been as high as 9.17 per cent p.a. This huge growth in marginal workers establishes, to a certain extent, the growing unemployment scenario of the State. However, the feature of educated unemployment cannot be established from such analysis. It may be recalled that during 1970s, after the declaration of Union Territory, government jobs were created just to employ people at a very large scale irrespective of public needs. The trend continued even after the attainment of the statehood in 1987. During 1990s huge burden of debt, unsustainable fiscal deficit, enormous growth in non-plan expenditure etc. had compelled the state government to put a stop to the growth of public employment that was already over saturated. The failure of successive state governments to understand the importance of private sector for the generation of employment has been primarily responsible for the growing unemployment in Mizoram.

TABLE 20.2

Organized Sector Employment in Mizoram

(Persons in thousands)

Sector	Year	
	1991	2000
Public Sector	33.5 {96.82} [4.86]	40.1 {96.63} [4.51]
Private Sector	1.1 {3.18} [0.16]	1.4 {3.37} [0.16]
Total	34.6 {100} [5.02]	41.5 {100} [4.67]

Source: Planning Commission, 2002.

Notes: {} figures indicate per cent of total Employment in organized sector.
[ ] figures indicate per cent of state Population.

Public sector in Mizoram, as in Table 20.2, provides around 97 per cent of total employment in organized sector. The decline in relative share of public sector from 96.82 per cent during 1991 to 96.63 per cent during 2000 is nominal as compared to national average of 71.29 per cent and 69.08 per cent respectively. However, the public sector employment relative to state population has dropped from 4.86 per cent to 4.51 per cent against the all India average of 2.25 per cent to 1.88 per cent and northeastern average of 2.63 per cent to 2.44 per cent. In 2000, the public sector employment relative to state population in Mizoram even though stands highest in the country the absence of effective private sector and other possible opportunities are responsible in this regards. Again, Planning Commission in 2002 recorded the Labour Force Participation Rate (LFPR) in Mizoram as 61.9 percent in 1993-94 and 63.8 per cent in 1999-2000 with an annual growth of 4 percent against the national figures of 64.5 per cent and 61.8 per cent respectively with a growth of 1.6 per cent only. The incidence of unemployment was recorded as 0.8 per cent in 1993-94 and 2.0 per cent in 1999-2000 against the all India figures of 2.0 per cent and 2.3 per cent respectively.

The relative position of the State among all-32 Indian states and Union Territories, estimated by the Planning Commission, in terms of Human Development Index in 1991, was seventh. This achievement in social sector was also supplemented by the evidence of sixth ranking in the country in terms of Gender Development Index. Mizoram,is, thus characterized with reasonably decent standard of human development and encouragingly low gender gap coupled with overwhelmingly low expansion of economic choices and opportunities. At this point one can argue that Mizoram, being the only state in NE region recording per capita income higher than national average (both in current and constant 1993-94 prices), the claim of low economic opportunities in the state appears to be contradictory. However, it may be referred to the study by Goswami and Gogoi (2004) in which 25 Indian states (excluding Jharkhand, Chhatisgarh, and Uttaranchal) are ranked on the basis of economic development–based on a composite index where the performances of four sectors viz.; agriculture, industry, infrastructure and social sector have been considered. Mizoram, according to their ranking, is placed second from the bottom – only above Arunachal Pradesh.

High per capita income especially in special category states does not indicate fair expansion of opportunities in these economies. It is gross central devolution which contributes the major component of the state income. During the fiscal year 1990-91 over 92 per cent of GSDP of Mizoram had been contributed by the centre in the form of grants etc. Though, that unprecedented phenomenon had been corrected, to a certain extent, in latter years of 1990s, during the fiscal year 2001-02 gross devolution from the centre contributed about 58 per cent of state's per capita income as compared to all states average of about 7 per cent. In other words, aggregate expenditure of the state accounted for about 71 per cent of state's income against the all states average of about 16 per cent.

TABLE 20.3

Key Macroeconomic Indicators of Mizoram

(as per cent Of GSDP)

Year	*Gross Central Devolution*	*Gross Fiscal Deficit (GFD)*			*Decomposition of GFD*		
		Revenue Receipt	*Aggregate Expenditure*	*GFD*	*Revenue Deficit*	*Capital Outlay*	*Net Lending*
1992-93	65.82	69.31	79.10	9:79	-7.76	15.76	1.79
1993-94	68.44	70.60	71.67	1.07	-11.78	11.63	1.21
1994-95	70.24	72.86	78.05	5.19	-10.14	14.29	1.04
1995-96	64.78	66.96	74.50	7.54	-6.65	13.24	0.95
1996-97	60.05	62.22	73.90	11.8	-4.38	14.87	1.19
1997-98	62.35	64.18	75.23	11.05	-5.33	14.88	1.49
1998-99	58.41	59.08	69.72	10.64	-3.55	11.46	2.72
1999-00	67.57	67.73	80.45	12.72	-4.21	14.55	2.39
2000-01	46.17	46.90	68.15	21.25	10.95	9.27	1.03
2001-02	57.69	57.38	70.67	13.29	2.14	9.84	1.31

Source: Computed from Economic and Political Weekly Research Foundation, May 2004.

The key macro-economic indicators of the state are depicted in Table 20.3.The fiscal deficit, considered in modern days as the summary indicator of macro-economic impact of the budget, has crossed the normal limit in Mizoram by all standards. Revenue surplus that the state enjoyed till the end of 1990s had suddenly converted into revenue deficit. Considerable fall in the 'state's share of central taxes' – a component of gross central devolution in the early years of new millennium has been primarily responsible for the fall in revenue receipt as well as in revenue surplus. To harness the macroeconomic imbalances, acceleration of income growth, however, appears to be impossible since state's income reflects an abject dependency on central devolution. The very close relationship between central devolution and total revenue of the government implies that the state has miserably failed to develop its own revenue resources. Mounting fiscal deficit at staggering rate indicates simply that in near future the state's economy is likely to spill over into severe macroeconomic instability. In addition, this situation attenuates the state government to undertake new developmental projects when it finds hard to fund the ongoing ones due to the huge burden of interest payment.

IV

Strategies of Development

Plan strategies pursued by the successive governments in Mizoram since the attainment of Union Territory in 1972 give an idea of thrust areas. The plan objectives were outlined to improve the income and quality of life of the common people to attain self-reliance in food production, to create alternatives for the age-old practice of shifting cultivation, to generate job opportunities for addressing the problem of unemployment and to improve the standard of education and health of the citizens. With 95 per cent tribal population whose traditional livelihood is cultivation, the plan documents obviously emphasized agriculture and the welfare of the people engaged in this sector. All successive state governments with different political moorings surprisingly came up with almost identical programme of agricultural reforms. A bird's eye view reveals the fact that all such reform programmes were aimed primarily at the reduction of the areas under shifting cultivation to protect environment and to raise productivity. Since 1972 at least five reform programmes viz.; Garden Colony (1979), Land Use Policy (1984), Jhum Control Project (1987), New Land Use Policy (1990), and

Mizoram Intodelhna Project (2002) have been undertaken. Emphasis has also been given to reduce the burden of huge labour force in agriculture through creation of viable alternatives so that primary goal of improving income level as well as living condition of agricultural population can be achieved. Proposals have been made to change the crop pattern from popular crops to cash crops. The policies adopted in this line included separating horticulture department from agriculture, establishing an independent rural development department and agricultural research laboratories, expanding irrigated areas through small irrigation projects, etc. Every state budget had been liberal enough to allocate huge expenditure without noticing the sustainability, financial feasibility, and most importantly without considering whether the targeted population is going to benefit from such allocation or not. Although the state is having much lesser rural population compared to national average, i.e., 50 per cent of its population against the national average of over 72 per cent and NE average of over 84 per cent, surprisingly it has much higher percentage of population employed in agriculture. The growth of agricultural income during 1990s was registered even less than 2 per cent p.a. with a growth of labor force of over 4 per cent. In addition,

TABLE 20.4

Rural and Agricultural Population

(As per cent of total population)

	Rural Population	*Agricultural Population*			*Working Population (main + marginal)*
		Cultivators	*Agricultural Laborers*	*Total*	
Mizoram	50.50	28.41	3.09	31.50	52.70
NE Region	84.49	15.92	4.77	20.69	38.06
India	72.22	12.45	10.48	22.93	39.26

Source: Census, 2001.

the relative share of agriculture to NSDP (at constant 93-94 prices) has dropped to about 22 per cent during 2001-02. This, however, does not match the claims of significant rise in agricultural productivity (Table 20.5) in recent time.

TABLE 20.5

Agricultural Productivity of Mizoram

	Jhum Rice			*WET and HYV Rice*		
	Area Cultivated in ha.	*Produc-tion in MT*	*Producti-vity in MT per ha.*	*Area Cultivated in ha.*	*Produc-tion in MT*	*Producti-vity in MT per ha.*
1990-91	36,716	35,283	0.96	14,607	28,511	1.95
2002-03	41,356	67,076	1.62	15,711	42,129	2.64
Growth (%)	12.64	90.00	68.75	7.56	48.00	37.44

Source: Directorate of Agriculture, Government of Mizoram.

During the first phase of development (1947-1972) under the administrative status of Mizo Hills District of Assam, scant attention had been paid towards the process of industrialization. Little effort had been made for the first time in 1962 by the Rural Industries Project to develop the cottage and village industries. Major thrust area was the cotton weaving on handloom–a traditional practice of Mizo society. However, Lalkhama Committee Report (1971) mentioned clearly that by that time no industrial unit of worth mentioning had been existed. In the second phase of development–a period from 1972 to 1987, Government of India initiated a central programme which authorized District Industries Centre (DIC) to distribute grants and loans to different units of the area. Under the provision of the programme with 25 per cent central subsidy at least 1925 units were reported to have come up by 1980. The Central Government sanctioned a sum of Rs. 6 crores. The first industrial convention was convened during the transitional phase of U.T. to statehood in 1987.

A planned effort towards industrialization has been initiated after the attainment of statehood with the declaration of First Industrial Policy of Mizoram in 1989. The objectives of state industrial policy were not only rapid industrialization in the state but also an all round development with an aim to provide gainful employment and self employment to the rural poor engaged in shifting cultivation. The emphases were given on handloom and handicraft, agro-forest based industries, sericulture, electronic industries etc.

The new industrial policy of Mizoram was announced in 2000 after a decade of implementation of first industrial policy. The new policy was framed to accelerate the industrial process through the promotion and modernization of textile industry. The investment from outside the state 'on selective basis' along with the local entrepreneurs were proposed to be encouraged. Two major research works have already been done by M. S. Swaminathan Research Foundation, Chennai and Tata Consultancy Services, Mumbai, during late 1990s. The first one suggested to establish a solid resource-industry linkage through establishment of agro-forest based industry, while the latter emphasized on the long-term sustainable development through infrastructure building. Despite such efforts (Ray: 2002), the poor performance of the state in industrial sector has been a matter of concern. During the fiscal year 2001-02, according to the Directorate of Economics and Statistics, manufacturing (both registered and unregistered taking together) contributed even less than 2 per cent of NSDP (Ray: 2003). During 1990s sectoral income at 1993-94 constant prices grew at an alarming rate of (-) 12.61 per cent p.a. while the share to NSDP dropped by 1.52 per cent during the period from 1993-94 to 1999-00. Kabra (2005) alludes to a number of factors that had come on the way of industrialization of the state. The study categorizes such factors as exogenous and endogenous. The factors of former category hindering industrialization in the state include lack of marketing support, absence of database, restriction on outside entrepreneurs, poor infrastructure, disturbed ethno-political situation, etc. However, the factors of endogenous category include the defective capital base and operational plans, shortage of working capital, obsolete techniques of production and so on and so forth.

V

Border Trade: An Emerging Opportunity

Considering the geo-political location, agro-climatic conditions as well as requirement of investment in infrastructure, border trade with neighboring nation is being considered, in recent times, as one of the options for enhancing economic development. Studies by UN-ESCAP (1996) and Kabra and Singha (2003) observed that while exports to Bangladesh through Tlabung sector on Indo-Bangladesh border are basically local agro-horticultural products produced in Mamit, Lunglei, and Lawngtlai districts, the same to Myanmar through southwestern part of the state composed of consumer and luxury items produced by big Indian companies elsewhere.

Informal imports from both Bangladesh and Myanmar consist primarily of luxury and fancy consumer items produced in industrialized Asian countries of China, Thailand, Hong Kong, Singapore, South Korea, Japan, etc. The informal export to Bangladesh, as reported by UN-ESCAP (1996) consisted of mainly cotton which used to be largely produced in Mamit, Kolasib, Lunglei, Lawntlai and Saiha districts of the state. During early 1990s cotton production was encouraged as one of the major cash crops. But over time, the cotton production in Mizoram has been declining significantly. Both area under cultivation and yield of cotton, as reported by the Directorate of Agriculture, had dropped miserably in the early years of new millennium as compared to that of early 1990s (Table 20.6). This reduction in the trend of cotton production has a significant impact on informal trade in this sector.

TABLE 20.6

Cotton Production of Mizoram

(figures in M.T.)

Year	*Area Cultivated (in ha.)*	*Production*	*Productivity (per ha.)*
1990-91	948	408	0.430
1991-92	1066	489	0.458
2001-02	620	215	0.347
2002-03	388	175	0.451

Source: Directorate of Agriculture, Government of Mizoram.

Informal imports in this sector consist of second-hand garments: mainly winter wears, curtains, bed-sheets, pillow and pillow covers, ladies inner wears, ties, etc. Besides these, imports from Bangladesh also include leather items, quilts, blankets etc. It is commonly believed that Bangladesh, being one of the low-income countries in the world, receives these used garments and other items as aids from European as well from East-Asian industrialized countries. However, the faulty distribution system and completely different climatic condition and social likings stand on the way of their use in Bangladesh. On the other hand, Mizoram, being one of the largest consuming states in the country (in per capita consumption term), has huge demand for such articles. Second hand clothings also suit in the moderate climate of the state. This informal imports plays a crucial role in terms of trade and employment in the state. The wide range of variety of second-hand winter clothes and other articles enter into the consumption basket of the people of all sections. An unpublished survey conducted during 2002-03 has reported that the annual import of second-hand items from Bangladesh had been over Rs. 62 crore and over 7.6 thousand people were engaged in different capacities directly or indirectly in this trade. Thus trade in second hand garments provides a significant size of employment in the state–especially during winter season.

Mizoram contributes a significant share to the region's total export of agro-horticultural as well as forest products to Bangladesh. Products of Mizoram origin are exported mainly through Karimganj Land Custom Station of Assam. This activity has hardly been reported in a systematic manner. The surplus, generated in the rural blocks of northern Mizoram neighboring Cachhar and Karimganj districts of Assam, has been reportedly included into the export baskets. The products consist of ginger, banana, passion fruit, papaya, pumpkin, cardamom, hatkora, chillies, etc. The low transport cost and other favorable factors clearly indicate that there has been a further scope of accelerating the speed and space in this direction which would benefit the cultivators of Reiek and Zawlnuam blocks of Mamit district; North Thingdawl of Kolasib and Darlawn and Phullen of Aizawl.

TABLE 20.7

Items Proposed for Formal Trading between Mizoram & Bangladesh

(Figures in thousand M.T.)

Items for Export to Bangladesh (estimated Surplus in the 2004-05)	Items of Imports from Bangladesh
Bamboo (1.75 Crore in number)	Cement
Stone metal and chips	Iron and steel
Ginger (25)	Crockery and utensils
Orange (14)	Poultry products
Passion Fruit (0.9)	Clothes and readymade garments
Sesamum (0.5)	Toiletries
Tung Oil (2.1)	Cosmetics
Papaya (15)	
Hatkora (2.8)	
Pumpkin (40)	
Squash (9.6)	
Pineapple (1.5)	
Chillies (0.9)	

Source: Directorate of Trade and Commerce, Government of Mizoram.

Kabra and Singha (2003) had compared the relative merits of the trade possibilities between Mizoram and two neighboring nations of Myanmar and Bangladesh. They pointed out that so far as state initiative in opening formal border trade is concerned, Government of Mizoram significantly lags behind compared to other NE states. The incentives and infrastructural facilities that need to be taken care of by the state authority for the promotion of trade and commerce had never been adequate.

After the spot verification by Ministry of Commerce officials and release of over one crore by the Central Government, work has been initiated to set up a Land Custom Station (LCS) at Kawrpuichhuah under Lungsen rural development block of Lunglei district on Indo-Bangla sector. A plot of about 0.3 sq. km. has been acquired for the construction of border trade centre. On the other side of the border, an LCS at Thegamukh is being constructed by Bangladesh. However, the construction of the connecting road of about 123 km. between Thegamukh and Rangmati (district headquarters) remained as one of the unsettled issues.

Thus, border trade along Mizoram-Bangladesh sector primarily flows through informal channel. Efforts towards formalization of cross border trade has been initiated only recently. Once the structure is in place, it will no doubt boost up trading activities across the border. If Mizoram is to convert its geographical disadvantage into advantage, a strong cross border trade relationship with Bangladesh is must.

REFERENCES

Barua, S. (2000): 'Certain observations on informal border trade with neighbouring countries and economic prospects of NE region,' published in *'Border Trade: NE India and neighbouring countries'* edited by G. Das and R.K. Purkayastha, Akansha Publishing House, New Delhi.

Bhalla, S.S. (2003): *Imagine There's No Country: Poverty, Inequality and Growth in the Era of Globalization,'* Penguin Books, New Delhi.

Bob, J. (2003): 'The political economy of scale and the construction of cross-border micro-regions,' in Soderbaun, F. and T.M. Shaw edited *'Theories of New Regionalism- A Palgrave Reader,'* Palgrave, Mcmillan.

Das, Gurudas (2000): 'Trade between the NE region and neighbouring countries: structures and implications for development,' published in *'Border Trade: NE India and Neighbouring Countries'* edited by Gurudas Das and R.K. Purkayastha, Akansha Publishing House, New Delhi.

Deutsch, K.G. (2001): 'The EU: Contending for leadership' in *'The WTO-Millennium Round,'* edited by Deutsch K.G. and B. Speyer, Routledge, London.

Finger, J.M. and P. Schuler (2001): 'Developing countries and the millennium round,' in *'The WTO-Millennium Round,'* edited by Deutsch K.G. and B. Speyer, Routledge, London.

Fisch, G. (2001): 'Regionalism and Multilateralism – side by side in *'The WTO-Millennium Round,'* edited by Deutsch K.G. and B. Speyer, Routledge, London.

Goswami, H. & J.K. Gogoi (2004): 'Interstate disparities in economic development of India with special reference to NE states,' Seminal paper presented in the 'Workshop on Quantitative Analysis in Economics,' Shillong, 8–13th March.

Kabra, K.C. (2005): 'Business and Industry in Mizoram–A study of developments since 1872 and present status,' unpublished Ph.D. thesis submitted to J.R. Nagar Rajasthan Vidyapeeth University, Udaipur.

Kabra, K.C. and R. K.P.G. Singha (2003): 'Border Trade of Mizoram: Emerging trends and future prospects,' seminar paper presented at ICSSR-NERC, Shillong, 21-23rd October.

Madhab, J. (2002): 'Social conflict in the Northeast: An economic interpretation,' contemporary India, A NE special, 1(4) Oct.-Dec.

Murshed, S.M. (2003): 'Perspective on two phases of globalization' in self edited, *'Globalization, Marginalization and Development,'* Digital printing, Routledge, London.

Peet, R. (2003): *Unholy Trinity: The IMF, World Bank and WTO,* Zed Books, London.

Planning Commission (2002): *Human Development Report, 2001.*

Ray, Santanu (2002): 'Structural change and strategy for development: Resource- industry linkages,' seminar paper presented in ICSSR-NERC, Shillong, March.

Ray, Santanu (2003): 'Economic sustainability and structural transformation in Mizoram,' published in G. Das edited *Structural Change and Strategy for Development,* Akansha Publishing House, New Delhi.

Ray, Santanu (2004): 'Fiscal reforms and related issues: a critical assessment of Financial sustainability in post statehood Mizoram,' unpublished seminar paper, presented at the national seminar on 'Transforming the Hill Economy of NE region,' Itanagar, 26-28th November.

Soderbaum, F. and T.M. Shaw (2003): *Theories of New Regionalism – a Palgrave Reader,* Palgrave, McMillan.

Srinivasan, T.N. (2003): 'The cost of hesitant and reluctant globalization: India,' Indian Economic Review, Vol. XXXVIII, No. 2.

Stern, N. (2002): 'Building a climate for Investment, growth and poverty reduction in India,' speech delivered in EXIM bank of India, Mumbai, March 22, 2001 and published in 'A strategy for development' the World Bank, Washington, DC.

UN-ESCAP (1996): Survey report of 'Informal border trade in NE region' as a part of study by 'Research and information system for Non-Aligned and Developing Countries,' New Delhi on India's border trade with selected neighbouring countries.

World Bank (2005): *World Development Report: A Better Investment Climate for Everyone,* Oxford University Press, New York.

REPORTS

Perspective / Visionary Plan: for the State of Mizoram: formulated by Tata Economic Consultancy Services, Mumbai, 1998.

A Blue Print of Sustainable Agriculture and Rural Development (Agenda – 21, for the State of Mizoram), by the M.S. Swaminathan Research Foundation, Chennai, 1998.

First Industrial Policy of Mizoram, 1989.

New *(Second)* Industrial Policy of Mizoram, 2000.

Mizoram Intodelhna Project, 2002.

21

BORDER TRADE WITH BANGLADESH: A NOTE ON THE MIZORAM SECTOR

C. Lalzirliana

Government of Mizoram strongly feels that border trade should be operationalised as soon as possible in this sector. This is also in terms of clause 7 of the Mizoram Peace Accord, 1986.

The State Government is also in favour of starting formal trade with Bangladesh. For this purpose, Shri N. Mishra, Additional Secretary, Ministry of Commerce, also visited Tlabung in the month of November 1999. A decision has also been taken in the Ministry of Commerce that a border township having all infrastructure for international trade and commerce should be set up. Accordingly, under the CIB Scheme Rs. 5.00 crores was considered for this border trade centre, out of which a sum of Rs. 2.48 crores has been approved by Government of India out of which Rs. 1.13 crores has been released to Government of Mizoram. This project shall cover construction of buildings for customs, immigration and other Central and State level departments, besides other export / import infrastructural requirements.

The fund has been transferred to Mizoram PWD which is expected to start the construction during 2005-06.

Trade and Commerce Department has sent a trade delegation in June 2001 to Bangladesh in connection with marketing of ginger, chillies, etc. The different Chambers of Commerce & Industries of Dhaka, Chittagong, Sylhet, Rangamati etc. responded positively for opening of border trade between Bangladesh and Mizoram.

Land measuring 3,01,333 sq.meters (2424.99 bhigas) at Kawrpuichhuah near Tlabung has been acquired for the establishment of Indo-Bangladesh Border Trade Centre.

Government of Mizoram has all along been requesting the Government of India and Government of Bangladesh to open up traditional river route from Tlabung to Chittagong port. This matter had received positive response from the then Prime Minister of Bangladesh, when the Chief minister, Shri. Zoramthanga met her in March 1999. This route is the vital economic line for landlocked state of Mizoram. Fresh attempts are made by Government of India to get this route opened up early or if possible, a land corridor to Tlabung from Kaptai Dam in Bangladesh may be negotiated with Government of Bangladesh.

A team of 31 delegates from Federation of Bangladesh Chamber of Commerce & Industries visited Mizoram in October 1999 and signed a memorandum of understanding with the Mizoram Chamber of Commerce. Subsequently, a four member team from Syhlet Chamber of Commerce & Industry (Bangladesh) visited Mizoram for the promotion of cross border trade.

Issuess Need to be Addressed

Opening of LCS at Thegamukh (Bangladesh)

1. Government of Bangladesh need to be persuaded to

open an LCS at Thegamukh, counter part to Indian LCS at Tlabung (Demagiri) in Mizoram sector.

2. LCS at Thegamukh is known to have been active and operational prior to 1965 and is also known to have not been denotified by the Government of Bangladesh. This LCS has remained dormant since then. This may be reactivated on following considerations:

   - Government of Mizoram is keen to provide its bamboo (either in raw form or in semi-processed form) to Karnaphuli Paper Mill of Bangladesh on sustainable basis.
   - Mizoram can also provide stone metal and stone chips to Bangladesh for infrastructural development like road construction and buildings.
   - Mizoram is rich in ginger and other horticulture produce like hatkora, oranges, sesamum, cotton, papaya, pumkin etc. which may also be exported to Bangladesh.
   - Mizoram can import crockeries, cement, iron and steel, meat on hooves, poultry items, cosmetics and toiletries, garments etc.

Opening of Karnaphuli Riverine Route between South Mizoram (India) and Rangamati - Kaptai - Chittagong (Bangladesh)

This issue has remained pending for too long. This was discussed between Chief Minister, Mizoram, and Prime Minister, Bangladesh earlier. For mutual co-operation and economic benefit, Bangladesh may be impressed upon the necessity of opening this traditional riverine route between India (Mizoram sector) and Bangladesh. Bangladesh may be requested to agree to our proposal of inclusion of this route in the Chapter VIII of the Protocol for Trade and Transit between India and Bangladesh and approve Chittagong,

Kaptai, Rangamati and Tlabung (India) as ports-of-call under the said Chapter.

Construction of Road between Rangamati to Thegamukh

During the course of the last Secretary Level Talks in Dhaka, Commerce Secretary of Bangladesh contended that the proposal for opening an LCS at Thegamukh might be difficult due to its remoteness from District Headquarters of Rangamati. The assessed distance is about 123km. It is, thus, important to construct a road connecting these two places. Efforts in this direction need to be initiated.

Export of Bamboo

India needs to facilitate the export of bamboo from Mizoram to Bangladesh to feed the Karnaphuli Paper Mill (KPM). The KPM should identify importers who will tie-up with exporter from Mizoram.

Agro-horticultural Exports

Ginger

Ginger is the major cash crop of Mizoram. The average annual production of ginger is about 10,000 mt. The state is facing problems of marketing particularly during bumper harvesting season. About 80 per cent of the produce is marketed in Assam and another 20 per cent is exported to Bangladesh. As per information collected, ginger production may cross 25,000 mt. in the coming years.

Chilli

Chilli is the second largest cash crop of Mizoram. The average annual production is 3000 mt. About 90 per cent of the produce is marketed in Assam and about 10 per cent is exported to Bangladesh via Tlabung. There is enough scope to raise the production of chilli in the state. Operationalization of border trade with Bangladesh may act as a boost in this regard.

Sesame

The average annual production of sesame is 500 mt. It does not face much marketing problem. It is mostly grown in southern and western part of Mizoram and mostly exported to Bangladesh. There is room to increase its production.

Turmeric

The annual production of turmeric is not high as the demand is rather low. At present the annual production is 7500 mt. There is no processing plant installed in the state. Production can be further raised if processing and marketing can be improved.

Chow Chow

Chow Chow (squash) grows at an altitude of 1000 meters above sea level. It bears fruits in the first year of growing and harvested during the months of April to December every year. The peak period of harvesting is July to October. Annual production at present is 24000 mt. This can further be increased subject to the availability of market.

The tender leaves are as delicious as other vegetables like mustard leaves. Its tuber is mostly harvested in the months of December and January and it has a very flavoury taste. Because it is devoid fat, it is a recommended diet for those who are suffering from hypertension problem and it is very good for the people living in hotter place as it keeps the body cool. It can be produced more subject to the availability of market.

Marketing of Fruits

Hatkora

Mizoram annually produced huge quantity of hatkora

which is found to be in great demand in Bangladesh. Production can further be increased if there is market for disposal outside Mizoram.

Orange

Mizoram produces huge quantity of orange annually and there is not much problem in its marketing. However, increase in outside demand will certainly boost up its production.

Pineapple

Annual production of pineapple in Mizoram is 7000 mt. at present. Even though the production of pineapple is not very high; it could be increased subject to availability of market.

TABLE 21.1

Horticultural Products of Mizoram Having Export Potential to Bangladesh (2002 – 2005 Average)

Sl. No.	*Common name*	*Local name*	*Botanical name*	*Average Annual yield (M.T)*
1.	Passion fruit	Sapthei	Passiflora edulis	922.38
2.	Orange	Serthlum	Citrus reticulate	14125.80
3.	Banana	Balhla	Musa Cavendish	10000
4.	Pineapple	Lakhuihthei	Ananas commosus	1471.38
5.	Ginger	Sawhthing	Gingiber officinate	25255.22
6.	Turmeric	Aieng	Curcuma longa	1568.97
7.	Chillies	Hmarcha	Capsicum sps	3364.89
8.	Tung oil	Tung	Allecuritis sps	1200
9.	Iskut	Iskut	Sechium edule	9573.59
10.	Hatkora	Hatkora	Citrusmacrophylla	2817.17
11.	Arecanut	Areca	Areca Catechu	1142.33
12.	Anthurium	Anthurium	Anthurium Sp.	5628 Nos

Source: Directorate of Horticulture, government of Mizoram.

Banana

Banana production especially cavandish variety is

satisfactory in Mizoram. The average annual production is about 10,000 mt. Most of the product is consumed locally. If marketing prospect is good, production can be increased.

Tung (Aleurites Spp)

Tung belongs to euphorbiacea family and well suited to the agro climatic conditions prevailing in Mizoram. There are 5 different species of tung in the world. These are: Aleurites Montana, Aleurites Fordii, Aleurites Cordata, Aleurites Trispena and Aleurites Mulauna. In Mizoram, Aleurites Montana and Aleurites Frodii are only grown.

Tung oil is also known as china wood oil as China is the origin of this fruit. This oil is mostly used in laminate industry, printing ink industry and paint industry. It is also used for making brake lining, linoleum, oil cloth, plastic additives and modifiers for synthetic resins.

Mizoram started growing tung trees in large scale since early 1990s. As per census conducted by Rural Development Department, Government of Mizoram, there are more than 71,20,551 tung trees in 1996-1997 and there are more than 15,000 tung growing families in the state. Annual production of tung oil is 2100 mt.

Passion Fruit

Mizoram is ideal for the cultivation of passion fruits. But due to problems of marketing, many passion fruits farmers abandoned growing the fruit plant. It is mostly grown in the eastern part of Mizoram. The variety grown is passiflora edulis and the matured passion fruit in Mizoram is purple in colour. The taste is very flavoury. It can be consumed even without processing. The juice can be extracted and concentrated. Subject to availability of market, production can be raised to 10,000 mt annually.

Marketing of Other Agriculture Produces

Apart from the major produces mentioned, Mizoram also produces cardamom, citronella and mustard seed. These are being consumed within the state and a small part is also sold to the private traders coming from the neighbouring states. Their productions can be increased many folds within one or two season provided processing and marketing facilities are available.

Thus cross border trade with Bangladesh can revolutionize the economy of Mizoram. Cost effective access to Bangldesh market can boost up the local production and help in modernizing the agro-horticultural sector in Mizoram.

INDEX

■■■